Hunger, Horses, and Government Men

PATRONS OF THE OSGOODE SOCIETY

Blake, Cassels & Graydon LLP
Gowlings
Lax O'Sullivan Scott Lisus LLP
McCarthy Tétrault LLP
Osler, Hoskin & Harcourt LLP
Paliare Roland Rosenberg Rothstein LLP
Torkin Manes LLP
Torys LLP
WeirFoulds LLP

The Osgoode Society is supported by a grant from
The Law Foundation of Ontario.

THE LAW FOUNDATION OF ONTARIO

The Society also thanks the Law Society of Upper Canada
for its continuing support.

LAW AND SOCIETY SERIES
W. Wesley Pue, General Editor

LAW AND SOCIETY

The Law and Society Series explores law as a socially embedded phenomenon. It is premised on the understanding that the conventional division of law from society creates false dichotomies in thinking, scholarship, educational practice, and social life. Books in the series treat law and society as mutually constitutive and highlight scholarship emerging from the interdisciplinary engagement of law with fields such as politics, social theory, history, political economy, and gender studies.

A list of titles in the series appears at the end of the book.

Hunger, Horses, and Government Men

Criminal Law on the Aboriginal Plains, 1870-1905

SHELLEY A.M. GAVIGAN

PUBLISHED BY UBC PRESS FOR
THE OSGOODE SOCIETY
FOR CANADIAN LEGAL HISTORY

21 20 19 18 17 16 15 14 13 12 5 4 3 2 1

Printed in Canada on paper that is processed chlorine- and acid-free, with vegetable-based inks.

Library and Archives Canada Cataloguing in Publication

Gavigan, Shelley A. M.
Hunger, horses, and government men : criminal law on the aboriginal plains, 1870-1905 / Shelley A.M. Gavigan.

(Law & society, ISSN 1496-4953)
Co-published by Osgoode Society for Canadian Legal History.
Includes bibliographical references and index.
Issued also in electronic format.
ISBN 978-0-7748-2252-7

1. Criminal law – Saskatchewan – History. 2. Criminal courts – Saskatchewan – History. 3. Indians of North America – Criminal justice system – Saskatchewan – History. 4. Native peoples – Legal status, laws, etc. – Saskatchewan. 5. Criminal justice, Administration of – Saskatchewan – History. 6. Native peoples – Saskatchewan – Government relations. I. Osgoode Society for Canadian Legal History II. Title. III. Series: Law and society series (Vancouver, B.C.)

KE7722.C75G39 2012 345.71'00897 C2012-903971-3
KF8210.C7G39 2012

Canadä

UBC Press gratefully acknowledges the financial support for our publishing program of the Government of Canada (through the Canada Book Fund), the Canada Council for the Arts, and the British Columbia Arts Council.

This book has been published with the help of a grant from the Canadian Federation for the Humanities and Social Sciences, through the Awards to Scholarly Publications Program, using funds provided by the Social Sciences and Humanities Research Council of Canada.

UBC Press
The University of British Columbia
2029 West Mall
Vancouver, BC V6T 1Z2
www.ubcpress.ca

For Amy

Contents

Illustrations

Maps

Figures

Tables

Foreword

The Osgoode Society for Canadian Legal History

Shortly after Confederation Canada acquired the territories formerly owned and administered by the Hudson's Bay Company. Among the formidable challenges brought by this massive land acquisition, the most notable was the task of reconciling the Aboriginal peoples of the Plains to Dominion sovereignty. Much has been written about the treaty making process of the 1870s, and about the Métis resistance of the late 1860s and 1880s, but we know relatively little about the introduction of Canadian legal regimes. Professor Gavigan fills that historiographic gap, examining in considerable detail the introduction of Canadian criminal law and criminal justice institutions in the prairie west after 1870. Using newspapers, penitentiary records, Indian Department files, and, principally, the records of stipendiary magistrates, she shows the law's impact on the Aboriginal peoples of the West, as well as their use of it in coming to terms with the new political reality.

The purpose of the Osgoode Society for Canadian Legal History is to encourage research and writing in the history of Canadian law. The Society, which was incorporated in 1979 and is registered as a charity, was founded at the initiative of the Honourable R. Roy McMurtry, formerly attorney general for Ontario and chief justice of the province, and officials of the Law Society of Upper Canada. The Society seeks to stimulate the study of legal history in Canada by supporting researchers, collecting oral histories, and publishing volumes that contribute to legal-historical scholarship in Canada. It has published 84 books on the courts, the judiciary, and the legal profession, as well as on the history of crime and punishment, women and law, law and economy, the legal treatment of ethnic minorities, and famous cases and significant trials in all areas of the law.

Current directors of the Osgoode Society for Canadian Legal History are Robert Armstrong, Kenneth Binks, Susan Binnie, David Chernos, Thomas G. Conway, J. Douglas Ewart, Violet French, Martin Friedland, John Gerretsen, Philip Girard, William Kaplan, Horace Krever, C. Ian Kyer, Virginia MacLean, Patricia McMahon, R. Roy McMurtry, Dana Peebles, Paul Perell, Jim Phillips, Paul Reinhardt, Joel Richler, William Ross, Paul Schabas, Robert Sharpe, Mary Stokes, and Michael Tulloch.

The annual report and information about membership may be obtained by writing to the Osgoode Society for Canadian Legal History, Osgoode Hall, 130 Queen Street West, Toronto, Ontario, M5H 2N6. Telephone: 416-947-3321. E-mail: mmacfarl@lsuc.on.ca. Website: Osgoodesociety.ca.

R. Roy McMurtry
President

Jim Phillips
Editor-in-Chief

Acknowledgments

This book, which is devoted to the relationship between Aboriginal people and criminal law on the nineteenth-century Plains, has returned me to the people and the issues I encountered in the lower criminal courts in Saskatchewan as a law student and young lawyer in the 1970s. The research is grounded in the records of a nineteenth-century criminal court in the same region where one hundred years later my colleagues and I appeared as legal aid counsel. Most of our clients were members of First Nations and Métis communities, reflecting even then the over-policing and over-representation of Aboriginal youth and adults in the Canadian criminal justice system. In the course of research and writing, I have thought often of my clients and their struggles in the face of incredible odds, of my colleagues and friends in the Saskatchewan legal aid bar, and of myriad lessons it took me long to learn and longer to absorb. This work studies an earlier watershed period, but I am mindful that but for the experience a hundred years on I would not have found my way to this study.

The book began as a doctoral dissertation supervised by Jim Phillips at the Faculty of Law, University of Toronto. I thank him for his generous support of my research and writing and for his exemplary commitment to supervision, which I experienced as excellent in every respect. I acknowledge with thanks Carolyn Strange, who deepened my appreciation of research methodology, and Julia Hall in the Graduate Program at the Faculty of Law. I am indebted as well to members of the supervisory and examining committees, Martha Shaffer, Allan Greer, and Darlene Johnston for their support and advice, and especially Hamar Foster for his insightful interrogation as external examiner.

I am honoured that this book bears the imprimatur of the Law & Society Series of UBC Press and of the Osgoode Society for Canadian Legal History. I thank Randy Schmidt at UBC Press for his stewardship in this process, and I am indebted to Wes Pue and Jim Phillips, editors of each, for their support. The metamorphosis and production of this book has been supported by an author's dream team at UBC Press, led by Randy Schmidt and Ann Macklem. Every stage of the process was marked by the perfect combination of encouragement, support, and commitment to excellence. I am most grateful for the extremely helpful comments and advice offered by the three anonymous reviewers for UBC Press. I am deeply indebted to Ann Macklem for her expertise and her unwaveringly calm management of the production of the book and to her talented team at UBC Press: Francis Chow, copy editor; Lara Kordic, proofreader; Eric Leinberger, who drew the map of the Treaty 4 and Treaty 6 region; and Mauve Pagé, whose cover design beautifully captures the spirit and concern of the book.

Since 1986, Osgoode Hall Law School of York University has been my intellectual and professional home. Osgoode has given me the gift of time through sabbatical, research, and other forms of teaching release and leaves. Two Osgoode Hall Law School Research Fellowships awarded at different times over the last decade first made possible many research trips to the Saskatchewan Archives and then facilitated the revision from dissertation to book. I have had the opportunity to present portions of this research at Osgoode Faculty seminars and at Feminist Fridays sponsored by the Institute for Feminist Legal Studies. I am indebted to my Osgoode colleagues for their critical engagement with and generous support of my work as it progressed. Osgoode also provided excellent technical support when I needed it (which was often) and for this I acknowledge with thanks the work and support of Hazel Pollack, Miriam Spevack, Laurie Cormack, Gautam Janardhanan, Shahnoor Tilak, and the other members of the energetic IT team at Osgoode. I also acknowledge with great thanks the excellent research assistance of two different generations of Osgoode students, Karen Pearlston (LLB 1996), Sheetal Rawal (JD 2011), and Alexandra Matushenko (JD 2013).

Research for this book would not have been possible without access to court files and other public records housed and protected by publicly supported archives. I am enormously indebted to the Saskatchewan

Archives Board, especially to the archivists and staff of the Regina office. Catherine Holmes, Janet Harvey, Paula Rein, Tim Novak, Amanda Don, Becky Hahn, Susan Millen, and Bill Wagner were incredibly knowledgeable and unfailingly helpful; their support made the research process a pleasure. The Reading Room at the Saskatchewan Archives in Regina with its walls of windows is a wonderful place to do research and read court files. I acknowledge with gratitude the permission granted to reproduce the photographs and documents held by the Saskatchewan Archives Board that appear in the book. I also thank the now-beleaguered archivists and staff of Library and Archives Canada in Ottawa, especially Ritchie Allen and Patrick St-Jean Croft.

The librarians and staff of the Law Library of Osgoode Hall Law School and of the Scott and Frost Libraries at York University provided invaluable support and assistance for which I am most grateful. One never learns to love reading microfilm, but Hari Saugh and Wayne Mah in the Osgoode Law Library made it possible, and chats about sports with John Thomas made it bearable.

I have come to appreciate that writing is not always the solitary experience it is cracked up to be, a good thing as I have never been drawn to a scholar's monastic life. Many friends and colleagues have been generous in extending different forms of much appreciated support, advice, and encouragement. In particular, I would like to acknowledge and thank Dorothy Chunn, Mary Condon, Michael Gavigan, Renée Gavigan, Joan Gilmour, Janice Gingell, R.J. Gray, Balfour Halévy, Peter Hogg, Judith McCormack, Janet Mosher, Sidney Peck, Wes Pue, Gabriele Scardellato, Kathy Scardellato, Norma Sim, the late Otto Weininger, and the Deverell/Woroner clan. An intrepid few read earlier versions of parts of the manuscript and the most heroic, E. Ann McRae, Amy Deverell, and Balfour Halévy, read and offered detailed comments on full drafts, which were incredibly helpful and for which I am most grateful. Amy not only read with a sharp, critical eye, and very red pen, she also tackled the index, for which I am mindful no amount of thanks can fully be expressed.

I had the privilege of presenting portions of this work to colleagues and students in many academic settings, including the Canadian Law and Society Association, the Law and Society Association, the Toronto Legal History Group, University of British Columbia Faculty of Law's Institute of Feminist Legal Studies, Simon Fraser University's Department of Sociology and Anthropology, Monash University Law School, the National Law School of India University in Bangalore, the American Society of

Legal History, and at the inaugural Legal Histories of the British Empire Conference in Singapore in July 2012. I thank my national and international colleagues for their interest, comments, and advice. Earlier versions of Chapter 4 appeared in: "More Than Just *Mens Rea:* Indian Policy in Two Aboriginal Capital Cases from Regina, NWT" in Margaret E. Beare, ed., *Honouring Social Justice, Honouring Dianne Martin* (Toronto: University of Toronto Press, 2008) 108 and "'Prisoner Never Gave Me Anything for What He Done': Aboriginal Voices in the Criminal Court" (2007) 3 *Socio-Legal Review* 71, and I am grateful to these publishers for allowing me to reprint material.

As I embarked upon the writing, I received a precious gift, one of space and peace, from friends who made their beautiful cottage available to me during an equally beautiful autumn. From deep in the heart of Muskoka, I was able to write about criminal law on the nineteenth-century Aboriginal Plains, and I thank Beverley, Thomas, and Lorraine Burns for this generosity and hospitality. And in Umbria, where much of the thinking and some of the writing of the book has been done, *ci sono dei buoni vicini di casa, i nostri amici – Brunella, Luciano, Federica, Letizia, e Andrea – grazie mille.*

Historical research is inevitably about the past, and my own has been with me in this project. My life has been graced by people who think I can do anything, even when I have had reasonably held doubts. I thank my mother and late father, Edith Gavigan and Keith Gavigan, for their lifelong encouragement and support of my aspirations and endeavours. Judy Deverell can no longer be thanked in person, but her love, confidence, and trust remain with me. Thanks beyond measure go to Karen Andrews, my smart, irreverent partner and most precious critic, who for many years has lived and breathed this project with me – here, there, and everywhere. No one was called upon to make more sacrifices or to extend herself than was Karen, listening to and reading everything, never in silence, mostly without complaint, and never without insightful advice.

But, from beginning to end, this has been for Amy, my-our cherished daughter, with love and hope, as she continues along the path she has chosen, committed to the importance of ideas, the arts, and social justice.

Hunger, Horses, and Government Men

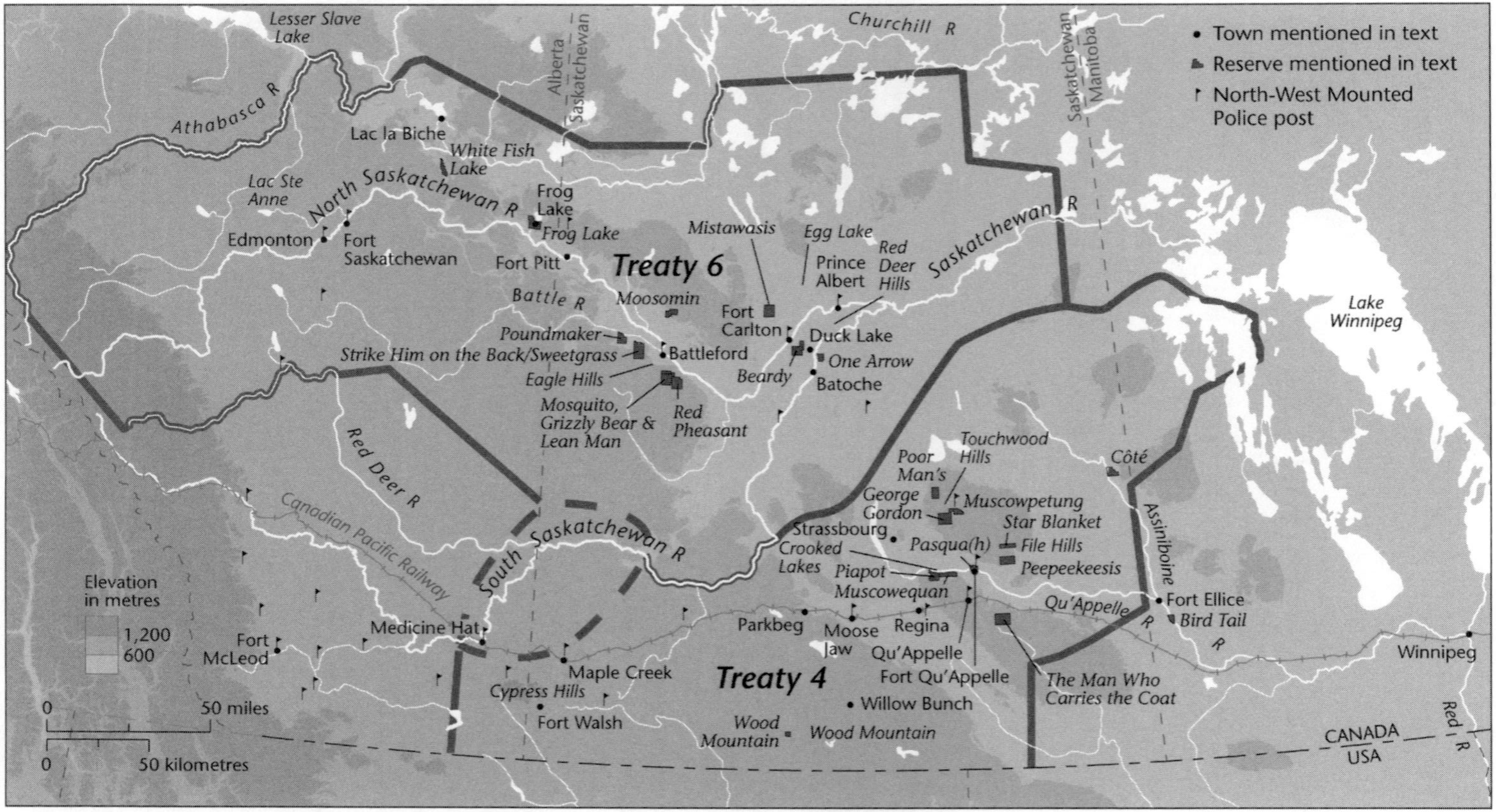

Map 1 Treaty 4, Treaty 6, and Indian reserves. | Cartographer: Eric Leinberger.

Introduction

One Warrior's Legal History

This book tells a little-known story, relying on voices seldom heard. It is the story of the relationship between the Plains First Nations and Canadian criminal law as it took root in their land. This is the first in-depth analysis of the relationship between the First Nations and the criminal law in the territory that is now Saskatchewan in the last quarter of the nineteenth century – a period of profound social, economic, and legal transformation for the First Nations of the region, of which the criminal law and criminal courts were a part.

The story begins in the Eagle Hills near Battleford, the first capital of the North-West Territories, where Pee-yan-kah-nik-oo-sit (Red Pheasant) was the long-time chief of the Eagle Hills Cree. In 1877, the year following the signing of Treaty 6, Red Pheasant's band consisted of twenty-seven men, forty-six women, and ninety-two children. This included the chief (and four women and three children for whom he received a treaty payment), four headmen (and their families), twenty-two other men and their families, and five families headed by women where no man was listed.[1] Peaychew, a signatory to Treaty 6 in 1876 and long-time headman to Red Pheasant, was listed and appeared as Number 4, "Pee-yah-Chew," on the Treaty Annuity Paylist. It is with his story that this book begins.

One Warrior's Watershed: Peaychew's Legal History

On 5 October 1885, Peaychew appeared as a prisoner before Stipendiary Magistrate Charles Borromée Rouleau, charged with the offence of treason-felony for his involvement in what for many years was known as the Riel Rebellion, and later as the North-West Rebellion and, still more recently, as the North-West Resistance.[2] Unrepresented by legal counsel, Peaychew pleaded guilty and was sentenced to two years in the Manitoba Penitentiary. On his admission to the penitentiary on 7 November 1885, the prison register recorded simply that he was an Indian, forty years of age, 5 feet, 8 inches tall, with dark hair, eyes, and complexion, whose occupation was indicated as "none."[3] This was not Peaychew's first encounter with Canadian criminal justice.

In early June 1880, his twelve-year-old daughter, M-c-s, had gone missing in the Eagle Hills. The girl had been living with her paternal aunt and her aunt's husband, Robert Saunders, since their marriage approximately three years earlier. Peaychew told the court that he had given his daughter to his sister and her husband because they asked to have her with them, and he had agreed so long as they remained in the area. He explained that he was always satisfied with their treatment of the child.[4] She had gone missing, however, during an egg-hunting trip with Saunders and two other men, and, perhaps surprisingly, Saunders had not informed her father of this on his return.[5] Instead, Peaychew learned that the child was missing only when another man, Tobacco Juice, indirectly alerted him by asking him whether she had returned. Tobacco Juice then informed him directly that she had been lost on the hunting trip. Peaychew later told the court that he went through the camp asking after the girl, and when he could not find her, he set out for Saunders's place. When he arrived, he found his sister, her husband, and two other men, Joseph Gouin and Louis LeToup. The men were working on a house. Peaychew asked Saunders what had become of the child; Saunders deflected this query with his own question: "Didn't she get to your place?" Peaychew told Saunders what he probably already knew – that the little girl had not turned up at his camp – and he warned that "if my child is lost there'll be some trouble."[6] Peaychew enlisted Saunders and Gouin in a search of the area where the child was last seen, but she was not found.

Peaychew may have feared the worst, but he did not take matters into his own hands. The trouble that he promised his brother-in-law came in the form of North-West Mounted Police (NWMP) constables Chassi and Prongua, dispatched by their sergeant to see after the missing child. It is clear from the court file that both Peaychew and Chief Red Pheasant spoke to Constable Chassi about the circumstances of the child's disappearance from Saunders's camp, and one of them may have alerted Chassi's commanding officer initially. Chassi dispatched some Indians to request

Saunders, Gouin, and LeToup to come and see him at the Eagle Hills Mission the next day, and then he went out to search for the child himself. Saunders presented himself at the mission the next morning and gave Chassi a statement explaining how the child had become separated from the hunting party. Saunders also gave Chassi a stocking that he said he had found, and which the child had been wearing the previous Sunday while out on the trip.

Saunders, LeToup, and Gouin were arrested on suspicion, brought directly before Magistrate Hugh Richardson in Battleford on 12 June 1880, and charged with an elaborate offence,[7] surely difficult to prove and dubious with respect to these facts: that they "unlawfully by fraud detained an Indian child under the age of fourteen years with intent to deprive her father of the possession of such child."[8] The court proceedings were interpreted into Cree by Peter Ballendine for the three prisoners ("all of whom understand that language"[9]), and into French by Constable Chassi for LeToup and Gouin.

Magistrate Richardson received Chassi's description of how he had come to the Eagle Hills Mission, of the search that had been undertaken, and of the statement that he had obtained from Saunders. The matter was adjourned to the following week at the request of the police. The record reveals that Saunders and LeToup were released on their own recognizance, and that Gouin was remanded into custody. At the next appearance, Peaychew's statement was taken; Richardson's apparent ambivalence about the case he called the "Case of the Lost or Stolen Child of Pee-Yah-Sew" was resolved in favour of the accused men, and the charge against them was dismissed.

The case of this missing child attracted the attention of the local paper, the *Saskatchewan Herald,* and was reported upon in considerable detail on the front pages of the 21 June and 5 July issues. The *Herald* reported that Gouin had been detained in custody as it appeared that he had been the last of the three men to see the girl.[10] The *Herald* also reported the warning given by Richardson to the three accused men before he ordered the adjournment:

> [T]he magistrate spoke in severe terms of the heartlessness of these three men in not following the child and making sure she was safe, and in not promptly notifying her father and instituting a search for her. He further explained that if she were found dead but without marks of violence they might be found guilty of manslaughter for their negligence; while if the body were found bearing such marks they might be put on their trial for

> the graver charge of murder. He also pointed out to them that it was their duty to conduct a vigorous search, and to aid by every means in their power the police and those engaged in the endeavor to clear up the mystery surrounding the case.[11]

According to the *Herald,* following the adjournment, an extensive search was undertaken by the NWMP commanding officer, two constables, and possibly even the prisoner Gouin, together with the people of the Eagle Hills reserve, all to no avail. Upon the reopening of court on the following Thursday, the statements of a number of Indians were taken (although only that of "Pee-Yah-Chew" is recorded in the court file), but the newspaper reported that they threw no new light on the case. The *Herald* indicated, although the court file did not, that when Richardson dismissed the case, he bound the three men "in their own recognizance to appear if called upon."

On 5 July, the *Herald* reported that on 20 June the missing girl had "walked into her father's house as unexpectedly as she had mysteriously disappeared, much to the surprise and joy of her family."[12] According to the *Herald*'s informant, the girl said that while she had been unhitching the horse from the cart, she saw two men on a hill whom she did not recognize, and so she ran and hid. She later saw the Indians who were searching for her and others on the Plain, but she was afraid and continued to hide, eating only roots, buds, grass, and the occasional egg for the fourteen-day period, before finally making her way to her father's house. The *Herald* reported that a great feeling of relief was experienced throughout Battleford when word of the child's safe return was received. Most especially, the paper added, the three men who had been under suspicion were relieved to learn of her safe return.

By 1882, Red Pheasant's band had declined in number to one hundred thirty-nine persons (twenty-three men, thirty-four women, seventy children, and twelve others).[13] That year, Peaychew received a treaty payment of $40 for himself, two women, and four children. In October, shortly after treaty payment time, Peaychew was again before Magistrate Richardson in Battleford, involuntarily and as a prisoner in custody, as a result of an Information sworn by Indian Agent Hayter Reed that he had engaged in conduct that in today's context would be regarded as akin to welfare fraud.

At the preliminary hearing before the justice of the peace, Reed alleged that Peaychew, by false pretences and with intent to defraud, had obtained

$15 in treaty annuities to which he was not entitled.[14] Reed deposed that when asked at treaty payment time for the numbers he had claimed as belonging to his family, the prisoner had named, among others, "a certain woman and two children," for whom Reed had paid him $15. Reed claimed that he had subsequently learned that "for the last two or three years he had discarded the woman and had refused to support her or the children, and that he claimed their pay last year." Reed also claimed that Peaychew had refused to return the money, and so he had him arrested.

A short deposition from Chief Red Pheasant was received by the NWMP officer sitting as justice of the peace; no interpreter is indicated. Red Pheasant's words were recorded, and he is said to have indicated that he had been present when the Indian Agent paid the treaty annuities: "I heard Mr. Reed say through [Thomas] Quinn the interpreter that Pee-ah-chew had drawn pay for a woman and two children that he had no right to. I know that Pee-ah-chew had drawn money for a woman and two children and that he had no right to the money. I promised Mr. Reed that I would try and get the money back."[15] In his Statement of the Accused, taken before the justice of the peace at the end of the hearing and before being committed for trial, Peaychew denied the statements made against him and indicated that he had intended to pay the money to the woman.[16]

His committal for trial was reported in the *Saskatchewan Herald* in almost precisely the same language as Reed's deposition: that Peaychew had discarded one of his wives, drawn the annuities for her and her two children, refused to deliver up the money when ordered to do so, and was arrested.[17] He was held in custody until 9 November 1882, when the court record indicates simply: "deft discharged."[18] In its account of the case, the *Herald* took the opportunity to edify its readers on the subject of Indian customary practices:

> One of the customs of the Indians is to take as many wives as they please, and to discard them when it suits their humour. Prisoner had, in pursuance of this custom, "thrown away" a wife and two of her children, and when payment was made he drew their annuities as of old ... The Judge laid great stress on the enormity of the offence of trying to rob the Government and explained to the Prisoner the danger he ran. Not being anxious to proceed to extremities for the first offence, and the agent being willing to withdraw the complaint if the money were returned, the court gave the prisoner the option of doing that or having sentence passed on him. The money was paid over and the case dropped.[19]

It may be trite, but nonetheless undeniable, to observe that the *Herald* would have had no access to reliable information on the marriage, separation, divorce, and other cultural practices of the Cree.[20] For the *Saskatchewan Herald,* "Indians" were men who "discarded" women at will. Hayter Reed and the *Herald* might well have characterized Peaychew as having "discarded" his daughter M-c-s, but the facts of the earlier case involving Saunders, Gouin, and LeToup do not indicate a disengaged, uninterested father. Red Pheasant's deposition provided a less than ringing endorsement, and likely not evidence beyond a reasonable doubt, of the charge against his headman, with whom he had stood in 1876 at Treaty 6 and again in 1880 when the child was missing. The perspective of the allegedly discarded woman is nowhere to be found in the court records or the press reports.

In the spring of 1885, "Pee-Yay-Chew" was one of five signatories to a letter to Louis Riel asking for ammunition and his support, evidence of which facilitated Poundmaker's conviction for treason-felony.[21] Described by one of Blair Stonechild and Bill Waiser's informants as a "hardliner" in Red Pheasant's band (Red Pheasant himself having rebuffed Riel's emissaries),[22] Peaychew is reported to have goaded some of neighbouring Cree chief Little Pine's men into joining the Métis in the fight: "You are cowards if you do not fight ... Anyone of you who refuses can don and wear his wife's dress."[23] For Peaychew's role in the events of 1885, Stipendiary Magistrate Rouleau accepted his guilty plea to treason-felony and sentenced him to two years in the Manitoba Penitentiary – a man who nine years earlier had been one of the Cree leaders whose "X" had graced Treaty 6.[24] Over the course of those nine years, Peaychew had made trouble for a man who had treated him with discourtesy by not informing him directly, or at all, that his young daughter was lost; had been prosecuted by the Indian Agent; had been publicly ridiculed by the *Saskatchewan Herald;* had been lectured but not convicted by Richardson; and finally – and for the first time – had been convicted as a result of his participation in the events of 1885. He was pardoned in March 1886 and released from the Manitoba Penitentiary,[25] as were others,[26] and he lived past the age of seventy.[27] Despite his pardon, the Treaty Annuity Paylists in the years that followed continued to list him as a rebel[28] – a Treaty 6 signatory and a father who had once invoked the assistance of the police and the court.

Peaychew's complex and uneven relationship with Canadian criminal justice between 1876 and 1886 lays the groundwork for the story and interpretation found in this book of the more general relationship between the First Nations and the criminal law in the region in the last three decades of the nineteenth century. Peaychew's experience with the criminal law exemplifies the transformation of the period: as a signatory to Treaty 6 in 1876, he had a personal experience and understanding of what the representatives of the Crown had promised and expected of the First Nations that entered into the treaty. As headman to Chief Red Pheasant, along with Poundmaker, he would have had occasion to consider matters of concern to the Eagle Hills Cree, and he stayed with Red Pheasant when Poundmaker established his own band (and reserve not far from Red Pheasant's reserve).[29] The legal records suggest that he might have been a man who knew his rights, who made good on a promise or threat, who was not easily intimidated, who stood his ground. He was prepared to make use of the law, and when first taken as a prisoner to court in 1880 he did not simply nod his head.[30] He did not share the misgivings of his chief about Louis Riel, and he joined the historic struggle in 1885.

The press report of his conviction and sentence for treason-felony, together with the skeletal entry in the prison register, provide at best the barest sketch of the Cree hunter and warrior. A more fully developed and complex portrait of Peaychew, and of his experiences with Canadian criminal law, clearly emerges from the court records of Hugh Richardson in the years before Peaychew's appearance before Charles Borromée Rouleau, who succeeded Richardson in 1883 as stipendiary magistrate in Battleford.

Peaychew's little-known guilty plea and conviction for treason-felony invites a reflection upon our knowledge of the trials and convictions of better-known First Nations leaders for the same offence in the aftermath of the events of the 1885 North-West Resistance. As other historians have demonstrated, the First Nations people of Treaty 4 and Treaty 6 paid a heavy price for modest to nonexistent forms of involvement and support in the events of the spring of 1885.[31]

The images of the 1885 Resistance trials loom large in the historical literature. Significant among them are photographs of Cree leaders in custody following the events of the spring and early summer. Among the most vivid of these are those of Mistahimusqua (Big Bear) in shackles at Fort Carlton,[32] of Big Bear and Pîhtokahanâpiwiyin (Poundmaker) at the time of their trials in Regina,[33] and of Big Bear in Stony Mountain Penitentiary, "shorn of his shoulder-length hair to humiliate him."[34] Images of the shackled, incarcerated Cree leaders have come to exemplify, for some historians, the nature of the relationship between Aboriginal peoples and Canadian criminal law (see Figures 0.1 to 0.3).

Historian Sidney Harring describes their prosecutions for treason-felony as "the most famous Indian criminal trials in Canadian history."[35] This not

Figure 0.1 Big Bear as a prisoner in June 1885. | Saskatchewan Archives Board, R-B3780.

Figure 0.2 Big Bear and Poundmaker at their trial in Regina, 1885, photographed with *(at the far left in front)* Big Bear's young son Horse Child (not Little Bear). Poundmaker is misidentified as a Blackfoot chief. | Saskatchewan Archives Board, R-A2146.

FIGURE 0.3 Poundmaker, 1885. | Saskatchewan Archives Board, R-B8775.

unreasonable claim warrants consideration as well as a brief analysis of the implications of those trials and how they have been interpreted by legal historians. The names and histories of other Cree, Assiniboine, and Dakota leaders also prosecuted (and some of them imprisoned) for treason-felony in the aftermath of the violent spring of 1885 are less well known: White Cap, One Arrow, Lean Man, Yellow Mud Blanket, Peaychew, to name but a few. Poundmaker's charisma (and his striking good looks, which made him the darling of some of the press, even if not the law[36]) and Big Bear's stature as a political and spiritual leader no doubt contribute to the attention. The Resistance trials have come to symbolize the defeat and subordination of the Plains Aboriginal peoples by the Canadian state and to define the role and contribution of the criminal law.[37]

It would be an error to dismiss, or even to minimize, the significance of the 1885 Resistance trials, and I do not intend this.[38] A hierarchy of knowledge and names does exist, however: we know more about the 1885 trial of Louis Riel[39] than about the companion trials of Poundmaker and Big Bear. Due to the press coverage at the time, as well as popular and scholarly accounts written since,[40] we also know more about the trials of Poundmaker and Big Bear than we do about those of the Willow Chief One Arrow[41] and the Dakota Chief White Cap.[42] We know less about the eighty-one First Nations and forty-six Métis prisoners also tried in 1885[43] or about Papamahchatwayo (Wandering Spirit), Apischiskoos (Little Bear), Manichoos (Bad Arrow), Papamakesick (Round the Sky), Wahwahwitch (Man Without Blood), Kittimakeguh (Miserable Man), Napaise (Ironbody), and Itka, the six Cree and two Assiniboine warriors hanged for murder at Battleford following summary trials or guilty pleas in Fort Battleford on 27 November 1885.[44] We also know more about the handful of prosecutions concerning the potlatch in British Columbia[45] and of religious dances on the Plains[46] than we do about the routine engagement of criminal law on the ground and the Plains Aboriginal people who for one reason or another found themselves before justices of the peace, magistrates, and – later – judges, before or after the events of 1885. This book renders visible some of these people and some of their stories. And from these stories images emerge of relationships rather more complex than are commonly understood at present.

"The Grist of the Law"

There is now more interest in the records of proceedings of lower criminal courts, characterized by some as "low law," and this book forms part of this reclamation.[47] The definition of and distinctions between high law and low law are important, if contested by some postmodern socio-legal scholars critical of the apparent primacy given to state law.[48] By "high law" Douglas Hay means "the law of appellate courts, most law professors, and most opinion makers."[49] Low law, in contrast, comprises the "most common daily manifestation" of law: summary proceedings, before a magistrate without a jury and without counsel.[50] The socio-legal, political (and arguably scholarly) implications of high law are important: rare and expensive high law – the "most loudly articulated account of law" – becomes the only form of law.[51] High justice is celebrated "as if low justice did not exist,"[52] and thus scarcely meriting a scholar's gaze or analysis or a law teacher's mention in the classroom.

It is low law, however, that affects most people, and certainly most directly affects the poor, the marginalized, the vulnerable, and the oppressed – those whose voices are muted in and by law, who cannot afford to retain lawyers even if lawyers are available and/or willing to represent them. In today's context, their ranks include social benefits recipients, tenants, the displaced and undocumented, the working poor, and the homeless, who find themselves vulnerable to prosecution for a plethora of small offences and municipal bylaw infractions for which legal aid is seldom available. The accused persons of low law appear before the lowest level of the judiciary, most of whom historically, and many of whom still, are not schooled in the law. The justice they experience is lean, unadorned, and summary at best. And when on occasion they find themselves in high-law contexts or reported on in the press, caricature and insult often compound the injury of poverty and oppression.

I have found that on the nineteenth-century Canadian Plains, "law" for most people, including most First Nations people, meant low law. When accused of crime, they appeared in court invariably as a prisoner, without legal counsel, without legal arguments, without grand juries, in proceedings conducted in a foreign language, where they had limited access, if any, to basic linguistic interpretation. This law meant confinement in a police barracks before the hearing and taking of depositions; and if the evidence was sufficient to warrant a committal for trial but was otherwise weak, release on bail or a recognizance until trial was possible – if indeed there was a trial (and often there was not where this form of interim release was granted). For most accused persons, it meant remaining in custody at the police barracks until trial, appearing before the magistrate in his office at the barracks, and serving a custodial sentence in the same police barracks. For most, it involved a preliminary hearing or possibly summary trial before one or two justices of the peace, who probably held that office because they were a Hudson's Bay Company factor, a North-West Mounted Police officer, an Indian Agent, or a medical man or other eminent member of the settler community. For many, then as now,[53] it involved a guilty plea and no trial, and, for almost all, no appeals to a higher court. For the most unfortunate, it meant a prison sentence to be served in the Manitoba Penitentiary, a form of death by incarceration for many.

Hugh Richardson was the first magistrate before whom the First Nations peoples of the Saskatchewan region, including Peaychew, had appeared. The research for this book derives from his court – a lower territorial trial court – in its everyday application of ordinary criminal law. My primary focus is on the Aboriginal people who appeared as deponents, witnesses, informants, and accused persons, and on the kinds of cases that were prosecuted, whether or not there was a trial or conviction – cases that Canadian legal historian Louis Knafla once characterized as the "grist of the law."[54]

"A Distinct Sense of Place"

In many ways, the space, terrain, and territory are easier to discern in the court records than are the people whose cases and experiences are set out therein.[55] The context whence these cases derived and found their way to the court defies capture through contemporary concepts of rural or urban, for it was neither. A way of life based on a different relationship to land, family, and work is described in many of the court records, together with the intersection of newer relationships and influences.

The Plain is omnipresent in these records – as space, place, and location. It offered some people sanctuary from a summons that would never be delivered or a sentence that would not be served, just as it readily delivered up others. People met each other on the Plain; assaults took place on the Plain; people sent word to the judge telling him of their inability to come to court because they were on the Plain; and those who were thought to be evading justice took refuge on the Plain. On the Plain, hungry indigenous people approached freighters' wagons filled with flour, sugar, and pemmican.[56]

The land, and people's relationship to it, animates and shapes the unfolding of the cases. We learn of the chilling discovery of the bones and charred remains of a mother and her children buried in the snow in the bush following their murder by her husband, their father.[57] The pond in the spring that promised ducks but brought death to an elderly hunter at the hands of his son-in-law;[58] another pond in another season that gave rise to the murder of another family by two brothers who claimed that their hunting territory was being encroached upon;[59] the lost child left behind on a hunting trip;[60] the bank of the lake where the body of a newborn infant was buried by a young mother;[61] the swampy place where a young girl was found crying while trying to wash herself, having been sexually interfered with by her mother's husband;[62] the place on the river where a hapless Mountie moored his canoe, perhaps not appreciating the invitation it represented;[63] the river again, where a Cree man was told he should fetch his water, rather than from the "water hole";[64] the distance of a mile – measured by telegraph poles – for a horse race outside Battleford.[65]

The court records also reveal the newcomers' different but no less significant relationship to land, disputes over it giving rise to criminal prosecutions: houses that were "taken down" by an aggrieved husband demonstrating his complaint about the homeowner's inappropriate intimacy with his wife[66] or thrown into the river by those who argued a prior claim;[67] empty homes and schoolhouses left unoccupied for a season or year,[68] one of which was used as a refuge by a fifteen-year-old British orphan immigrant who had been brought to Canada, who said, when found in the house, that he had wanted a home of his own;[69] piles of firewood intended only for the private use of owners.[70] The land, the distance, the space, the weather, the terrain, the seasons, the location – a "distinct sense of place"[71] – significantly form and inform the stories and the cases found in the early court files.

These are cases that did not, could not, wend their way to the higher courts, even if appeals had been permitted.[72] The spoken words, frequently through an interpreter (who was sometimes sworn in), were recorded by a justice of the peace, and depositions were marked with an "X." These cases of low law are those of the Plains Aboriginal people. To do them justice requires us to be attentive to complexity and contradiction and to avoid the trap of self-evidence, thereby adding to our understanding of the people and their relationship to and engagement with the criminal law in the land that became the North-West Territories.

How the Story Is Told

Historical scholarship reflects the writer's approach to research, method and techniques, ideas, and the writer's aspiration to understand and interpret the documents and data she has found. I accept completely the perspective that legal historical research into court records works with broader contexts, and take a broad view of the evidence in court records.[73] It is important, however, to be clear how one defines one's broader contexts. My study is of the relationship between Aboriginal people and the criminal law in the North-West Territories in the last three decades of the nineteenth century. On one level, the broader context of this study has encompassed two collections of one judge's criminal court records, and not simply the ones in which Aboriginal persons are named as accused persons. By reading all the criminal files of the two courts over which Hugh Richardson presided between 1877 and 1903, I was able to identify non-Aboriginal as well as Aboriginal accused persons and to develop a fuller understanding of the operation of criminal justice in the region during the period. Thus, I was also able to locate more cases involving Aboriginal peoples that enabled an analysis of a fuller range of Aboriginal experience of and engagement with criminal law in the North-West Territories.

Although my focus is on criminal law, I broadened the legal context of this study as well: I looked beyond the formal black letter of criminal law to identify and incorporate other forms of law that emerged as relevant: Treaty 4 and Treaty 6, the Dominion government's Indian legislation and policy, and Aboriginal "criminal law" prior to 1870. This broader legal context has enabled me to consider the relationship between the treaties, government policy, and the criminal law.

Stephen Robertson also has reminded interdisciplinary socio-legal historical researchers of the importance of engaging with the law.[74] For me, this involves paying close attention to the distinction and relationship between legal forms, legal institutions, and legal actors. Informed by the work of social historians that identified forms of agency and activism within the First Nations and forms of conflict within the state,[75] I eschewed an assumed relationship between the criminal court and government policy, and I looked for expressions of Indian policy in criminal prosecutions. I have proceeded from the premise that the coercive aspects of the *Indian Act* and government policy were a different form of legal coercion, and not simply another point along a supposed continuum of criminal law. This has led me to a critical engagement with criminalization and the exemplars offered in other social and legal historical literature, about which more will be said below.

I have drawn extensively on socio-legal, non-legal, and Aboriginal sources, as well as the nineteenth-century territorial press and Annual

Reports of the Commissioner of the North-West Mounted Police to enable me to develop a more fully social account of both the data and the dimensions of the court records.

Finally, I have made extensive use of direct quotations of the words attributed to First Nations participants in the criminal proceedings. The words they spoke were likely spoken in their own language, interpreted by a man charged with that responsibility, on occasion sworn in by the court, and then transcribed by a justice of the peace or a court clerk. Where possible, I have attempted to reproduce their words by quoting directly from their depositions, statements, and testimony in the court documents rather than summarizing or paraphrasing. I am mindful that lengthy quotations should be used sparingly, but on balance I think it is important in this writing to stay as close to their recorded words as possible (bearing in mind that the text is at least twice removed from the speaker). Although court proceedings do not give much space for the voices of the marginalized, what the marginalized have to say for themselves in these settings is worth repeating.

In identifying the themes around which the book is structured, I have departed from conventional legal methods to identify and analyze this complex relationship. Rather than take the analytic and substantive categories of criminal law as its organizing principle, forms of Aboriginal participation in the criminal law and its processes are used to organize the themes and chapters of the book. I looked beyond the dyadic relationship between the state and the accused to capture a wider spectrum of Aboriginal involvement and participation in the criminal law. This includes Aboriginal informants, complainants, interpreters, and witnesses, in addition to accused persons. In choosing this approach, a debt must be acknowledged to socio-legal historical work on law and colonialism that bears the influence of history, anthropology, legal pluralism, and international law – to scholars who have begun to re-examine the relationships between colonized and indigenous peoples and colonial law and the ways in which indigenous and other subordinated peoples actively participated as actors in colonial legal processes and in criminal justice systems.[76]

In the Western Canadian context, historians R.C. Macleod and Heather Rollason argue that considerable evidence can be found that in the period 1874-85 Aboriginal people in the North-West Territories experimented, negotiated with, and used the law when it appeared to them to be useful.[77] Tina Loo also emphasizes that First Nations peoples were active agents in the development of legal institutions and processes in the Canadian West – who, as guides, trackers, constables, court interpreters, and Crown witnesses, "brokered the extension of European state power in the form of law."[78] Loo offers this assessment of First Nations peoples who used the law, cooperated with the police, erected gallows, worked as constables, and so on: *"[T]hey helped reproduce the system that contributed so much to their domination.* However, their engagement with the law and their victimization by it was more complex than simple, straightforward oppression ... [N]ative peoples' engagement with the law speaks to and for the ambiguities and contradictions of power, complicating our understanding of agency and oppression and hegemony and resistance."[79] In explaining the role of Aboriginal men as special constables, or that of chiefs and communities in turning over alleged murderers, she argues that they were deploying the law to serve their private interests.[80] Emphasizing the importance of Aboriginal agency, she nonetheless appears to suggest that the participation by Aboriginal people in the legal system was tantamount to collaboration with legal authority against their community.

Context is important, and the situation and experience of the Plains First Nations, signatories to Treaties 4 and 6, suggest something different from that suggested by Loo above. In the North-West Territories, many chiefs who were prosecuted or who as informants turned to law were protecting their people or pursuing their community's interests. Cree chiefs Beardy and Lucky Man, Assiniboine chief Lean Man, and Cree-Assiniboine chief Piapot were prosecuted criminally at different times for attempting to assist or protect their people; Cree chiefs Beardy, Red Pheasant, and Strike Him on the Back (through his headman) invoked the law to seek assistance or redress for their band members; and Assiniboine chief Bear's Head was permitted to post bail in 1884 for his fellow chief Lean Man. chief Mosquito testified as a character witness in another case, on behalf of one the members of his band charged with horse theft. Blackfoot chief Stamiscotocar (Bull Head) was thrown in police cells for refusing to hand over one of his men to the NWMP,[81] and in another case he was the informant in the prosecution of an apparently private matter – that is, he accused a Métis man of stealing one of his horses.[82]

Indigenous and colonized peoples around the world have participated within the legal systems and have used and resisted laws,[83] and the Plains First Nations were no exception. Although the fact of participation of colonized peoples in colonial legal processes is not unique, as others writing of other colonial contexts have shown,[84] understanding its forms and significance remains a more difficult challenge, which we take up in this book.

And What of Criminalization?

Criminal law is generally understood to be the perfect expression of a coercive legal form, expressing as it does the power of the state to criminalize, to enforce, to detain, and to punish. Even so, this coercive legal form is replete with contradictions. While it is undeniable that criminal law legitimates, enforces, and reinforces relationships of inequality, it also mediates these relationships.[85]

A central argument of this book is that the discourse of criminalization fails to capture the complexity of the relationship between the First Nations and the criminal law, because it directs our gaze only to the criminalized and away from others. As with Peaychew, many forms of engagement with the criminal law are described in this book. I have found cases in which First Nations individuals laid Informations against white men as well as men from their own communities, alleging different types of offences, such as theft and assault;[86] cases in which Aboriginal women and girls appeared as informants and witnesses and charged white and Métis men, as well as men from their own communities, with forms of sexual interference with, or "carnal knowledge" of, them or their daughters;[87] cases in which only a handful of First Nations women and girls appeared as accused persons, charged with or implicated in the theft of small items, such as a tea kettle from an empty house,[88] a silver spoon from an empty schoolhouse,[89] the clothes that First Nations children were wearing when they ran away from the industrial school,[90] or, in the case of Betsy Horsefall and Benjamin Gordon, in the theft of a horse that Betsy said was hers.[91]

Perhaps the strongest argument of this book concerns the form and content of law and reflects my long-standing commitment to the importance of attending to the specificity of different legal forms and the relationship between them.[92] The book represents a sustained call for a more precise definition and use of the concept of criminalization, one in which distinctions between criminal law as a legal form and other forms of law are recognized, and that seeks to apprehend the contexts, circumstances, and sites in which actions and practices of Aboriginal peoples were prosecuted – as crimes or as regulatory or other statutory offences.

Some of the historical literature reveals a certain imprecision with respect to the definition and scope of criminal law. Many scholars adopt a wide approach to criminal law, in which all legal forms that have an air of compulsion, coercion, or sanction are coloured with a criminal law brush. Recent work examining the efforts of the Canadian state to restrict and curtail traditional forms of Aboriginal expression and activity, including dances and ceremonies, hunting, and fishing, uses the language of criminalization to characterize them.[93] For instance, a now iconic exemplar of criminalization is said to be found in amendments to *Indian Act* in 1884 that prohibited particular kinds of dances and celebrations (such as the potlatch in British Columbia).[94] For the Plains First Nations, the most expansive and relevant *Indian Act* restrictions were introduced in an 1895 amendment to s. 114 that prohibited dances involving giveaways and wounding or mutilation.[95] Although historical evidence implicates the police as well as Indian Department officials in efforts to enforce the prohibitions and prosecute these offences, the historical evidence also indicates that these prohibitions were resented, resisted, and ignored as well as only occasionally and unevenly enforced (indeed, they were almost unenforceable) on the ground.[96] In any event, these provisions fell outside the ambit of criminal law.

Admittedly, caution is in order here. Interdisciplinary scholarship in socio-legal studies argues for a broader notion of crime – one that challenges the historical preoccupation with crimes of individual wrongdoers and the historical neglect of crimes of the powerful, including the state and corporate actors and institutions,[97] as well as the historical neglect of the experience of the environment, culture, and entire communities as victims of forms of seldom criminalized violence.[98] If one proceeds with criminal law narrowly construed (excluding some of the coercive provisions of the *Indian Act,* for instance), one may risk proceeding with too narrow an understanding of crime. The importance of critical engagement with a self-referential notion of true "criminal law" cannot be denied.[99] The content of criminal law is neither universal nor transhistorical; and, importantly, criminalization is not self-evident.

The process of criminalization occurs when people are criminally prosecuted and convicted for forms of conduct that have become defined by the state as crimes. It may encompass the extension of criminal law over formerly non-criminal behaviour, or it may involve the systemic targeting, overpolicing, and criminal prosecution of particular groups and communities for particular kinds of offences. Inevitably, it is intended to express and enforce social denunciation for socially injurious conduct. In legal scholarship, it is important to be attentive to the analytic distinction between legal and extra-legal forms of compulsion and legal coercion, between prohibition and regulation, and between committal and conviction, in order to precisely identify the nature of the law under discussion.

To insist upon specificity in the scope and definition of criminal law need not lead one to an uncritical acceptance of the legitimacy of its norms. It is important, however, to be attentive to questions of form, content, and diversity of legal instruments deployed by the state, many of which contain offences but which do not involve the denunciation and sanction normally associated with criminal law.

An important and related line of inquiry concerns the way in which legal historians have or have not addressed the specificity of the two legal regimes of the *Indian Act* and the criminal law, and the sites of intersection between the Canadian government's "Indian policy" and the criminal law component of its national policy. The Indian policy of the Canadian government intensified over the last two decades of the nineteenth century with the introduction of increasingly oppressive amendments to the *Indian Act.*[100]

In recent work examining the efforts of the Canadian state to restrict and curtail traditional forms of Aboriginal expression and activity, the language of criminalization has been invoked.[101] For some scholars, the prohibition of some forms of religious ceremonies and dances, together with special practices and policies, such as the pass system,[102] offer evidence of the nature of the Canadian state's treatment of Aboriginal peoples.[103] For the most part, these initiatives occurred under the legislative auspices of the *Indian Act* or the administrative initiatives of the Commissioner of Indian Affairs and his Indian Agents in the field. It has become commonplace in some of the literature to refer to the criminalization of Indians and Indian religious celebrations.[104]

There are other voices in the historical literature that offer different emphases. It is significant, in my view, that one recent study expressly devoted to law, colonialism, and First Nations addresses the struggle over the right to fish and the regulatory framework, including offences, of the *Fisheries Act.*[105] Nowhere in Douglas Harris's careful study of the restriction and regulation of the Aboriginal fishers of British Columbia does he characterize the process as one of criminalization. Similarly, Katherine Pettipas's equally rigorous study of the interference with and prosecution of First Nations ceremonies on the Prairies characterizes government policy as one of regulation.[106]

We can also, however, find instances and forms of NWMP resistance to federal Indian policy. Pettipas's carefully researched study of the regulation and repression of indigenous religious ceremonies on the Prairies provides irrefutable evidence of the legalized campaign of repression of forms of religious celebrations. Nevertheless, although her work demonstrates the lengths to which the government went to circumscribe and curtail these forms of religious expression, including the prosecution and imprisonment of a number of Aboriginal celebrants, she also notes that some members of the NWMP actually ignored orders to prevent dances and instead facilitated the events.[107] Both Pettipas and John Jennings cite Stipendiary Magistrate Macleod's refusal to convict Indians who had been arrested for performing a sun dance. Macleod, a former commissioner of the NWMP, is said to have delivered "a scathing rebuff" to the police who had made the arrests, likening their conduct to having made an arrest in a church.[108]

In sum, Pettipas's study of the regulation of Plains Indian religious ceremonies evinces a nuanced analysis, showing the uneven and contradictory tensions that accompanied this damaging legislative initiative. She reminds her readers that only some forms of dances and celebrations (those involving "giveaways"' and "piercings") were prohibited by the *Indian Act;* that because of its vagueness, the police often declined to enforce the infamous s. 114 of the *Indian Act;*[109] and that even Indian officials were of the view that a prosecution should be undertaken only as a last resort.[110] It is also clear that some First Nations people were prepared to "test" the strength and limits of the law.

In conclusion, the "self-evidence" of criminalization is a trap for the unwary. Criminal law becomes all law; criminalization becomes an umbrella that covers all manner of legal forms (from liquor violations, to hunting and fishing offences, to the *Indian Act,* and sometimes even criminal law). In critical legal historical work on criminal law, criminal law is depicted "in one dimensional terms"[111] – criminal law "acts against" subordinate people (women, indigenous peoples, workers, and so on). This is the dominant account in the critical literature – inequalities of class, race, and gender are reinforced as the criminal law bears down on those brought before it. And yet some of the literature may also be read to offer a more relational notion of criminal law,[112] even in a colonial context.

This book takes a different view and makes a different argument: the offences and prosecutions under the early *Indian Acts* did not criminalize the First Nations; rather, they "Indianized" the First Nations.[113] They were prosecuted as "Indians" – not as criminals – for violating the *Indian Act,* for not conforming to the behaviour required of Indians by this legislation.

The question of how to identify and interpret forms of participation and treatment of subordinated peoples, such as Aboriginal peoples of the Canadian Plains, in criminal processes is important. Against the "coercive domination" story of criminal law is set and celebrated instances and forms of "resistance" to it. It is clear from the literature, and appears to be confirmed by the court records I have examined, that the experiences transcend one-dimensional notions of oppression coupled with victimization. Few historians today would suggest that the Aboriginal peoples were the passive victims of the new dominant order that was being established in the Territories. At the other extreme, it is also an error to regard every act of defiance or criminal activity as a form of resistance. The challenge is to identify forms and expressions of resistance while resisting an impulse to portray every act in heroic terms. In the middle is the vexing matter of participation, and here again the challenge is to avoid the worst excesses of misunderstanding.

This book reinserts criminal law into criminalization and, through the stories yielded by the court records, offers new evidence – and a new interpretation – of its role and relationship with the First Nations on the Aboriginal Plains.

I

Legally Framing the Plains and the First Nations

The adverse impact of criminal justice upon Aboriginal people in Canada today is a matter of public record, aided in part by the research findings of many commissions of inquiry, the provenance of which invariably has been a wrongful conviction, a suspicious or wrongful death, or another form of injustice or mistreatment.[1] The 1991 Manitoba Aboriginal Justice Inquiry, for instance, was commissioned in response to two specific incidents: the 1987 trial of two men for the 1971 murder of nineteen-year-old Helen Betty Osborne in The Pas and the 1988 death of a prominent First Nations leader, J.J. Harper, who had been shot during an encounter with the Winnipeg City Police. The two judges who served as commissioners examined all aspects of the Manitoba criminal justice system, including the issue and possible contribution of systemic discrimination against Aboriginal people. The Manitoba Inquiry still stands as a beacon for its commitment to historical perspectives and to a community-based approach, which took the commissioners to Aboriginal communities to meet with Aboriginal people, and to receive, in their own languages, their accounts and reflections on the justice system.[2] In its *Final Report,* the commission paid close attention to what it characterized as Aboriginal Concepts of Justice, and identified an underlying philosophy of resolution, healing, and harmony within the community in dealing with crime.[3]

It is difficult to imagine a greater contrast between such an approach to crime and punishment and the one introduced to the North-West Territories in the 1870s. Incarceration, with or without chains, hard labour, and corporal punishment, and much less a penitentiary, formed no part of the "atonement" process in Aboriginal communities, although self-imposed exile of many years might be undertaken by murderers who were "palpably in the wrong."[4] The introduction and imposition of a new legal regime; new notions governing property, marriage, and sexual relations; and the redefinition as crimes of past practices associated with the hunt, sport, and inter-tribal relations, such as capturing and recapturing horses, represented a historic cultural assault. Added to this was an armed cavalry of white men mandated to enforce these new laws, many of whom also had the authority to adjudicate, to convict, and to sentence. And yet a still greater threat was posed by men who did not need to wield weapons or wear uniforms to announce their power, men who dispatched the police, magistrates, and others to administer the new regime, the most senior of whom never once set foot in the North-West Territories. Government men in Ottawa devised law and fashioned policies that would govern the most intimate and important aspects of everyday life, intent on redefining and transforming the First Nations into "Indians."

The criminal court records upon which this book relies involved criminal prosecutions, many of which occurred before the 1895 amendments to the *Indian Act* (which extended earlier "Potlatch" prohibitions to the giveaway dances of the Plains First Nations). The primary purpose of the *Indian Act,* including its offences, was not to criminalize but rather to Indianize the First Nations[5] – a distinct, separate, and no less damaging project.

Despite, or perhaps because of, its undoubted significance today, criminal law, especially at its lowest echelons, is not the most examined area in historical scholarship concerning First Nations and Aboriginal peoples and Canadian law. That position is occupied, understandably, by studies that have focused on Aboriginal rights, generally expressed through Aboriginal title[6] and treaty rights.[7] More recently, colonialism and self-government,[8] and the scourge of Indian government legislation and policy,[9] have jockeyed for position.

In this chapter, I introduce the legal framework and institutions of, and actors in, the criminal law in the Canadian Plains after 1870. I widen the frame of conventional understandings of criminal law and the administration of criminal justice in the North-West Territories to introduce the particular contribution of the Canadian state to the First Nations of the Plains and the relationship between them.[10]

I begin with the legal legacy of the *Royal Charter of 1670,* which effectively deeded the entirety of Rupert's Land to the Hudson's Bay Company (HBC) and delegated the administration of justice to the Company. One might be forgiven for simply saying "and the rest is history." But, of course, what followed from this imperial conceit was not a simple unfolding of history. Complex and contradictory relationships were forged between the Company and the First Peoples over the next three hundred years, until, without a word to its indigenous partners, the Company signed off with the Crown for £300,000, with some entitlement to land and mineral resources remaining with it, and (sort of) walked away.[11]

Mindful of the overarching importance of the "numbered treaties," I also identify the criminal law dimensions and implications of Treaties 4 and 6. A brief overview of the legislative framework of the North-West Territories follows, with the introduction of the principal legal offices and officers responsible for law and the introduction and administration of criminal justice, notably the North-West Mounted Police (NWMP) and the stipendiary magistrates in the early period. With the creation of the Supreme Court of the North-West Territories in 1886, the office of stipendiary magistrate ceased to exist, and in the next section I introduce this new court, to which Hugh Richardson was appointed until his retirement in 1903. In the last section, I introduce Hugh Richardson himself.

New Legal Frameworks and Relations for the Canadian Plains

The Legal Legacy of a Royal Prerogative: Secrets and Lies

> *Many, many years ago, before we were born, one of the Kings gave the [Hudson's Bay] Company certain rights to trade in this country. The Queen thought that this was not just neither to the white nor the red man. She considered that all should be equal.*
>
> – *Alexander Morris (1874)*[12]

The legal framework and institutions of, and actors in, criminal law in the Canadian Plains changed dramatically after 1870, when Canada acquired land from the Hudson's Bay Company and created the North-West Territories. This is a story that cannot be told, however, without acknowledging the legal legacy of the *Royal Charter of 1670*. It is easy to underestimate and difficult to overstate the importance of this Charter to the legal history of the North-West Territories, through which, by royal prerogative, King Charles II bestowed upon the Hudson's Bay Company a vast area called Rupert's Land along and stemming from the shores of

Hudson Bay.[13] In the years following 1670, the Company construed the terms and boundaries of its Charter in increasingly wide terms.[14]

In addition to proprietary and trading rights, the *Royal Charter* purported to confer legislative and judicial power over the inhabitants of the territory.[15] The administration of justice for Rupert's Land, such as it was, rested in the hands of the Company. All HBC factors (managers) were regarded as magistrates,[16] but the precise scope of the Company's judicial authority has been a matter of some differing interpretation.[17] While the legislative authority conferred by the Charter covered officers and employees of the Company, the judicial authority appeared to be couched in broader terms, and to apply to all persons "that shall live under them."[18]

The First Nations of the Plains came to have more than passing, casual contact with Europeans, thanks to their long-time trading relationship with the HBC. The norms and protocols governing those contacts were established through many decades of trading and barter. Two aspects of the HBC's approach to the administration of justice are of particular relevance: first, it seems that, in practice, the HBC seldom interfered with the internal affairs or disputes of Aboriginal people, appearing to accept Aboriginal rule of law for Aboriginal matters;[19] and, second, the Company never established a regularly convening court in Rupert's Land.[20]

One significant change occurred after 1870, when Rupert's Land and the Indian Territories were acquired by Canada. The HBC's policy of non-intervention in internal Aboriginal disputes had extended to areas of social life and social relations that in other contexts would attract the attention of the criminal courts. Aboriginal self-governance and the policy of non-intervention changed, however, with the restructuring of the legal foundation of the land they called home, together with the arrival of a police force and the signing of the treaties.[21]

The Canadian State and the First Nations of the Plains after 1870

> *This land provided us with many things, gave us a good life and we were able to survive by all the resources available to us ... The Creator had placed them on the land for our use, and though they were taken, continues to protect us, which is why we were never completely destroyed and why we are still here today. If the whiteman had a better understanding of what the land meant to us he would have thought differently about us.*
>
> – *Senator John Tootoosis (1976)*[22]

> *We heard our lands were sold, and we did not like it; we don't want to sell our lands; it is our property, and no one has a right to sell them.*
>
> – *Chief Sweet Grass (1871)*[23]

One theme in the historical literature speaks to symmetry in the earlier and later acquisitions of this land: in 1670, the imperial authorities knew little about the land and the peoples who were by royal decree transferred to the HBC;[24] two hundred years later, Canadian officials regarded the North-West as untamed land, "occupied by a flawed people,"[25] without any system of law and order – land that was theirs for the taking, and a bridge that had to be taken in order to anchor British Columbia's place in the Dominion and to fend off the aggressive Americans. The image of a vast and ungoverned land concealed a substantive contradiction that the central government failed, perhaps refused, to recognize: there was an indigenous legal tradition as well as a democratic political tradition in the North-West, one "which drew its strength from indigenous forces and the consent of the majority."[26]

It is difficult to say with certainty what the population of the indigenous peoples was when Rupert's Land and the Indian Territories were incorporated into Canada as the North-West Territories. The territory was home to the Cree (Plains, Swampy, and Woodland), the Assiniboine (Nakota, Stone Sioux, or Stonies), and the Saulteaux (Plains Ojibway) peoples.[27] In a few years, the North-West Territories would shelter the Dakota Sioux led by Sitting Bull, who fled there following the battle, and their victory, against the American military at Little Big Horn. Farther to the west lived the Blackfoot Confederacy (the Blood/Kanai, Siksika, and Peigan) and Tsuu T'ina (Sarsi) peoples.[28] People of mixed indigenous and European ancestry with strong associations, including familial, to both the HBC and the First Nations also called the territories home. In the official records and documents of the period, these many peoples were invariably referred to as "Indians" and "Half-Breeds," respectively. The decade following 1870 witnessed a "Métis" exodus from the Red River into the Territories, settling in areas connected to Oblate missions such as St. Albert (which had received Métis migrants as early as 1866), St. Laurent, Duck Lake, and Fort Qu'Appelle, as well as Wood Mountain and Cypress Hills.[29]

Although maps of the region tend to situate the Cree, Saulteaux, and Assiniboine in discrete geographic territories, Aboriginal scholars of the region and period emphasize the interrelatedness of the Plains First Nations.[30] Cree appears to have been the *lingua franca*,[31] but the lines between the nations may have been fluid, as suggested by no less than the lineage of many of the leading Plains leaders of the period,[32] and the fact that many "Cree" bands were in fact mixed Cree and Saulteaux (as was the case, for instance, for Chief George Gordon's band in the Touchwood Hills) or mixed Cree and Assiniboine (as was the case for Piapot's followers).

Precision with respect to the population figures in the North-West Territories is elusive and probably impossible. The total population of the Plains in 1870 has been estimated at between 40,000 and 50,000 persons, with the First Nations accounting for about 35,000 (see Table 1.1).[33] The 1884-85 Census of the North-West Territories reported that the Territories were home to at least 21,990 people of English, Irish, Scottish, and French origin (the major non-Aboriginal population groups), 4,848 "Half-Breeds – Métis" (English, 577; French, 3,387; Scotch [*sic*], 762); Irish, 65; and Unidentified, 57), and an Indian population of 20,170.[34]

By 1891, the population of the Territories was reported to be 66,799 (Table 1.2).[35] It is difficult to ascertain the population figures for the First Nations in the Territories at the time of this census, as no separate category for "Indians" appears (although the number of Indian chiefs is listed as 13[36]); however, from the figures reported for "Canadian born" persons in the North-West Territories districts of Eastern Assiniboia (5,936), Western Assiniboia (2,247), and Saskatchewan (7,659) in 1891, we can infer a dramatic drop in the Aboriginal population.[37] Confirming this inference, the 1901 Census of Canada reported that the total population of the four districts of the North-West Territories was 158,940.[38] Of this, the Half-Breed (Métis) population was said to number 11,636, and the "Indian" population was reported to be 14,669 (by district: Saskatchewan, 5,836; Western Assiniboia, 292; Eastern Assiniboia, 2,921; and Alberta, 5,620).[39]

In the thirty years following the incorporation of the North-West Territories into Canada, the population of the Plains First Nations was reduced dramatically, possibly by half or more. The fate of one band, Lean Man's small band of Assiniboines, who had been forced to relocate to the Eagle Hills from the Cypress Hills in the south, offers evidence of the devastation of the period. Lean Man's Band did not last much beyond 1891 (see Table 1.3).[40] The ravages of disease, such as smallpox, alone cannot account for this tragic attrition and loss of all their children and others; one has to consider the demise of the buffalo, the loss of the commons,[41] the relegation to reserves, restrictions on movement, and the determination of the Dominion government not to ameliorate but rather to pursue policies that ensured immiseration and starvation, designed to enforce the transition from the traditional way of living to the new. In the midst of

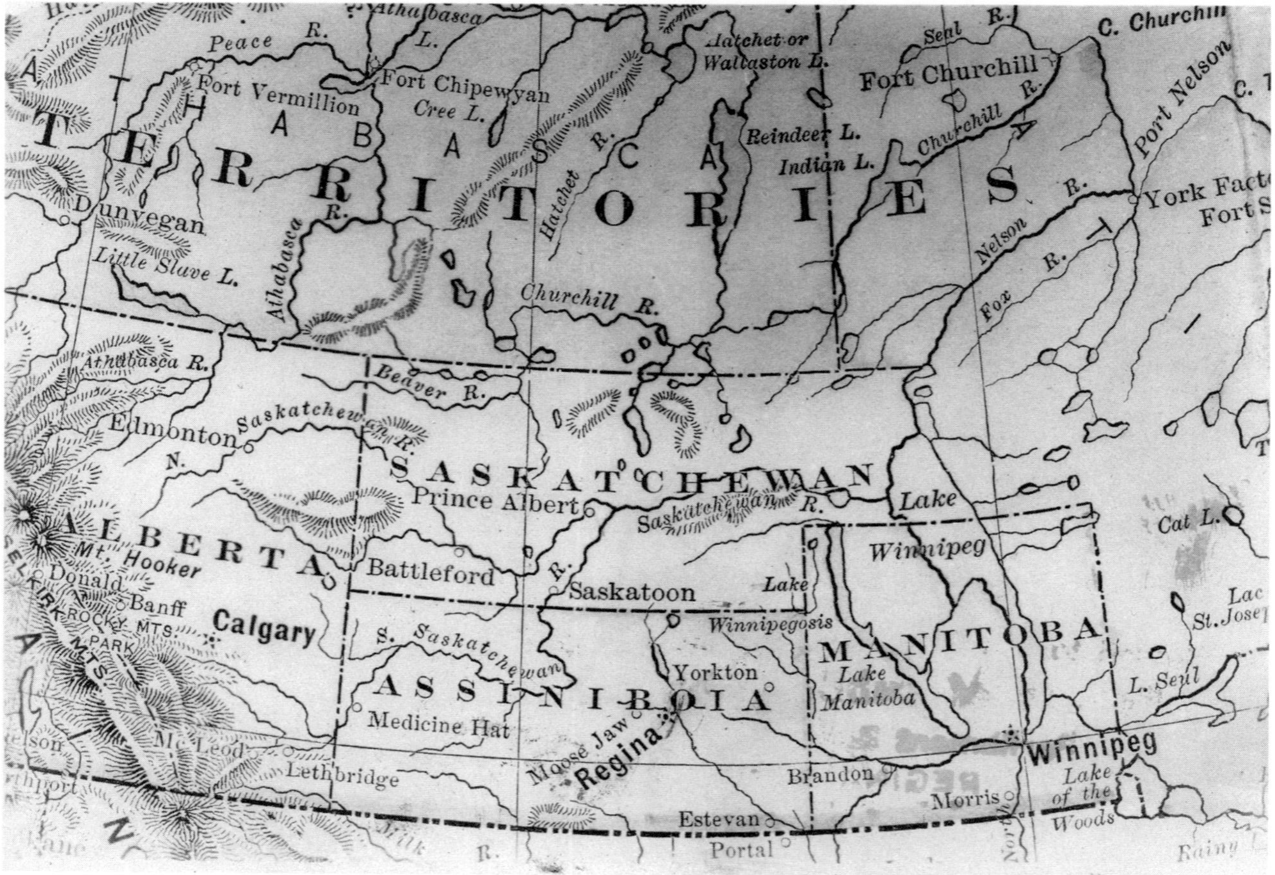

Map 2 The North-West Territories before the inauguration of Saskatchewan and Alberta. | Saskatchewan Archives Board, R-A5123.

Table 1.1 Population of the Canadian Plains, 1870-1901

Year	Total population	First Nations population
1870	40,000-50,000	35,000
1884-85	48,097	20,170
1890-91	66,799	–[a]
1901	158,940	14,699

a Figures not reported.

Table 1.2 Census data: North-West Territories, 1884-1901

	1884-85 Census		1890-91 Census		1901 Census	
North-West Territories	Total	Indian	Total	Indian	Total	Indian
Total population	48,362	20,170	66,799	NR	158,940	14,669
Saskatchewan	10,646	6,260	11,150	NR	25,679	5,836
Assiniboia	22,083	4,492	30,372	NR	67,385	3,213
Western Assiniboia	–	[319][a]	9,890	NR	17,692	292
Eastern Assiniboia	–	[4,173][a]	20,482	NR	46,693	2,921
Alberta	15,533	9,418	25,277	NR	65,876	5,620

Note: NR = not recorded.

a The Districts of Western and Eastern Assiniboia did not exist in 1884-85; the totals here have been compiled from the figures reported for the sub-districts.

Table 1.3 Lean Man's Band Treaty 6 Annuity Payments, 1882-85; 1891

Year	1882	1883[a]	1884	1885[b]	1891
Men	9		6	6	1[c]
Women	16		10	10	3
Boys	22		11	11	1[d]
Girls	23		7	7	
Other persons/relatives	4		3	3	
Total	74		39	39	5

a Information is missing.

b Bands that were involved in the North-West Rebellion did not receive treaty payments in 1885.

c Lean Man.

d Born in 1891.

Sources: Library and Archives Canada, RG 10, Treaty Annuity Paylists for Treaties 4, 6, and 7: reel C-9415, vol. 9415 at 118 (1882); reel C-7146, vol. 9417 at 92 (1884); reel C-7146, vol. 9418 at 128 (1885); vol. 9424 at 612-13 (1891).

this well-documented catastrophe, the criminal law, while neither neutral nor benign, played a modest and often mediating role.

Treaty 4, Treaty 6, and the Administration of Criminal Justice

> *This is our land! It isn't a piece of pemmican to be cut off and given in little pieces back to us. It is ours and we will take what we want.*
>
> – *Poundmaker (1876)*[42]

> *I had ascertained that the Indian mind was oppressed with vague fears; they dreaded the treaty; they had been made to believe that they would be compelled to live on the reserves wholly, and abandon their hunting, and that in time of war, they would be placed in the front and made to fight.*
>
> – *Alexander Morris (1876)*[43]

A full consideration of the form and content, nature and implications of the numbered treaties – all issues of critical importance – exceeds the scope of this study. Suffice it to say that if the treaties are to be regarded as the foundation of the relationship between the First Nations and the Canadian government, that foundation has been shaky and flawed from the beginning. It is now widely recognized that the official texts were essentially boilerplate templates, and that the signed versions of the treaties represent only the version of the Canadian government and at best only an imperfect and incomplete expression of what the leaders of the First Nations regarded as the agreements that were being negotiated.[44]

It is clear that the primary concerns of the First Nations involved economic survival and well-being, and the need to ensure a future for their children and their children's children, including education and access to health care, for as long as the sun shines and the water flows. Needless to say, not everyone trusted the government or the treaty process. Big Bear, the most reluctant signatory and the longest holdout, is said to have likened the invitation to make treaties to bait for a trap.[45] Cree chief Mistawasis is said to have responded to critics and skeptics at the Treaty 6 negotiations at Fort Carlton by invoking the terrible losses they had experienced already: "I speak directly to Poundmaker and The Badger and those others who object to the signing of this treaty. Have you anything better to offer our people? I ask, again, can you suggest anything better that will bring these things back for tomorrow and all the tomorrows that face our people?"[46]

The arrival and role of the North-West Mounted Police did not loom as large in the negotiations. Still, the argument attributed to Mistawasis suggests an explanation why, as the court records reveal, Plains First Nations people also turned to the criminal court for assistance and redress. Referring to American whiskey traders as "cutthroats and criminals who recognized no authority but their guns ... [and who] murdered Indians without fear of reprisal," and to the "Red Coats" who were sent by the Queen Mother, Mistawasis is reported to have said: "The Police are the Queen Mother's agents and have the same law for whites as they have for the Indians ... I, for one, look to the Queen's laws and her Red Coat servants to protect our people against the evils of white man's firewater and to stop the senseless wars among our people."[47]

The treaties made the First Nations subject to new law and imposed upon the chiefs the obligation to assist in bringing to justice and punishment any of their people who infringed Canadian criminal law.[48] The written text of the treaties that purported to protect their hunting, trapping, and fishing rights also contemplated legal encumbrance, regulation, and restriction.[49]

Finally, in addition to the general prohibition on the manufacture, importation, sale, and possession of intoxicants in the North-West Territories,[50] a prohibition on sale or possession on Indian reserves also was incorporated into the treaties.[51] These prohibitions on alcohol would also be buttressed by the *Indian Act* in 1876.[52]

A new approach to law and governance via Canadian criminal law, and the institutions and actors of policing and adjudication, were all contemplated by Treaty 4 and Treaty 6.[53] The chapters that follow demonstrate from the court records that in the early years following the signing of the treaties and the arrival of the stipendiary magistrate, chiefs and their headmen made demands on the police and the court when the well-being of their people was at risk or required redress.

The Arrival of Canadian Criminal Justice in the North-West Territories, 1870-1905

The Early Period: 1870-86

The matter of law and its territorial administration was certainly not the central government's highest priority for the region.[54] Beyond paying compensation to the Hudson's Bay Company for its surrender of Rupert's Land, Canada proceeded to reconfigure Rupert's Land and the Indian

Territories into the North-West Territories,[55] without consultation with the other inhabitants of the Territories or their representatives. Neither law enforcement nor judicial institutions were established in the newly acquired territory.[56] By an order-in-council in 1870, however, the Lieutenant-Governor was authorized to provide for the administration of justice and to appoint justices of the peace.[57] This was the first in a series of steps in the piecemeal development of a legal framework.

In 1873, the Dominion government enacted legislation to enable the Governor-in-Council to make laws for the peace, order, and good government of the North-West Territories;[58] this statute continued the requirement that all laws passed by the Council were to be laid before both Houses of Parliament.[59] Three other federal statutes of 1873 provided both the infrastructural form for the administration of criminal justice in the North-West Territories and the federal department that would be responsible for the Territories more generally. The legislation underscored the central government's view of the inseparable connection between "Indian Affairs" and the Territories. The federal Department of the Interior was created by the statute that bore its name.[60] Under this legislation, the Minister of the Interior was to have control and management of the affairs of the North-West Territories,[61] to act as Superintendent General of Indian Affairs, and, as such, "to have control and management of the lands and property of the Indians in Canada."[62]

By another of the 1873 acts,[63] several federal criminal statutes were made to apply in the North-West Territories, including statutes that governed substantive offences (such as forgery, larceny, offences against the person, perjury, and high treason) as well as criminal procedure (including the duties of justices of the peace and the availability of summary justice). With respect to summary trials, Schedule A of that act provided that in the North-West Territories, a "competent magistrate" was to be construed as meaning any two justices of the peace sitting together, whose jurisdiction was to be absolute without the consent of the parties charged.[64]

The North-West Mounted Police

The most prominent, almost axiomatic, image of law and order on the nineteenth-century Canadian Plains is that of the North-West Mounted Police. The presence of the NWMP in the Territories represented and involved more than the enforcement of Canada's criminal law. Its arrival in 1874 has been characterized in the historical literature in various terms, but no historian denies the monumental significance of its presence, whether it is said to represent the implementation of the National Policy in the consolidation of the Confederation of Canada, to be an expression of colonial domination, or to act as the coercive and repressive arm of the young Canadian state. Scholars of all perspectives generally equate the Mounted Police with "The Law" in the Territories, which is understandable, given the duties imposed on the force to act as police officers, prosecutors, justices of the peace, and jailers in the Territories.[65]

The most significant piece of 1873 legislation created the formal apparatus for the administration of justice: the office of Stipendiary Magistrate and the NWMP, a force of three hundred men.[66] A series of disparate provisions in the legislation combined to place almost complete responsibility for all aspects of the administration of justice with the police. In addition to policing duties in relation to preventing crime and preserving the peace, enforcing the ordinances of the North-West Territories, and apprehending offenders, the NWMP was to attend upon the stipendiary magistrate or justice of the peace, to execute their warrants, and to escort prisoners and lunatics to their respective places of confinement.[67] And if jail or prison was "at a distance," the sentencing magistrate was authorized to order that the convict be imprisoned at the police station.[68]

The NWMP commissioner and senior officers were *ex officio* justices of the peace,[69] as were senior Indian Affairs officials, as well as Indian Superintendents and Indian Agents, initially only for the purposes of the *Indian Act.*[70] It appears that despite the fact that there were more lay justices, the police justices adjudicated most of the criminal cases that came before justices of the peace,[71] including trials of accused persons they themselves had apprehended.[72]

The historiography of the NWMP in relation to Aboriginal peoples is dominated by the scholarship of R.C. Macleod[73] and John Jennings.[74] Macleod expressly situates the work of the NWMP in relation to the Aboriginal peoples within the framework of government Indian policy, which he argues proceeded in three stages: the signing of treaties, persuasion to give up the hunt and settle on reserves, and the attempted integration of Indians into the dominant economy and society.[75]

Macleod and others identify an early period (1874-85) and a later period (post-1885) in Aboriginal/NWMP relations; this periodization of relations roughly corresponds with pre- and post-Rebellion/Resistance. For Macleod, credit for law and order in the "early period" rests with the NWMP.[76] Jennings also has characterized the 1885 Rebellion/Resistance as "an obvious watershed both in Police and in Indian history," but he cautions against emphasizing it as a "moment" of demarcation and argues that the Rebellion caused no dramatic change in police-Indian relations.[77] For Jennings, the creation and enforcement of the reserve system was a "more fundamental deep-rooted" cause of deterioration in the relationship between the First Nations and the NWMP.[78]

Given the official or quasi-official nature of much historical work on the North-West Mounted Police,[79] Walter Hildebrandt has argued that it is "difficult to find a balanced history of the NWMP."[80] Even the scholarly account found in Macleod's work is, for Hildebrandt, "as unsatisfactory as those of earlier police historians."[81] Hildebrandt acknowledges that there is "evidence of fair treatment of Aboriginal people by the NWMP," and he concedes that Macleod replaced the image of the police as enforcers of law and order with an image of the National Policy and "a new society."[82] Hildebrandt argues, however, that Macleod's account of the failure of the National Policy and, in particular, of the failure of the Aboriginal people of the Plains to share in the profit of the new economy reflects his own assumption about their culture and abilities.

A more complex relationship to Aboriginal peoples and the forms of law and policy that the police were called upon to enforce may be pieced together by a careful reading of the historical literature. For instance, Jennings suggests that "hardening" of NWMP attitudes toward Aboriginal peoples preceded the 1885 Rebellion. Historians (including Jennings) also note the significance of shifts in Indian policy and the role the police were called upon to play, either in bailing out zealous Indian farm instructors by arresting Indians who threatened or assaulted them (often as a result of provocation or inflexible adherence to government policy), or by enforcing a form of apartheid, following the introduction of the now-notorious pass system. The pursuit of this "policy of repression," says Jennings, is usually thought to have been caused by the Rebellion; he argues, however, that the Rebellion "merely made the policy more blatant."[83] But even here historians have pointed to the NWMP's disagreement with the "work for rations" or "starvation" policies pursued by Indian officials, whose intransigence caused hardship for the Aboriginal people and frequently triggered violence. John Tobias has suggested that Indian Commissioner Edgar Dewdney came to recognize that a policy of withholding rations triggered violent responses from the Cree (in other words, "starving the Cree into submission was not the means to control them"). As a result, Dewdney turned to a policy of "sheer compulsion," which he was able to pursue for only a few months in 1884. This policy, says John Tobias, also proved to be ineffectual and put the Mounted Police who were called upon to enforce it at great risk in the confrontations that ensued (in which they were inevitably significantly outnumbered).[84]

Recently, Tobias, Sarah Carter, Walter Hildebrandt, and Katherine Pettipas have re-engaged with the relationship between Aboriginal peoples and these law officers of the Crown. Carter has argued for a reallocation of credit for the relatively peaceful transformation the West: "The fact that the non-Aboriginal settlement of Western Canada proceeded relatively peacefully, and that 'law and order' was to a great extent observed, has almost entirely to do with the strategies and actions of First Nations."[85]

Carter's research on government policies regarding Indian farming has challenged the conventional wisdom that the First Nations were not amenable to pursuing a different way of life, an interpretation that Carter acknowledges she had thought would remain intact in her own research, but for which she soon found little support. She found that the First Nations peoples were amenable to learning to live and work in this new way, but were thwarted and demeaned by the bad faith of government policy and practices, implemented on the ground by farming instructors. Government policy reflected less a commitment to construction of a new mode of life than to compulsion, confinement, and curtailment of the old.[86] In her discussion of the government's Indian policy more generally, and specifically of the pass system introduced after 1885, Carter notes the dubious legality of the pass system.[87] Katherine Pettipas, relying on Jennings's work, also notes NWMP Commissioner (and Stipendiary Magistrate) Irvine's position that the enforcement of the pass system was a breach of treaty rights.[88] In Carter's words,

> Officials of the NWMP were never comfortable with the absence of any legal foundation for the pass system. The lack of a legal basis in this case undermined the validity of all NWMP operations: they were trying to demonstrate to the Indians that the police enforced a rational system of laws that operated to the benefit of all. In 1892 Commissioner L. Herchmer was advised by circuit court judges that the system was illegal and that the police would surely lose if their right to enforce it was challenged in the courts. The legal opinion of government law officers was sought, and they proved to be "unequivocally opposed to continuation of the practice." In 1893, a circular letter was issued directing all police officers to refrain from ordering Indians without passes back to their reserves.[89]

Carter observes that Assistant Indian Commissioner Hayter Reed (known as Iron Heart by the Cree, Saulteaux, and Assiniboine) "would have none of these weak-kneed legalistic concerns"[90] and ultimately succeeded in having the NWMP reverse its position.

The historiography of the NWMP and Indian relations thus reveals tensions within the Canadian state and challenges conventional causal explanations for the shift or hardening of the attitude of the police in relation to the First Peoples of the Plains. Indeed, further evidence supporting the minor theme of intra-state discord is found in Tobias's research, which demonstrates not only Indian Commissioner Edgar Dewdney's efforts in pursuit of a "policy of compulsion" but also its limits. Dewdney was committed to legal coercion and incarceration of the Cree, but Tobias suggests that he did not trust the rule of law of the regular criminal courts: "[W]hat was needed in his opinion were trial judges who 'understood' Indian nature at first hand and who would take effective action to keep the Indians under control. Therefore, Dewdney wanted all Indian Department officials in the West to be appointed stipendiary magistrates in order that all Indian troublemakers could be brought to 'justice' quickly."[91]

Indeed, as both Jennings and Pettipas demonstrate, and Roderick Martin confirms,[92] the police and the court did not always conform to popular or political expectations. In contrast to the official view typified by Dewdney, the scrupulous fairness of Stipendiary Magistrate and former NWMP Commissioner James F. Macleod toward Aboriginal accused stands out. Despite his prior relationship with the NWMP and his reputation for eschewing the legal niceties, Macleod's understanding of "Indian nature" led him to insist on fair and respectful treatment of them by officers of the Crown and court.[93] This was illustrated notably but not exclusively in his acquittal of Star Child, who had been charged with the murder of an NWMP officer.

In sum, this historical work offers another explanation for the difficulty in finding good accounts of the history of the NWMP in relation to Aboriginal peoples in the prairie west. Within the overarching context of the National Policy and the enforcement of Canadian criminal law, it appears that, although Macleod's assessment of the NWMP's role as agents of government policy is sound. Canadian historians have been able to point to instances of ambivalence, if not outright resistance, to the enforcement of the larger policy and regulatory initiatives of the Canadian government, notably Indian officials' policies.

The Office of Stipendiary Magistrate

The stipendiary magistrate was to be the senior judicial officer within the Territories, with the magisterial, judicial, or other functions appertaining to any justice of the peace, or any two justices of the peace.[94] None was appointed until 1876, however. Thus, for the first five years following Canada's acquisition of the Territories, the significant local judicial actors continued to be HBC men acting as justices of the peace; after 1873, they were joined by NWMP justices. Serious criminal matters were sent for trial to the Manitoba Court of Queen's Bench.

On 1 January 1876, NWMP Commissioner James F. Macleod and Matthew Ryan, a member of the Quebec Bar who had been appointed in 1875 to enumerate Manitoba Métis,[95] received their commissions as stipendiary magistrates for the North-West Territories. Hugh Richardson received his commission in July 1876. Although the magistrates had jurisdiction throughout the Territories, three judicial districts (Saskatchewan, Bow River, and Qu'Appelle) were established in which regular courts were to be held "presided over by a Stipendiary Magistrate, resident in the judicial district."[96]

The criminal law jurisdiction of the stipendiary magistrate was increased through four legislative amendments between 1873 and 1880,[97] when the office was replaced with the creation of the Supreme Court of the North-West Territories in 1886.[98] Initially, a stipendiary magistrate sitting alone could hear only a narrow range of criminal offences, including relatively minor property offences, for which the maximum penalty was less than two years.[99] The 1873 act provided that offences for which the maximum punishment did not exceed seven years were to be tried summarily, without either a grand or petty jury, by two stipendiary magistrates sitting together, or by a judge of the Manitoba Court of Queen's Bench.[100] A justice of the peace, stipendiary magistrate, or judge of the Manitoba Court of Queen's Bench was empowered to commit persons charged with offences punishable by death or by imprisonment in the penitentiary for trial in Manitoba before the Court of Queen's Bench.[101] The extra-territorial jurisdiction of the Manitoba Court was significant as no stipendiary magistrates for the North-West Territories were appointed until 1876.

The *North-West Territories Act* of 1875[102] authorized the Governor-in-Council to appoint no more than three stipendiary magistrates who had jurisdiction to hear and try a broad range of criminal matters, although the Manitoba Court of Queen's Bench continued to play both a companion and a supervisory role.[103] The federal government revisited the issue of the criminal jurisdiction of the stipendiary magistrate again in 1877, by which time the three magistrates had been appointed. The new legislation[104] provided that a stipendiary magistrate sitting alone could try summarily any charge that had been set out in the 1873 act as well as, with the consent of the accused, any offence where the maximum punishment was less than seven years' imprisonment; for offences with a maximum penalty of more than seven years (other than the death penalty), the stipendiary magistrate was to sit with a justice of the peace and a jury of six.[105] For offences punishable by the death, the stipendiary magistrate was to sit with two justices of the peace and a jury of six.[106] Thus, by 1877 all criminal offences could be tried in the North-West Territories. Appeals involving convictions for which a sentence of death had been imposed were to go to the Manitoba Court of Queen's Bench.[107]

Finally, in 1880, the jurisdiction of the stipendiary magistrate as well as that of the justices of the peace was broadened yet again.[108] Now a stipendiary magistrate or two justices of the peace could try summarily property-related offences involving less than $200, as well as all forms of assault, except rape, and offences related to escape custody, obstruction of peace officer, and so on. All other offences were to be tried by a stipendiary magistrate, sitting with a justice of the peace and a jury of six.[109] Again, appeals of convictions with the death penalty were to continue being heard by the Manitoba Court of Queen's Bench.

In sum, the stipendiary magistrates figured prominently in the administration of justice and in the governance of the North-West Territories between 1876 and 1886. Their judicial powers increased steadily following the appointment of Macleod, Ryan, and Richardson in 1876. As *ex officio* members of the small Territorial Council, their influence extended beyond their courtrooms. Richardson, the former Justice Department clerk, credited with having drafted the 1875 *North-West Territories Act*,[110] appears to have played an active and important role on the Council, and is said to have been the principal draftsperson of territorial ordinances.

When the legal administration of the North-West Territories was reconfigured yet again in 1886,[111] the office of stipendiary magistrate was eliminated and the Supreme Court of the North-West Territories was created, as a supreme court of record of original and appellate jurisdiction.[112] The new Supreme Court, composed of five puisne judges, was given all the powers, rights, and privileges of the Court of Queen's Bench with respect to civil and criminal jurisdiction. The Court sat *en banc* in Regina

Figure 1.1 The North-West Territories Supreme Court was made up of *(from left to right)* E.L. Wetmore, James F. Macleod, Hugh Richardson, Charles B. Rouleau, and Thomas H. McGuire. Dixie Watson, clerk of the court, is at the far right. | Saskatchewan Archives Board, R-B3813.

Figure 1.2 Hugh Richardson. | Saskatchewan Archives Board, R-B1400-1.

to hear all questions or issues of law or points reserved for the opinion of the Court, and all appeals, motions, and so on; the Court *en banc* required a quorum of three judges and was presided over by the senior judge.[113]

Three sitting stipendiary magistrates (Macleod, Richardson, and Rouleau) were elevated to the five-member Supreme Court of the North-West Territories, joined by Edward Wetmore and Thomas H. McGuire (see Figure 1.1).[114] Thus, Stipendiary Magistrate Colonel Hugh Richardson became Mr. Justice Richardson, presiding over the judicial district of Western Assiniboia in Regina until his retirement in 1903.[115] Wetmore sat in Moosomin, McGuire in Prince Albert, Rouleau in Calgary, and Macleod in Fort Macleod and later Calgary. In 1902, Edward Prendergast was appointed to the Court and joined the ailing Richardson in Regina.[116]

Hugh Richardson: Stipendiary Magistrate and Justice of the North-West Territories Supreme Court

Before turning to the stories of the First Nations and Aboriginal peoples that are found in the court records of the North-West Territories from the last three decades of the nineteenth century, it is appropriate to introduce the jurist before whom they appeared and whose records significantly inform this book. Hugh Richardson, who dispensed criminal and civil justice in the North-West Territories for the last twenty-three years of the nineteenth century, was by all accounts and appearances a dedicated, hard-working jurist. He retired in 1903, before his region of the Territories was reconfigured in 1905 as the province of Saskatchewan, and before his court was succeeded in 1906 by the Supreme Court of Saskatchewan (see Figure 1.2).

Hugh Richardson is not a household name, even for Canadian legal historians. A flicker of acknowledgment tends to occur when his name is mentioned in relation to Louis Riel, the most famous accused person to appear in his courtroom. His formal contribution to Canadian legal history appears to be simply a controversial flash in the pan. He sentenced Riel to hang in 1885, and for many this is his claim to infamy.

And yet he was the first magistrate before whom the First Nations peoples of the Saskatchewan region would appear who was not also an officer of the Hudson's Bay Company or the North-West Mounted Police. He issued the first cautions and deferred sentences and imposed the first terms of imprisonment that the First Nations experienced. His was the first trial court to dispense a new form of justice based on new concepts

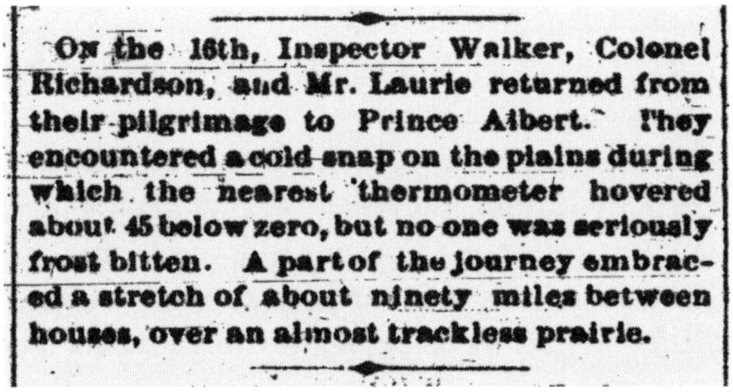

On the 16th, Inspector Walker, Colonel Richardson, and Mr. Laurie returned from their pilgrimage to Prince Albert. They encountered a cold snap on the plains during which the nearest thermometer hovered about 45 below zero, but no one was seriously frost bitten. A part of the journey embraced a stretch of about ninety miles between houses, over an almost trackless prairie.

FIGURE 1.3 This *Saskatchewan Herald* clipping from 27 January 1882 describes Hugh Richardson's return trip from Prince Albert.

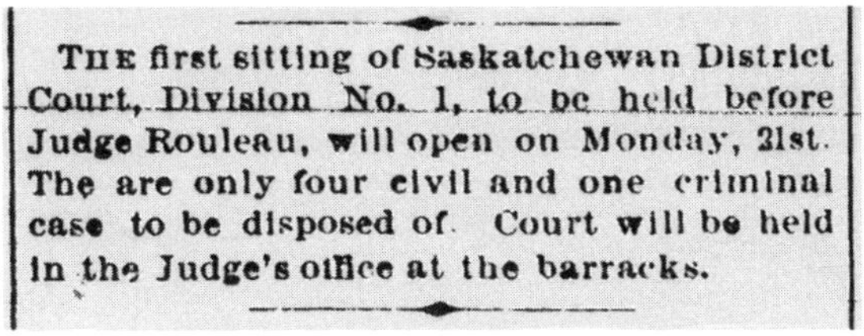

The first sitting of Saskatchewan District Court, Division No. 1, to be held before Judge Rouleau, will open on Monday, 21st. The are only four civil and one criminal case to be disposed of. Court will be held in the Judge's office at the barracks.

FIGURE 1.4 *Saskatchewan Herald*, 12 January 1884. Court was held in police barracks.

of wrong, bringing new forms of punishment to the Cree, Nakota (Assiniboine), and Saulteaux peoples. There would have been as many firsts for him as well.

Several months after his 1876 appointment, Lieutenant-Colonel Hugh Richardson arrived in Battleford, the territorial capital, to take up his judicial duties.[117] One wonders what in his previous life in Ontario would have prepared him for the bush and the plain of the North-West Territories. Born in England in 1812, he had come with his family to Canada as a young man. He was admitted to Osgoode Hall and called to the bar in 1847. He practised law in Woodstock until 1872, when by order-in-council he was appointed chief clerk at the Department of Justice in Ottawa,[118] an appointment he held until July 1876, when he joined Macleod and Ryan as the third stipendiary magistrate appointed for the North-West Territories.

A unilingual Anglophone whose adult life and professional career were spent mostly in the softer land of southwestern Ontario, where cultural diversity came in the form of the Irish, he presided over matters requiring Cree, Assiniboine, Saulteaux, Sioux, and French interpreters in remote, far-flung outposts, along the old fur-trade route of the north Saskatchewan River, reached only by horse and cart or York boats in good weather and horse-drawn sleds in winter, where courthouses or inns would not appear for decades (see Figures 1.3 and 1.4).

Richardson left behind few personal words – there is no autobiography or biography, and there appears to be no personal diary or correspondence.

To the extent that he is recalled at all, it is for his role in the 1885 treason trial of Louis Riel, and more recently for his role in the other trials in the legal aftermath of the events of 1885.[119] In *The Queen v. Louis Riel,* Desmond Morton intimates that Richardson's judicial experience prior to the Riel trial derived from "the police court at Regina [where] liquor offences were the most common item on his docket," although he acknowledges that Richardson had tried four other men for murder.[120] J.M. Bumstead is less charitable: "He was a lawyer with limited trial experience and a very limited imagination who was not likely to have independent views. He had a strong dislike of the Métis, but his racial attitudes would probably not have disqualified him in the eyes of either the Crown or the legal system. Hugh Richardson – unimaginative, weak, inexperienced, and prejudiced – was probably the perfect instrument for a government looking to convict and execute Louis Riel."[121] More recently, the *Globe and Mail* marked the ninetieth anniversary of Richardson's death with the following remembrance in its "Died This Day" column: "In 1885, he secured a place in history when he presided at the trial of Louis Riel, the leader of the North-West Rebellion. Sadly, he was not up to the job and may have been selected for just that reason. The trial was a plodding, procedural affair that remains controversial to this day. In 1887, he was made chief justice of the NWT Supreme Court."[122]

Leaving aside the fact that the office of Chief Justice of the North-West Territories Supreme Court did not exist in 1887, and that Richardson was not appointed to the position when it was later created, the basis of these assessments that intimate judicial inexperience and incompetence is less than clear. That these commentators understand the nature of the jurisdiction or the workload of the territorial magistrates is not an inference easily drawn. By the time of the Riel trial, Richardson had sat as a stipendiary magistrate for nine years, during which time the jurisdiction of his court had expanded on more than one occasion. By 1885, he had presided across the length and breadth of the Territories over at least 250 matters, and probably more, both civil and criminal in nature. Contrary to Morton's assertion, liquor offences were far from the most common item on Richardson's docket in Regina: between 1883 and 1885, only 11 of the 100 or so matters over which he presided involved liquor violations.[123]

Sandra Bingaman,[124] Peter Ward,[125] and Wilfred Bowker[126] found that Richardson was well respected in the Territories as a magistrate, that his reputation did not include political bias, and that he expressed no public opinions about the guilt or innocence of the accused persons who were charged in the aftermath of the events of the spring of 1885.[127]

While it is counterintuitive to criticize a judge for being attentive to procedure, as Morton does, Richardson does in fact appear to have taken matters of procedure and jurisdiction very seriously. It is clear that he sought advice from the Minister of Justice on procedural matters from time to time,[128] and that he had a definite sense of the public duty owed by public servants. In one file, he queried the right of an NWMP officer, as a government official, to receive the informer's fee, a portion of the fine imposed in a liquor violation. When he realized that this had caused offence to the officer, he relented in that instance, but indicated that he would refer the question to Ottawa.[129]

Questions of jurisdiction, in many forms, arise time and again in Hugh Richardson's court files. Often the question is implicit; at other points, a question of jurisdiction was raised by a person caught by the criminal processes, and occasionally by the judge himself. The North-West Territories was a vast region with many borders. And, as with all borders and boundaries, it was life and law at the margins that provided particular challenges.

For instance, the extent of the reach of long distance law arose in an 1879 case in which the authority of the HBC factor as justice of the peace and the jurisdiction of the Stipendiary Magistrate of the North-West Territories was challenged. Daniel Williams of Fort St. John was charged with a number of offences arising out of a dispute he had with the Hudson's Bay Company. Initially accused of shooting and wounding three of the Company's horses as they grazed in his field, he was later charged with arson and with threatening the lives of the chief trader and one of the clerks. He was arrested and taken in chains (following an escape attempt) down the river to Fort Saskatchewan for trial. He was held in custody for several months, and also sued the HBC men for false arrest and imprisonment.

Williams was firmly of the view that he should not be tried in the North-West Territories, and it appears that Richardson too had his doubts. In response to Richardson's letter to the Minister of Justice in Ottawa, the Deputy Minister offered pragmatic advice: if the evidence is good, assume jurisdiction; if the case looks weak, decline.[130] Although Richardson ultimately dismissed Williams's complaints of wrongful arrest and imprisonment, it is not clear from the file what, if any, disposition was made in the criminal charges against him.[131]

Richardson also exhibited a strong sense of one's moral duty to protect others, especially those he regarded as vulnerable.[132] In 1892, George Glover, a Regina man, was indicted and tried for theft of a sum of money from one William Park. Park, while extremely drunk, had spent the night with a young woman at an establishment described in the court file as a "whore house outside Regina." In the morning, he pulled out a roll of bills and offered her $100 if "she would go with him for two weeks and not let another man touch her." This was said within Glover's hearing, and shortly thereafter Park realized that his roll of money was missing. The woman who ran the house insisted that the police be sent for; when the police arrived, the "girl" was searched but nothing was found. Something about Glover made the police officer suspicious, and on searching him on the spot he found a roll of $100 in Glover's under-drawers.

Richardson convicted and sentenced Glover to two years of hard labour at the Regina jail. During the sentencing, he commended the fairness of Crown prosecutor David Lynch Scott and the efforts of defence counsel T.C. Johnstone, and then continued at length:

> [I]f this man was drunk it was the more your duty to have protected him or to have seen that he was protected, and not assist in making him worse; you should have done with him as you say was done with you in a like condition, and knowing that he had money about him it was your duty to have seen that that also was taken care of, and the police would have taken

> care of both; if anyone is to blame in this matter who can be said to be more to blame than yourself.[133]

In the following year, when sentencing Pierre Bourassa to five years and twenty lashes of the cat-o'-nine-tails for unlawful carnal knowledge with a young Aboriginal girl who was apparently under fourteen,[134] Richardson lectured the prisoner:

> The Schools like the Industrial School where she has been for the last 6 years were established with the purpose of elevating these girls and putting them in a position where they would be perfectly civilized and of removing any distinction between as we say their colour and that of the whites and if ever there was a duty incumbent upon a young man even if she had that night asked you to cross the prairies with her it was your duty above all to have avoided anything wrong even if she proposed it herself.[135]

On the other hand, he appears to have been prepared, perhaps out of necessity, to sit on matters where he was the informant/complainant, as in the (ultimately unsuccessful) prosecution of Constable Henry R. Elliott for a series of offences in relation to his unauthorized marriage to Luders

FIGURE 1.5 Battleford, 1884. | Saskatchewan Archives Board, R-A12657.

FIGURE 1.6 Regina, 1887. | Saskatchewan Archives Board, R-B1136.

FIGURE 1.7 Richardson House, Victoria Avenue, Regina. | Saskatchewan Archives Board, R-A2024.

Richardson, Richardson's daughter,[136] or the prosecution of a man for the theft of a shotgun that appears to have belonged to Richardson himself (although he was not the named informant).[137]

When the territorial capital was moved from Battleford to Regina, Richardson moved with it (see Figures 1.5 to 1.7). Once based in Regina, his circuit more closely followed and reflected the new iron route of the Canadian Pacific Railway. The distances he travelled were not as great as when he was based in Battleford; he heard matters in Regina as well as in Moose Jaw, Wood Mountain, and Maple Creek to the west, and Qu'Appelle immediately to the east.

Conclusion

In this chapter, I have introduced the framework of legal institutions and relations that transformed the Plains region of North America from 1670, when the Hudson's Bay Company acquired its rights, and following 1870, when Rupert's Land and the Indian Territories became the North-West Territories under Canadian authority. Just as it is impossible to overstate the significance of the Hudson's Bay Company in the development of the North-West Territories, so too it is impossible to overstate the relevance of the *Indian Act* in reshaping and governing the lives of the First Nations peoples who were subject to it. The outcome of the negotiated numbered treaties was disappointing, but at least the representatives of the First Nations were there. As others have noted, the treaties made no mention of the legal and bureaucratic regime that would be administered by an Indian Commissioner and overseen by the Minister of the Interior of the Dominion government. Indian policy was devised in Ottawa but administered and enforced at the local level.

If the treaties fundamentally altered the nature of the relationship of the First Nations to the land, so too did the *Indian Act* fundamentally alter the nature of the relationship of the First Nations to the Canadian government. But what of other forms of Canadian law?

It is to the criminal law and criminal courts over which Hugh Richardson presided, and their complex on-the-ground impact on the lives of First Nations of the Plains that we now turn.

2
"Of Course No One Saw Them"
Aboriginal Accused in the Criminal Court

Felix Plante appeared as a prisoner before newly arrived stipendiary magistrate Hugh Richardson at Fort Saskatchewan on 15 December 1877. He entered a plea of guilty to a charge of assaulting his father with a rake, seriously wounding him and rendering him insensible. Following the guilty plea, the magistrate ordered that the younger Plante be released on a recognizance to keep the peace and be of good behaviour. He recorded his reasons in the following handwritten disposition:

> That it appearing from the medical statement offered that the said Felix Plante is insane although not now a dangerous lunatic and upon the recommendation of W. Herchmer the medical staff constable of the Fort that confinement is not likely to result in any good effect and being informed by Ins Jarvis that prisoners [*sic*] friends have offered to [watch?] in charge if released – I decline to pass any sentence but direct that upon one surety to keep the peace for one year in $400 be given as surety or two sureties in two hundred dollars each [subject to] Ins Jarvis approval Felix Plante be released.[1]

Felix Plante's case is demonstrative of the many mysteries shrouded by lower-court records. Little about his troubled life is revealed in the thin criminal court file consisting of four sheets of paper: the initial remand dated 27 November 1876 to 30 November 1876, a warrant of committal dated 30 November 1876 and signed by Jarvis JP, the disposition by Richardson, and the surety entered into by Xavier Plante, farmer, of Lake St. Anne, in the amount of $400.

There is neither an Information nor any depositions from any witnesses, including the victim, Xavier Plante, describing the incident and assault. There is no record of the medical officer's statement or any record of any medical evidence. Clearly, the medical officer persuaded Hugh Richardson that Felix was insane although not a dangerous lunatic, but we learn neither the symptoms nor the basis of the diagnosis. It appears also that W.D. Jarvis participated in the process in multiple roles: as senior North-West Mounted Police (NWMP) officer, as the justice of the peace who committed Felix Plante for trial, and possibly as the prosecutor who approved the conditions of his release and approved the surety. Finally, there is no Statement of the Accused.

The court record does not reveal that the Plante family was Métis.[2] It is silent as to Felix Plante's age and the identities of the friends and family members who agreed to keep an eye on him. If the dates in the file are correct, he had been held prisoner in the NWMP guardhouse for a year; if so, the NWMP might have been happy enough to see him discharged from their responsibility.[3]

To further complicate the story, the *Saskatchewan Herald* published the following short item in the fall of 1878: "A half-breed named Felix Plante is under arrest at Fort Saskatchewan, charged with attempting to kill his father. Prisoner is undoubtedly insane, as he says that he is divinely commissioned to kill off the whole human race."[4] It may be that Felix Plante was charged with another attempt on his father's life, or he may have been brought back before Richardson on the original charge and breached recognizance. The NWMP court returns for 1879 contain an entry indicating that "F. Plante" was prosecuted by "X. Plante" as a "Lunatic" under a Territorial Ordinance and convicted by W.D. Jarvis JP at Fort Saskatchewan; the penalty is recorded simply as "committed," and for a final disposition one has to look to the prison records of the Manitoba Penitentiary, which indicate that on 21 October 1880, Felix Plante was "received to the Penitentiary as a Lunatic under the authority of Lieutenant-Governor Laird."[5] There is no indication if or when he was released. A decade earlier, there were no police and no magistrates in the North-West Territories. One wonders what Felix Plante's family would have done with this troubled, violent son who attacked his father had the police and the magistrate not been on their land to deal with him as a prisoner and lunatic.

Having an appreciation of the manner in which the Plains First Nations defined harms or wrongs, as well as how they dealt with "culprits" or wrongdoers before the arrival of Canadian criminal law, is of unquestionable significance to what came after. This line of inquiry is fraught with uncertainty, however; even the naming of the nations and identification of their norms cannot be claimed with confidence. Many of the accused persons in the court records are identified as "Cree," "Assiniboine," "Treaty-Half-Breeds," or often simply as "Treaty Indian" – but were they? For instance, were David Mandelbaum's informants in his landmark ethnographic study, *The Plains Cree,* in fact "Cree"?[6] Neal McLeod suggests that Mandelbaum's designation may have been imprecise and overinclusive.[7] Still, Mandelbaum's informants described their understanding of the nature of a Plains chief's responsibilities in matters related to crime and justice: "It was incumbent upon the chief to maintain order and peace in his camp ... Gift giving was the socially accepted method of mollifying an aggrieved person and in this way the chief eased troublesome situations."[8]

Some of the sources of information about how wrongdoing was handled come in the form of legends, stories, and reminiscences, all redolent of ideological significance. For instance, Edward Ahenakew recounts a story from Chief Mistawasis's band of a dispute between a man who blamed the chief's nephew (Ahenakew's uncle), Ē-pay-as, for having provoked a Blackfoot raid on the camp in which the first man's son had been killed; he pressed Ē-pay-as to give him two horses, but was refused. Tired of the man's insistence, Ē-pay-as, his brothers, and their families left and set up camp elsewhere. When a large party from the main camp followed them to their camp, they refused to leave their tent. In this way, says Edward Ahenakew, "the three refused to obey the camp law."[9] The large party began to cut up their possessions while the three brothers watched. When Mistawasis's son arrived on the scene, one of the brothers (his cousin) teased him, telling him that he had mistaken him for a white man. Mistawasis's son responded in anger with a crushing blow to the man's head. Things then took an even more serious turn, as Ē-pay-as shot and killed the man who had led the party. Ē-pay-as fled with his injured brother, saying to the young Edward, "Go away, my nephew. We have no relatives now. Go away."[10] In Edward's recounting, a sorrowful Mistawasis is said to have assembled his people and told them he wanted no more trouble. The chief arranged for two of his finest horses to be delivered by Edward's father (Ē-pay-as's brother-in-law) to Ē-pay-as so that he might give them, or two of his own, to the son of the man he had killed. Edward's father delivered the chief's horses as a peace offering and Ē-pay-as, holding his dying brother, said he would do as his chief had asked.

Drawing on another story from the Sweetgrass Band, Mandelbaum suggested that this role of a chief continued to be important well into the twentieth century: "A bitter quarrel broke out between two men over the disputed ownership of a heifer. The chief of the reserve gave one of his own cattle to the man who claimed that his animal had been stolen. By this act the dispute was settled, the possibility of bloodshed averted, and the prestige of the chief was enhanced."[11] Moreover, a chief was expected to conduct his own affairs "with the highest restraint":[12] "Even if one of his relatives should be murdered, a chief was supposed to forgo the blood vengeance which ordinary tribesmen would be impelled to take."[13] Mandelbaum was told a story of prominent chief Big Bear's response to an assault as an example of this "restraint," as well as the extra-legal fate of the wrongdoer: "[Big Bear] was once wantonly assaulted and knocked unconscious by a drunken member of his band. In retaliation, Big-bear's daughter immediately ran to the attacker's tipi, slashed it, and bore off his possessions. When Big-bear was revived, he ordered all the man's goods taken back and decreed that no further retaliatory measures be taken. The attacker later tried to make propitiatory gifts, but he was never thenceforth able to regain his former prestige status."[14]

The rules of the hunt are said to have been of particular importance, and these were policed by members of a band's Warrior Society, whose responsibilities also included caring and providing for the needy (including divesting oneself of one's possessions if need be); protecting women, children, and the elderly when the band moved camp; and attending to rituals associated with preparing a body for funeral.[15] Individual hunting was not permitted when preparations for a hunt involving a herd of buffalo were being made, and *mens rea* was not necessary if the hunt was jeopardized. A hunter who either intentionally evaded the watch of the Warrior Society or one who, because he could not control his horse, unintentionally caused a herd to stampede received the same sanction, swiftly administered: his tipi was slashed and his possessions destroyed. If he accepted the action and responded without anger or resistance to this sanction (as Ē-pay-as and his brothers had not done), restitution for his lost possessions would be made.[16]

David Mandelbaum's study concluded that theft was rare.[17] Murder is said to have demanded blood vengeance by the relatives of the murdered man[18] – a practice, of course, not unique to the Plains Cree.[19] According to Mandelbaum, however, "disastrous blood feuds" were averted by the intercession of Worthy Young Men[20] through a ceremony with the Sacred Pipestem.[21] Apparently, also, a payment of horses could commute blood vengeance.[22]

The legal transformation of their land into the North-West Territories had profound implications for the First Nations. In addition to new legal norms governing property, property relations, and marriage and sexual relations, and the redefinition as crimes of certain past practices associated with the hunt, sport, and inter-tribal relations, the hardening of the "medicine line," now known as the United States–Canada border, was also significant to the First Nations who previously had travelled from north to south and back without legal encumbrance. One consequence was the amplification of ordinary horse theft into the smuggling of stolen horses. Some of the cases, however, suggest that the Cree and Assiniboine who engaged in the cross-border horse raids were mindful both of the nature of the risks and the protection the border afforded.

The themes that emerge from the court records provide compelling evidence of a wrenching transition, one that was simultaneously negotiated, avoided, resisted, and painfully experienced by the First Nations of the Plains. Old forms of relations met and mixed with new relations and forms of enforcement that came with the arrival of Canadian criminal law.

Old Relations, New Relations, Differently Defined, Differently Enforced

The time period covered by this book demarcates a watershed: from the period prior to 1870, when the Hudson's Bay Company's criminal law norms were not applied to the internal relations of the indigenous peoples of Rupert's Land, to 1899, when Bear's Shin Bone was convicted of polygamy under the *Criminal Code* for having married two women according to the marriage custom of the Kainai,[23] and to 1902, when Ce Tan (or Chaton), a Dakota man, was charged with failing to provide the necessaries of life to his wife and children after briefly leaving them for a young woman, whose parents objected and invoked the law.[24] In thirty short years, Canadian criminal law redefined as criminal many of the most personal aspects of First Nations life.

The relationship between the First Nations and Canadian criminal law as seen through court files involving First Nations persons who stood as prisoners in the North-West Territories criminal court is the central focus of this chapter. The court records reveal some of what might be anticipated about the criminal law's contribution to the substantive inequality of Canada's Aboriginal peoples. A number of stories lend support to a "criminalization" thesis, and applying this thesis does not present a particularly significant challenge. Indeed, the fact that 71 of the 243 ordinary criminal cases (29 percent) between 1876 and 1886[25] involve one or more accused persons described in the records as "Indian" tends to support the argument that many First Nations peoples' experience of the arrival of the police, criminal law, and the criminal court was one of criminalization. At least one hundred First Nations men, and a handful of women,[26]almost all without benefit of defence counsel, found themselves charged, arrested, and prosecuted. Most were convicted of something; some, but not all, were sentenced to terms of imprisonment at hard labour in a jail at the police barracks, and a few were sentenced to penitentiary terms in Manitoba.

A number of themes in the court records fit well under the rubric of "old relations, new relations, differently defined, differently enforced." This captures the criminal law's contribution to the enforcement of new forms of legal relations (such as wage labour) and an entirely new approach to disciplining children (locking them up), as well as the challenges the criminal law posed to family forms (and relationships such as marriage) and traditional practices (such as horse raids, blood feuds, and child rearing). In short, the court records provide further evidence of the nature of the contribution of Canadian criminal law to the transformation of social relations and legal regulation of life on the Plains. In the last part of the chapter, these themes and the evidence are drawn together in a reconsideration of this relationship between criminal law and the First Nations in the North-West Territories in the decades before the province of Saskatchewan was established.

"I Didn't Kill Anybody's Children but My Own": Homicide and Familial Relations

The fur trade, Christian missionaries, and later the Indian Department all intervened and reshaped First Nations relations in ways that were intrusive and intimate. These institutions and socially transformative forces affecting the personal and family lives of the indigenous peoples of the Plains were as important as the criminal law, if not more important. Certainly, no definition of family, community, or a people could have been more dramatically rewritten than through the intermarriage of fur-trade men with First Nations women and the social, cultural, and demographic transformation that resulted.[27] Evidence of the close interrelationships between First Nations and "Half-breeds" of the North-West may also be found at the more formal level, as in the interventions and advocacy by the chiefs and spokesmen at Treaty 4 and Treaty 6 negotiations,[28] and the more informal, as seen in the court records, where Cree, Saulteaux, and Half-breeds travelled and camped together.[29]

Many of the family-related assaults[30] and homicides that can be identified in the court records bear evidence of the prior or co-extensive involvement of the church, the Hudson's Bay Company, or the government, which were either directly or indirectly implicated in precipitating the events that gave rise to an alleged offence, or were an animating presence in the prosecution. The presence of religious influence and the active role of clergy can be seen in both the earlier and later records. In some of the court files, the fact of religious influence or interference within a family appears to have been a contributing factor to the distress resulting in a crime.

Five early homicide cases, while not typical of the criminal activity among First Nations in the North-West Territories, nonetheless demonstrate the extent of the rupture between the old and the new, and the ways in which the latter supplanted the former. In all but one of the five homicides between 1876 and 1886, the deceased was killed by a family member.[31]

The fifth homicide,[32] while not intra-familial, was familial in another sense, as it involved an attack on an entire Assiniboine family, the Susseys, by two men who were themselves brothers. The killings occurred "when the leaves were getting withered and two winters [had] passed" near a lake about four days' travel from Lesser Slave Lake. It appears that the killings were the result of a dispute over beaver-hunting territory. The informant, Alexis Sussey, described the encounter between the accused, his brother Bear, and his deceased father. The accused had accused the boy's father of hunting in a place where he had promised not to hunt; according to Alexis, his father said, "God put the beaver for anybody. Bear then said you don't do what you agree to. My father said you have ill-treated some of my relations and you think you will do the same to me. The prisoner walked up to my father, told him not to say two words more or he would lie there." Shortly, he did, having been shot by the two men. Alexis described the shooting of his mother: "[B]efore he shot her she asked for her life, and called him her son. The prisoner said I am no son of yours, you Blackfoot wife. He shot her in the back, and then began to stab her." Alexis deposed that he and his brother then shot and killed Bear, at which point the prisoner threatened to kill them all.

Four siblings – two sisters and two brothers – survived. Some of them had witnessed the killing of their father, their mother, the baby she was holding, and two little brothers. One of the attackers, Bear, was killed by one of the Sussey boys; Bear's brother, Kee-chee-qua-pi-e-ka-wa, was later prosecuted for murder. One of the surviving daughters, Monique, told the justice of the peace that their lives were spared only by the intercession of their grandmother. After the prisoner had burned their tent and threatened to kill her as well, the old woman offered him a horse to spare the children's lives and her own. Monique said that her grandmother died two weeks later, without having recovered from the fright.

It is not clear what precipitated the formal criminal process, how the surviving siblings found their way to NWMP inspector W.D. Jarvis, or under what circumstances Kee-chee-qua-pi-e-ka-wa came to be arrested. On 30 August 1877, the depositions of Alexis (who was also the informant), Monique, and Jean-Baptiste Sussey were found to be sufficient to warrant the committal of Kee-chee-qua-pie-ka-wa (also known by the names Johnny, The Son of the Big Man, and Tis-ta-mous-noui) for the murder of their parents and siblings. Kee-chee-qua-pie-ka-wa declined to make a statement, "on account of his health." The process that had been undertaken by the surviving children was not one that a previous generation of Susseys would have pursued to avenge the deaths of their parents and siblings at the hands of the two brothers. Perhaps there was no one else to help them, nowhere else to turn. Less than a decade earlier, the hunter Kee-chee-qua-pie-ka-wa would not have contemplated ending his days in a police guardroom or on a gallows. He died in custody ten days after the hearing before the NWMP justice of the peace.

At the 10 September 1877 inquest into his death, George Herchmer, described in the files as the NWMP medical officer who had attended both him and Charles Cardinal, another prisoner, who had died in July, stated that in his medical opinion, the prisoner had died of consumption, but added: "From the experience of these two prisoners that have lately died, it is my opinion that Indian prisoners should be kept at labor during the time of their imprisonment and dieted differently to other prisoners, as they are physically unable owing to their habits of life, to stand close confinement."[33] Herchmer neglected to refer to anything he himself might have done, including cutting the prisoners' hair when they were ill, which undoubtedly would have exacerbated the negative impact of the experience.

The other prisoner to whom Herchmer referred was Charles Cardinal, who had been accused in 1877 by Margaret Gladieu, his mother-in-law, of shooting and killing her husband, Naboise, the previous year.[34] The origin of the problem between Cardinal and herself and her husband was said by Margaret to have been the admonition by a Roman Catholic priest that it was not proper for a man to have two wives. Charles Cardinal had two wives: two daughters of Naboise and Margaret Gladieu. He had been married to one of their daughters for approximately twelve years when, as Margaret explained in her own words,

> he bought another daughter from us for whom he paid a horse, he lived with both for two years, then the Priest told me it was not proper to have two wives, and urged me to take the last one away. I told the Priest I was afraid to do it, that he was a bad man and would kill some of us for it. The Priest then told me he would not do such a thing, and if he attempted to do the like to take a stick and maul him. At that time, he was only living with the one and put the other one away. I told the priest that I would tell them of it when I had an opportunity. When Charles came with his wife I told him of it. I then took my daughter and gave him his lawful wife. I went off with my daughter and kept her with me for the whole winter. He did his utmost to take her from us the whole time.[35]

It is certainly not evident from this account that the Cardinal/Gladieu family had observed a customary practice of "in-law avoidance." When Naboise, Margaret, and their daughter Mary Anne (Cardinal's second wife) were making their way from Beaver Lake to White Fish Lake in June 1876 to join a band of Indians under treaty, Cardinal shot and killed Naboise. The Gladieu party had stopped to make camp near the Large Beaver River, and Naboise went to hunt ducks by a pond. Cardinal had been tracking them. No one witnessed the shooting, but Margaret and Mary Anne heard the shots. When they saw that no ducks flew after the shots were fired, they knew that something was wrong. Margaret found her husband's body and confronted Cardinal. He knocked her down and made off with Mary Anne to his father's camp. Margaret eventually made her way to White Fish Lake and asked for help with her husband's body.

Cardinal disputed his mother-in-law's interpretation of the shooting and her version of what took place after the older man was shot. Although he later claimed to the NWMP interpreter that his father-in-law had aimed at him first and that he had shot in self-defence, the men and boys from White Fish who were sent to find and bring the body back said that it looked to them like Naboise had been shot in the back. In Reverend Henry Steinhauer's words, "on examining the body, we found the mark of the ball, where it had entered between the shoulder blades and came out immediately below the left breast. I am satisfied that the ball entered the back. I have seen gunshot wounds before and am therefore satisfied that

that was the case."[36] One cannot help but recall Margaret's account of the priest's advice to her – to take a stick and maul him – in response to her prediction that Cardinal would kill them if they interfered in his relationship with their second daughter, his second wife. Although Margaret invoked the priest's intervention as the reason for taking her daughter back, it is also possible that she and her husband regarded Charles as a bad man, but one of whom they were afraid. It is also distinctly possible that they did not approve of the fact that he was living only with the second daughter, having "put the other one away," and hence no longer providing for her in his camp.

The facts giving rise to the dispute between the elder Gladieus and their son-in-law, as recounted by the widowed mother-in-law, are suggestive of the difficult transition in social and familial relations and the disruptive influence of a missionary upon one Cree family, together with the deleterious effects that the new system of criminal justice – including prisoners in police custody being placed in irons, enforced confinement, a white man's diet (bread and milk as rations when sick), and the cutting of their hair – had on Aboriginal prisoners.

Not surprisingly, members of the clergy participated as informants, both formally and informally, in the criminal justice process. Different forms of these informal roles can be seen in the two other family homicides, also from the northwest region of the North-West Territories (now the province of Alberta). The earlier of the two, Ka-ki-si-kut-chin (The Swift Runner)[37] attracted enormous interest in the territorial press, and later in popular true crime accounts of "outlaws" in Western Canada.[38] He was the first man to be executed in the North-West Territories. There were extensive reports of his arrest, trial, confession, and execution at Fort Saskatchewan at the end of December 1879, and, following his execution, an account of his spiritual reclamation written by the Oblate priest who had ministered to him in the days before his death.[39] Ka-ki-si-kut-chin, a forty-year-old Cree trapper, onetime HBC trader, and possibly a former guide for the NWMP,[40] was accused of murdering his wife and six children at their winter camp over the course of the previous winter. The intense interest in his case derived from the accusation that he had eaten his family after killing them. There was a suggestion that he was "a lunatic," and one recent biographer has suggested that in the year or two prior to the murders he had undergone a personality transformation: from a gentle, trustworthy man to one who had a penchant for whiskey and violence and who was drunk for months at a time.[41] According to Colin Thomson, "Windigo seized his brain like a bad migraine."[42]

Ka-ki-si-kut-chin was charged with the murder of his wife, Charlotte, on 1 February 1879, "at the Open Hill Creek near the Athabasca Trail."[43] It appears that Charlotte's father may have been the first person to suspect the murders, when he saw his son-in-law return alone from the bush earlier in the spring, at which time he was told by Ka-ki-si-kut-chin that he was the only one of his family left.

Ka-ki-si-kut-chin maintained his innocence even as he took the police and interpreter on a long circular march in the bush, until finally human remains were found. He initially claimed that his wife and children had starved to death. At his trial, the police witnesses, including the NWMP medical officer, described the scene and were clearly of the view that none of the deceased had been buried in graves but appeared to have been cut apart. Essentially, all that appears to have been left were bones, ashes, and bits of hair.

At his hearing on 15 June 1879 before the justices of the peace (Inspector William Drummond Jarvis and Sub-Inspector Sévère Gagnon), it was alleged that "during the last six months, in the woods at a place south of Muskeg River, between the Saskatchewan and Athabasca Rivers," he had murdered several members of his family. He confessed at the conclusion of this hearing, and a document described as his "voluntary confession" was later tendered as exhibit "A" through the evidence of Inspector Jarvis. In this confession, he said: "I am going to tell the truth; I have done a great deal of harm, that is the reason I was backward in telling about it. I did not kill anybody else's children but my own."[44] He admitted killing his wife and five of his children, but denied killing his eldest son (who he said had starved to death), his mother, and his brother, who had also disappeared. He concluded by admitting that he had come out of the bush after he had eaten his last boy, and by denying that he had previously threatened to kill and eat his wife.

At his trial on 6 August 1879, before Stipendiary Magistrate Hugh Richardson and two justices of the peace, Ka-ki-si-kut-chin had the assistance of an interpreter but was "otherwise undefended." The prosecution's case was presented by Inspector Jarvis, who was both the police officer who had obtained his confession and justice of the peace who had committed him for trial. Jarvis, among other police witnesses, also testified, and it was through him that the critically important confession was admitted into evidence. It is fair to observe that Ka-ki-si-kut-chin's confession was the only evidence that identified and linked the human remains to him, and thus directly implicated him in the deaths.

His father-in-law, Kis-sic-kow-way, testified that he had last seen his daughter and her family the previous autumn at a place where his entire family had been camped. When they all broke camp, Ka-ki-si-kut-chin, Charlotte, and their six children, as well as Ka-ki-si-kut-chin's mother and brother, had forked off in another direction and went off on their own. It was the father-in-law's opinion that his daughter's family could "readily have got into the Hudson's Bay post at the River landing without risk of starvation, even if no game could be found."[45] Kis-sic-kow-way testified at the trial in August that his son-in-law had told him that Charlotte had shot herself, that two children had died, and that the rest had left him.

The six-man jury, four of whom were said to be able to converse in Cree,[46] deliberated for twenty minutes before returning a verdict of guilty.

It is difficult to assess just what the accused's mental state was, either at the time of the alleged murders or at the time of his trial. No evidence of this was presented at the trial, and the NWMP medical officer appeared not to have examined him (or at least he made no reference to this in his evidence). Ka-ki-si-kut-chin's confession appears to have prompted Sub-Inspector Gagnon to contact the Roman Catholic mission to send a priest to minister to the prisoner and prepare him for death. Father Hippolyte Leduc arrived at Fort Saskatchewan the week prior to the 20 December date that had been set for the execution and ascertained that his soul could be saved. In a long article in the *Saskatchewan Herald* published after the execution, Father Leduc wrote of his first meeting with Ka-ki-si-kut-chin: "After questioning him, I found him far enough advanced in his religious instruction to warrant me advising him to avail himself of the presence of the Bishop and to receive the sacrament of confirmation. He at once expressed a wish that the holy sacrament would be given to him, and received it from the Bishop with evident satisfaction."[47]

Leduc heard confessions that were both secular and religious in nature; the condemned man told the priest that he wanted to correct the statements he had made when first interrogated, and the priest said that he received Ka-ki-si-kut-chin's express permission to publish the particulars of the secular confession. In this final account, Ka-ki-si-kut-chin told the priest that in the early part of the winter, all had been well, that he had been able to find enough moose and bear to keep the family fed, but then he had fallen sick, and those with him had not been able to find any game. He had not yet fully recovered when he was able to travel to an HBC post, where the officer in charge gave him a few provisions, which did not last them long. They were starving, and so his brother and mother set off on their own. He urged his wife and children to follow, saying that he would stay on his own in the woods. One of his little boys would not leave him when the others left. The two of them camped together for a period of time when "an abominable thought crossed my mind": he shot his child while the boy was sleeping, and then ate parts of the boy's body and bone marrow. He left that place and carried on, coming across his wife and other children; he told them that the son who had been with him had died of starvation, "but [he] remarked immediately that they suspected the frightful reality." After a few days together, he realized that his family wanted to leave him, "from fear of meeting the same fate as my boy." And so one morning he rose early, his entire family sleeping around him: "I was mad. It seemed to me that all the devils had entered my heart." He killed his wife and three little girls in their sleep. He kept his starving and bewildered seven-year-old boy alive for a while. But when they had travelled a distance and arrived close to Egg Lake, where some of his relations lived, "the devil took possession of my soul; and in order to live longer far from people, and to put out of the way the only witness to my crimes, I seized my gun and killed the last of my children, and ate him as I did the others."[48]

Father Leduc reported that Ka-ki-si-kut-chin repented sincerely and asked God's pardon: "I had no knowledge of God, although three of my children had been baptized. I am the worst of men."[49] As he had promised, Father Leduc remained with the condemned man until the very last, hearing his last confession, arranging for a Mass to be celebrated, and investing him with the scapular of Our Lady of Mount Carmel. The thought of the impending execution affected the priest, who revealed to his readers that when he first saw the scaffold while walking Ka-ki-si-kut-chin back to his cell the day before his execution, he encouraged his charge to have courage, but "it was with utmost difficulty I was able to keep my feelings under control."[50] In the end, Ka-ki-si-kut-chin went to his death, accompanied by the priest and his prayers, and was reported by the priest to have been courageous to the end: "Poor Indian; human justice had to condemn him, but I have the sweet confidence that he found mercy at the tribunal of God."[51] Still, one rather hopes that, having experienced an earthly redemption through the intervention of Father Leduc, Ka-ki-si-kut-chin nonetheless had to meet Charlotte and her children at God's tribunal before he entered Leduc's kingdom of heaven.

Leduc's lengthy eulogy published in the *Herald* was undoubtedly designed to reinvest a measure of humanity and a soul into the image of an Indian man who had had been convicted of a heinous murder and condemned as a cannibal. Leduc celebrated the transformative impact of religion upon the man who had committed savage murders. He said that, following initial religious instruction by another priest, Ka-ki-si-kut-chin showed repentance and obedience to God's grace: "O, depth of the mysteries of the wisdom and mercy of God! A pagan – an infidel – a cannibal – will undergo under the influence of holy religion, a complete transformation."[52] It is also clear that the priest was mesmerized by the possibility of reclaiming this condemned soul and overwhelmed by his own terror of "human justice." It is distinctly possible that Ka-ki-si-kut-chin played the priest, and if so, who could blame him? As he apparently said to the priest, everyone else shunned and despised him, yet Leduc came to him "in the name of God to console, fortify and encourage [him]."[53] (It was reported that no Indians had attended his trial, and one might reasonably infer that he was being shunned by his people.[54])

This case, together with Felix Plante's case (discussed at the beginning of this chapter) and perhaps the case that follows below, are suggestive of yet another level of complexity in social relations and the clash of old and new, but perhaps also of a shared conundrum with respect to mental illness. Felix Plante's family clearly turned to the law, and the law tried to send him home – as clearly neither had the resources to handle the mentally ill boy. The horror of the police at their discovery of the charred remains of Ka-ki-si-kut-chin's wife, Charlotte, and her children and the horror and fascination of the territorial press at the reports of the aggravating expression of cannibalism are palpable in the file. There is no discussion of mental illness, and there appears to have been no doubt that he should be executed – not, however, as a lesson to his people (who appear to have abandoned him) but as a denunciation by the law of a heinous crime, a vile expression of violence, betrayal, and evil. Father Leduc attempted to explain the murders by invoking Ka-ki-si-kut-chin's lack of faith and to transform the events into a religious experience. One cannot know whether Magistrate Richardson thought that this was a crime that only an Aboriginal man could commit, but there is no evidence that the police, court, or press regarded it as anything but an abhorrent act by an individual (Cree) man, not his people.

Three months after Ka-ki-si-kut-chin's execution, a *Saskatchewan Herald* headline announced "Another Murder, An Indian Kills His Son."[55] Here again, a member of the Roman Catholic clergy played an important role, but in this case it was the suspicion of a priest that facilitated a criminal prosecution of another Cree father for the murder of his seventeen-year-old son. And, but for an apparently devout Roman

Catholic Cree man, the dead boy's paternal uncle, this particular homicide might never have come to the attention of the priest or anyone else outside the family.

At his uncle's insistence, the body of Moise Cardinal, said to be seventeen, had been brought to the mission at Lac la Biche for burial. Although the coffin had been closed by a blanket sewn over it, the priest was concerned. It appears that he did not open the coffin, but perhaps given the circumstances of its arrival (possibly accompanied by Moise's brother St. Luke Cardinal, perhaps with a message from the dead boy's uncle), Father Groward quickly sent a letter to the local justices of the peace, suggesting that the young man had suffered a violent death and asking them to come to examine the body before it was buried.[56]

A post-mortem examination was held on 22 February 1880, presided over by two justices of the peace, Edward Traill and James Pruden, and twelve Métis and First Nations men as "witnesses." The coffin was opened, and the fourteen men observed that the head of the young man was entirely severed from the body, having been cut off with a heavy knife or axe; there was what was described as a terrible gash to the back of the head, and other deep gashes to other parts of the body. From the smell, they concluded that the young man had been dead for some days. As the clothing was not torn, it was clear that someone had taken care to dress him and put a pair of "Indian shoes" on his feet. They also observed that the right hand held a small metal cross. Traill wrote to the commanding officer at Fort Saskatchewan, asking him to come immediately with the coroner and informing him of the steps that he had taken to apprehend Joseph Cardinal and to arrange for the attendance of witnesses.[57]

The case can be read differently, depending on the source of information: the court file or the *Saskatchewan Herald.* The depositions of the relatives, including the deceased's eleven-year-old brother, who was with his father and older brother when the latter was killed, tell a story of a menacing young man who was not in his right mind. After Moise had accosted and frightened his stepmother, Angelique, Joseph sent her and the little girls to his father's place across the lake. Angelique told the justices of the peace that her husband had said to her, "Tell my father to make haste and come. In the meantime, I will be keeping my son."[58] When she returned with her father-in-law, they found Moise already dead and the house in disorder; Angelique ended her deposition by saying that Moise had been "wrong in his head for some time before the murder." J-B (the youngest brother) gave an unsworn deposition at the hearing. His narrative portrayed a terrifying scene, in which, he said, his brother "wanted to kill us," and he ended his deposition by saying that his brother "had been beside himself for two days." He described his brother knocking a cup or pot out of his father's hand. The child's deposition continues in narrative form, but with words that may have been attributed to him rather than being his own:

> The deceased then had hold of his father by arm and at the same time trying to get at me. I ran away crying and my father then struck the deceased with the axe on the head. The blow seemed to give deceased more strength. He was more vigorous after the blow. My brother then asked for holy water. My father called for a knife. I gave my father the knife and I ran out crying. He was still breathing when I left the house.[59]

The justice of the peace noted in the body of the boy's deposition: "The witness is a boy, is aged 11 years. His evidence is very much confused so that the court was obliged to question him very closely."[60] Thus, in addition to the trauma from what he had witnessed and experienced, the child was subjected to close questioning by the white men at a hearing where his father was a prisoner, accused of murdering his older brother.

Antoine Cardinal, brother of the accused, had seen nothing himself, but his deposition provides a moving account of his response to the killing. He said he arrived at the house the following day and saw the body:

> I knelt down and said as many prayers for the dead as I know. When I finished praying over him, I took off the covering from the body. I tried to take off the two shirts that the deceased had on, but was unable. I then took some printed cotton and wrapped the body in it after which my wife and sisters-in-law sewed up the cotton. When done with that we took wood and made a coffin as best I could. After I finished I put the corpse into the coffin. Only after the above proceedings I began to speak to my brother (the prisoner). I told him that body could not remain there. The pères must see the body. All of those that were present consented that the body should be brought to the church. I then asked two young men to take the body to the mission.[61]

When asked by the justice of the peace whether he had ever seen anything that would lead him to believe the deceased was crazy, Antoine said that he had never seen anything, as they lived some distance away.

Joseph Cardinal gave an extremely long account of the events in his Statement of the Accused at the end of the hearing. In it, he repeated what his wife and youngest son had said, that Moise was not in his right mind, and that he, Joseph, had acted to defend himself.

Having been charged with the murder of his son, Cardinal was committed to stand trial. The record of the trial is simply a record of a conviction entered by Richardson, who presided at the trial with Sévère Gagnon, as justice of the peace, and a jury. The jury convicted Cardinal of manslaughter on 12 July 1880. No sentence is indicated in the file, but an item later that autumn in the Saskatchewan Herald suggests that Cardinal was sentenced to a term in the Manitoba Penitentiary. The Manitoba Penitentiary admission register confirms that Joseph Cardinal Prisoner 65, thirty years of age and married, arrived on 21 October 1880 to begin serving a seven-year sentence, and that he was released on 3 June 1886.[62]

The Saskatchewan Herald offered a slightly different account of the incident. It reported, based on a "special dispatch" apparently received prior to the arrest, that Joseph Cardinal had barricaded himself in his house with four guns, and intended to resist to the death any attempt to arrest him.[63] The Herald's report indicated that "the [deceased] lad had evidently been laboring under temporary insanity for two or three days before his death, but it does not appear that he was in any way dangerous."[64] The newspaper reminded its readers that Cardinal was a "hard case" and a "dangerous character" from a family that had produced several criminals;[65] its theory of the case was that Joseph had recently married a younger woman and that he suspected his second son, Moise, of having been intimate with her.[66] The Herald reported that although Cardinal claimed to have acted in self-defence, the neighbours said that the death was due to his jealousy. Questions surely remain, however, not least of which is whether Joseph Cardinal had really been the thirty-year-old father of a seventeen-year-old son.

In the previous decade, none of these men who were prosecuted for murder would have faced this form of white man's justice, and the intervention of white man's religion may not have been so significant. It is difficult to say whether vengeance by blood would have followed any of these homicides. In some of the families, it appears that the patriarch was killed (Naboise Gladieu; the Sussey children's father) and we do not know whether there were other relatives who could and would have retaliated. In the other two cases, the father himself had killed his family member(s). Perhaps Charlotte's father and his remaining family could have retaliated against Ka-ki-sit-kut-chin, but it is difficult to imagine that St. Luke Cardinal would have avenged his brother's death by killing their father (or whether such a response would have been appropriate under the circumstances). In any event, members of the Cardinal family had turned to the church even before the law intervened.

These homicides all occurred in the remotest part of the North-West Territories, where the Hudson's Bay Company and the church had preceded the arrival of the law. The bush, more than the Plain, is evident here. There is less a sense of new relations being forged than of old relations being differently defined and enforced. We now turn our focus to life on the Plain, with new forms of relations, including employer/employee relations, as well as new forms of protection of new and old property relations.

Economic and Property Relations

The Hudson's Bay Company was an important participant in the criminal law process, especially in Treaty 6 territory in the early period. Between 1877 and 1883, HBC officials figured prominently as informants in a number of cases involving non-Aboriginal and Aboriginal persons accused of break, enter, and theft, as well as other offences.[67] In one case involving a young Cree and three young Half-breeds who were charged with stealing and killing an HBC ox,[68] the initial letter of informal complaint lamented: "Of course no one saw them kill him. I hope you will take means to put them through, they deserve to be punished very severely." Although no one saw Shakes His Wings (The Youngest Son of the Netmaker) and his party kill the ox, a man recounted meeting their carts on the trail on his way to Fort Pitt, "at the side of the Red Deer Hills, near the west on the right hand side near the lake." At this point, it seems that the ox was pulling the cart of the Netmaker's son. The informant said he had asked for some tea, and was obliged, but he was told that they had no food. Later, in Duck Lake (many miles to the southeast of Fort Pitt), The Youngest Son of the Netmaker hired a horse from this man's brother and paid for the hire with a shirt, seven shillings, and a shoulder of beef. When asked where he got the beef, "laughing he said it is funny for a man to kill his ox and tie his carts together." On the basis of a case stitched together with circumstantial evidence, not least the Youngest Son of the Netmaker's joke about himself, the four young men were arrested. All made statements that were, to greater or lesser extents, exculpatory, each minimizing his own involvement, but all four pleaded guilty before Magistrate Richardson, who sentenced each to three months of hard labour.

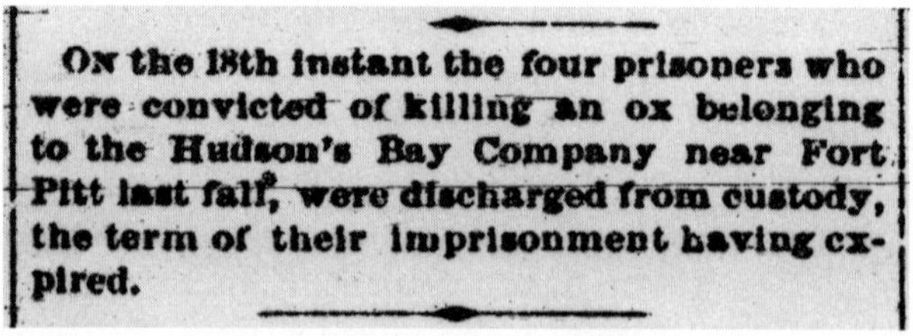

On the 18th instant the four prisoners who were convicted of killing an ox belonging to the Hudson's Bay Company near Fort Pitt last fall, were discharged from custody, the term of their imprisonment having expired.

FIGURE 2.1 On 27 January 1879, the *Saskatchewan Herald* announced that the young men had been released after serving their three-month sentence.

Despite the fact that no one saw them kill the animal, their case suggests that the Plain in this instance offered no protective anonymity to The Youngest Son of the Netmaker and his companions.[69] The chance encounter on the trail, the exchange of pleasantries and tea, and his joke about himself in Duck Lake – the case bears the hallmark of a misadventure of four young men who might well have been hungry and indifferent to the possibility that anyone "owned" the ox. Richardson appeared to recognize this when he specified that their hard labour was to involve cutting wood and ordinary labour for every working day of their sentence.[70] This is the only court file in which he gave express direction concerning the form of labour to be performed during the sentence. Figure 2.1 shows the *Saskatchewan Herald*'s report about the young men's release.

One gathers from another court file that prisoners serving their sentences at the Fort Battleford police barracks had some measure of freedom of movement. Napesis (or Joseph) pleaded guilty in 1881 and 1882 to theft from two different employers and was sentenced on each occasion to six months of hard labour in Battleford. Shortly after the 1882 conviction, he was back in court entering another guilty plea to another theft charge: on this occasion, he had lifted two silk handkerchiefs belonging to the NWMP men who were responsible for the prisoners. This netted him an additional six months in jail.[71]

Recourse by the Company and other employers to the criminal court to police and discipline wage labourers is found in Richardson's court records. An Assiniboine man named Thomas (or Joseph) was charged in 1883 with the theft of one fisher, one marten, and about two pounds of bacon from his employer, the HBC at Fort Saskatchewan; he had sold the furs to a man named Carey, who suspected they were stolen because he knew that Thomas worked at the HBC fort and that he had not been out hunting. Alerted regarding Carey's suspicions, Thomas's boss placed a fisher skin in an area where he sent Thomas to work and then later found that the skin was missing. As Thomas was working alone, his boss locked him in the building and went around outside to see whether he had thrown the skin out the window. Apparently he had not done this; rather, the boss found bacon on the ground. He confronted Thomas, who eventually admitted that he had thrown the bacon out the window and stolen the other furs. At the hearing before the justice of the peace, Thomas asked one question of his boss: "Did you see with your own eyes that I took the furs and sold them to Carey? Answer: No."[72] Thomas was committed for trial and appears to have been held in custody for four months before entering his guilty plea before Richardson on 16 July 1883, at which time he was sentenced to a further one month of hard labour at Fort Saskatchewan.

In cases involving theft from an employer, or from the Company both as employer and as retailer, it bears noting that most of those convicted received a custodial sentence for their offence, even, as in the case of the "stolen bacon," where the item was recovered on-site (one is left to wonder whether Carey returned the stolen furs to the HBC).[73] There can be no doubt that the Company had more property than most in the North-West Territories (rivalled only by the Canadian government), and hence certainly more to lose than most.[74]

An 1880 case involving a man named Peecoose (Sandfly) (Figure 2.2), apparently a member of Big Bear's band, is interesting because of the suggestion that his prosecution was motivated less by a desire to protect the HBC than by a desire to ensure that the government man who had taken up with his wife could proceed unimpeded by Peecoose's presence and interference. Charged with theft of goods from the Hudson's Bay Company at Fort Pitt, Peecoose spent several months in police custody before being brought before the magistrate. The Information sworn by James Keith Simpson before HBC factor W. McKay JP on 8 October 1879 was a model of efficiency for criminal justice, setting out both the particulars of the alleged offence and the evidence:

> [O]n or about the night of the fourth of August last the store of the [HBC] ... was feloniously entered and a quantity of goods and chattels – that is to say (among other things) – two blankets, three tweed coats, one vest, one L'Assomption belt, two shirts, one scarlet wool shawl, one single rein bridle, one single barrel shotgun, one felt hat and two towels, and that he hath just and reasonable cause to suspect and doth suspect that the said goods and chattels were feloniously stolen by one Pee Coose (or Sandfly) a Cree Indian,

Figure 2.2 Sandfly, 1915, in a photo taken at Onion Lake. If this man is in fact the same Peecoose (Sandfly), it would appear that he was a person of some stature in his community. | Saskatchewan Archives Board, R-A9450-6.

> the said Pee Coose – otherwise said Sandfly having on the thirtieth day of September last hand [*sic*] to the said James Keith Simpson, the above-mentioned goods & chattels, confessing that he had stolen the same the said [HBC].[75]

The list of items he was said to have stolen was longer than that of Thomas; as with Thomas, the goods that were the subject of the particular charge were returned to the Company (although Simpson's Information hints that there were more items taken). The record of Peecoose's prosecution is remarkably thin: a mere five pages, containing simply the Information, cover letter dated 24 April 1880 from W. McKay forwarding the Information to Richardson ("I do not think it necessary to put the Government to the expense of sending any witness but one – Mr. J.K. Simpson – who will deliver this letter to you"); a letter of 29 April 1880 from Inspector French of the Battleford NWMP confirming "an Indian named Sandfly in our custody for the last six months awaiting his trial on a charge of felony"; a further letter of 2 June 1880 from Inspector French, still at Battleford Barracks, apparently responding to a request earlier that morning from Richardson for the documents concerning Peecoose, and asking Richardson to inform him of the date and place of the trial so that he could arrange for the attendance of the prisoner. The file also contains a piece of paper indicating Peter Ballendon [*sic*], "Interpreter"; James Keith Simpson, "Evidence"; and the names of eleven jury men under the heading "jury men"; next to the names of nine of the men is the word "mark."[76] One finds no record of a hearing before the justice of the peace (if indeed one was held), nor any record of the proceedings before Richardson.

The *Saskatchewan Herald* (whose editor, P.G. Laurie was listed as one of the jury men) chortled that "[a]n Indian rejoicing in the innocent name of Sandfly" had pleaded guilty to a charge of stealing of a large quantity of goods from the HBC at Fort Pitt and was sentenced to "two and half years' exile to Manitoba."[77] This sentence ranks with the most severe Richardson handed out for theft of recovered goods (although the facts contained in the Information suggest a break-in, which, if true, would have warranted the more serious charge of break, enter, and theft). The sentence appears especially severe when one considers that Peecoose was in custody, apparently in Battleford itself, for eight months prior to his appearance before Richardson. One can only infer that Richardson did not receive the April correspondence, and that Peecoose languished for a further two months due to paperwork that went missing. Given the seriousness of the offence, it is surprising that the file contains no depositions taken before justices of the peace prior to committal unless there was no hearing. It is also possible that the court file in the Saskatchewan Archives is not the complete file, but its sparseness, combined with the delay in bringing Peecoose before Richardson and with the harsh sentence, does raise questions about the process as well as the result.

On this point, others have inferred a more sinister motive by a real culprit. Hugh Dempsey suggests that this particular prosecution was something of a put-up job.[78] Dempsey implicates Frog Lake Indian farm instructor John Delaney, who had "stolen" Peecoose's wife. When Peecoose protested, Delaney apparently had him charged with assault: "This failed to have him jailed, so a further charge of theft was levied against the Indian, and he was sentenced to two and a half years in prison."[79] Dempsey draws upon correspondence from Hayter Reed to Indian Commissioner Edgar Dewdney: "The feeling was general that 'Mr. Delaney had the man arrested so he could accomplish his designs,' and he cohabited with the prisoner's wife all winter."[80] It has also been suggested that, "to add insult to injury, when he tired of the Indian woman, Delaney married a white woman, Theresa Delaney,"[81] whose "capture" by Big Bear's band in 1885 has been chronicled and re-examined.[82]

I have found no court record of the assault charge to which Dempsey refers, and there is nothing in the court file that expressly supports Dempsey's account. Peecoose's case raises questions, however, and Dempsey, among others,[83] suggests a compelling answer. For his mistreatment of Peecoose and others, as well as his earlier reputation for contributing to the debauchery of young Indian women, Delaney was said to have been despised by the First Nations people with whom he worked. Peecoose escaped from the NWMP barracks before he could be transported to the penitentiary; the *Saskatchewan Herald* reported that when the guard left the guardroom for a short time, Peecoose unscrewed the lock plate and walked away unobserved.[84] It appears that he remained at large and was said to be back in Big Bear's camp during the spring of 1885. Peecoose did not kill Delaney at Frog Lake, but Delaney's death at the hands of the Cree at that location was not a random event. Others in the community clearly remembered; few accounts of Delaney's violent death at Frog Lake in 1885 fail to refer to his mistreatment of Peecoose, and other victims, and the implicit settling of accounts.[85]

Some accounts and records suggest that he was arrested in 1885 as a "suspected rebel," convicted of treason-felony, and sentenced by Stipendiary Magistrate Charles Borromée Rouleau to three years in the penitentiary.[86] The Manitoba Penitentiary admission register tells a slightly different story.

The prison record indicates that "Peecoos" (Sandfly), Prisoner 121, age twenty-seven, was admitted on 20 October 1885 and released on 19 April 1890. The register indicates that he had been sentenced by Rouleau for "escape."[87] Unlike many other Indian prisoners sentenced in 1885, Peecoose received no pardon and served a full five and a half years in prison.

Criminalizing Aboriginal Children

One of the challenges posed by court records is the lack of identifying information with respect to the accused persons – for example, whether they were Métis or Cree, children or adults.[88] Thus, the *Saskatchewan Herald*'s brief report of 9 May 1881 (see Figure 2.3) offers one sliver of evidence that John Thomas and the Widow Conata's son, known by the nickname Thomas A. Beckett, were children (the fact that the *Herald* did not refer to them as "bucks," the paper's preferred term for Indian men, supports this inference). The court file refers to two, not three, accused, who are described as "2 Cree Indians."[89] The fact that Hayter Reed, the Battleford Indian Agent, appeared on behalf of the prisoners also suggests that they were not adults. The facts of their case strongly suggest a prank on an old(er) man, John Burnett, by boys who hinted that they had brought a woman for him. Burnett's furious embarrassment and hyperbole packed a criminalizing punch.

Burnett, a labourer, laid an Information on 27 April 1881 before his neighbour, a justice of the peace named Scott, claiming that the boys had fired a revolver at him, "with intent, feloniously and of their malice aforethought to kill and murder" him. At their trial on 3 May, he claimed that John Thomas had come to his tipi late in the evening and said that he was with two others. Burnett said that when he asked why John Thomas had come, Thomas replied that he had come with another boy, and "someone else" who was out on the road. Thomas asked Burnett if he had any money, and continued to press Burnett when he said he had none. Finally Thomas A. Beckett, the second boy, joined them in the tipi, and Burnett decided to see who else was outside. When Burnett could find no one else, he came back into the tent and saw that Thomas A. Beckett had something in his hand, pointing at him: "I saw a flash, heard a report of either a pistol or revolver fired off. I backed out feeling as if there was a hole thro' my head. I picked up an axe. They both then ran away."[90] Under cross-examination, Burnett denied that he had any clear understanding why the "two men" had come that evening; he maintained that he could see clearly who they

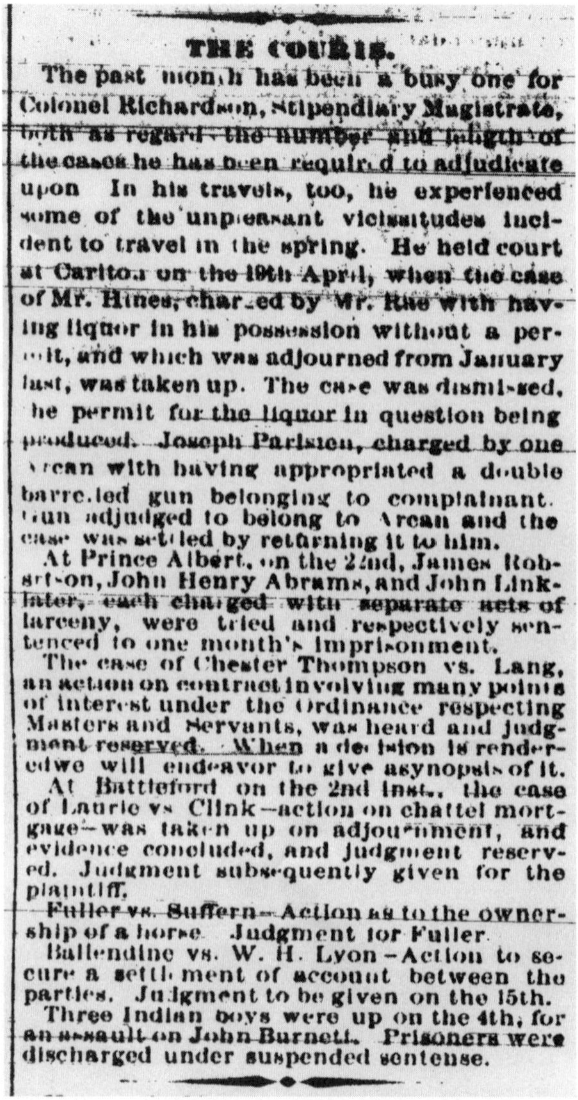

THE COURTS.

The past month has been a busy one for Colonel Richardson, Stipendiary Magistrate, both as regards the number and length of the cases he has been required to adjudicate upon. In his travels, too, he experienced some of the unpleasant vicissitudes incident to travel in the spring. He held court at Carlton on the 19th April, when the case of Mr. Hines, charged by Mr. Rae with having liquor in his possession without a permit, and which was adjourned from January last, was taken up. The case was dismissed, the permit for the liquor in question being produced. Joseph Parisien, charged by one Arcan with having appropriated a double barrelled gun belonging to complainant. Gun adjudged to belong to Arcan and the case was settled by returning it to him.

At Prince Albert, on the 22nd, James Robertson, John Henry Abrams, and John Linklater, each charged with separate acts of larceny, were tried and respectively sentenced to one month's imprisonment.

The case of Chester Thompson vs. Lang, an action on contract involving many points of interest under the Ordinance respecting Masters and Servants, was heard and judgment reserved. When a decision is rendered we will endeavor to give a synopsis of it.

At Battleford on the 2nd inst., the case of Laurie vs Clink—action on chattel mortgage—was taken up on adjournment, and evidence concluded, and judgment reserved. Judgment subsequently given for the plaintiff.

Fuller vs. Suffern—Action as to the ownership of a horse. Judgment for Fuller.

Ballendine vs. W. H. Lyon—Action to secure a settlement of account between the parties. Judgment to be given on the 15th.

Three Indian boys were up on the 4th, for an assault on John Burnett. Prisoners were discharged under suspended sentense.

FIGURE 2.3 *Saskatchewan Herald*, 9 May 1881.

were, as he had a good fire in his tipi; and he admitted that he had never known either prisoner to have any firearms. A member of the NWMP, described as a surgeon, testified that he had examined Burnett the next morning. In his opinion, Burnett had not been shot; he did not think it possible that the lump he had examined on Burnett's head could have been caused by a bullet.

At the close of Burnett's case, Richardson, probably on Hayter Reed's motion, discharged John Thomas, as there was no evidence against him. Thomas was then sworn, and through his testimony the boys' story came out: they had not been able to get back to their own tent that night, and they had agreed "to play a practical joke on Burnett about a squaw."[91] After they had induced Burnett to go out and look for the woman who was not there, he came back into the tent angry and swearing at them. Thomas A. Beckett struck Burnett in the head with a small stick, and they ran away because Burnett went after them with an axe and they feared for their lives. The file contains no indication of the final disposition for Beckett, but it is likely he was convicted by Richardson of assault and discharged on the suspended sentence (as perhaps partially correctly reported by the *Herald*). For their practical joke, the boys had spent a week in custody in the cells in the police guardroom at the behest of the private prosecutor. Perhaps Burnett's embarrassment was amplified by the public trial, although clearly the *Herald* spared his feelings in its report – and we are left to ponder just how young these "Indian boys" were.

John Thomas and Thomas A. Beckett were not the only children – Aboriginal or white – who appeared as prisoners in the criminal courts in the Territories. It is quite likely that many of the accused who appeared before Richardson were young people, including a few settler boys and adolescent labourers.[92] The 1882 returns of the North-West Mounted Police indicate that five Blood boys appeared (and were discharged) at Fort Macleod, and that a nine-year-old Sarcee boy was discharged on a charge of larceny.[93] The 1883 returns indicate that "Patrick, half-breed boy," was sentenced by Stipendiary Magistrate Macleod in Calgary to two years in the penitentiary for horse stealing.[94] These were children for whom the twentieth-century *Juvenile Delinquents Act* could not come soon enough.

In 1999, John S. Milloy made the now axiomatic observation that "the residential school experience was, beyond question, intolerable."[95] A century earlier, two First Nations youngsters agreed, and did their best to extricate themselves from the intolerable experience. They found that the industrial school (see Figure 2.4) and the government's Indian education policy packed not only a punch but also a legal wallop, and they spent close to a month in jail as a result.

The legal wallop was experienced by Alex Bone, a boy,[96] and Julia Coté, a girl,[97] after they ran away from the Indian Industrial School in Regina. Given the industrial school provisions of the *Indian Act*, it is reasonable to infer that they were under the age of sixteen.[98] The girl was from Coté's Reserve in the Treaty 4 area; the Information alleged that the boy was from

FIGURE 2.4 Regina Industrial School as it stood when Julia Coté and Alex Bone fled from it in 1894. | Saskatchewan Archives Board, R-A2025.

Muscowpetung's Reserve, but the Treaty Annuity Paylists indicate that he was originally from Moosomin's Treaty 6 band in Treaty 6 near Battleford. In 1894, his mother applied to transfer to Pasquah's Treaty 4 band near Fort Qu'Appelle.[99] He was included in her application but she died before the transfer could be completed. The Treaty Annuity Paylist indicates that he was a pupil at the industrial school and that his $5 treaty payment was paid to the school.

The charge against Alex Bone and Julia Coté was that on 21 September 1894 they "stole, took and carried away" clothes that were the property of the Indian Department: in the girl's case, this was one dress and one suit of underwear. The boys in the industrial school may have been better clothed because Bone was charged with stealing a coat, a vest, a shirt, a pair of knee pants, and a pair of long stockings. These items were the school clothes they were wearing when they ran away,[100] their own clothes likely having been taken from them when they arrived at the school. The principal deponent in the hearings into the charges on 28 September before senior NWMP officer Sévère Gagnon, who sat as justice of the peace, was the principal of the school, Angus J. McLeod, who said that the prisoners knew that the clothes belonged to the Indian Department. They were committed for trial and remained in custody until their trial date. On 13 October, they were arraigned by Crown Prosecutor W.C. Hamilton. Assistant Indian Commissioner Amédée Forget ("at request of Mr. Hamilton & with desire of prisoner") was granted permission to address the court, and he spoke on behalf of both prisoners. There is no record of any plea by Julia Coté: the court file contains a simple endorsement that "at the request of ass't Indian commissioner [*sic*] Mr. Forget and Rev'd. Mr. McLeod Principal of Regina Industrial School, accused discharged."

Bone entered a guilty plea and Mr. Forget asked for leniency. By this time, he and Coté had been held in jail in Regina for over three weeks. Who could blame him if at that point he simply nodded his head? Bone's court file suggests that the authorities either regarded his case as more serious or held out greater hope for him. Principal McLeod addressed the court in support of Forget's plea for leniency; he told the court that the boy's character was "generally good, & truthful" and that he had been in the school about a year. The principal indicated that he was willing to take Bone back. The endorsement indicates: "Boy states willing to go back – & on boy's promise to behave himself & if when required will come up to receive sentence, discharged –." As Bone had been recently orphaned and recently moved from his original band, they may have thought he had nowhere else to go, but his flight from the school suggests that he himself had thought otherwise.

Aboriginal children were not the only children during that period to face criminal charges and to be held in jail prior to their trials or guilty pleas. For them, however, it was an experience that probably reinforced that of the industrial school and would have been a fate beyond the vision or contemplation of their grandparents, much less the approach that the latter would have taken to helping their young ones become good people.

"Nobody Saw Me Steal the Horses"

This undoubtedly true statement[101] did not save eighteen-year-old Ka-ka-wusk from conviction and a lengthy penitentiary sentence, which ultimately took his life at the age of twenty. While most property thefts in the Territories involved small movable or wearable pieces of property (rings, watches, and wallets, left in pockets or on wash stands; or shawls, belts, socks, shirts and pants, and occasionally ribbons and shawls; household items from empty houses, and so on) the most significant and challenging form of theft involved horses. And here, as others have observed, the Canadian government faced the formidable challenge of transforming the meaning of horse raids into horse theft.[102] Given that horse raids appear to have been an important part of warfare, the objective of which was to make off with as many horses as possible from an enemy camp,[103] Brian Hubner argues that in the 1880s and 1890s, horse stealing replaced warfare as an important expression of Native autonomy.[104] He also argues that the NWMP initially took a lenient view of horse stealing, but a crackdown commenced in the 1880s that resulted in Aboriginal "horse thieves" receiving penitentiary sentences when they were convicted of bringing stolen property (namely, horses) into Canada from the United States. And here, more likely, was the crux of the conflict: that the Indians could no longer retrieve horses stolen from them by American Indians, who were able to take refuge south of the border. If they ventured across the border and took back or stole American horses, they faced the more serious offence of smuggling once they were back in Canada.

Hubner appears to be on solid ground when he argues that the desire to prevent the practice of cross-border horse raids weighed heavily in the decision to move the closely aligned Cree bands of Piapot and Little Pine, and the Assiniboines led by Lean Man and Grizzly Bear's Head, to reserves far away from the Cypress Hills,[105] but it is not clear that Hugh Richardson's court records support his more general claim that the Indians received increasingly harsh sentences for horse stealing as the 1880s went on. The aggravated offence of smuggling or bringing stolen property across the border could draw a more serious sentence, but even here Richardson's records suggest a more tempered approach than Hubner conveys. Hubner's view is supported in the case of eleven Cree men who were sentenced by Stipendiary Magistrates McLeod and A.G. Irvine (who was also NWMP Commissioner) to two-year terms in the penitentiary in 1883.[106] Given the composition of that bench, and the fact Irvine, when sitting either at Fort Walsh or Fort Mcleod, did not hesitate to impose penitentiary sentences for these offences and for cattle killing,[107] it is understandable that Hubner would be inclined to conflate the NWMP with "the law." Although Richardson did not routinely sit at either Fort Walsh or Fort Mcleod, he did preside over horse stealing and smuggling cases that were committed to Qu'Appelle for trial. From these cases, it is not clear that his approach to sentencing was as harsh as described by Hubner.

In a set of companion cases before him in 1882, the sentences he imposed were modest. Three Cree men, Chac-a-Chas,[108] Wa-ya-koo-la-ya-hoo, and

Weka-repee-asoo, each pleaded guilty to "bringing stolen horses and mules into Canada, knowing them to have been stolen and having same in their possession" and were sentenced to thirty days' imprisonment at hard labour.[109] Seven Cree men and one Saulteaux man also pleaded guilty to having possession of stolen horses belonging to John [*sic*] Baptiste Champagne. It seems that the two sets of men may have been part of what the NWMP described as a "war party of thirty-two Crees"[110] that had arrived at the end of April that year at the camp of Jean-Louis Légaré, a trader based in Willow Bunch, Wood Mountain, North-West Territories. In his deposition, Légaré indicated that his party, which included a Teton Sioux and a Half-breed man, was camped somewhere between Fort Buford, North Dakota, and Wood Mountain in the Territories. The "war party" asked him for something to eat, and he gave them supper. Later in the evening, they began to go through his carts, taking what they wanted, and refused to stop despite his order to do so. Overnight, he said, he heard them planning to kill the Teton Sioux man who was with him[111] (the Annual Report of the Commisioner of the North-West Mounted Police indicated that the "war party" had said they were going to kill Légaré as well[112]). Seven Cree men (The Bear, The Man That Walks There, The Man That Takes Them in His Canoe, The Man That Thinks Most, Short Thunder, Dry Grain, Stony Hair) and one Saulteaux man (The Man That Makes Noise in the Sky) were ultimately arrested and charged with theft of tea, sugar, and blankets from Légaré, threatening to take the life of Légaré and the Teton Sioux, and possession of stolen property (horses) that belonged to Champagne. They were also charged with possession of a stolen blanket belonging to yet another man, Mathias Sansregret.

The eight men apparently gave a collective Statement of the Accused taken with respect to both sets of charges, which warrants reproduction. In response to the Légaré and Sansregret charges, they said: "We were with the party who met Mr. Legare [*sic*] and his party and did not want to take anything from him but the majority of our party wished to take the goods and kill Mr. Legare [*sic*] and the Sioux Indian and we were too few in number to do anything towards protecting them so we were forced to join the majority of the party."[113] In response to the charge concerning Champagne's horses and Sansregret's blanket, they said: "We took the horses from John Baptiste Champagne at night but next day was overtaken by the owner who got them back. We would not have taken them had we known they were half-breed's horses. Pie-a-Pot told us not to steal any horse on this side of the line."[114]

Both sets of accused appear to have been held in custody from 12 May until they entered their guilty pleas before Richardson in Qu'Appelle on 9 October. The Légaré charges appear not to have proceeded. Chac-a-Chas and his two colleagues pleaded guilty to having brought stolen horses into Canada knowing that they had been stolen. The Bear alone pleaded guilty to possession of the stolen Sansregret blanket, and he and his seven colleagues pleaded guilty to the Champagne charge, for which they were sentenced to twenty days at hard labour. Of course, the sentences were not as light they might first appear, given the five months they had spent in custody awaiting trial. A sentence of twenty days or one month, served closer to home, does not come close to a term in the Manitoba Penitentiary, however.

Similarly, in a series of cases two years later, on 26 August 1884, Stipendiary Magistrate Richardson sentenced seven Cree men to two months and one Assiniboine man (Ah-kee-tap) to one month in jail for "smuggling stolen horses into Canada."[115] There is an interesting connection between one of the "horse smugglers" (Ah-kee-tap) and Buffalo Calf, a sixteen-year-old Assiniboine boy who also appeared before Richardson that year, and here the story is suggestive of intrigue and possible arrangements or inducements that are not made explicit in the court files. Buffalo Calf's arrest on 22 June 1884 and his prosecution could not have occurred without the cooperation of his fellow Assiniboines, Ah-kee-tap and O-see-wat-a-tao (also named Empty Belly in other records), the only witnesses who could have seen him commit the offence. In fact, Ah-kee-tap, Empty Belly, and another man, Little Eye, had been charged with the offence of "placing obstruction on C.P. Railway track" on 18 June 1884; the charges against them were dismissed by NWMP superintendent Deane JP on 19 June.[116]

Three days later, on 22 June, Buffalo Calf was charged with obstructing the Canadian Pacific Railway line at a place "six days march west of Regina": specifically that he "unlawfully and maliciously put upon the line of the Canadian Pacific Railway at or near Parkbeg ... an obstruction, to wit, a piece of iron rail, with intent to endanger the safety of some person or persons unknown travelling or being upon the same railway."[117] Before Justice of the Peace Deane, three witnesses were examined: NWMP Sergeant Blight, Ah-kee-tap, and O-see-wat-a-tao. Corporal James Thompson was sworn as interpreter; he translated the evidence of Sergeant Blight and "explained to the Prisoner the nature of the charge." After each witness, Buffalo Calf is recorded as having declined to cross-examine. The two lay witnesses were brothers; Ah-kee-tap was married to Buffalo Calf's sister. Their depositions indicated that they saw Buffalo Calf place the iron rail across the track. At the end of the evidence, Buffalo Calf declined the offer to make a statement: "I will not say anything." The record of his trial before Richardson indicates simply a plea of "not guilty" and "verdict of jury guilty" on 25 June 1884.

It seems that the jury recommended mercy, and perhaps his age was a factor in this recommendation. It may be that prior to sentencing, Richardson canvassed the range of possibilities: perhaps he could simply discharge Buffalo Calf or perhaps the Executive might intervene after sentence was passed. No record of his inquiries is found in the file, but the NWMP Commissioner delivered the following message to "Colonel Richardson":

> I saw the Lieut. Governor this evening and he is not disposed to interfere with the ordinary course of law in the case of "Buffalo Calf" and prefers to let the recommendation to mercy of the jury stand on its own merits – if circumstances should subsequently justify a mitigation of punishment he will not be averse to recommend it but considering the improbability of obtaining sufficient evidence to convict in future similar cases should they occur and the desirability of impressing upon the Indian mind that such crimes cannot be committed with impunity, he prefers to leave the matter to your judicial discretion.[118]

While the court file is silent with respect to the disposition, the 1884 Annual Report of the NWMP Commissioner indicates that Buffalo Calf was sentenced two days later, on 27 June, to two years in the penitentiary.[119] The returns of the NWMP for 1884 indicate that on 19 July, Empty Belly, or O-see-wat-a-tao, was sentenced in Regina by Stipendiary Magistrate Colonel Irvine to two years in the penitentiary for horse stealing.[120] They also indicate that three days earlier, in Regina, Richardson had sentenced Corbert Peltier, Baptiste Peltier, Alexandre Peltier, and Brisbois Brier to two years for theft of horses on 15 June.[121] Thus, it appears that Richardson arranged for Irvine to deal with the Assiniboine man, perhaps because he knew that Empty Belly would be appearing before him as a witness during the trial of Buffalo Calf, which was yet to take place.

One can only imagine what sixteen-year-old Buffalo Calf felt as he arrived at the Manitoba Penitentiary to become Prisoner 269, one of only two sixteen-year-olds among the 315 prisoners admitted between 1871 and June 1885.[122] When, or if, he was ever released from prison is not known; the prison register is silent.

Later that summer, on 14 August, Ar-ki-tap was charged, on an Information sworn by Louis Leveille, with bringing two stolen horses into Canada earlier that spring, on 30 April 1884. On 16 August, "Ka-ke-tap, Assiniboine Indian" (likely the same man, Ah-kee-tap or Ar-ki-tap) is named as Informant in an Information laid against three Cree Indians – The Rock, Little Fish, and Is-te-wah – charging them with bringing into Canada one horse "stolen or unlawfully obtained" in the United States on 30 April.[123] Also charged on 16 August on Informations sworn by Louis Leveille of Maple Creek were three other Cree men: Ah-sti-ni-ah,[124] Day Thunder,[125] and Little Fish.[126]

The Statement of the Accused made by Ar-ki-tap on 14 August is telling: "I have told already that I took the horses and all about the men who were with me."[127] For his part, The Rock, who was charged on Ka-ke-tap's Information, said simply: "I have nothing to say. I have a few words to say to 'Big Bull.'"[128] Ah-sti-ni-ah's statement similarly referred to the Big Bull: "I brought five horses over. All I have to say I will say when I see the Big Bull."[129] Finally, in the statement of the one of the accused men, named as "The Cree" in the court file, we encounter the grievance pointed out earlier in this chapter about American Indians stealing Canadian Indians' horses with impunity: "Five times they did me wrong from the other side. Four times I stood it. The fifth I could not."[130]

Richardson accepted the guilty pleas of all the accused, and sentenced the seven men to two months of hard labour; Ar-ki-tap was sentenced to one month of hard labour. As noted above, his brother Empty Belly (sentenced by Irvine) and the four Half-breed men sentenced earlier by Richardson received much longer penitentiary terms. In this complex web of charges, Ar-ki-tap emerges as a central figure – as informant, witness, and accused – in the chain of events that followed his initial arrest on 18 June on a charge that was summarily dismissed. His brother and brother-in-law did not fare as well, of course, but once again, at the end of the day, Hubner's concern that Indians received increasingly harsh sentences for horse theft and bringing stolen horses into Canada is not supported by this series of cases (although the sentences handed down to the "Half-breed gang" and Empty Belly offer some support for his argument).

Not all horse thefts involved raids and cross-border activity. On 23 May 1879, Na-tox-kris-tok-ka (The Only Mountain) of the Blackfoot Nation appeared before Hugh Richardson and, through interpreter Jean L'Heureux, laid an Information to obtain a search warrant. In his declaration, The Only Mountain charged that on 1 May, his large bay horse (fully described with white star on the forehead and black points) had been stolen by The

Little Person, a Cree Indian, son of Running Crow.[131] Richardson issued the search warrant, but it appears that it was never executed by the police. On 10 September, Superintendent Walker of the Battleford NWMP explained, apparently in response to a letter sent by Richardson the day before, that he had intended to execute the warrant at Sounding Lake during the treaty payment time, but he had not gone there himself. Rather, he reported that he had transferred the warrant to Major Irvine, who took it to the Cypress Hills, as he believed that "the parties implicated are in that neighbourhood."[132]

It is doubtful that Major Irvine ever executed the warrant, and more likely that this horse from Blackfoot territory at the junction of the Red Deer and Saskatchewan Rivers became a Cree horse that accompanied its new owner to and from the Cypress Hills.

One wonders whether The Only Mountain experienced a sense of loss, or perhaps shame, at having to ask the NWMP for assistance in finding the horse stolen by Running Crow's son. Could the Blackfoot no longer take back what was theirs from the Cree? Or did he feel that he had a right to call on the white man's law to help him, to use its power, influence, and police, to show a young Cree that he could no longer make off with a Blackfoot horse and not expect trouble? Did The Only Mountain want The Little Person punished by the law, or did he simply want his horse returned? Was the young Cree following a traditional path, or was he just a thief? Had there been a raid or simply a dispute? Was he trying to become a Worthy Young Man through the taking of the Blackfoot's horse, or did he just need a way to get home? Was the (possibly older) Blackfoot following a new path? Was the Blackfoot right?

The Only Mountain's complaint about his lost or stolen large bay horse represents one small unresolved case in the court records, and not the only file in which members of different First Nations charged others with horse theft. In the summer of 1881, three horses went missing from William Wolf's pasture on the Eagle Hills Cree Reserve near Battleford. It appears that Peter Ballendine alerted Wolf in early October that his three horses were in the possession of some Stonies to the south, heading in the direction of the Cypress Hills. (Ballendine may have encountered the party in his travels as mail carrier.[133]) Wolf's Information was based on information and his belief that four Stoney (Assiniboine) men had his horses. The Information named: A Small Bull, A Soul, The Thunders Home Son, and A Deceiving Man. On 31 October, the *Saskatchewan Herald* convicted them in advance of their trial: "The Assiniboine horse thieves brought in from the Red Deer Forks will be tried today" (see Figure 2.5).[134] Three trials

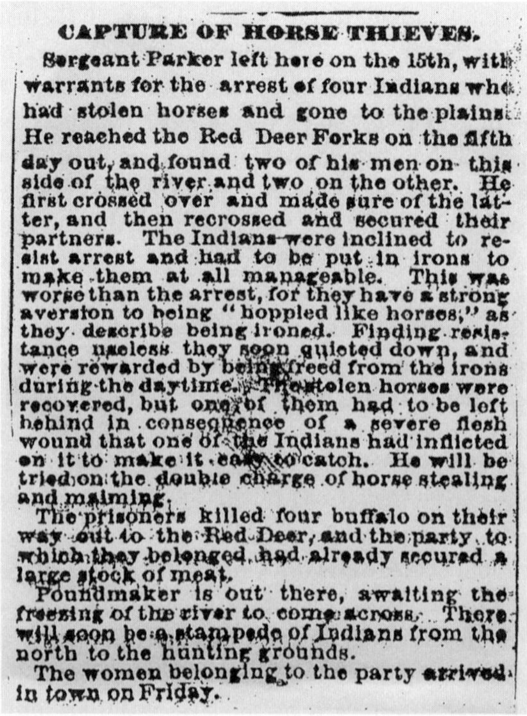

CAPTURE OF HORSE THIEVES.

Sergeant Parker left here on the 15th, with warrants for the arrest of four Indians who had stolen horses and gone to the plains. He reached the Red Deer Forks on the fifth day out, and found two of his men on this side of the river and two on the other. He first crossed over and made sure of the latter, and then recrossed and secured their partners. The Indians were inclined to resist arrest and had to be put in irons to make them at all manageable. This was worse than the arrest, for they have a strong aversion to being "hoppled like horses," as they describe being ironed. Finding resistance useless they soon quieted down, and were rewarded by being freed from the irons during the daytime. The stolen horses were recovered, but one of them had to be left behind in consequence of a severe flesh wound that one of the Indians had inflicted on it to make it easy to catch. He will be tried on the double charge of horse stealing and maiming.

The prisoners killed four buffalo on their way out to the Red Deer, and the party to which they belonged had already secured a large stock of meat.

Poundmaker is out there, awaiting the freezing of the river to come across. There will soon be a stampede of Indians from the north to the hunting grounds.

The women belonging to the party arrived in town on Friday.

FIGURE 2.5 *Saskatchewan Herald,* 31 October 1881.

were held in Battleford; the files contain only Richardson's handwritten notes from the three, in which two of the three accused testified for each other and against the third. No other legal documents are in the four files. It appears that a Mr. Forget cross-examined the witnesses on behalf of the prisoner, Esktope, who emerges from the record as the principal accused and for whom Mosquito, chief of the Eagle Hills Assiniboines, testified as a character witness.

The three Assiniboines tried for stealing Wolf's horses were Esktope, The Ghost, and The Bull That Walks Painted Red. Given that Wolf, a Cree, spoke no English, his initial complaint, including the names of the Stonies who had allegedly stolen his horses, would have been translated into English for the initial Information, and then back into Cree for him; for the purpose of the trial, the Information would have had to be translated into Stoney for the three accused. The trials required a Stoney interpreter (Thomas Quinn) for the accused and a Cree interpreter for the witness, Wolf. Finally, the proceedings were transcribed in English, apparently in

Richardson's handwriting. Thus, it is distinctly possible that The Ghost was the person named as "A Soul" in the Information, that The Bull That Walks Painted Red was the person named as "A Small Bull," and that Esktope was either "A Deceiving Man" or "The Thunders Home Son."

The challenge of the Plains is once again revealed through the evidence of the prosecution witnesses. Sergeant William Parker, who arrested the prisoners at their camp on the south side of the South Branch of the South Saskatchewan River, testified that he found the horses at the Stony Creek on the north side of the river. He brought only one of the horses back with him, leaving the other mare, who was "hobbled," and the colt; Wolf identified this horse as his.

When cross-examined, Parker testified that he "understood that these Indians were after buffalo and were waiting a chance to cross the river going southward." Parker also admitted in the trial of the Bull That Walks Painted Red that he "explained on arrest the nature of the charge through the interpreter but can't say if my words were properly translated."[135] Wolf also admitted under cross-examination that his horses had wandered off before, but added that they had come back of their own accord. It is possible that if this had been the only evidence, all three accused might have been acquitted. The Bull That Walks Painted Red gave unsworn evidence in The Ghost's trial, however; as a non-Christian Indian, he was warned in accordance with the provisions of the Indian Act.[136] He testified that Esktope brought the horses into camp, and that The Ghost was with him hunting ducks when Esktope arrived with the horses. He also testified that Esktope had had no horses when their party had left the reserve.[137] The Ghost testified for the prosecution in Esktope's trial, stating that Esktope had not been with them when they left the reserve, and that he had not known that Esktope was coming. He testified that Esktope caught up to their party five days after they had left, and that Esktope said that he had found the horses. Esktope called two witnesses in his defence, one of whom was his chief, Mosquito, who testified to the prisoner's good character: "I don't think he would steal a horse."[138] Mosquito also testified that he remembered when the party had left the reserve for Red Deer River and Esktope had left on foot five days later. He added that both the party and Esktope had headed off to the west, whereas Wolf's place on the next reserve was to the east.

Hugh Richardson's court files contain no record of the disposition, but the NWMP Commissioner's Annual Report indicates that on 31 October "The Bull Painted Red Who Walks," "The Ghost," and "The Cloud Old Man" were acquitted of horse stealing, and that Esktope was acquitted of shooting a horse.[139] Here again, there is a less than perfect fit between the press, court, and police records. No mention of the case or the outcome was made in either of the next two issues of the *Saskatchewan Herald*;[140] perhaps the *Herald*, satisfied with its own pre-trial pronouncement on the guilt of the "Assiniboine horse thieves," could not bring itself to admit that the men had been acquitted.

Conclusion: Criminalization Revisited

In this chapter, I have analyzed cases of First Nations persons who found themselves criminally prosecuted for activities that a few short decades earlier would not have caused them to be prosecuted for anything, much less punished by the white man's law. Like Macleod and Rollason, I have found that Aboriginal accused persons represent less than one-third of the accused persons in the court files. Most of the numbers are even smaller fractions: four First Nations children prosecuted in two very different circumstances, one scarcely less spurious than the other; seven women and girls charged (and discharged) over the entire period; eight homicide files, one of which was a trumped-up charge of accessory after the fact to murder.

These records enable – indeed, require – one to reassess the discourse of criminalization and its exemplars. One might well say that the very fact that seventy-one files in the early period (1876-86) involved accused persons described as "Indian" is evidence of their criminalization. They were prosecuted for the most part for small thefts – some for ridiculously minor items – others for assault, smuggling stolen horses into Canada, and a few for murder. They appeared in court as prisoners but many, if not most, were not imprisoned when convicted. Many pleaded guilty without benefit of legal advice or counsel; a fortunate few had someone to speak for them, such as their chief. Other than horses, the property alleged to have been stolen tended to be items of clothing, foodstuffs, and money, and really not much in any case.

The cases discussed here demonstrate the central argument of this book: the First Nations peoples did experience criminalization through prosecutions for criminal offences that hitherto had not been dealt with in their communities in this way – admittedly not in the systemic or overwhelming numbers that "-ization" usually connotes, but still they were criminally prosecuted. To the extent that this occurred, it occurred through the ordinary criminal law. To point this out is not to deny the overarching importance of the *Indian Act* or of the government's increasingly coercive policies, but here again the concept of criminalization needs to be revisited, contextualized, and applied with greater precision. Although the intersection of the criminal law with the First Nations did mark a watershed in Aboriginal societies, the "criminalizing" aspects of the *Indian Act* have been overstated in other studies. As Chapter 4 will demonstrate, the criminal courts did not reliably act as the "best friend" of the government's Indian officials.[141]

3
"Prisoner Never Gave Me Anything for What He Done"
Aboriginal Voices in the Criminal Court

In colonial law ... it is tempting but wrong to view any participation in an imposed legal system as collaboration, on the one hand, and to represent any form of rejection of the law's authority as resistance.

– *Lauren Benton (2002)*

On 7 August 1878, a man named Oo-pie-too-kah-han-up-ee-we-yin, also referred to in the court file as "The Pondmaker" swore an Information accusing another man of stealing his horse.[1] "The Pondmaker" of this court case was surely the man now known to us as Poundmaker (Pihtokahanapiwiyin), headman of the River People, spokesperson at Treaty 6 negotiations, one of the most prominent First Nations leaders of his generation, and one of the chiefs convicted of treason-felony in 1885 and sentenced to three years in the penitentiary.[2]

Poundmaker's Information was sworn before Stipendiary Magistrate Hugh Richardson in Battleford and interpreted by Peter Erasmus;[3] in it, he accused one John Ballendine of having stolen his horse. The horse in question had been the subject of a wager between Ballendine and Poundmaker on a horse race that they had agreed would be run over the distance of a mile. Sporting events involving horse races were popular in Battleford (see Figure 3.1). Ballendine told Poundmaker that twenty-seven telegraph poles measured the distance of one mile; however, Pierre

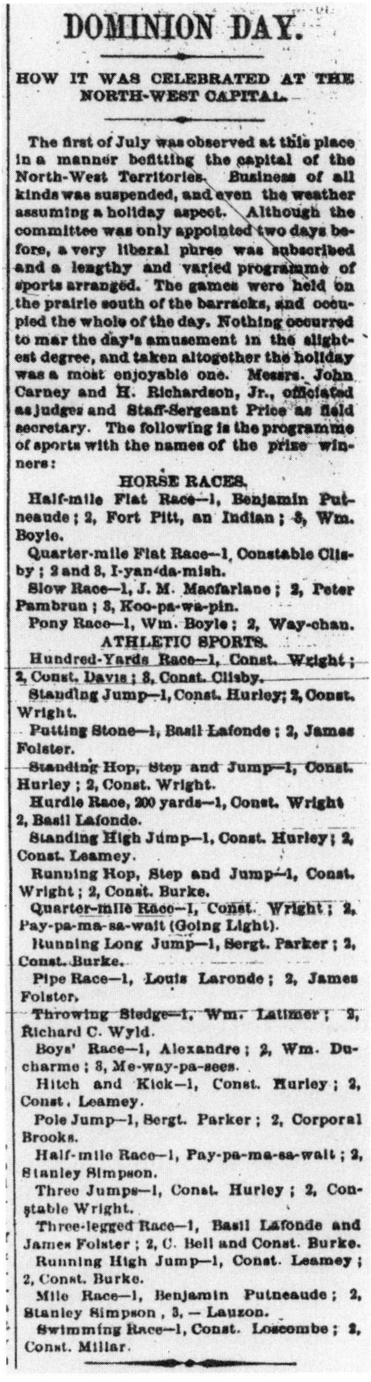

DOMINION DAY.

HOW IT WAS CELEBRATED AT THE NORTH-WEST CAPITAL.

The first of July was observed at this place in a manner befitting the capital of the North-West Territories. Business of all kinds was suspended, and even the weather assuming a holiday aspect. Although the committee was only appointed two days before, a very liberal purse was subscribed and a lengthy and varied programme of sports arranged. The games were held on the prairie south of the barracks, and occupied the whole of the day. Nothing occurred to mar the day's amusement in the slightest degree, and taken altogether the holiday was a most enjoyable one. Messrs. John Carney and H. Richardson, Jr., officiated as judges and Staff-Sergeant Price as field secretary. The following is the programme of sports with the names of the prize winners:

HORSE RACES.

Half-mile Flat Race—1, Benjamin Putneaude; 2, Fort Pitt, an Indian; 3, Wm. Boyle.

Quarter-mile Flat Race—1, Constable Clisby; 2 and 3, I-yan-da-mish.

Slow Race—1, J. M. Macfarlane; 2, Peter Pambrun; 3, Koo-pa-wa-pin.

Pony Race—1, Wm. Boyle; 2, Way-chan.

ATHLETIC SPORTS.

Hundred-Yards Race—1, Const. Wright; 2, Const. Davis; 3, Const. Clisby.

Standing Jump—1, Const. Hurley; 2, Const. Wright.

Putting Stone—1, Basil Lafonde; 2, James Folster.

Standing Hop, Step and Jump—1, Const. Hurley; 2, Const. Wright.

Hurdle Race, 200 yards—1, Const. Wright 2, Basil Lafonde.

Standing High Jump—1, Const. Hurley; 2, Const. Leamey.

Running Hop, Step and Jump—1, Const. Wright; 2, Const. Burke.

Quarter-mile Race—1, Const. Wright; 2, Pay-pa-ma-sa-wait (Going Light).

Running Long Jump—1, Sergt. Parker; 2, Const. Burke.

Pipe Race—1, Louis Laronde; 2, James Folster.

Throwing Sledge—1, Wm. Latimer; 2, Richard C. Wyld.

Boys' Race—1, Alexandre; 2, Wm. Ducharme; 3, Me-way-pa-sees.

Hitch and Kick—1, Const. Hurley; 2, Const. Leamey.

Pole Jump—1, Sergt. Parker; 2, Corporal Brooks.

Half-mile Race—1, Pay-pa-ma-sa-wait; 2, Stanley Simpson.

Three Jumps—1, Const. Hurley; 2, Constable Wright.

Three-legged Race—1, Basil Lafonde and James Folster; 2, C. Bell and Const. Burke.

Running High Jump—1, Const. Leamey; 2, Const. Burke.

Mile Race—1, Benjamin Putneaude; 2, Stanley Simpson, 3, — Lauzon.

Swimming Race—1, Const. Loscombe; 2, Const. Millar.

FIGURE 3.1 Dominion Day horse races (*Saskatchewan Herald,* 8 July 1882). Poundmaker's horse race in 1878 may have had its origin in an event like this, with First Nations, police, and settler participants competing together.

Daignault, a Métis man in Poundmaker's party (and occasional interpreter in the criminal court) disputed this, saying that in fact thirty-one poles comprised one mile. Ballendine stood by what he had said, and Poundmaker accepted his word. They shook hands on the wager. The race was run and Ballendine's horse won.

After the race, Poundmaker recounted, a man named Todd approached him and said that he had heard that he had lost the race and "that there was some foul play about it." With the assistance of the surveyor's camp crew, a measure was taken, and indeed a further seven poles beyond the twenty-seventh made up the distance of one mile. Ballendine had lied when he gave his word to Poundmaker. Poundmaker then went to Ballendine, told him where the horse was, but proposed another race, as he was satisfied that a mile had not been run. Ballendine declined to race his horse again, and no new race was run.

Faced with Ballendine's intransigence, Poundmaker "consulted Mr. Brelland who told me to go to Mr. Richardson and lay a complaint. I was afraid to do so as I had heard from Daignault and others I might be punished for gambling. Mr. Brelland insisted I should go and I went." Poundmaker continued: "After seeing Mr. Richardson I went with Lazare to Ballendine and Lazare told him as I understood what Mr. R had directed. Ballendine made rough reply in English. Ballendine afterwards in my absence went to my camp and took my horse." Ballendine, apparently neither moved nor awed by the indirect intervention of the magistrate, responded by surreptitiously making off with the horse when Poundmaker was not at his camp. And here the court file ends. There is no evidence in it that Ballendine ever faced this charge in court. As is often the case, however, the process is perhaps of more interest than the resolution.

In this matter, Poundmaker had been assisted by the white and Métis men of Battleford: Todd, the telegraph survey crew, Peter Erasmus, Lazare (possibly Richardson's emissary), and, apparently, Richardson himself. He had access to and invoked the highest levels of authority in Battleford, consulting with "Mr. Brelland" (likely Paschal Breland, Métis member of the North-West Territories Council), who sent him to Magistrate Richardson (who was also a member of the Council).[4] Clearly, Richardson had sent a message to Ballendine through Lazare, and Poundmaker's English was sufficiently good to understand Ballendine's "rough reply." Poundmaker's Information had been laid not before a justice of the peace but before the more senior and recently arrived magistrate. Whether or not he experienced being cheated as a humiliation, Poundmaker's indignation at the "foul play" is matched by the unresolved nature of the matter in the court file. And, regardless of the unresolved state of the criminal file, one can well imagine that a man of Poundmaker's stature, intelligence, and ability would have found a path to resolution and to his stolen horse. Seven arduous years later, Poundmaker would again be in front of Richardson, but this time as a prisoner in his court in Regina, facing the charge by the Crown that he had committed treason-felony in the 1885 North-West Rebellion. He was convicted by a jury on disputable evidence and sentenced to three years in prison.

Aboriginal Voices in Court

The voices of Aboriginal people in the criminal law form the heart of this chapter through their transcribed, often interpreted, words when appearing as informants, complainants, and witnesses in the criminal court. This focus represents a shift from the traditional if understandable preoccupation of legal historians of criminal law with the Crown and the accused, through or against whom the coercive form of the law is expressed, and by whose numbers it is counted and its efficacy measured. The criminal process involved many more ordinary people as well, some of whom invoked the criminal law for support, protection, and redress. To say that the criminal law is simply the coercive arm of the state against the people is to identify only the most visible aspect of this legal form, and to miss its more contradictory contribution, in which social relations of inequality are not simply enforced but also mediated. This is one of the partial, contradictory "truths" of criminal law and First Nations in the late nineteenth-century North-West Territories.

The criminal court records of the North-West Territories provide little information concerning any of the participants (informants, deponents, prisoners, police officers, judges) in the criminal proceedings. For instance, the actual age of any of the accused persons, complainants, or other witnesses is seldom disclosed.[5] There is very little of the prisoner's voice to be found, other than in the "Statements of the Accused" at the end of a preliminary hearing before the justice of the peace, and occasionally in cross-examination of a prosecution witness.[6]

In possibly the first actual criminal trial before Stipendiary Magistrate Richardson, William Turner, a labourer, was tried in Battleford on 1 December 1877 on a charge of assault upon John Eye (another name, "Oskjec," was struck out), a Cree man, the complainant and informant.[7]

The court record from 30 November indicates that Richardson had issued the following summons to Pierre Daignault:

> Whereas information was laid before me In [*sic*] that William Turner on the thirtieth day of November instant in and upon one John Eye did make an assault and him the said John Eye did beat and wound and illtreat and it hath been made to appear to me you are qualified to interpret the Indian Cree language into English on the trial.
>
> These are therefore to require you to be and appear on Saturday the first day of December at my office in Battleford to interpret as required.[8]

The assault followed a dispute regarding whether John Eye could get his water from the water hole. The incident was described in John Eye's words, through Daignault as the sworn interpreter:

> When I went for water I met Turner near the water hole. He told me to go to the river. I told him I would not. I went to the mill and took a bucket full. He came behind me and told me to throw that water in the hole I asked him what for. He repeated this order. I put the water in the hole and stepping back called Turner a "son of a Bitch[.]" Turner struck me on the side of the head with his hand. I jumped for a stick but did not take it. Turner took a stick and I ran away.[9]

To the defendant he said:

> My reason for making use of the expression I did use was because you spoke so roughly to me. I was going to take up a stick but when you [picked] up one, I ran away.[10]

Here, John Eye was clearly responding to a question put to him by Turner. Richardson convicted Turner, but "owing to the provocation," he stipulated that the fine would be a nominal one of $1, "not enforced at this time," plus costs in the amount of $1 for the interpreter's fee.

Evidence of alleged offences contained in the territorial criminal court records is found primarily in the Informations and depositions taken down before two justices of the peace, and in the warrants of apprehension or of committal to jail, with cryptic, abbreviated endorsements by the trial judge. The depositions appear as first-person accounts, as uninterrupted narratives, but they would have been the product of examination – perhaps by a North-West Mounted Police (NWMP) officer or a private prosecutor

– and some cross-examination, including on occasion by the accused prisoner. Many deponents in criminal matters were First Nations women, children, and men. Their words taken before the justices of the peace and reduced to writing having been interpreted in many cases from Cree, Sioux, Saulteaux, or French. Some of these languages would have no words for the legal concepts and terms (such as guilt, manslaughter, wilful murder).[11] The written versions of the depositions were signed before the justice of the peace. Less than a handful of the depositions given by Aboriginal witnesses are signed with a signature; in place of a signature is simply an "X" – "their mark" – accompanied in some, but not all, instances by the signature of the interpreter.

These pre-trial depositions do not necessarily reflect the evidence given by the witnesses at trial, nor is it safe to assume that they reflect the entirety of the evidence ultimately presented by the prosecution at trial. Many of them contain all manner of hearsay, character, and reputation evidence concerning accused and complainants alike, some of which may or may not have been admitted into evidence at trial.

Some historians express ambivalence regarding the probative value of depositions.[12] Mindful of Carolyn Strange's injunction against seeing court files as "textual productions of truth,"[13] these depositions may be described as textual productions of allegations. As Edward Muir and Guido Ruggiero have opined, however, "not just any lie will do in testifying about a crime. Usually lies must have the ring of credibility."[14] The depositions do represent a form of first-person account by informants and witnesses of events that gave rise to the matters in the criminal courts. Indeed, John Beattie has characterized the depositions of victims and witnesses and the examinations of accused persons as "among the most useful" supplements to the indictments he was studying in his landmark study of crime and courts in seventeenth- and eighteenth-century England.[15] And, for all their frailty, the depositions and the Statements of the Accused tend to be the only words in the file that tell us anything about what gave rise to the criminal prosecution before the court.

The information in these records is sketchy, but there can be no doubt that these texts are anything but disembodied legal discourse. Many voices in the court files are lay voices, the voices of ordinary people coming or being brought to law, as well as those of the NWMP, men of standing, such as Hudson's Bay Company (HBC) men, other merchants, government men, and, of course, other lay witnesses, some of them less reluctant than others. The only professional experts to be found are the medical officers in the NWMP who, on occasion, offered opinion evidence as experts on Indian medicines and potions.[16] Peter Hourie (who was allowed by Richardson to be qualified as an expert on the interpretation of certain Cree and Saulteaux words in Tom Lemac's 1902 murder trial[17]) and latterly veterinary surgeons, midwives, and medical doctors began to appear in the court records as well.[18]

When they appeared in court, Aboriginal deponents and witnesses, as recently as 1902 in Tom Lemac's murder trial, were also called upon to give forms of expert evidence (for example, on the entry and exit of bullets in the wounds on a dead body,[19] or on the effect of alcohol on Indians), or to act as cultural interpreters of the ways and meanings of Indian gestures and forms of courtesy.[20]

The nature of the evidence in the court files suggests the mediated nature of law and law's construction of experience. The mediation is multi-layered: complaints appear to have been made to a chief or husband, who then complained to the police or to a justice of the peace or stipendiary magistrate, after which an Information was taken and sworn. As to what is revealed about Aboriginal voices in the criminal law, it may be best to eschew the metaphors of a window or a camera in favour of a prism,[21] which by definition contemplates a partial and refracted image of the experiences caught by the records. The images are partial, the stories fragmentary and incomplete; nevertheless, we can begin to draw some conclusions.

Going to Law: Aboriginal Informants

In a document neither sworn nor dated, one Is-pinik-hah-kee-toot complained that in the winter of 1875 (or possibly 1874: see Figure 3.2), his brother-in-law Apistatim had taken seven horses, without authority, from Is-pinik-hah-kee-toot's father (since deceased).[22] With the assistance of the police at Tail Creek, Is-pinik-hah-kee-toot, described throughout the document as "Complt," had recovered six of the horses, but his brother-in-law had come again and made off with six horses that he (Is-pinik-hah-kee-toot) owned. Friends of Is-pinik-hah-kee-toot had recovered these horses, but in October 1877 Apistatim had returned in the complainant's absence and taken three horses, which he never returned. Apistatim is described in the complaint as being "non-treaty" and "in Big Bear's camp." Is-pinik-hah-kee-toot estimated that the three horses were worth $75 each. His witnesses were said to be "the whole camp," and he concluded by saying that he himself would be back at his camp in about seventeen days.

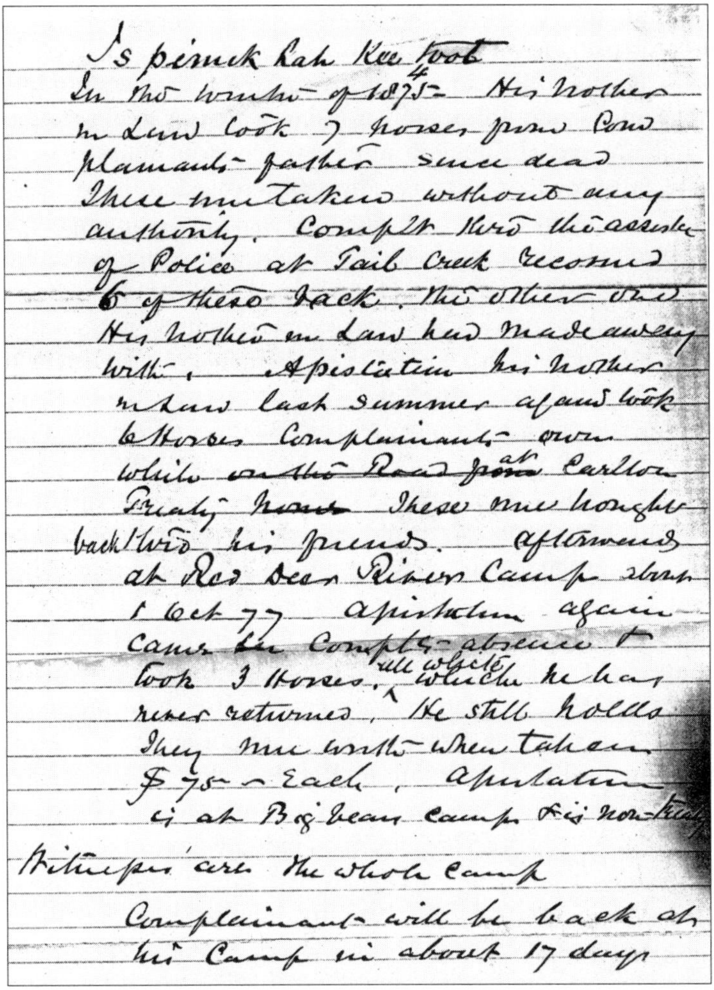
Is pinik hah Kee toot
In the winter of 1874-5 His brother
in Law took 7 horses from Com
plainants father since dead
These were taken without any
authority. Complt thro the assistce
of Police at Trail Creek recovered
6 of these back. The other one
His brother in Law had made away
with. Apistatim his brother
in Law last summer again took
6 Horses Complainants own
while on the Road at Carlton
Treaty Money These were brought
back thro his friends. afterwards
at Red Deer River Camp about
1 Oct 77 apistatim again
came in Complts absence &
took 3 Horses all white which he has
never returned. He still holds
They were worth when taken
$75 - Each. apistatim
is at Big Bear camp & is non-treaty
Witnesses are the whole Camp
Complainant will be back at
his Camp in about 17 days

FIGURE 3.2 Information of Is-pinik-hah-kee-toot, 1878. | Apistatim [1878], SAB AG (GR 11.1) CR-Regina, 1st series, 1876-86, file 42.

The court file is a single sheet of paper; not surprisingly, there is no record of either a hearing or a disposition.

That the matter was not resolved is less significant than the fact of the complaint itself. Clearly this was a dispute between extended family members; it appears that Is-pinik-hah-kee-toot was acting in a capacity akin to that of an executor in his efforts to reclaim his father's horses from his brother-in-law. The dispute over the horses is not one that less than a decade earlier would have witnessed the involvement of police or the white man's court, and yet a clearly exasperated Is-pinik-hah-kee-toot turned to the law for assistance, not once but twice. Perhaps he was a Treaty Indian who felt he had a right to assistance from the Canadian authorities in dealing with his non-Treaty brother-in-law who kept stealing his horses.

While not overwhelming in numbers, it is clear from the territorial court records that First Nations individuals invoked the assistance of the criminal law. Many of the cases discussed in earlier chapters and in the chapters to follow have involved First Nations complainants and informants: Peaychew, William Wolf, Na-tox-kris-tok-ka (The Only Mountain), Margaret Gladieu, Alexis Sussey, and so on. In addition to these files, the court records indicate that a number of Aboriginal women turned to the law and charged their husbands with forms of assault.[23]

In 1880, Joseph Jack, described as a Sioux farmer on the Sioux Reserve at Bird Tail Creek, charged one Paskada (also known as Whitehead) with administering poison with intent to kill Solomon Tankansaecije, described in the court file as a Sioux Indian minister, who had drunk tea and eaten a dinner of bread and pork at Paskada's home. The evidence against Paskada was not particularly compelling: it was suggested that he did not like the minister, that the minister had eaten alone when invited to Paskada's home for dinner, and that he had become sick after dinner, but there was no evidence that Paskada had in any way been involved in the preparation of the offending meal. The "expert" evidence of poison was provided by a witness described as NWMP surgeon Robert Miller: "I was and am of the opinion Solomon got poison in a liquid state and in the tea he drank and the long continued affects [*sic*] described indicate those of digitalis which is indigenous in this country. Digitalis is a strong poison with various affects [*sic*] on persons taking."[24] The jury acquitted Paskada.

The participation of First Nations leaders, notably chiefs and their headmen, figures significantly among the thirty "Indian" Informants in the early period. The Richardson court files suggest that even when not named formally as Informants, chiefs such as Red Pheasant, Beardy, and Strike Him on the Back were prepared to use the police and the court to gain assistance for their people.[25]

Even when not named in the Information as "Chief," some chiefs clearly laid charges in that capacity, on behalf of their band members (or to protect the band's resources). For instance, at Chief Beardy's instance, Francis Deschaw was charged and convicted in 1878 for theft of clothing and money, the property of Beardy's band.[26] Deschaw had accompanied Beardy and his councillors to Winnipeg shortly after their treaty money had been paid. He had helped himself to a pair of trousers and a coat from the goods they had purchased, had worn them on the trip back but never paid for them, and, upon conviction for theft, was sentenced to six months of hard labour at the Battleford police station.

On 6 October 1882, a man described as a Cree Indian named Ka-nah-pic-a-nah-hew, also known as The Snake Indian, was accused in an Information sworn on information and belief by "Metchewais, a Councillor of Strike Him on the Back's band" (his name is spelled Mee-ta-way-wis in the Treaty Annuity Paylist[27]) before NWMP superintendent and justice of the peace W.M. Herchmer: "that Ka-nah-pic-a-nah-hew or The Snake Indian a Cree Indian of ________ band on the fourth day of October inst. At Strike him on the Back's Reserve by force and against her will, feloniously ravished and carnally knew Kutenay, an Indian girl, a daughter of Kaa-out-a-pew a Cree Indian under the age of twelve years. I was told this by some who knew of it."[28] One of Metchewais's informants may have been Ka-na-do-tac, a woman who later testified at the trial and who described herself as the girl's grandmother. She may have gone to the chief, Strike Him on the Back, and perhaps the chief delegated this matter to his headman, Metchewais; or perhaps she went to Metchewais directly, although this is probably less likely. The Snake Indian was brought to court as a prisoner, and it appears that the child's mother was herself held in custody until after the trial, perhaps to ensure her attendance as a witness.[29]

The court file contains no record of such a hearing or order of committal for trial by the justice of the peace. Herchmer must have held such a hearing, however, because the file does contain a Statement of the Accused taken by "Supt. Herchmer JP," a statement that was to have been taken after the witnesses for the prosecution had been examined in the accused's presence, and to which he was invited to say something in answer to the charge. The document bears only the date, October 1882, and states that The Snake Indian said only, "Not guilty."

He was tried in Battleford by Magistrate Richardson on 11 November 1882. Three witnesses, two women and the girl he was alleged to have sexually assaulted, testified at the trial. Richardson's transcript describes each as a "non English, non Christian" who was cautioned by the magistrate under the provisions of s. 85 of the *Indian Act.* The girl, Kutenay, gave her evidence first and described through the interpreter, Louis Laronde, how she knew the prisoner, what he had done to her, and what she had done afterwards.

She said that she lived at the Battle River Indian Reserve and that she knew the prisoner, whom she described as her mother's present husband.

She provided the context for the offence, saying that it happened "when Indian treaty money was paid at the reserve." On that day, the prisoner had sent her off to get potatoes from another Indian man named "Black," who lived some distance from their house. In order to get to Black's place, one had to walk along a road that went through some bush. On her way, and on the stretch of road that passed through the bush, she was overtaken by her mother's husband, who told her to go into the bush.

> ... and he went with me. When in the bush, Prisoner caught me by my shoulders, and laid down on the ground holding me, pulled up my clothes and got on top of me. He unfastened his trousers and with his privates penetrated my private parts I screamed and cried out. When prisoner had done this he got up and went away. I got up and went towards home and on the way met an Indian woman whom I told this woman what had occurred – I was then in a swampy place washing the blood off my person.

In Richardson's handwriting, the last line of her evidence is crossed out: "~~When I got home soon after I told my mother.~~" Richardson perhaps contemplated the issue of a "recent complaint," but it seems that the evidence did not establish that she had told her mother of the assault right away. The prisoner, unrepresented by counsel, asked no questions of her.

The second witness was her mother. Magistrate Richardson appears to have been more cautious at the prospect of her as a witness, as he seems to have questioned her closely in order to impress upon her the importance of telling the truth. He noted that she "appear[ed to be] destitute of the knowledge of God and of any fixed ~~belief~~ and clear belief in religion being cautioned pursuant to the *Indian Act* ... and has only solemnly declared that she will tell the truth, the whole truth and nothing but the truth." Kutenay's mother told the court that the prisoner was her present husband and that Kutenay was her daughter by her previous husband. She said that Kutenay was "past seven years of age." She recollected at treaty payment time, "Prisoner sending the girl off for potatoes. Prisoner followed shortly after. Late on the same day I was told by an Indian woman called Ka-na-do-tac that prisoner had outraced the girl. I then examined the girl and found her privates injured and blood flowing. Prisoner at this time was away." She then appeared to direct herself to the prisoner, in response, it seems, to questions by him that may have challenged the thoroughness of her examination and perhaps intimated that she had given him permission to do this. She rejected any such suggestion: "To Prisoner: I examined the child carefully. Prisoner never gave me anything for what he did. I never consented that prisoner should sleep with the girl, nor did he ever ask me to do so."

The third and final witness, Ka-na-do-tac, was also cautioned and solemnly declared that she would tell the truth; she testified that the girl was her granddaughter and said that she recollected, "one morning at payment time meeting the girl or coming near her she was standing in water and crying. I asked what was the matter She replied that prisoner had had connection with her in the bush motioning to a bush nearby. The girl's legs were cover with blood – I then told the girl's mother."

It may be that The Snake Indian was not a member of Strike Him on the Back's band, given that his band was left blank on the Information, which may also explain why Metchewais and Ka-na-do-tac each pursued the matter. It may also be that the child's mother, for a range of possible reasons, was a reluctant witness; if so, this would explain why she too was held in custody. And, although the prisoner appeared to have asked no questions of the child and the grandmother, he seems to have asked a questions of his wife, which gave rise to her answer that she examined the child and she never consented to his sleeping with the child.

It is possible that The Snake Indian had not apologized to his wife and offered no compensation for the assault upon her child and the consequent injury to her. Or perhaps his question to her addressed this; perhaps he had attempted a form of reparation and she had not accepted it or simply denied that it had been offered. Clearly, she denied that she had consented to his conduct.

Although Richardson's file does not indicate the disposition in the case, the Annual Report of the Commissioner of the North-West Mounted Police indicates that a prisoner named Ka-na-pic-a-nahon (Snake Indian) was convicted of illegally and carnally knowing a girl under the age of ten years by Magistrate Richardson and was sentenced to five years at the Manitoba Penitentiary.[30] The penitentiary admission register records that The Snake Indian was Prisoner 199, a single twenty-four-year-old man, when he arrived to serve his sentence, and that he was discharged "By death" on 14 March 1885. The Snake Indian was one of many First Nations prisoners for whom a prison sentence meant a slow death sentence.[31]

Other Aboriginal people laid Informations before a justice of the peace or the stipendiary magistrate, including women complaining of mistreatment by men who were not their husbands. A Battleford man, William Williams, was convicted in 1882 of assaulting a woman described as "A certain Cree Indian woman know as Little Duck"; he was required to pay a fine of $5.00 and $4.50 to Little Duck.[32]

Sometimes, the accused was a husband or a man with whom the woman had wintered, as in the 1891 case involving a woman from a Treaty 4 band. The informant was a woman named Swaspekoke, who charged a man named Wa-chin (or possibly Wa-chan) with theft of her pony: "I wintered with the Defendant and when he left me he took the pony away with him. Five days after he went away I sent my little boy after the pony. When the little boy came home he told me that the Defendant would [not?] let anybody have the horse. Two days after the boy came home I saw Lemac and he brought me downtown and laid the information next morning. The horse now here in the possession of the police is my property."[33] NWMP Constable Andrews arrested Wa-Chin on Pasqua's reserve: "When I arrested him he was riding the pony."[34] For his part, Wa-chin's statement to the court conceded: "It is true I took the horse away without asking for the use of it, but I intended to return the horse when I was done with it. I asked my little half-brother for permission to sell the colt, but that was neither here nor there."[35] The court file ends with a record of Wa-chin's plea of not guilty and a note that "Horse restored to prosecutor."

In other cases, the accused was a member of the NWMP accused of theft following "connection" for money, or a prominent merchant, such as Battleford's J.B. Mahoney.[36] A Mrs. Mary Hamblyn (who required a Cree interpreter) accused Mahoney of indecently assaulting her when she went to his store for some biscuits. She said he owed her some money. After she pushed him away, he gave her the biscuits. After he received her Information, Richardson sent a letter to Mahoney, indicating that the complaint had been filed and asking whether Mahoney would prefer to attend at the Registry Office in order to receive his summons without formal police service: "Might I suggest that the case as presented is one which the parties concerned have a right to adjust between themselves it should it should [*sic*] not gain [much?] publicity" (see Figure 3.3). Mahoney replied, indicating that he would attend on Richardson's summons and service thereof without formal police service, adding that he thought "it best to have the matter settled by yourself and have done with it" (see Figure 3.4). There is no disposition indicated in the file.

On 18 February 1878, Madeleine Wallace testified that John Smith had come to her house on the previous Saturday and told her that her husband was jealous of him last fall and asked her if she would sleep with him and told her that he would give her all the money that she wanted. John Smith was being tried at Fort Carlton before Justice of the Peace Lawrence Clarke on a charge of common assault (with intent to commit adultery).[37] Madeleine Wallace's husband appears to have been an animating presence

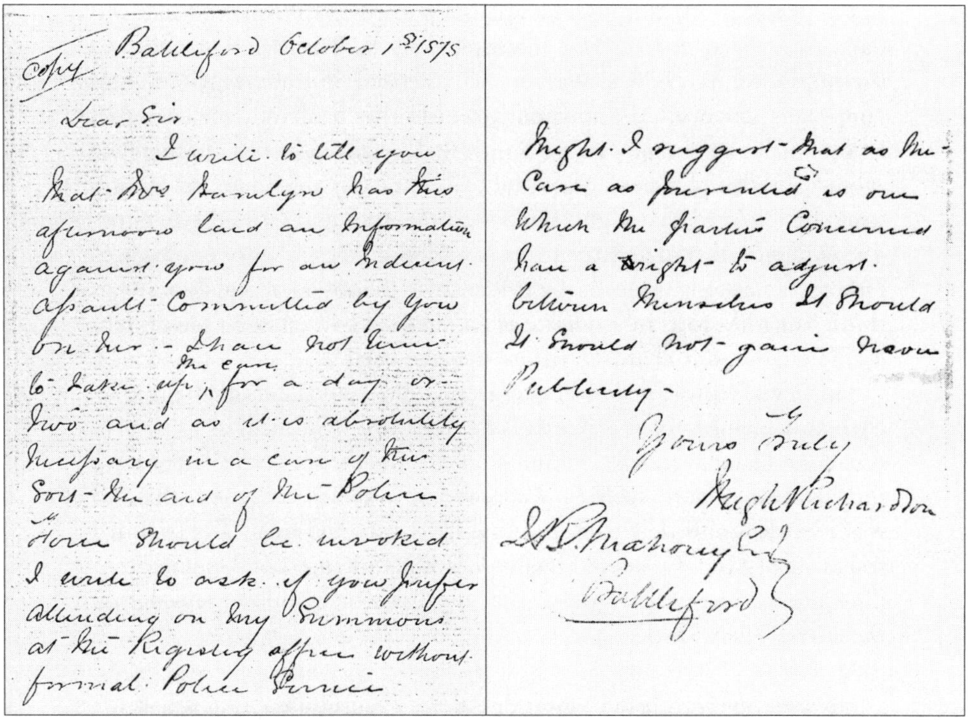

Copy Battleford October 1st 1878

Dear Sir

I write to tell you that Mrs Hamlyn has this afternoon laid an Information against you for an Indecent Assault Committed by you on her – I have not time to take up the case for a day or two and as it is absolutely necessary in a case of this sort the aid of the Police Force should be invoked I write to ask if you prefer attending on my Summons at the Registry office without formal Police Service

Might I suggest that as the case as presented is one which the parties Concerned have a right to adjust between themselves it should it should not gain more Publicity –

Yours truly

Hugh Richardson

J.B. Mahoney Esq

Battleford

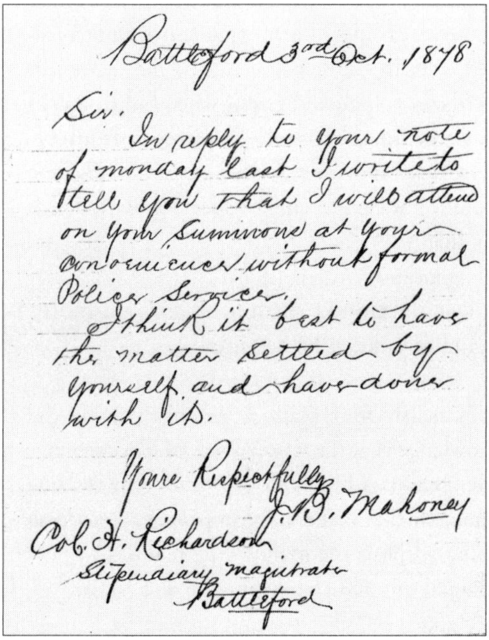

Battleford 3rd Oct. 1878

Sir.

In reply to your note of monday last I write to tell you that I will attend on your Summons at your convenience without formal Police Service.

I think it best to have the matter settled by yourself and have done with it.

Yours Respectfully

J.B. Mahoney

Col. H. Richardson
Stipendiary Magistrate
Battleford

▲ FIGURE 3.3 Letter from Hugh Richardson to J.B. Mahoney, 1 October 1878. | James B. Mahoney [1878], SAB AG (GR 11.1) CR-Regina, 1st series, 1876-86, file 54.

◄ FIGURE 3.4 Letter of reply from J.B. Mahoney to Hugh Richardson, 3 October 1878. | James B. Mahoney [1878], SAB AG (GR 11.1) CR-Regina, 1st series, 1876-86, file 54.

in the prosecution, although he was not named as Informant.[38] Her evidence was given in Cree and interpreted by William McKay, who was sworn as interpreter. Mrs. Wallace characterized Smith's behaviour as an "improper advance." She apparently sent for her husband, who reported to the justice of the peace that Smith had persisted in offering his wife money and troubled her a great deal before she was able to get rid of him; when he returned that night, she bolted the door and refused him entry. The evidence at trial appears to have addressed the "improper advance" rather than assault (indeed, the evidence at trial of an actual assault was thin). The most forceful evidence of an assault is contained in a letter sent by the Clarke to Richardson before the trial itself.[39]

Smith was represented by Hayter Reed, who would later rise to prominence as a member of the North-West Territories Council, as an Indian Agent, and later as Indian Commissioner.[40] The theory of the defence was that Smith had gone to Mrs. Wallace's home at her invitation, that she was a woman of little virtue, and that he was a good man. The recorded responses of Mrs. Wallace to his cross-examination, most of them negative, illustrate the line of questioning that Reed pursued, and her rejection of the answers he was suggesting:

> He visited me twice before I made this charge. He made improper advances on his previous visits. I do not know what his errand was to my house when he made the improper advances or if he had any errand. I did not meet Smith two days before to invite him to visit my house. I did not ask Smith why he did not visit me. There was no person present when Smith was in my house. I never asked him for ear rings or jewelry as presents. Smith offered me no dress or any other article on that day. I did not ask him to come and see me when alone. Do not remember seeing or speaking with Smith within a week of making this charge.[41]

The position of the defence was developed further by the testimony of blacksmith William Giles of Duck Lake, who testified:

> I have known the prosecutrix nearly four years. I met her first on the plains. I know of my own knowledge that the woman was of bad character then. I would not estimate her character highly now. I think that any one going to her and making arrangements could have improper intercourse with her – I saw her cohabiting without the man on the plains – I know the defendant since last fall – he is of good character as far as I know.[42]

Clarke J.P. appears to have pressed Giles on this, because in response to questions by the court he admitted that he had first met Mrs. Wallace when she was single, and conceded, "I know nothing against the woman's character since she has been married." The defendant, being duly cautioned by Clarke, made the following statement under oath, in which he acknowledged calling upon Mrs. Wallace and indeed the conversation in which he told her that Mr. Wallace was jealous of him:

> At one time I met her she asked me why I did not come to visit ... I told her that her husband was jealous of me and I did not wish to make any trouble between her and him. She replied that she was not afraid of her husband. Some few nights afterwards I call in to her place. She and her brothers were there. She said there was not much chance for conversation then. She invited me to call upon her when she would be alone two days later. I called according to her invitation and she asked me if I had any more ear rings and said that she owed me for a pair since the fall. She said would like a dress of [?] and I told I would give her money to purchase one. She refused to accept the money.[43]

Smith was convicted at trial by Clarke J.P. The less than novel defence strategy of impugning Mrs. Wallace's character[44] while celebrating his own proved to be unsuccessful. He was fined $5.00 and required to pay $9.20 in costs.[45]

Aboriginal women also laid Informations complaining of mistreatment by their husbands and other men. In 1882, a Saulteaux woman, The Little Girl, charged her Assiniboine husband, Hoh-pie-sah-pah (Blacknest), with assault after he split her head open with an axe.[46] The *Saskatchewan Herald* reported that owing to the great (but nowhere described) provocation, Blacknest's sentence was a modest ten days at hard labour in the Battleford police station.[47] In another case, a Cree man named Jean Marie was charged by his wife, Kah-kiche-inew, with assaulting her with a knife. One of the witnesses against Jean Marie was Thomas Quinn, an Indian farm instructor to whom the assaulted woman had gone for assistance. Although Jean Marie was committed for trial on the assault charge, it was withdrawn before Magistrate Richardson, apparently at Kah-kiche-inew's request.[48]

In October 1880, the *Saskatchewan Herald* celebrated the successful arrest and conviction of two Cree men, William Gladieu and I-ah-pee-coo-cah, for assaulting John Delaney, an Indian farm instructor.[49] The men had been arrested in the bush near Frog Lake, and the *Herald* reported that the police party transporting them, first to Fort Pitt for a court appearance (before the NWMP justice of the peace), and then to Battleford to serve their sentence, had been stopped more than once by "several parties of Indians" seeking to liberate their friends. It appears from the press report that Delaney was the principal witness against the men; once again, no particulars of the assault were disclosed, but there was evidence of sustained but unsuccessful attempts to prevent the two men from being carted away.

I-ah-pee-coo-cah (or I-ah-pee-coo-caw) would have just completed serving his two-month sentence when his wife, Margaret, laid an Information and complaint before William McKay, HBC factor and justice of the peace, on 12 January 1881. McKay recorded Margaret as saying "in the words to the effect" that on 7 January she had asked her husband for permission "to go to the Indian farm instructor's for provisions for their child who was crying from hunger."[50] She said that he gave her permission to go, but then told her that "if she did not get provisions she should not come into the house again."[51] As she was about to leave, her husband jumped up, tried to find something to use as a weapon, and, settling for a chisel, threatened to kill her. His brother was there and tried to restrain him, but he made several attempts to stab her. She was able to run into her mother's house, and other men kept him from following her and striking her. In her Information and complaint, she asked that he be placed on a peace bond, with sureties, citing his threats and her fear that he would injure her.

Although it is not completely clear from the file, I-ah-pee-coo-cah may then have been held in the cells at Battleford until April, when his three sureties were brought from Fort Pitt. On his posting $100 and his three sureties posting $35 each, he was released on a twelve-month recognizance to keep the peace and be of good behaviour, especially toward his wife. In this case, we see the indirect implication of John Delaney in I-ah-pee-coo-cah's violence against his wife. Delaney would have been the farm instructor to whom Margaret would have had to go to ask for provisions for their hungry child – undoubtedly a galling prospect for her husband, who had just served a jail sentence for assaulting him.

Delaney was also widely reputed to make a practice of demanding or expecting sexual services from First Nations women in exchange for rations[52] – an abuse of authority, according to Sarah Carter, drawing from Department of Indian Affairs files in Library and Archives Canada, and one that was not unique to him.[53] As we have seen in the previous chapter, he was also said to have orchestrated the 1879 prosecution of Peecoose (or Sandfly) for theft from the HBC, because he had taken up with Peecoose's wife.

The relationships of I-ah-pee-coo-cah, Margaret, Peecoose, his lost wife, and John Delaney suggest the myriad disruptions that accompanied the presence of Indian farm instructors in First Nations communities, which displaced some forms of patriarchal relations while reinforcing others. The next chapter will consider in greater depth the significance of the presence of government policy and government men in the lives of the First Nations as well as in the criminal court.

O-cha-nah-kis and the Bad Cop

On 11 September 1889, a warrant for the arrest of one James Ford was issued by NWMP officer and justice of the peace John Cotton. A Cree woman named O-cha-nah-kis had laid an Information charging Ford with stealing $12 from her.[54] Two nights earlier, a man went to a Cree camp near Regina, kicking at tents and calling for a woman. He entered one tent and asked if there were any policemen there. The people in the tent told him no, and told him to go home. Then, according to O-cha-nah-kis, "he asked me if I was 'doing it' for money, I said yes for two dollars – he said that it was too much – I said 'one dollar.'" The man who went to the tent and who paid O-cha-nah-kis $1 for sexual connection was Constable James Ford of the NWMP. He went back to the tent later that evening with two other police officers, demanding that O-cha-nah-kis turn money over to him, intimidating her and her husband with a show of handcuffs. Ford seems to have thought that he had lost some money in O-cha-nah-kis's blanket, and when he came back with the other police officers, she became frightened and asked her husband to give him all their money, which he did.

Ford had been engaged with the NWMP since May 1885, when he joined at the age of twenty-two.[55] In his application he indicated that he was single and in good health, and that his religious faith was Roman Catholic; a reference letter from a man who said he had employed Ford for the previous two years described him as a "sober, industrious and hard-working young man."[56] His NWMP service record tells a different story, however: on Christmas Eve that same year, he was reported to have been drunk at the NWMP barracks, discharged his rifle, and resisted the efforts of other police officers to subdue him, for which he was convicted criminally and sentenced to three months in jail. Other disciplinary infractions netted him, at different times, loss of pay as well as fourteen days in the guardroom. In October 1886, he was again disciplined by his commanding office at Maple Creek for being drunk and causing a disturbance; on this occasion he was fined one month's wages and sentenced to six months at hard labour. There is no record of this in the NWMP returns for 1888, only in his service record.[57] After completing his sentence the following spring, Ford was transferred to Regina, and it was here some months later that he accosted O-cha-nah-kis and her family in their tent, calling for a woman.

One theme in the historical literature concerning Aboriginal women and Canadian law and society concerns the rapid and pervasive construction, by settlers, missionaries, and government officials alike, of Aboriginal women as a menace[58] and as sexually promiscuous, such that any expression of sexual independence or agency was interpreted as illustrative of a "wildness" that had to be "tamed" while being simultaneously exploited by male newcomers.[59] In the context of colonial British Columbia, for instance, Jean Barman has noted, drawing on a range of archival sources and press accounts, the "rapidity with which Aboriginal women became sexualized as prostitutes."[60]

Thus, this case from Regina is striking because it illustrates not only the sexual exploitation of a First Nations woman but also her response to it. O-cha-nah-kis's complaint to the court said that the police officer had returned and extorted $12 from her and her family. Her identification of him was a bit shaky, as she said she was nearly blind, but Ford was convicted by Richardson of the theft of the $12, and although the one hour in jail he received as a sentence was insignificant, it may have been one hour longer than he ever thought he would spend in jail as a result of his behaviour toward her.[61] It was also the shortest jail sentence he received during the little over four years that he was in the NWMP. His application for discharge from the force, the second in as many years, was granted in early November 1889; he was permitted to purchase his release for $50.[62] His NWMP service record is silent with respect to the conviction on 13 September for theft of O-cha-nah-kis's money.

Maria's Story: Secret Love and Public Shame

Roman Catholic priests and educators such as Father Joseph Hugounard, principal of the Lebret Industrial School, also appeared as informants or intervened when they believed that their female students had been raped or sexually exploited and cast aside.[63] In one such case, Baptiste Robillard, a young Métis man who had been acquitted of unlawful carnal knowledge with a girl between twelve and fourteen years of age because the onerous corroboration requirement could not be satisfied, was charged with perjury when it was revealed that he had given a written acknowledgment of paternity and undertaking of some restitution (two horses) to the young woman who had given birth to a baby as a result of her relationship with him.[64] The priest who had extracted the secular "confession" and undertaking testified at the perjury trial.

A complex layer of social and familial relations and the interventionist role of the Roman Catholic clergy are but two aspects of this particular case. On 20 August 1898, Maria Thorne swore an Information before Justice of the Peace Guernsey in Fort Qu'Appelle, alleging that "she being a girl under the age of sixteen years and over the age of fourteen years was seduced by and had illicit connection with one Baptiste Robillard near Fort Qu'Appelle on or about the 25th day of September last past" – which led to a criminal prosecution in September. During the hearing, at which Baptiste was represented by legal counsel, Mr. Hamilton, Maria Thorne described her relationship with him and what transpired when he went to see her at the home where she was working as well as at her mother's home the previous year (1897):

> I cannot say in English what happened, in Cree it is qemistotak.[65] My clothes were off. I was in bed when accused came to the house. He did not take off his clothes, he got on top of me, he had connection with me three times. It was not the same night. He did not have any connection with me after that night – he gave me whiskey out of a bottle – I had 4 drinks that night before he had connection with me. I am now 16 years old. Accused promised to marry me. I promised to marry him. I had a child by accused, it is nearly 6 months old.

In response, Baptiste swore under oath: "I never had connection with Maria Thorne at any time, her statement that I had connection with her at her mother's and at Anderson's is not correct." When pressed under cross-examination, Baptiste skated around the issue of an apparent admission he had made to a priest and resorted to a seemingly cross-cultural and transhistorical tactic in his own defence: he besmirched her character, said she slept around, and recounted a rather far-fetched account of his time in her bed:

> I had a conversation with one of the Fathers but did not say I had had connection with Maria Thorne. I told the Father's [*sic*] I would not marry that kind – I saw so many young fellows around her house.[66] I was there once in a while. I was at Anderson's with her last fall. I was in bed with her. It was dark & I couldn't say if her clothes were off. I was in bed with her for 6 or 7 minutes, I had a bottle, she got it, but I did not give it to her, she asked me to get into bed with her to get warm and she did not want me to leave. In the summer, one Sunday I was at her place, we stayed in the house. This was before I was at Anderson's with her.

His defence counsel argued that the Maria Thorne's evidence had not been corroborated under s. 684 of the *Criminal Code* and that the case should be dismissed. The Crown prosecutor who reviewed the file agreed and made the following notation on the back of the Information: "In this case there is the lack of evidence of chastity & aside from the evidence for the defence there is no corroboration (which is material) of intercourse and the case should I think be dismissed. Sept 1/98 T.C. Johnstone, Crown Prosecutor, W.A."

Baptiste's denial was sufficient to facilitate the dismissal of the illicit carnal connection charge but it led to the laying of a perjury charge against him. At the perjury hearing, the transcript of the earlier September hearing was filed as an exhibit and, through the evidence of Baptiste's brother, Thomas Robillard, and Father Joseph Campeau, an agreement dated 18 June 1898, signed by Baptiste Robillard, witnessed by his brother and the priest, and accepted by Maria Thorne, was produced. Father Campeau explained that he became involved in the matter because "the relatives wished us to act and to get accused to marry the girl or settle it." Maria lived with her mother, Harriet Thorne, who was married to Thomas Robillard, Baptiste's older brother. Baptiste told the priest that he did not wish to marry her, but was willing to "recompense her for the damages he had done to her." Initially Baptiste admitted to the priest that the child was his, but after a few weeks he apparently had second thoughts and suggested that the child was not his. The priest pressed him further; finally, on 18 June, Baptiste signed a fulsome "confession" drafted by Father Campeau, in which he "willingly" agreed to give Maria Thorne a mare and a colt "to help the mother to bring up her boy and to indemnify the mother Maria as much as I can for all the trouble and harm I have caused her, and by giving Maria Thorne these two horses – I settle forever our difficulties with Maria Thorne and her relatives." Maria Thorne accepted the two horses as a "true settlement" between herself and Baptiste. Baptiste clearly had second thoughts about the agreement after he signed it, and never came through with the horses.

The two witnesses for the prosecution at the perjury hearing were Father Campeau and Baptiste's older brother, Thomas, who, as mentioned above, was also the husband of Maria's mother. In response to the perjury charge, Baptiste swore in his own defence that Father Campeau's evidence was not true, and further: "Father Campeau told me I would go to jail if I did not marry Maria Thorne and give her something. I didn't want to marry her or give her something for nothing, he then said I had better give her a colt and things would be left alone. I saw Father Campeau next morning at the church and he drew up the papers and I signed it because I wanted to be left alone." After Baptiste's trial for perjury on 1 November 1898, Justice Richardson reserved his decision for several months. Finally, on 14 February 1899, he convicted Baptiste of perjury, sentenced him to one month in jail at hard labour, and placed him on a recognizance for two years. Having neither married Maria nor settled the matter, Baptiste had one short month to be left alone.

Ce Tan's Wife and Her Husband's Lover's Parents

A final case from the south illustrates a somewhat different set of law, state, and gendered relations. In mid-November 1901, a Sioux woman informed a staff sergeant of the North-West Mounted Police at Wood Mountain that her husband, Ce Tan, had left his camp and gone off with another woman. Ce Tan was charged with deserting his family. His wife's deposition appears not to have been taken down by the justice of the peace, so we do not know her name or even her words through an interpreter. Staff Sergeant Watson, however, deposed that the man's wife had "stated that she had no food for herself and two children and being left alone with these two children she was unable to support them. First she was afraid to leave them alone in the tent while she went out to work, and secondly she was in an advanced state of pregnancy, about seven months gone, and unable to do any hard work." It appears that Ce Tan's wife worked as a cleaner for the NWMP, as Watson further deposed that he himself had observed her inability to do heavy work: "I know this latter statement to be a fact as coming here to work she was unable to finish the work and had to go home and leave it." Watson was unable to locate Ce Tan, as there appeared to have been many conflicting reports as to his whereabouts. On 29 November, on his way to the Willow Bunch, he was stopped on the trail by a woman, Mrs. Bokas: "[S]he stated she wanted her daughter recovered who had run off with Ce Tan. She also informed me that she had reason to believe that Ce Tan and her daughter were living as man and wife at the Willow Bunch." When he arrived at the Willow Bunch, Watson asked a constable to go to the Indian camp and tell Ce Tan to return to his wife and family, which the constable said he did. Upon his return, the staff sergeant was approached by "Bocas Sr and his wife" and asked again to endeavour to recover their daughter for them.

Further evidence before the justice of the peace was provided by Fred Brown of Wood Mountain, who indicated that after Ce Tan went away, his family went to Brown's place and Brown gave them something to eat. Brown stated that he had known Ce Tan for twenty years, but could not say that "he is married to the Indian woman ... only that he lives with her." Another deponent was a man named W.H. Ogle:

> Well about the time that Ce Tan went away Mr. and Mrs. Bokas came to me and told me that they wanted to get their daughter back and what was the best way to go about it. I told them to come up to the police post and apply to Dr. Watson through the Gov't interpreter which they refused to do and several days afterwards kept bothering me with the same complaint. They informed me that they considered that they had some claim to my services, it being chiefly through my representations that they sent some of their grandchildren to school, and they considered that being one of the few Indians who had obeyed the wishes of the Govt. in that respect that the Law ought to protect them in the case of their daughter. I went with them and reported to Dr. Watson that they wanted their daughter taken away from Ce Tan.

Ce Tan eventually returned home under what is described in the court file as "police escort," to face the charge that "from Nov 13th 1901 until Dec 8th Chaton Sioux Indian in company with Lilla Bokas did visit Willow Bunch & during that time did leave his wife and two children without providing the necessaries of life for them and his wife being in an advanced state of pregnancy he did thereby endanger her health."

When given the opportunity to make a statement at the hearing before the justice of the peace, Chaton is said to have stated: "I am sorry for what I have done and did not understand that I was doing any wrong." Ce Tan, or Chaton, was committed to stand trial at the next sitting of the Supreme Court of the North-West Territories, and was released from custody pending trial on a recognizance signed by W.H. Ogle.

This case may appear to be simply another unreported case, of limited legal significance and certainly of no precedential value. Indeed, it is not even clear what happened, legally or otherwise, to Ce Tan, for although he was committed to stand trial at the next sitting of the territorial Supreme Court in Regina, the court documents contain no endorsement of the Supreme Court justice. There is no record that he ever appeared at court in Regina. The statistical information contained in the crime reports of the Annual Report of the Commissioner of the North-West Mounted Police for 1901 and 1902 reveals that one case involving the same offence as Ce Tan's was dismissed.[67]

Ce Tan's case provides a modest illustration of the complexity of relations between the First Nations, the police, and the law, suggesting different forms of demands and expressions of entitlement. Ce Tan's wife had been abandoned, and although the formal charge against him concerned his failure to provide her with the necessaries of life, it also appears that the parents of the woman with whom he had gone off were an animating presence in the criminal process. They may not have had a legal claim to police intervention but they appear to have articulated a moral claim, demonstrating an understanding that the white community owed them something for their loyalty.

Clearly, a number of First Nations people now turned to the law for assistance, and admittedly the criminal justice "returns" were modest. Of greater interest, however, are the clear expressions of agency of First Nations women and men notwithstanding their socially subordinate positions, which neither denies their oppression nor supports the suggestion that in going to law or using the law they acted as brokers of their own oppression.

Speaking in Court: Aboriginal Witnesses

Contemporary Aboriginal legal scholars remind us of the importance of language in expressing and understanding different approaches to and concepts of justice,[68] not least when one speaks of Aboriginal law or Aboriginal criminal law. *Mens rea* (the mental element, or guilty mind), so important, if imprecise and contested, in contemporary criminal law principles, appears not to have been a prominent or even essential element of Aboriginal law. Some forms of harm that are central to Canadian criminal law norms formed no part of Aboriginal law; other forms, central to Aboriginal law, formed no part of Canadian criminal law. We are told that there are no indigenous words for criminal law concepts such as "guilty."[69] Nonetheless, Freda Ahenakew and her colleagues have found that "pleading guilty has become so accepted by Aboriginal people ... it has become part of [contemporary] folklore" in the Battleford region of Saskatchewan – the local Cree say *ê-nitawi-nâh-naêmiskwêyiwan cî,* which means "Are you going to nod your head?" (perhaps accompanied by a *Ganootamagaagewinini,* "the man who begs for someone" – the word used for a defence lawyer).[70]

An often repeated story in the historical literature of the 1885 North-West Rebellion trials tells of Chief One Arrow's response when his treason-felony indictment was read to him. Having heard the indictment, which, when interpreted into his own language, accused him of knocking the Queen's bonnet off her head and stabbing her in the behind, One Arrow is said to have asked the interpreter if he was drunk.[71] One Arrow was offended as he had never met the Queen, much less knocked off her bonnet.

Big Bear, who was also tried in 1885 on the same charge as One Arrow and Poundmaker, among others, had long been misunderstood. In 1876, he arrived at the Treaty 6 negotiations at Fort Pitt after Sweet Grass and the others at the fort had agreed to the treaty, and after the most experienced interpreter, Peter Erasmus, had left. Erasmus had emerged from the Treaty 6 meetings as the most competent, respected, and trusted interpreter; his assessment, for instance, of Peter Ballendine (who had been retained by the treaty commissioners to act as one of their interpreters) was that Ballendine had neither the command of the Cree language nor the rhetorical skills to interpret and convey the complex legal concepts that were involved in the treaties.[72] Big Bear's words to Alexander Morris may have been interpreted by Ballendine, and it is now generally accepted that his meaning was not conveyed properly. At one point, he told the commissioner that he feared the white man's rope being placed around his neck; this was conveyed to and understood by Morris to mean that Big Bear feared the death penalty, rather than the yoke of indenture and the loss of freedom.[73] Although the idioms and metaphors of the Cree language, as well as customary practices and courtesies, were probably lost on Morris, Big Bear's comparison of the treaties to bait for a trap was likely conveyed well enough and understood by both of them.

That many Aboriginal people appear as witnesses in the Richardson records is not particularly surprising;[74] what is surprising, given the legal and cultural issues involved, is the paucity of legal scholarship in the area of linguistic interpretation, including issues of cross-cultural interpretation.[75] Thus, the receipt of the evidence of Aboriginal witnesses posed two major challenges, one that might be characterized as linguistic and another that went to the issue of their competency as witnesses. We turn our focus now to these issues raised by Aboriginal witnesses, their interpreters, and the interpretation of Aboriginal culture in court.

A considerable challenge is the issue of transcription of the interpreted statements or depositions in the court files. When an Aboriginal deponent spoke in Cree or Saulteaux, for instance, we have no record of what was actually said. The records contain transcriptions that surely involve both cultural and linguistic forms of interpretation. Every level was surely fraught with uncertainty: the fact that many of the concepts and phrases relevant to an Anglo-Canadian criminal legal process had no counterparts in the indigenous languages, the weakness of the interpretation (especially when the first language of the interpreters was not the Aboriginal language), the standing of the interpreter, and the transcription of the interpretation by a court official. And, in addition to questions regarding the text, contextual questions of how the Aboriginal deponent or complainant came to be in court and the personal and inter- and intra-community relations that may have been important and relevant must not be forgotten.

The most prominent Cree interpreters in the early records were Peter Erasmus, NWMP constable Washington Brazeau, William McKay, Pierre Daignault, Louis Laronde, Peter Ballendine, and, later in the south, Peter Hourie (see Figure 3.5). Ballendine of Battleford, in particular, emerges as a man of influence (although, as I have indicated above, his ability to interpret more than ordinary conversation was questioned by Erasmus at the time of the Treaty 6 negotiations[76]): he appears not only as a sworn interpreter but also as informant/prosecutor and witness in a number of files, and is described variously as a merchant, mail contractor, and Crown timber agent.[77] He was also later employed by Edgar Dewdney as a special agent or informant (some say spy), and he was one of the witnesses for the Crown against Poundmaker in his 1885 treason-felony trial (although he apparently testified that Poundmaker took no part in the "sacking" of Battleford).[78] Ballendine, Erasmus, and Hourie were certainly Métis,[79] which is probably also true of the other interpreters named above. Ballendine and Hourie (see Figure 3.5) also had close ties to the government. From time to time, justices of the peace complained about the difficulties they encountered in finding a suitable interpreter, and of course, in the end the files contain only the English words ascribed to the Cree, Assiniboine, French, and Sioux witnesses. Only occasionally is the actual Cree word is reproduced in the transcript, as well as the discussion of its (possible) meaning.

FIGURE 3.5 Peter Hourie and Judge Hugh Richardson, undated photo. | Saskatchewan Archives Board, R-B1401.

Interestingly, there were few challenges to the competency of "non-Christian Indians" to testify. Richardson appears to have routinely followed the procedure set out in the *Indian Act,*[80] and then proceeded to receive their evidence. For instance, in the trial of The Snake Indian in November

1882, three Cree witnesses, including a young child, gave evidence through interpreter Louis Laronde at the trial before Richardson.[81] The child witness, K, was described as "non English non Christian Cree Indian girl"; her mother was also described as "non English speaking Cree Indian who appears destitute of the knowledge of God and of any fixed and clear belief in religion"; the third witness testified that she was the child's grandmother. The evidence of all three witnesses was received after they were "cautioned" pursuant to the *Indian Act.*

In 1902, Tom Lemac, described in court as "a Christian Indian who formerly went under the name of Wingegee,"[82] was tried for the 1894 shooting death of his friend Oskinaway (also named and referred to in the court file as Josiah Matoney). The evidence indicated that Lemac had last been seen a few days after Oskinaway's death, and then had been in the United States until his arrest eight years later. There were no witnesses to the shooting and no direct evidence that Lemac had shot Oskinaway. One witness testified that he had seen Lemac and Oskinaway leave Fort Qu'Appelle on horseback on the September evening when Oskinaway was shot. The wounded Oskinaway was found alone near the trail the next morning, and was taken to the nearby home of William and Elizabeth Daniels, where he died. Elizabeth Daniels testified that she had heard two people passing by late at night, talking in Saulteaux in an angry manner: "I could not take up their words but still it is easily known when people speak angrily with each another she speak roughly. I understand Saulteaux. I could not hear what was said but I knew they were angry." There was also evidence that Lemac returned in the morning looking for his friend.

The Crown's theory was that Lemac blamed Oskinaway for the death of his sister. The Crown's case rested largely on the evidence of Cree and Saulteaux witnesses who spoke to Lemac and who saw him shortly after Oskinaway was killed. The defence counsel objected to the receipt of the evidence of these Crown witnesses. The following exchanges occurred during cross-examination of Crown witness Aka Moose after she had been sworn as a witness:

Q: You say you believe in God. What kind of God?
Witness: I believe in the God the white people pray to.
Q: What do you know about that God?
A: The reason I say so is that the white man prays to a god and are always prosperous and get on well.
Q: What has that God done for you?

His Lordship: You are going too far. If anybody has done wrong it is myself and you have your redress against me if I have done wrong.

The transcript reveals Richardson's impatience with the defence lawyer's insistence upon challenging each of the non-Christian witnesses. He asserted that he had been following the same procedure in court since 1877, and reminded the lawyer: "I may just as well say that I have taken a little trouble in looking this matter up in English law."

Besides the issue of the competency of the Indian witnesses to testify, Lemac's trial revealed important issues of linguistic and cultural interpretation and their inseverable connection. At the heart of the matter was the meaning of the words Lemac had spoken to the witnesses on the night Oskinaway was shot. Aka Moose testified that about eight years earlier, Lemac had entered her tent where she had been camped beyond Star Blanket's reserve:

Aka Moose: I heard Tom Lemac say when he came into the tent "I think I have done wrong." In Cree when anybody talks like that we get afraid. We know he has done something very bad.
Q: What else did he say?
A: When he came to the tent the fire was a little low. We were in bed but not asleep. He said "Are you all asleep?" Then he said "I think I have done something very wrong."
Q: When he said "Are you all asleep?" Did not any one answer?
A: Yes I said I was not asleep. He said "I fired two shots at him and I think I have killed him." I then asked him Whom? He named the man and said Oskinaway.

The witness, Kakoom, described as a Cree Indian woman whose sister, Peewusk, was married to Wingegee, testified that she heard him say: "I fired two shots at Oskinaway and I think I may have killed him."

Q: Did he use the word murder?
A: He said "I think I have killed him."
Q: Did he use the word murder?
A: Yes, that was what he said.
Q: What was he then saying?
A: He said "I killed Oskinaway."
Q: What was he saying when he used the word murder?
Interpreter: Kill and murder are the same word in Cree.

Peter Hourie, the court interpreter was then sworn as the last Crown witness to give evidence as to the meaning of the Indian words.

> *Q:* During the evidence of several witnesses the expression "I have done wrong" was used. What is the Indian word for "wrong"?
> *A:* Ne-mi-ye-too-tin.
> *Q:* The meaning is?
> *A:* That he has done wrong.
> *Q:* What is the Indian word for "Killed"?
> *A:* NeNepaha, that is the Cree, the Saulteaux is Ginesah.
> *Q:* The interpretation of the word "wrong" has the same meaning as in English?
> *A:* Not with the Indians.
> *Q:* What is the meaning of the word with an Indian?
> *A:* He might have stolen or killed and is the first expression he would use in his language to relate what he had done.
> *His Lordship:* What you mean is that when an Indian uses the expression "I have done wrong" he means he has committed a crime.
> *A:* To that effect.
> *Q:* When the word "killed" follows "I have done wrong" what meaning has the word to an Indian?
> *A:* There is no word for murder. I cannot find a word for it. The two expressions taken together mean I have committed a murder, the two expressions "I have done wrong" and "I have killed my fellow Saulteaux."

When pressed by defence counsel on cross-examination, Hourie maintained that "there is no word for murder in the Indian language."[83] Lemac, a former interpreter, guide, and assistant to the police,[84] was convicted of murder and sentenced to death. His sentence was commuted to life in prison. It appears that he was about sixty-five years of age at the time of his conviction.[85]

Two points are worth making here. First, the express consideration in Lemac's trial of the meaning and interpretation of language, of concepts from two different cultures, offers evidence of the ever-present concern that the interpreted and transcribed words of the Aboriginal deponents may or may not represent their original meaning. Without the original words in their original language, we are left with imperfect sources and, inevitably, imperfect understandings.

The second point concerns the issue of the interpretation of culture, and by whom.[86] In Lemac's case, the Indian witnesses time and again attempted to explain the significance of a symbol, a gesture, a measure of time, to the judge and jury. This is what Mrs. Aka Moose seems to have been doing when she said, "When an Indian says this ..." Although it is a distinct and unsettling possibility that Peter Hourie was editorializing in his interpretation, it appears nonetheless that the Aboriginal witnesses were attempting to make their culture understood. For instance, in responding to a question that implied that a conversation must have taken a long time, a witness answered, conveying the courtesy expected to be shown when listening to another:

> *Q:* How long was he with you?
> *A:* It would be about an hour. When Indians meet like that we listen till he is through and then we separate.

Or, when asked in cross-examination about the effect of liquor upon Indians, Bazil Mozine offered an explanation as well as a gentle reminder that, in his experience, liquor also affected the behaviour of white men: "As far as I know about this liquor business let a man be ever so quiet and if he gets full of drink it makes him foolish and he loses all memory of what he does. It has a little of that effect upon white people. I have known certain white person and when he got drunk he wanted to fight me but when he was sober he was very quiet."

Conclusion

The focus of this chapter has been on another aspect of the engagement and relationship between Plains Aboriginal people and Canadian criminal law in the last quarter of the nineteenth century – cases in which Aboriginal people participated as informants, complainants, and witnesses.

Clearly, First Nations leaders, especially in the earlier period, made demands on the law and the police. It is difficult to say whether they went to the law because they regarded this as an obligation owed to them under the treaties or simply because the police and the magistrate represented the new way. The fact and implications of treaty rights and obligations appear to be implicit in some of the cases. For instance, it does seem that Is-pinik-hah-kee-toot was of the view that the police were there to help him deal with his non-Treaty brother-in-law, who time and again made off with his late father's horses. The Cree chiefs and their headmen who acted as Informants, or who appeared to be supportive of the investigation or prosecution, were advancing the interests of their band members or the band more generally. Admittedly, Beardy, chief of the Willow Crees, was taken to law more often than he went to law, and it is a testament to his obvious abilities that he appears never to have lost in court. Even Poundmaker's disputed horse race involved more than his individual loss and complaint. The broader community, including those who placed wagers on the race, was affected, and a number came to his assistance.

Poundmaker's horse race addresses another important issue, that of inter-community relations. Based on this research into the North-West Territories court records, it is at best premature to speak of the criminal law and criminal court as the site of inter-communal norms.[87] The relations and relationships, however, as well as the court records discussed in this and other chapters, are suggestive of a fair degree of interaction and communication between the First Nations and the newcomers. The newspaper clipping shown in Figure 3.1, reporting on the results of the Dominion Day races in Battleford on 1 July 1882 (with Hugh Richardson acting as one of the judges) illustrates this in a small way. And when these relations were strained or ruptured, as occurred with Francis Deschaw, John Ballendine, John Smith, and James B. Mahoney, among others, aggrieved Aboriginal persons, including Aboriginal women, turned to the criminal law for assistance. The Snake Indian's case, and the case of Peaychew's missing daughter discussed in the Introduction, came to the criminal law from within a particular Aboriginal community, at the instance of the band's leadership. Some of the cases discussed here and in Chapter 2 also demonstrate, however, that different forms of intra- and inter-community matters began to be taken to court – for example, between Cree and Assiniboine neighbours in William Wolf's complaint against the three men of Chief Mosquito's band, or between the Cree and Blackfoot nations, in the case of The Only Mountain's complaint that his horse had been stolen by Running Crow's (Cree) son. The Snake Indian's wife also reminds us of the protocols followed by her people when someone injured or hurt another: her husband, the prisoner, had offered her nothing for what he had done to her daughter.

The layers of mediation of the voices are many, and certainly the scale and complexity of issues of linguistic and cultural interpretation are seen in Tom Lemac's murder trial, where, despite the arguably controversial role and interpretation of Peter Hourie at the trial, Aka Moose and Basil Mozine appear to have done their best to make important things understood by the white judge and jury.

These stories add another dimension to our knowledge of the relationship between Aboriginal peoples and the criminal law. By broadening the scope of inquiry to focus on more than accused persons and to look through more than the lens of criminalization, they have made possible a fuller and deeper account of this relationship.

4
"Make a Better Indian of Him"
Indian Policy and the Criminal Court

The image of criminal law in the North-West Territories in the later nineteenth century has been long associated with the North-West Mounted Police (NWMP), acting as both the symbol and, for some, the source of law.[1] The police are often seen as the enforcers of the government's Indian legislation and policy, an unfortunate if understandable impression given the multiple roles of the most senior officers (police officers, prosecutors, justices of the peace, and jailers). The NWMP Commissioner's annual reports to Parliament offer evidence of a close relationship between the police and Indian Department officials.[2] It is clear from these and other accounts, however, that this relationship in the field was also marked by disagreement over the creation and escalation of conflicts.[3]

This chapter focuses on what the court records reveal about the relationship between the Dominion government's Indian legislation and policy and the criminal law. Just as the records of the NWMP offer some evidence of tensions between the police and the government, so do the court files. When conflicts resulted in criminal charges being brought against First Nations persons, the result in court was not invariably what was desired or expected by the Indian Department officials who were the informants and complainants. The post-conviction process is also analyzed as another site of government intervention through the cases of two First Nations men convicted of murder and sentenced to death by Richardson.

Stark examples of the expression of government policy in criminal justice, and the profound change it wrought in the lives of First Nations people, are not difficult to find. Indeed, one need look no further than the prosecution of Alex Bone and Julia Coté, youngsters who were charged by the principal of the industrial school with stealing the clothes they were wearing when they ran away from the school,[4] and who spent a month in jail while awaiting their court appearance, which occurred under the watchful eye of an Indian Department official (see Chapter 2).

Less formal but no less important interventions within and outside the criminal process are also not difficult to find. For instance, Simon Crow Moccasin's theft charge in 1898 provided the opportunity for a larger, if less legal, indictment by an Indian Agent. Crow Moccasin from the File Hills was charged with theft of another man's pony, which served as a platform for indicting him for his general failure to conduct himself in a manner expected by the Indian Agent of a young man who had had seven years of education at the industrial school.[5] Indian Agent William Graham's moralizing narrative at the hearing before the justice of the peace described Crow Moccasin as lazy, indolent, unreliable, and untruthful (which were not in and of themselves criminal offences, even in 1898):

> I expected as a discharged pupil from the school, he would have been a good reliable man ... As evidence of his unreliability, when discharged from the school, he got married and I gave him a house on the reserve, the school furnished him with furniture and he had 9 or 10 head of cattle. During the winter of '97 he killed one of his cattle without my permission, he disposed of his furniture and became degraded and was in a worse state than before going to school ...
>
> [To the accused] As an instance of your untruthfulness, you assaulted your wife and then denied you did so. When you disposed of your furniture, you denied it. I did not order you off the reserve, you left without my permission.[6]

Simon Crow Moccasin later entered a guilty plea before Richardson and was sentenced to one year of hard labour, severe by Richardson's standards. The sentence clearly addressed more than the pony with which he had absconded; rather, it was a condemnation of the litany of failings and character flaws in which the particulars of the actual offence had figured scarcely at all for the Indian Agent.[7]

Indian Agent Graham and the industrial school principal derived their power, authority, and influence from the legislative framework of the *Indian Act.* No piece of legislation occupies a more important place in the history of the relationship between the Canadian government and the First Nations of Canada than the *Indian Act.* It is useful to recall Alexander Morris's lament at the commencement of the Treaty 6 negotiations: "[T]he Indian mind was oppressed with vague fears; they dreaded the treaty; they had been made to believe that they would be compelled to live on the reserves wholly, and abandon their hunting."[8] With the benefit of hindsight, research, and analysis, we are able to say that the Indians were right and Morris was, at best, wrong.

In 1876, the same year that Treaty 6 was signed, Parliament enacted a new *Indian Act,*[9] which consolidated previous amendments and established a new regulatory regime, defining who could be an Indian, who could live on Indian reserves, what and how they could hold as property, what happened to their property at their death, who could do business on and in relation to reserve land, and so on. In 1996, the *Report of the Royal Commission on Aboriginal Peoples* characterized this regime as a "legislative straitjacket" that had "regulated almost every important aspect of the daily lives" of the people.[10] Unlike the treaty-making process, flawed as it was, there was not even the pretence of consultation or negotiation as to the form and content of the *Indian Act.* The *Indian Act* made no reference to the treaties. For the Royal Commission, this amounted to a deliberate act of forgetting, from which one could infer that Canada had attached little importance to the treaties and their status as "nation-to-nation" agreements.[11]

Through the *Indian Act* and the government policy it facilitated, the First Nations people were legally transformed into children of the state.[12] The operation and legacy of Canada's destructive Indian policies, notably its contribution to the infantilization and immiseration of First Nations peoples and its regulation of everything from the most basic to most sacred, has been documented by historians, policy analysts, Aboriginal legal scholars, Aboriginal justice inquiries, and Royal Commissions, to name but a few.[13] The *Indian Act* left no aspect of Indian life and governance untouched and untransformed; again, however, the provisions that are of most interest to this book are those that created offences and touched the administration of justice more generally.

The responsibilities of Indian Agents increased during the period covered by this book to include a judicial function, an important aspect of the criminalization of the *Indian Act.* The 1876 *Indian Act* was silent on this, but in 1881 Indian Agents, and a few designated senior Indian officials, were made justices of the peace *ex officio,* for the purposes of offences under the *Indian Act.*[14] By 1895, this magisterial role had been expanded to empower Indian Agents to hear offences under Parts XIII and XV of the

Criminal Code (offences against morality and vagrancy offences), as well as two sections of the *Criminal Code* dealing with the prostitution of Indian women.[15] The Indian Agent's jurisdiction as a justice of the peace extended to the entire North-West Territories; in other words, his jurisdiction was not confined to matters involving Indians in his own region. This significant expansion of the Indian Agents' legal powers undoubtedly reflected dissatisfaction with the justice enforced and dispensed in the regular criminal courts.

The formal powers granted the Indian Agent by Parliament were matched, and perhaps outstripped, by aggressive government policy hatched in Ottawa and deployed in the field. Within the criminal court records, one encounters the names of many associated with Indian policy administration in the North-West Territories (Edgar Dewdney, Hayter Reed) and with the events of 1885, including Indian Department men who would be killed: Thomas Quinn, James Payne, and John Delaney, to name the most prominent.[16] The presence of Indian officials in the court files is significant, and their attempts to use the criminal law to enforce their policy and to punish Indian wrongdoers are evident.

The court records do not contain two of the most important names associated with the government's Indian policy during the period of this book: John A. Macdonald, Prime Minister and Superintendent of Indian Affairs, and his loyal deputy, Lawrence Vankoughnet, Deputy Superintendent General of Indian Affairs (1874-93). These men were the principal authors of the policies that were to be implemented on the ground. Vankoughnet was so keen to do Macdonald's bidding that it seems Macdonald was scarcely required to make it explicit: Vankoughnet's loyalty to Macdonald, together with his reputation for inflexibility, parsimony, and by-the-book administration directly contributed, as Douglas Leighton has argued, "to the rigidity so characteristic of the department's decision-making processes just when it needed to be as flexible as possible, particularly in regard to the Plains Indians."[17] In the years following 1876, Vankoughnet, often over opposition from those in the field, required government officials to pursue policies of starvation, to use food as a means of subjugating the Plains Cree, to require Indians to work for rations, and to cut or deny rations as punishment.[18] Both Brian Titley and John Tobias argue that Edgar Dewdney, Indian Commissioner (and after 1882 also Lieutenant-Governor of the North-West Territories) differed somewhat with Vankoughnet on the efficacy of attempting to starve the Cree into submission.[19] By the winter of 1885, however, they were of the same mind about pursuing a more coercive approach to Indian unrest and resistance. As Titley recounts, both Dewdney and Macdonald liked Vankoughnet's idea to "throw the instigators of agitation in jail ... but [Dewdney] pointed out it hadn't worked very well in the past mainly because the magistrates rarely handed down sufficiently lengthy jail sentences to act as a deterrent or to keep trouble-makers out of the way when their presence was least desired."[20]

Titley adds that Macdonald "encouraged Dewdney to use his personal influence on magistrates to secure their cooperation on sentencing."[21] Through this we get a glimpse of the regard in which the Superintendent General of Indian Affairs (and Prime Minister) and his most senior bureaucrats held the court, and their expectation of it: to be an instrument of their will as expressed through government policy. The worst fears, or fondest hopes, of a conspiracy theorist are realized: "Have a word with the judges."

The criminal court was not necessarily the government's best friend, however. A number of prosecutions demonstrate the presence of Indian policy in the court, through efforts to use the criminal court to enforce and advance Indian policy – "to make better Indians" – as well as forms of resistance to and mediation of government policy. Paradoxically, the cases from the territorial court records demonstrate that only in the criminal court was the legal subjectivity of Aboriginal peoples and a measure – modest, to be sure – of formal equality recognized. This had been its appeal to Chief Mistawasis at the time of Treaty 6 – the same law for whites and Indians – but this notion of formal equality was a problem for the government, which preferred a special law for Indians and a criminal court to do its bidding.

Prosecuting Leaders

Who can say when the discourse of the "bad Indian" and the "good Indian" entered the vernacular? Both Dewdney and Vankoughnet are reported to have been particularly offended at the prospect of "saucy" Indians,[22] but by 1876, Cree leaders Big Bear and Kah-mee-yis-too-way-sit[23] (Beardy), chief of the Willow Cree, were firmly in the ranks of "bad" Indians, and those who sought to discredit them were vociferous. The territorial press was a spirited and frequent contributor to these efforts. Beardy, whose band settled near Duck Lake, was not a chief or religious leader of the stature of Big Bear or Piapot, but records suggest a man with what might be characterized in current popular discourse as "attitude," and who was certainly saucy.

The reputation constructed for him by the *Saskatchewan Herald* was that of a liar and a thief who had a facility for evading the long reach of the law. Beardy appears to have been prosecuted and convicted in the pages of the *Herald* more often than in court;[24] despite the *Herald*'s regular accounts of his alleged activity (killing cattle, theft, idleness), he appears in the Richardson records twice as an accused (apparently he was never convicted)[25] and once as an informant.[26] On 11 September 1879, Lawrence Clarke, HBC factor and justice of the peace at Fort Carlton, wrote to Richardson, forwarding an Information that had been laid before him the previous day. The informant, Owen Edward Hughes, was described in the Information as the "duly authorized agent of Stobart Eden and Company," the owner of a horse that was the object of the criminal charge. The Information alleged that Beardy had possession of a horse that he was "illegally detaining" and refusing to give up. Clarke's letter informed Richardson that Clarke and the NWMP sergeant had decided that it was too risky to serve the warrant on Beardy. He asked Richardson to decide what to do with the warrant, warning that "if this man is not arrested, it is very probable that the settlers will take the law into their own hands, as this Indian has become a public nuisance."[27] Richardson issued a warrant on 17 September, but it appears that the informant withdrew the warrant on the same day and a summons was issued for "25 October at Duck Lake, 3 pm." The file contains no disposition, so we do not know whether Beardy responded to the summons. A reasonably safe inference is that the process ended with the summons.

In late July of the following year, Beardy and fellow chiefs One Arrow and Cut Nose were charged after some of their people killed cattle. It was alleged that the three chiefs had caused the cattle, property of the Indian Department, to be stolen, shot, and killed two days earlier. At the hearing before the justices of the peace, two men gave depositions based on their affirmation that they had killed the cattle on the orders of the chiefs. Omenakaw's deposition told the story, which also contained the seed of the chiefs' defence should the matter have proceeded to trial: "Some of us, I among the number, killed the cattle as we had nothing to eat and we were told they belonged to us (the Indians) it was the [?] told us. The council decided that the cattle were to be killed, the three chiefs were there and were the headmen at the council. They gave us the orders."[28] There is no warrant of committal and no disposition in the court file. Only from the NWMP returns for 1880 do we learn that Beardy and his fellow chiefs were acquitted by a jury on 27 July,[29] supporting both contemporary[30] and more recent assessments[31] that Beardy had a facility for successfully testing and withstanding the authority of white men. And, despite the *Saskatchewan Herald*'s fervent hope and confident prediction, Beardy was never convicted or deposed as chief. One Arrow appears to have continued to regard the cattle on the reserve as belonging to his band, not to the government: in 1881, Indian Agent Rae charged a Métis man with acquiring two oxen from Chief One Arrow without the written consent of the Superintendent General of Indian Affairs; no conviction is recorded, but a warrant of distress was issued.[32]

Both One Arrow and Beardy suffered as a result of the events of 1885, One Arrow to a greater degree given his disputable conviction and three-year sentence for treason-felony. The elderly One Arrow would never make it home, dying en route shortly after his release from the penitentiary in March 1886. Although Beardy's band was characterized by Hayter Reed as having been disloyal during the events of 1885,[33] Blair Stonechild maintains that Beardy, among many other Cree chiefs, did not support Riel because he (and his fellow chiefs) respected and felt bound by what they regarded as their obligations under the treaty.[34]

One of the clearest efforts to prosecute, punish, and discredit Plains chiefs who sought to protect or advance their peoples' interests comes from the NWMP annual reports, and an incident involving the Indian Agent, the police, and the head chief of the Sarcee, Stamiscotocar (Bull Head).[35] In May 1884, the Indian Agent on the Sarcee Reserve complained to the NWMP that a Sarcee man named Crow Collar had destroyed property in the reserve's ration house. NWMP superintendent McIllree dispatched one of his men to arrest Crow Collar, but his chief would not give him up. McIllree himself then went to the reserve and demanded that Bull Head deliver Crow Collar to him. When Bull Head refused, McIllree attempted unsuccessfully to arrest the chief himself. He withdrew rather than risk bloodshed, but sent word the next day to Bull Head that Crow Collar and Bull Head were to be brought in. Crow Collar was delivered up to the police, and Bull Head sent word to McIllree that he would go in on the next day. This he did, arriving accompanied but unarmed. McIllree locked him up for three days, releasing him only when Bull Head "promised he would give no more trouble."[36] Like other chiefs and their people, Bull Head had used the law and also experienced its high hand. It was the locus of struggle where, as in this case, he had been abused by the law in an attempt to undermine his authority and bring him to heel.

Assiniboine chief Lean Man, whose band no longer exists, is not well known, although the incident giving rise to his criminal prosecution has been mentioned by others.[37] His little-known case sheds light on the plight of the Assiniboines in the early 1880s, provides a context for some of the events of 1885, and provides evidence of the criminal law's mediation of the unequal and antagonistic relations between some Indian Department officials and Aboriginal people. Lean Man, his fellow chief Grizzly-Bear's Head, and their bands had asked for and been promised reserves in the Cypress Hills (as had the Cree chiefs Little Pine and Piapot); government officials changed their mind, however, fearing both the proximity to the United States border (and the problem of cross-border horse raids) and, more importantly, the potential perils of creating a large Indian territory in the Cypress Hills.[38] The Cree and Assiniboine were forced to move or starve.[39] Over the summer and fall of 1882, Lean Man and Grizzly Bear's Head were required to move onto the reserve of Mosquito's Assiniboine band in the Eagle Hills, near Battleford, until their own reserves could be set aside. The newly arrived Assiniboines had suffered great hardship the previous year; the addition of over 250 people to Mosquito's reserve created even more hardship and stretched the already overextended resources of the Battleford Indian district.[40] In this situation of sickness and hunger, the "work for rations" or "let them suffer"[41] policy could scarcely have been more unworkable, as little of either work or rations was available to the Assiniboines.

In January 1883, Lean Man was charged on an Information sworn by farm instructor James Payne; the charge was that, after being ordered to leave and then being forcibly ejected from Payne's house, he persisted in attempting to gain entry and at length pointed a loaded firearm at the instructor.[42] The deposition of Alphonse Carrier, who had been in the house (and who may have been his interpreter), indicated that the farm instructor had told Lean Man "that he had better go as he might get mad and put him out." Further, "the prisoner was very much excited and so mad that while Mr. Payne was holding him he spat in his face."[43]

For his part, Lean Man's Statement of the Accused (probably given through an interpreter, although no one is indicated) offered the following explanation:

> There was one of my children sick and another child so I went to the Instructor's house to tell him. When I arrived at the house Mosquito and Left and Right were inside. The Instructor told me motioning with his hand to go off. I opened the door a second time and the Instructor shut the door.

> I opened the door a third time – rather [violently?] ... when my daughter came and tried to take the revolver away from me. I refused to give it saying that seven of our people had been turned out already. I have been a good Indian ever since I took the medal.[44] Colonel Irvine told me to come here and make a living and I have been trying to take his advise [*sic*]. I did not take the revolver into the house. I did not intend to use it against the Instructor.[45]

On 16 January, Lean Man was committed for trial and remanded in custody. A letter of 21 February 1883 in the file, addressed to Richardson over T.T. Quinn's signature, advised Richardson that "Chief Bear's Head" was willing to post bail for Lean Man; later that day, the recognizance in the amount of $200 was entered into and Lean Man was released. There is no record of the trial in the file, only an endorsement on the reverse of the Information that he was "tried 20 May 83, convicted of common assault, sentence deferred." The *Saskatchewan Herald*'s report was only slightly less cryptic and probably less accurate: the paper indicated that Lean Man pleaded guilty to pointing a pistol at Payne, and received a deferred sentence.[46] Other records reveal that Lean Man was charged with treason-felony in the aftermath of the events of 1885, and that he was discharged.[47]

Lean Man's case is extraordinary in many ways in the context of the criminal law during the period: although the legal record does not indicate that he was a chief, the fact that another chief came forward to post bail, and the fact that Lean Man was released on bail notwithstanding the informant's claim that he had been threatened with a loaded pistol, is remarkable, to say the least. Lean Man was charged by a government employee engaged in his duties with having threatened him with a loaded firearm. And yet, at his trial in May 1883 he was convicted only of the lesser offence of common assault and discharged, presumably to return to what remained of his people, his home, and family. It is difficult to imagine that this was the lesson that James Payne wanted to teach the chief when he charged him with the more serious offence.

There is no record of what was said in court, and the *Herald*'s report could not be briefer. It may be that Magistrate Richardson accepted an account of the incident that more closely resembled Lean Man's than Payne's; the result suggests as much. Faced with a desperate chief acting on behalf of his sick and dying people and (from all accounts) an ill-tempered, despotic farm instructor, Richardson's disposition of the case could not have been more favourable to the Assiniboine chief.

Like Peaychew, the Cree warrior who was arrested in 1882 on a fraud charge (apparently withdrawn upon Richardson's intervention), Lean Man was a prominent leader in the region. Perhaps it should have been satisfaction enough for the Indian department officials to have had them arrested, charged, and held in police cells for a short period of time (as Superintendent McIllree had done with Chief Bull Head). The evidence marshalled by other historians suggests, however, that this was not the case for the Indian Department officials, who wanted stiffer responses from the court, which they did not get in these cases.

As indicated above, James Payne was shot and killed during the spring of 1885, around the same time as the events that came to be known as the Frog Lake Massacre. Payne was killed not by the Cree at Frog Lake but in a separate and apparently unrelated incident.[48] He was shot at his home during the Rebellion by Itka, an Assiniboine man from Mosquito's band. An eyewitness is said to have attributed his killing to Payne's reputation for violence toward Aboriginal women and his drunken mistreatment of his common-law wife, a young Assiniboine woman.[49] Stonechild and Waiser suggest that Itka knocked on Payne's door (as Payne apparently insisted be done) and shot him when he opened the door.[50] Itka, a grieving father, is said to have been avenging the death of his young daughter, who had been staying with her aunt, Payne's wife, and who had been thrown out of the house and to the ground by Payne.[51] In Cree elder John Tootoosis's account, the girl died of tuberculosis not long after, and Itka blamed Payne for her death.[52] In either version, it is clear that Payne died when Itka took the occasion of the troubles to settle a personal account. Based on all the accounts, it is unlikely that many tears were shed for Payne. Itka, without legal counsel, pleaded guilty to his murder before Magistrate Charles Borromée Rouleau and a justice of the peace on 9 October and was hanged at Fort Battleford on 27 November 1885 with his fellow Assiniboine, Man without Blood, and six Cree warriors from Frog Lake. Rouleau is reported to have addressed Itka directly when he sentenced him: "You, Itka, have confessed to having killed a connection of your own, the late farming instructor on your reserve. If the instructor had done you any wrong, you could have come to me and I would have given you redress. I am here for that purpose."[53]

This may have been a rhetorical statement, but, following E.P. Thompson, it was not necessarily empty rhetoric. It may be that the magistrates did hold themselves out as a recourse for people who wanted to complain about the abuses of Indian Department officials. Richardson was also quoted by the *Saskatchewan Herald* as having made this same kind of offer in 1881, when Yellow Mud Blanket, Poundmaker's brother, appeared before him on a charge of attempting to strike George Gopsill, an Indian farm instructor, with a knife for refusing to release provisions to him. According to the *Herald:* "The Colonel [Richardson] censured the Indian [Yellow Mud Blanket], and cautioned him that he must not on any account interfere with the instructors, who had but to obey orders. In future, if anything went wrong, they were to apply to the local Agent; if he failed to give satisfaction, then application was to be made to him. With this caution the gentleman of Mud took his leave."[54] This tends to support the view that the government men were not confident of support when they took their charges (in both senses of the word) to court. The chiefs were prosecuted criminally for trying to vindicate or protect their peoples' interests in the face of intransigent officials on the ground, on their reserves. Lean Man's struggle, of course, did not end with his modest victory in Richardson's court, but as modest as this victory was, the deferred sentence he was given could not be understood as anything but a setback for the Indian Department.

Enforcing and Resisting Indian Policy

In the years before he moved to Regina, Magistrate Hugh Richardson travelled widely and, in the period between Matthew Ryan's departure from the bench in 1881 and Ryan's replacement by Rouleau in 1883, he covered the southern and eastern districts (Fort Ellice, Fort Qu'Appelle, and Prince Albert) as well. Lean Man's case would have been one of the last criminal matters over which he presided before moving from Battleford. Criminal prosecutions arising out of many of the incidents associated with "pre-rebellion" activity or organizing would have been in the Duck Lake, Fort Pitt, and Battleford regions and would have come before Rouleau or have been dealt with by justices of the peace, either sitting alone or with another.

The court records from Richardson's early period as a stipendiary magistrate (1876-85) reveal different ways in which Indian policy was an issue in different cases. The North-West Territories was to be "dry" – an alcohol-free territory; only those with permits issued by the Lieutenant-Governor were permitted to have or transport specified amounts of alcohol (it is likely that many applicants sought a generous interpretation of an exemption for "medicinal purposes"). The *Indian Act* also made it an offence to provide intoxicants to Indians. Bazil Lafond[55] was convicted in Battleford in 1878 of giving John Longman, an Indian, one quart of intoxicating liquor; although the statute supporting the charge is not indicated in the court documents, it is clear from the evidence that the offence was under the *Indian Act.*[56] Longman testified that he was invited to Lafond's house on 22 October, and that Lafond "treated me to liquor. I went there again and got more. It made me tipsy." The clerk of the Indian superintendency testified that he knew Longman, a Treaty Indian. Nothing else is revealed about Longman, except that one of the defence witnesses testified that Longman was funny after he had had a drink. Peter Ballendine, a frequent presence as an interpreter and prosecutor in the Battleford court files, testified that he had seen Longman in a state of intoxication on the 22nd, but that his only knowledge of where he obtained the liquor had come from Longman himself.

Lafond's defence was advanced through evidence that he had a permit issued by Lieutenant-Governor David Laird permitting him to have three gallons of alcohol for medicinal purposes, that the date of the alleged offence (set out in the summons to the defendant and to the witnesses) was said to be 21 October (not the 22nd), and that two witnesses who had been present on the 22nd said that they had not seen Lafond offer liquor to Longman. Still, Lafond was convicted and fined $100 and costs (including $6 in interpreter's fees). As with Longman, we learn nothing more from the file concerning Lafond, but it is likely that he was "Basile Lafond," a former HBC man who had settled permanently in Battleford in 1876.[57] He is said to have worked along the Saskatchewan River with Ballendine, also a former HBC man, who had been among the first to stake a claim in Battleford in 1874. It seems that Lafond was sufficiently well off, as he was able to pay the fine and costs immediately. The file contains no formal Information, but it would appear from a receipt in the file, that Lafond's former colleague, Peter Ballendine, was the informant, as Ballendine received $50 from Richardson (one-half the fine, to which an Informant was entitled[58]).

A trio of similar liquor-related prosecutions in 1881 included a tit-for-tat pair in which Indian Agent John Rae and Reverend John Hines successfully prosecuted each other for supplying intoxicating liquor to Indians.[59] Despite this little flurry of such cases in 1880 and 1881, very few of the files involving Aboriginal accused appear to have involved alcohol. In a couple of the later files, notably Tom Lemac's murder trial in 1902 (discussed in the last section of this chapter), it is clear that the Aboriginal accused had been under the influence of alcohol at the time of the alleged offence; in files from the early period, however, hunger and illness are far more prevalent and discernible than alcohol.

Indian Agent Hayter Reed used the court to enforce contracts of employment involving Aboriginal men whom he had hired.[60] Again, the facts in these cases are sparse, but it is clear that Reed was prepared to use the court to prosecute for non-performance, as in the case of Wachan, a Sioux man, although no sentence was imposed by Magistrate Richardson. In a handful of other cases, Aboriginal men were charged with forms of assault against government men. Some of these cases, such as Ah-tim-musis-sequine in 1881, contain just three documents with no particulars or records of evidence: the Information sworn by Indian farm instructor Daniel Clink, charging that he had been assaulted with a knife with intent to wound; the Warrant to Apprehend (both documents issued on the same day); and the Record of Conviction dated the following day, with a sentence of two months being imposed by Richardson.[61]

In a number of the early cases, notably some emanating from the Fort Pitt/Frog Lake area, Indian farm instructor John Delaney is implicated either directly or indirectly in prosecutions of Peecoose (Sandfly),[62] The Dancing Bull and Moostus,[63] and I-ah-pee-coo-caw.[64] As discussed in Chapter 3, Hugh Dempsey has suggested that Peecoose's conviction for theft from the HBC store at Fort Pitt, as well as his lengthy sentence, was orchestrated by Delaney, who had taken up with Peecoose's wife, and that Delaney's treatment of him was resented by the people at Frog Lake. One of Peecoose's aggrieved supporters is said to have been his brother, The Dancing Bull, who, with Moostus, was charged by Delaney with having stolen and killed a heifer that had gone missing in October 1882. Delaney's Information was based on information and belief and sworn before Richardson at Frog Lake on 1 December 1882. Again, no record of any evidence in support of the charge is found on the file; other than the Information, there is only the Record of Conviction, which indicates that each man pleaded not guilty but was found guilty by Richardson. The Dancing Bull was sentenced to two months' hard labour at Battleford, Moostus to four months. Dempsey suggests that Delaney may have regarded The Dancing Bull as a threat and accused him of witnessing the killing of a government ox in order to have him removed as well.[65]

Yellow Calf and Tom Gopher from the Treaty 4 region offer two further illustrations of the harsh conditions in 1884. Yellow Calf, one of the

Crooked Lake leaders, was tried, together with two of his men, in the winter of 1884 for breaking into the "Government store" at Crooked Lake and stealing flour and bacon.[66] The trial was covered in the Regina *Leader*. It appears that Yellow Calf and his colleagues were represented by counsel, Mr. Forget. They pleaded guilty to the charge, and in speaking to the matter of sentence, Forget is reported to have told the court that at the time of the offence, the prisoners had been in a "starving condition" and "being under the impression that those store were placed there by the Queen for the relief of the needy Indians, and having applied to the agent for relief and refused" they did what they believed they had to do, and had a right to do. They voluntarily surrendered to the police, and offered to make reparation. Richardson reserved their sentence, but is reported to have directed the interpreter to tell Yellow Calf and the others that "he had been informed that they had threatened to use firearms to resist arrest," but they had not been charged; he warned them that this was a serious crime, and if it ever happened again they would lose their firearms.

That same winter, Tom Gopher from Peepeekeesis's band was also charged with breaking into the storehouse on the reserve and stealing flour and bacon.[67] The Regina *Leader* reported on his case, in particular that Magistrate Richardson addressed the prisoner in encouraging terms when he sentenced him to one month of hard labour after his guilty plea. The *Leader*'s headline said it all: "Gopher Tom Says He was Starving, Cree Indian From File Hills." The story stated: "The Judge told the prisoner that it was his duty both to protect the Indian from harm and to punish him when he did wrong, he sentenced him to a month's imprisonment but in a kindly manner gave him some good advice which from the expression of the Indian's face he evidently appreciated."[68]

Hunger, like government men, is a constant presence in the court records. From Beardy, One Arrow, and Cut Nose at Duck Lake, to Lean Man in the Eagle Hills, to Crow Collar on the Sarcee Reserve, to Margaret and her hungry child and angry husband at Frog Lake discussed in Chapter 3, to Jean Felix Callilouis at Rivière Qui Barre in the Edmonton district,[69] and to Yellow Calf at Crooked Lake and Gopher Tom (also known as Tom Gopher) in File Hills[70] – in all these cases, to the experience of poverty and starvation was added the injury of violence and the threats and harassment of criminal prosecution. These court records give names and recurring voices to the unrelieved hardship and misery experienced by the Cree, Assiniboine, and Saulteaux across the Territories during the late 1870s and early 1880s – and constitute but a fraction of the stories that could have been told.

The Criminal Court after 1885: *E-mâyi-kamikahk* ("Where It Went Wrong")

In the aftermath of the events of 1885,[71] the seemingly impossible occurred: things became even more dire as, under the leadership of Hayter Reed (now Assistant Indian Commissioner), increasingly punitive policies were devised and imposed.[72]

Most of the Treaty 4 bands had not been active participants in the violence and resistance of 1885, but even though they were not labelled disloyal, their bands were not broken up, and their people were not scattered to other bands, they still felt the scourge of hunger and of changes in government policy in the years following 1885.

In 1885, Richardson's Regina docket included the majority of Métis and First Nations men charged with treason-related offences as well as his regular court docket. The number of Aboriginal accused in the regular criminal court was not overwhelming before 1885, and even fewer such cases are found in his post-1885 records. After 1886, Richardson sat as a member of the Supreme Court of the North-West Territories in Regina. Due largely to the removal of the Cree and Assiniboine from Cypress Hills, the demographics of his judicial district, Western Assiniboia, were such that far fewer Aboriginal people appeared before him than when he was a stipendiary magistrate based in Battleford. Other than a few Sioux from Wood Mountain and the occasional case that came in to him from the western part of Qu'Appelle or the Touchwood Hills, Richardson presided largely over property and assault offences in and around Regina and Moose Jaw, involving settler farmers, young labouring men, and businessmen enforcing or dodging their promissory notes. The isolation of homestead life, the vulnerability of children in those homes and barns, and the failure of the law to offer them any meaningful protection, then as now, are also expressed in his records.

A handful of cases involving Aboriginal men accused of livestock-related and other offences provide evidence, however, that life on the southern reserves were just as difficult as in the northwest. Evidence of struggle and resistance in the pre-1885 period can also be found. For instance, in 1889, a man named Mequanis (The Little Quill) (see Figures 4.1 and 4.2) was charged with inciting Indians to violence, at that time an offence under the *Indian Act*.[73]

Mequanis was a member of Peepeekeesis's band in the File Hills, which consisted of fewer than ninety people (see Figure 4.2). It is possible that a more correct version of his name is found in the Treaty Annuity Paylist,

Figure 4.1 Mequanis, in a studio portrait (likely 1915). | Saskatchewan Archives Board, R-A20995.

where he appears as Number 13, bearing, in fact, two names: Tipiskow Keesekow Awaksis, or Mequanis (the English translations of these two names were indicated to be "Night and Day Child" and "The Quill," respectively).[74]

The informant was Indian Agent Harry L. Reynolds, of the Peepeekeesis Band of the File Hills Agency. Mequanis (or Mequaness) had refused,

FIGURE 4.2 Mequanis and Buffalo Bow among the File Hills Elders, November 1914. Mequanis (spelled "Mekwinness" on the back of the photograph) is the last person at the far right of the front row, kneeling. Buffalo Bow is the third man from the right in the front row. | Saskatchewan Archives Board, R-B1854 (also R-A18).

when ordered, to go and cut hay. The Indian Agent withheld the band's rations, a tried and true method of discipline. Chief Peepeekeesis had died not long before, and the band did not have a chief. Mequanis appears to have been regarded as a leader by both the people of the band and the Indian Agent. He was taken into custody and charged with "inciting a number of named others to make demands of the Indian Agent in a riotous, disorderly and threatening manner." When he appeared in court, Mequanis did not nod his head; rather, he informed the court that he required the attendance of a number of witnesses for his trial. Correspondence in the court file reveals a recommendation that, rather than proceed further with the prosecution, the matter ought to be dropped "in the public interest." Clearly, a decision had been made that prosecuting this man would only backfire on the Indian Agent, and perhaps further compromise his shaky authority.

In 1896, two men also from Peepeekeesis's band, Shave Tail[75] and Jean Baptiste, were charged with unlawfully killing a steer that belonged to

Buffalo Bow, also of their reserve. The Indian officials did not regard Jean Baptiste as the main culprit but as an "involuntary agent" who was controlled by Shave Tail. The Commissioner of Indian Affairs wrote to Justice Richardson that "Jean Baptiste has always been well-behaved and not troublesome"; he trusted that the judge "will consider this when it comes before you."[76] At trial the jury entered a verdict of guilty; Richardson granted a deferred sentence, and Jean Baptiste was discharged on his own recognizance.

Correspondence in the court file, dated "August 8 '96," from "S. Hockley, Temporarily in charge of Agency," to the Indian Commissioner in Regina indicated: "'Shave Tail' says he did not do any shooting himself but is responsible for the shooting and says his reason for doing so was because he was hungry."[77] Later correspondence in the court file, dated 25 September 1896, from the Indian Agent forwarded by the Commissioner of Indian Affairs to Justice Richardson by letter dated 29 September 1896, indicated that Shave Tail was the son of the deceased chief, and that neither he nor his mother owned any cattle: "I hope whatever sentence he gets, that it will make a better Indian of him. Being the son of the deceased Chief Peepeekeesis he has considerable influence with the Band and does not, I am sorry to say, always show a good example – in fact he gives me more trouble than any other Indian in the Agency."[78] On 1 October, Shave Tail pleaded guilty to the charge before Justice Richardson; he was remanded in custody until 9 October, when Richardson resisted the position advanced by the Indian Agent and declined to make a further example of him. As with Jean Baptiste, Shave Tail was discharged on a suspended sentence.

Earlier, in the spring of 1896, Richardson had imposed a similar sentence on a man from Muscowequan Reserve, Eopiassis, Son of the Old Blind Man, who had been convicted of "unlawfully and wilfully without legal justification or excuse and without colour of right" wounding a cow that belonged to the Government of Canada.[79]

The criminal law had been invoked against these accused men for engaging in the only form of hunting now available to them, and, in Mequanis's case, for outright resistance to the authority of the Indian Agent. And yet the violence of the law was tempered by the court. The Indian Department officials appear to have encountered resistance not only from the First Nations but also occasionally from Richardson's court.

These cases reveal the coercive face of the law, the resistance of the people in the context of their immiseration, and the mediating role of law in relation to Indian Department officials and the First Nations peoples. Again, the relations found here are complex. The illustration of hunger, oppression, and dire poverty is clear. Recourse by the authorities to the criminal law's coercive force in order to enforce compliance when mere threats and compulsion failed is also clear. Less straightforward is the contribution of the criminal law once invoked. Although it would be foolish to doubt even for an instant that Richardson shared the desire to "make better Indians" – he expressed such a sentiment at least once from the bench[80] – the dispositions in these cases, and the earlier ones, suggest that Richardson did not simply rubber-stamp the approach taken by the Indian Agents, or their use of his court to enforce the Indian policies, to punish hungry people even further.[81]

In the spring of 1903, Shave Tail, son of the late Chief Peepeekeesis, continued to be a good Indian, but not in the way the Indian Agent had hoped when he wrote to the court in 1896. Shave Tail once again found himself prosecuted for an alleged violation of the *Indian Act,* specifically that he encouraged another Indian to celebrate a dance of which the giving away of goods consisting of provisions forms a part.[82] On 22 May, the depositions and notification from the jailer that the accused was in his custody were filed with the Supreme Court of the North-West Territories. On 13 June, the Crown prosecutor, probably T.C. Johnstone, filed the formal charge against him, and on 15 June, at the request of the same prosecutor, Shave Tail was released, or, as the clerk recorded in the docket book, he was allowed to go free on promising to appear in Regina to answer the charge when called upon to do so.

Shave Tail spent three weeks in jail, but on this occasion he was not convicted. As in 1896, he was released from custody on his promise to return to court when required to do so. Earlier that spring, another man, Etchease from Muscowpetung Reserve, had not navigated the criminal court quite so ably as Shave Tail. Etchease too was charged with assisting in celebrating a dance of which giving away goods were a part, and also with encouraging another Indian to celebrate a dance.[83] At his trial in May, the jury convicted him on both charges, and Richardson sentenced him to three months in the Regina jail.

At the Mercy of Indian Policy: Eugana and Tom Lemac

During his tenure on the bench, as both a stipendiary magistrate and a justice of the North-West Territories Supreme Court, Hugh Richardson presided over nine capital cases, including eight murder trials.[84] Of these prosecutions, five involved First Nations men accused of murder and one involved a young woman, described as a "Treaty Half-breed," charged with murder and concealment of birth. Of the three First Nations men convicted of murder, only one (Ka-ki-si-kut-chin, or The Swift Runner) was hanged following his conviction; the death sentences of the other two men – Eugana (The Fast Runner) in 1885 and Tom Lemac (Winegee) in 1902 – were commuted.[85]

The process and evidence in the criminal trials of Eugana and Tom Lemac are reviewed below, including the difficulty in establishing the facts of the case, the evidentiary basis for anything, and the conduct (and in Eugana's case, the lament) of the defence counsel of an Aboriginal accused in a murder trial. Given the focus of this chapter, however, the nature of the interventions and recommendations of Territorial and Indian Department officials, as well as Indian policy in the post-conviction processes, are of particular interest.

Eugana: "The Gallows" and the Reprieve (1885-88)

In the summer of 1885, Eugana (The Fast Runner), the twenty-three-year-old second brother of Assiniboine chief The Man Who Carries the Coat, was vexed by a complicated relationship involving himself, another man, and their wives. The exact contours of the vexation are not clearly revealed in the court documents. It may be that the other man, Eagle Child, was after Eugana's wife, and/or that Eugana was interested in Eagle Child's wife, The Peigan Woman. In either event, Eugana faced a dilemma: to yield or to challenge Eagle Child, or try to find a way to avoid further conflict as a result of his wife's refusal to go to Eagle Child.[86]

Eagle Child, the source of Eugana's distress, was a prominent man on his reserve, older than Eugana and with a reputation for bravery. Before the end of the summer, Eugana was charged with murdering Eagle Child. By the end of September 1885, he was convicted and sentenced to death (see Figure 4.3). By the end of October 1885, his death sentence was commuted by order of the Governor-in-Council to a sentence of life imprisonment. By the end of October 1888, he was freed from prison.

Eugana's story was told in two ways at the two (fundamentally) different stages in the process:[87] first, through evidence that was admitted at the trial, and second, through evidence that was either ruled inadmissible or not presented at the trial. The former ensured his conviction; the latter facilitated the commutation of his sentence and secured his release. That Eugana had shot Eagle Child was clear, but nothing else was. Any

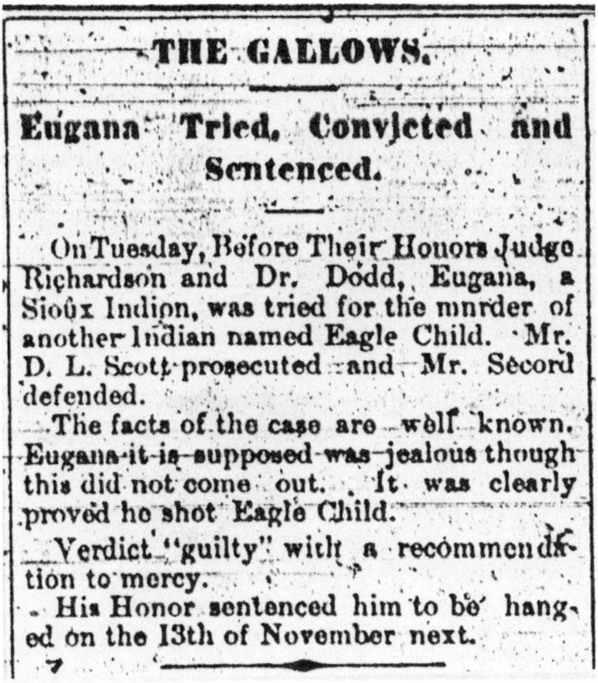
THE GALLOWS.

Eugana Tried, Convicted and Sentenced.

On Tuesday, Before Their Honors Judge Richardson and Dr. Dodd, Eugana, a Sioux Indian, was tried for the murder of another Indian named Eagle Child. Mr. D. L. Scott prosecuted and Mr. Secord defended.

The facts of the case are well known. Eugana it is supposed was jealous though this did not come out. It was clearly proved he shot Eagle Child.

Verdict "guilty" with a recommendation to mercy.

His Honor sentenced him to be hanged on the 13th of November next.

FIGURE 4.3 Regina *Leader*, 1 October 1885.

confidence that the legal system, casting its white eyes on the intricacies of Assiniboine cultural practices and relations, domestic and otherwise, could elicit the facts, much less the truth, could not have been more misplaced. At the end of the day, however, another, more familiar form of cultural practice facilitated the commutation of the sentence and Eugana's release from prison three years after his conviction: politics and the recognition of political debts due.

During the summer of 1885, Eagle Child was building a new house; it was said that as he lay dying, he continued to give instructions regarding the work still to be done to complete the house.[88] There was undisputed evidence at trial that Eugana had come upon Eagle Child at the construction site and that he had fired two shots that struck Eagle Child, resulting in a flesh wound to the abdomen and a wound to one of his upper arms. Directly after the shooting, Eugana and his wife looked for Indian farm instructor Arthur Taylor to tell him what had happened. Eagle Child's wounds were attended to by his brother and his cousin; they removed at least one of the bullets from his body.

The Indian Agent and a medical doctor from town were called to the reserve. The doctor examined Eagle Child and, given the grave nature of the injury to the arm, he recommended that it be amputated. Eagle Child and the people with him "stoutly refused" the procedure. The people from the reserve who were attending to Eagle Child had given him a purgative that the medical doctor believed had weakened him and "would be against recovery." There was some suggestion that the Indians caring for Eagle Child had not given him the nutritional rations that the medical man had recommended, which had been provided by the farm instructor. Eagle Child died on 10 August 1885, and Eugana was charged with his murder.

On 19 August 1885, five weeks before the trial, Edgar Dewdney, in his capacity as Indian Commissioner, advised the Superintendent General of Indian Affairs in Ottawa that one of the brothers of Chief The Man Who Carries the Coat had shot and killed another man of the band, resulting in a great deal of excitement but no further violence on the reserve. Dewdney's letter contained the particulars that had been provided to him by the Indian Agent, including the Agent's understanding that The Fast Runner (Eugana) and the deceased "had for some time past been attentive to each others wives, which after a while caused jealousy and ended by one shooting the other."[89] Upon arriving at the reserve, the Indian Agent had made his way to the chief's house, where a large number of people had gathered. He expressed his regrets to the chief for the reason for his visit, but told the chief that it was important for the guilty party to give himself up to the police and stand trial: "The Chief said his brother was ready to go and he would accompany him to Regina."[90] They met the police on the way to Regina, and Eugana was turned over to them.

Dewdney also noted that the Indians refused to allow the coroner to perform a post-mortem examination on the body of Eagle Child. He closed by observing that "the Indians had behaved very well although labouring under great excitement and the law will now take its course."[91]

The Evidence at Trial

The theory of Eugana's defence counsel, John Secord, was that Eagle Child was a bad man who had been trying to take Eugana's wife away from him; that Eagle Child had assaulted Eugana shortly before the shooting, resulting in Eugana's being injured; and that he had caused Eugana to fear for his life. Eugana told his lawyer that he had "offered on several occasions to give up his [wife] to Eagle Child in order to prevent trouble, and on one occasion shortly before these troubles, he told his wife to go to Eagle Child, but she refused."[92] Secord faced the unenviable challenge of attempting to elicit that evidence from the Aboriginal witnesses for the prosecution, all of whom were Eagle Child's relatives or friends.

Ha-wa-he (The Arrival) testified in the examination-in-chief that he remembered witnessing a quarrel between Eagle Child and Eugana two days before the shooting. Although he was present when Eagle Child was shot, he maintained that he did not see the shooting when it happened; he only heard it. He also testified that he knew that Eugana had been poisoned four years earlier and that he had never been well since. When asked in cross-examination whether Eugana had been struck or injured in the earlier quarrel, he could not say; he had not seen anything. When he was asked to say how Eugana had not been well following the poisoning incident, the discourse of the good Indian was invoked, through the interpreter who answered for the witness in the third person: "Well he says he never knowed the Indian to be a bad Indian, but sometimes he knowed that he was not in good humour – it was not a man to be always in exact humour."[93]

Eagle Child's cousin, The Man That Comes First (who with Eagle Child's brother was one of the people who had attended to Eagle Child after the shooting) testified that he had never heard of any trouble between Eagle Child and Eugana with reference to Eugana's wife. He had been at the house with Eagle Child when Eugana arrived, and said: "[Eagle Child] threw in his axe that way (down) he says Eugana says he, if you are mad, there is nobody holding you, do what you like."[94] When asked what Eagle Child meant by that phrase, he answered: "If you are mad, he says, there is nobody holding you, content yourself, content yourself, he means I suppose if her feeling like shooting him, to shoot him, that there was nobody holding him. This is what he says."[95] At this point, Eugana appears to have intervened: "Prisoner thinks the witness does not tell all he knows." The witness was reminded by the interpreter and the defence counsel that he was required to tell the truth, but the witness said he could say only what he saw with his eyes.

The last Indian witness for the prosecution was Eagle Child's widow, The Peigan Woman, who testified that she heard that her husband and Eugana were not on good terms. When asked about a conversation she had had with Eugana the day before the shooting, she remembered nothing, knew nothing.[96] She did admit that she had heard Eugana say to her and the woman she was with, "I could do something if I wanted." She did not know to what he was referring, did not know what he meant, and denied saying that if Eugana did not keep away, Eagle Child would kill him. When pressed by Secord, the interpreter expressed what she had said: "She just meant the same, if he wanted to talk to this woman, to try to revenge on this woman – of course the other one he was blaming that Eagle Child want to take his wife away from him, he wanted to do the same, and did not feel like it, that is why she told him to keep away, or else Eagle Child will kill you."[97] According to The Peigan Woman, she said that because "Eagle Child was a wicked man, he had beaten her, and that is why she told the Prisoner to be quiet, to keep away from him or her like, for if Eagle Child was to know it, he would kill him."[98] The Assiniboine women emerge as less than compliant: just as Eugana had told Secord that his wife had refused to go to Eagle Child, so it appears that The Peigan Woman "did not feel like it" if Eugana "wanted to do the same."

This is as much evidence of the basis of the quarrel between Eagle Child and Eugana as could be elicited from the witnesses.

In advancing the case for the defence, Secord faced a dilemma (or what should have been a dilemma for him): in order to defend his client, he had to deny the nature and significance of the relationship that was apparently the very heart of the case. Secord wanted to call Eugana's wife as a witness for the defence, but in order to do so, he had to take the position that she was not in law his wife, that she was simply living with him. Richardson made short shrift of this line of argument: "If she says she is his wife, her evidence is inadmissible, because the wife is – according to the Indian custom, just as much a wife in law under that decision in Lower Canada courts which went to the court of appeal – just as much a wife as our wives. I refer to the Connolly case."[99] Secord called her and asked if she was the prisoner's wife; she replied yes, and that was that – she was not permitted to testify on behalf of her husband. One other witness had been called by the defence to testify that she had seen Eugana's mother and wife attending to him two days before Eagle Child was shot (evidence that was intended to support the defence's theory that Eugana had suffered a serious injury as a result of the earlier assault by Eagle Child). Thus ended the defence's case.

Secord was permitted great scope and he took full advantage in his address to the jury, coming perilously close to giving evidence himself:

> Now gentlemen I may mention or point out to you that there is difficulty in defending an Indian charged with any of these crimes. You have seen the difficulty that I have had to get answers from questions, and I may say that

> I had the same difficulty with the prisoner in getting instructions in order to defend him properly ...
>
> I have felt that I have been in a manner handicapped in the defence of this case, and I am satisfied from what the prisoner tells me, that there is evidence that could have been brought out if the witnesses were not adverse to him. But you must take it as you find it ... upon the evidence that is given.[100]

For the Crown prosecutor, Scott, the question at the heart of the matter was a simple one: if Eugana was afraid of the deceased, why did he go to him, to the place where Eagle Child was working: "What did Eungana [*sic*] go to that house on that occasion for?"[101] The Crown's case was so strong that it was as easy as it was apparently irresistible for the Crown prosecutor to claim the high ground:

> Gentlemen, my duty as a crown prosecutor does not direct me to ask for a conviction at your hands if you think the prisoner should not be convicted. I am merely endeavouring to place the case as fairly as possible before you in order that you may see all points of evidence that have arisen in this case and consider all questions. That is as far as my duty leads me to go. I have no intention of asking for a conviction at your hands – I merely ask you that you should do your duty ... and as my learned friend says, give the prisoner the benefit of every reasonable doubt.[102]

Richardson's charge to the jury was a careful summary of the evidence and explanation of the law concerning causation, and he outlined the difference between murder and manslaughter. He reminded the jury that the doctor had testified that the cause of death was the wound, "accelerated, however, by foolish attention," and that if Eagle Child had received no treatment at all, he would have died.[103]

The jury deliberated for thirty minutes before returning with a verdict of "guilty with recommendation to mercy." Richardson sentenced Eugana to be hanged on 13 November 1885.

The Other Story: The "Inadmissible" and Absent Evidence

John Secord's formal letter of petition against the death sentence was in Lieutenant-Governor Dewdney's office the day after the trial. He cited the legal issues in the case and the difficulties he had encountered in conducting a proper defence for his client, including the refusal, on the morning of the trial, of an Indian witness he had intended to call to testify. Secord expressed the view that the witness who refused to testify was really implicated in the troubles, having stirred things up between Eugana and Eagle Child; on the morning of the trial, however, the witness denied any knowledge of anything. Secord closed with this lament and plea for his client: "The difficulty of getting the Indians to understand the nature of evidence is very great, and I cannot help but feel that the prisoner is not deserving of the death penalty, although no doubt he should be punished to some extent."[104]

Secord also referred to the facts that had not come out at the trial: that Eugana had offered to give up his wife to Eagle Child, and shortly before the incident he had told his wife to go but she refused. Secord stressed his understanding that Eugana had been led to believe that Eagle Child would kill him, and that he had fired the shots on the spur of the moment, after Eagle Child had provoked him.

On 2 October 1885, Richardson forwarded a full copy of the proceedings and evidence report to the Minister of Justice, drawing to the Minister's attention the jury's recommendation for mercy. By way of explanation for the recommendation, Richardson informed the Minister that the deceased and Eugana belonged to the same band (which Richardson incorrectly described as Sioux), and that there was "evidently some bad feeling between them, resulting from jealousy over their women." Richardson's reference to jealousy is interesting, because of course this had not been established in the evidence during the trial. He added that the medical evidence adduced at trial indicated that the deceased's life might have been saved "but for the ignorance of the deceased, and the ignorance and negligence of his friends attending him" and their refusal to allow amputation.

Dewdney forwarded Secord's petition to the Secretary of State, expressing the hope that it would receive favourable consideration and noting the prevailing opinion that the crime was committed "under extenuating circumstances, hence the strong recommendation to mercy" by the jury. Dewdney then added what surely was the real reason he was requesting favourable consideration:

> The chief of the band, who is the brother of the prisoner and some other relatives of the latter acted in a most commendable manner at the time of the commission of the crime, in holding the prisoner and sending word to the Police for his arrest. This conduct on their part would be gratiously [*sic*] rewarded by an act of clemency towards their unfortunate relative, and I have no doubt would go a great way in maintaining their present good

> feeling towards the authorities. The prisoner is an Assiniboine Indian and member of the band of the Chief, "The man that took the coat" – During the Rebellion the conduct of the whole band, including the prisoner was exemplary.[105]

The Minister of Justice's recommendation to the Governor General was contained in his letter of 29 October 1885. He repeated Richardson's point that Eagle Child had been weakened by the treatment he had received from his people, and noted their refusal of the course of treatment recommended by the medical doctor. Although he acknowledged that this did not lessen Eugana's culpability, he noted the uncertainty that flowed from the possibility that the deceased might have recovered had he received proper treatment. It was, however, the recommendation from the Lieutenant-Governor of the North-West Territories that appeared to carry the greatest weight for the Minister of Justice, as he reproduced Dewdney's letter verbatim. The legal and cultural issues raised by Secord in his petition were not referenced. The loyalty and exemplary behaviour of the band, including Eugana, during the Rebellion and their responsible behaviour in the matter of Eagle Child's death were to be rewarded. On 31 October 1885, the Governor General signed the order commuting Eugana's sentence to one of life imprisonment at the penitentiary in Manitoba.

At the time of Eugana's trial and conviction, Edgar Dewdney had also been the Indian Commissioner, and this fact would not have been lost on the chief. It is surely difficult to say in which capacity Dewdney had derived his knowledge of the exemplary behaviour of the band during the events of 1885. So, while his formal intervention in Eugana's capital case was as the Queen's Representative in the Territories, he was also known to all as the Indian Commissioner.

Three years later, the Indian Commissioner of the North-West Territories, now Hayter Reed, intervened again on behalf of Eugana and his band. Reed wrote to the Superintendent General of Indian Affairs about the case, citing reasons "which induce me to recommend to the Department that it should exert its influence to have him now released."[106] Reed referred to Secord's concerns expressed immediately after the trial about the witnesses who would not speak the whole truth, and the out-of-court assertions that Eagle Child had been persistently endeavouring to take away Eugana's wife, and that but for her refusal he would have agreed to part with her in order to avoid trouble. Reed intimated that the fatal encounter was accidental (a rather dubious construal of the facts), but more importantly, he reminded the Superintendent General that Eugana had surrendered, and that the pain of imprisonment was experienced more acutely by Indian prisoners. He proclaimed his strong support for the band's desire to have Eugana released, and concluded with what he clearly regarded as insight derived from his expertise: "Another aspect of the Indian's criminality, to which no small consideration should be given, is the fact that he only carried out the prevalent Indian view of justice; and the reclamation, of the Indians from their own deeply rooted ideas, must be a gradual process."[107] Two weeks later, Deputy Minister of Justice Robert Sedgewick recommended the release of the prisoner and the Minister of Justice and the Secretary of State indicated their concurrence;[108] Sedgewick then asked that the Indian Commissioner and the Superintendent General of Indian Affairs be informed of this recommendation.[109] A rather long two months later, Eugana was released from the Manitoba Penitentiary. The significance of the advocacy and pressure of his brother and the band must not be understated or underestimated, but it is equally important to note that his fate from the beginning to end of the process was shaped, if not driven, by the most senior government officials in the area of Indian Affairs.

Tom Lemac's Reprieve (1902)

The quality of the Indian Department's mercy experienced by Tom Lemac[110] fifteen years later was less vivid and somewhat less beneficial than that experienced by Eugana. Lemac, it will be remembered, had been convicted of murder in Regina in 1902 for the 1894 death of Josiah Matoney (Oskinaway). There had been evidence at the trial that both Lemac and Matoney had been intoxicated at the time of the shooting, which occurred on the plain in the middle of the night, as the two men were riding back to the reserve from Fort Qu'Appelle. There had been no witnesses to the shooting, and the fatally wounded Matoney had been found near the trail the following morning. A great part of the trial focused on what Lemac had said to others later that night, and how the words he spoke in Saulteaux to the women in their tents related to the offence of murder with which he was charged. The Indian witnesses at Lemac's trial were asked to recall with certainty the events that had taken place eight years earlier, and to act as cultural interpreters for the judge and jury in order to explain Lemac's conduct and the importance of his words and his departure (and long exile) after the shooting.

Lemac was convicted of murder, although it was surely open to the jury to have convicted him of manslaughter. He was sentenced to death. Almost immediately, a petition for clemency was circulated, and in the end the signatories included every businessman in the town of Regina as well as a few prominent Aboriginal individuals. Lemac, a former interpreter, guide, and special constable for the NWMP, was clearly held in high regard and respected for his work with the police. The sheriff and future mayor, P.M. McAra, was a strong supporter of both the reprieve and Lemac's early release. Lemac and McAra corresponded while Lemac was in the Manitoba Penitentiary, and later on in 1906, as mayor, McAra asked Premier Walter Scott for his support for Lemac's release. That August, the Premier obliged and sent a petition in support of Lemac's release to the Minister of Justice.

The capital case file reveals the active and serious intervention in the matter by the Department of Indian Affairs, including a lengthy memorandum of law prepared by Indian Department law clerk, Reginald Rimmer (former legal adviser to the Lieutenant-Governor of the NWT who later returned to the NWT and subsequently was appointed to the Saskatchewan bench). Rimmer's memorandum outlined several reasons in favour of clemency for Lemac. In case the Minister was not in favour of recommending clemency, Rimmer pointed out that there was also a ground for asking for a reserved case and, if this was refused, an application for leave to appeal.[111]

It is clear that the Minister of Justice read the memorandum, because he inserted a marginal note of his disagreement with one point of law advanced by Rimmer. The memorandum argued that the trial judge should have instructed the jury that if they were satisfied that the accused, being an Indian to whom the sale of intoxicants was prohibited, killed Matoney when he was in a state of intoxication in which he was utterly unable to form any intention, and that the prisoner had not intended to kill, they should find him guilty of manslaughter, not murder. The basis of the Justice Minister's disagreement is not clear; one possible inference is that he disagreed with the memorandum's emphasis on giving special consideration to the fact that Lemac was an Indian to whom the supply or sale of intoxicants was prohibited.

Rimmer's memorandum outlined the basis for a possible appeal, but acknowledged: "I can conceive that it may not be thought desirable, as a matter of policy, to create in the minds of the Indians in the Northwest, by a new trial and consequent publicity, the impression that they will be protected by the Department [of Indian Affairs] if they become intoxicated and commit homicide in that condition. Practically the same end can be obtained by commutation."[112] Rimmer's ambivalence is palpable. Clearly of the view that Lemac should not have been convicted of murder and that there were compelling legal arguments for an appeal, he understood the terrain on which he was treading. He was fully aware that the best he could hope for was a commutation of Lemac's sentence but was clearly uncomfortable resituating himself within that discourse, and he reminded his seniors of how he regarded Lemac's culpability and the death penalty itself:

> I can see no weighty reasons of policy in this case which outweigh the value of a human life if the Minister of Justice decides that the sparing of it would be consistent with justice. The effect of the trial and sentence will be sufficient warning to the Indians of the Northwest without the infliction of the most abhorrent form of death upon a man who may be considered to have had no real intention to kill and who is shown by the evidence to have passed the ordinary span of life.[113]

Lemac of course was not granted a new trial, but his death sentence was commuted in 1902. On 14 November 1908, Premier Scott's petition was granted; at the age of sixty-six Lemac was pardoned and released. He died at Pasqua's reserve ten months later on 4 September 1909.

In the post-conviction phase of the capital cases of both Eugana and Lemac, the importance of the government's Indian policy, even more than "Indian culture," is evident. The Indian Department is everywhere in these files, advocating for the condemned men, albeit in Lemac's case in the discourse of admonition of Indians about the evils of alcohol. Yet even in this case the department's law clerk urged that a human life not be sacrificed in the pursuit of policy.

The agency and activism of the Indians, including Eugana and Lemac themselves, in pressing the case for their release following commutation is evident. No general claim is made here about the clemency process involving other Aboriginal people convicted of murder as detailed in other capital case files; rather, the conclusion concerns only the experience of Eugana and Lemac. In these two cases, the rule of law, the specificity of Indian culture, and political interests combined to ensure that the men were eventually released. The paradox is that these Aboriginal men had supporters in high places, and in neither case was Indian policy or the rule law determinative; instead, there is evidence that a form of reciprocal mediation was at play, more relevant, perhaps, than questions of "Indian culture."

One last case, the 1901 criminal prosecution and imprisonment of Chief Piapot, the elder statesman of Treaty 4, highlights this difficult period.

Piapot: A Powerful Chief and the Power of Law

> *The dancing, which has always been carried to excess on this [Piapot's] reserve has ceased; in fact I only know of one small dance taking place during the year.*
>
> *– Indian Agent William Graham (1902)*[114]

> *I was surprised to see the Police on the Reserve.*
>
> *– Chief Piapot (1901)*[115]

On 21 October 1901, Piapot, the most prominent chief and major spiritual leader of the First Nations of Treaty 4, was brought before two justices of the peace in Fort Qu'Appelle, charged with the criminal offence of interfering with a police officer in the execution of his duty.[116] Piapot stood as a prisoner in court, as had Lean Man, Beardy, One Arrow, Cut Nose, and Stamiscotocar (Bull Head) – other Plains chiefs who had placed themselves between government men and police on behalf of their people. Like the others, Chief Piapot found himself criminally prosecuted for challenging or resisting the government's Indian policy or legislation (see Figures 4.4 and 4.5).

Earlier that month, a dance had been held on his reserve. The people of Piapot's band called it a "tea dance," but the Indian farm instructor on the reserve characterized it as a "giveaway" dance. On 17 October, he laid six Informations before Justice of the Peace G.W. Guernsey at Fort Qu'Appelle, charging six men of Piapot's band with participating "in a dance at which certain articles were given away." One of the men, Charles Fox, later testified at his own trial and described the dance and his understanding of the law:

> I live at Piapot's Reserve when I got home on the 6th October the people were ready to dance. I asked who would make it & I was told Big Sky – I let them in my house to dance, I went in when the drumming started, I took a drum & beat it. I heard some women behind my back giving away something either a horse or dog. The agent told us not to give away anything in a dance but you can make a present to your friends as long as it is not in

FIGURE 4.4 Piapot at the Regina Industrial School. | Saskatchewan Archives Board, R-A21256.

a dance, this was Mr. Mitchell [the former agent] – the present agent never told us anything & I thought it was all right – it was not a giveaway dance I didn't stop the women giving things away.[117]

FIGURE 4.5 Piapot *(second from right)* and other First Nations leaders in front of Canadian military, summer of 1885. Indian Commissioner Edward Dewdney is on the far left of the photograph. | Saskatchewan Archives Board, R-B741A.

On 18 October, police officers attempted to execute the warrants for the arrest of Piapot's men, including Charles Fox, and the elderly chief intervened. Although the arrival of the police armed with warrants drew a large crowd, there was no violence. Piapot engaged in talks with the police for two hours. While there can be no doubt that Piapot did not want his men arrested, it appears that his major concern was where they were to be taken. The police insisted that they were to be taken to Fort Qu'Appelle. Piapot said they would go to Regina. It was clear from the evidence of the two police witnesses and the farm instructor that Piapot had been very plain with them. One of the arresting officers testified: "Piapot stated he would not allow his men to go to or to be taken to Fort Qu'Appelle, I explained that we had to do our duty & we did not wish any trouble, the answer was that he & the police were good friends but he would not allow them to go to Fort Qu'Appelle but that they would go to Regina, he told them to get their horses ... Piapot put on his uniform & ordered his horse to go to Regina."[118]

Staff Sergeant Fyffe also testified that there was "no passion showed on either side & when Piapot was going away he shook hands." Despite his stature, reputation, and statesmanship, Piapot did not prevail. One can only speculate on why he preferred Regina to Fort Qu'Appelle. Perhaps the senior chief preferred to speak to the senior judge in Regina, not the justice of the peace at the Fort. Perhaps he was trying to cut the losses that his people were about to experience with the new agent. These things are not clear. What is clear is that Piapot faced down the police at great personal cost to himself. In the end, probably thanks to his efforts, only one of his men who had been charged with the dance was convicted.

For Piapot, however, there would be no deferred sentence, no discharge as there had been in an earlier period for Lean Man. One wonders whether the justices of the peace at Fort Qu'Appelle flinched inwardly, if at all, when they criminalized the eighty-five-year-old chief through his conviction and the insult of two months in jail for the criminal offence of interfering with a peace officer in the execution of his duty – for standing between his men and the authorities, for once again attempting to protect his people.

Historians who have studied this incident or Piapot's biography have suggested that the prosecution was instigated and used by William Graham, the new Indian Agent for the Qu'Appelle Agency, to legitimize the government's move to depose Piapot as chief.[119] Here again, one sees the importance of identifying when, how, and with what results government policy found its way into the criminal court. The hardening of the government's hand on Piapot in 1901 foreshadowed the trajectory of the twentieth century, the century that ushered in an era of criminalization of the First Nations. Historicizing this process of criminalization has been a central concern of this book.

Conclusion

In this chapter, I have demonstrated different ways in which the *Indian Act* and Indian policy are found in the ordinary criminal court records of the North-West Territories: through the prosecution of First Nations leaders, and through the role of Indian Agents and farm instructors as informants, either complaining of assault or attempting to enforce government policy through criminal prosecutions. Although this is not unexpected, it is significant that the criminal court was not always the government's best friend. The expansion of the judicial powers of the Indian Agent reflected a desire on the part of the government to have matters decided by Indian Agent justices of the peace, whose dispositions in matters involving Indian people would be more certain and more consistent with government policy.

Throughout the period, the most striking aspect of the court records is the consistent evidence of hunger and material deprivation across the First Nations communities. It drove the cases. The homicide cases – those discussed in Chapter 2 as well as those of Eugana and Lemac – account for a tiny fraction of the small fraction represented by First Nations accused, and are of a different order. And yet, as is to be expected, they offer extensive evidence of life on the reserves and the challenges involved in the relationship between First Nations and the criminal law.

And, of course, the ubiquitous Indian policy in its myriad forms may be seen at every stage of the criminal process. In some ways, in the capital case files of Eugana and Lemac, we see the Indian Commissioner and the officials of the Indian Department at their "best," advocating on behalf of the condemned men. And here we see the convergence of politics and policy: one can almost hear Dewdney's pleading, as much for himself and his reputation as for the condemned young Assiniboine man. One can only imagine the fallout for Dewdney and the government had Eugana been hanged in the autumn of 1885, within a month of the mass hanging of the eight Cree and Assiniboine men in Battleford.

The cases discussed and analyzed in this chapter do not lead one to deny the coercive role of the criminal law, even in relation to the government's Indian policy. It is clear, however, that this is far from the most interesting or compelling lesson one can draw from the many different cases. Did government officials turn to the criminal law to prosecute and hopefully convict and discredit leaders such as Beardy, Yellow Mud Blanket, Yellow Calf, Lean Man, Peaychew, Shave Tail, Mequanis, and Piapot? Clearly they did. Was there a close relationship between the police and the Indian Department officials? Clearly there was. Did Judge Hugh Richardson acquiesce in the use of his court to enforce the worst failures and excesses of government policy? The cases discussed here show that the answer is not always what one might expect, or what the government of the day clearly wanted.

5
Six Women, Six Stories

The symbolic importance of violence – whether the violence of the state and law or the violence of protest – may have no direct correlation with quantities.

– E.P. Thompson (1976) [1]

The women of the First Nations are difficult to locate, their voices almost indiscernible, in the legal history of the Plains. This chapter examines that phenomenon, evaluates the scholarly writing on and analysis of the relationship of Aboriginal women to criminal justice, and introduces six women's stories. According to Sarah Carter, "[a] major problem for historians is with the nature of the evidence, which rarely provides the first-hand voices of the women of this era ... Historians rely upon documentary evidence generated by predominantly male Euro-Canadian government officials, missionaries, or other observers ... they regarded as insignificant or misunderstood the role of women in Aboriginal society."[2]

The analysis of criminal law as a gendered and gendering practice[3] is not prominent in Western Canadian or Aboriginal legal history. Here again, the concept of criminalization is demonstrably overinclusive with respect to forms of law captured and under-inclusive in relation to gender.[4] For the most part, criminalization passes over and subsumes Aboriginal women, rendering their experience impossible to discern, much less understand. And yet some Aboriginal women were involved in and engaged by the criminal law on the nineteenth-century Plains, although more participated as informants and complainants than as accused persons.

In a recent essay, Val Napoleon captures my concern when she argues in another context: "In aboriginal rights jurisprudence, it appears that indigenous women have been erased off both the land and the legal landscape."[5] Napoleon identifies Aboriginal women's relegation to issues that in today's context tend to be framed as those concerning membership, family, poverty, health, education, and so on, and omission from others, such as the "big-ticket" items encompassed by Aboriginal rights jurisprudence in Aboriginal law.[6]

British Columbia historian Jean Barman also engages with these issues of invisibility, omission, and relegation, and adds to them the significance of forms of construction of Aboriginal women, both historically and in the historiography: "[W]e have become entrapped in a partial world that represents itself as the whole world. Records almost wholly male in impetus have been used by mostly male scholars to write about Aboriginal men as if they make up the entirety of Aboriginal people. The assumption that men and male perspectives equate with all persons and perspectives is so accepted that it does even not have to be declared."[7] Barman poses a question that raises both epistemological and methodological issues: "[W]hat happens when we turn the past on its head and make our reference point Aboriginal women instead of Aboriginal men?"[8] Historians interested in accepting this challenge face methodological hurdles, not least of which is the fact that the names of First Nations women and children are often "hidden from history"[9] or "forgotten in the mistiness of the past," as Hugh Dempsey has observed in relation to Big Bear's mother.[10] Women tended to be recorded under their husbands' names in the Treaty Annuity Paylists. Their names do begin to appear in early census records, but even the census records leave us to wonder, for instance, who were "Mrs. Daybird 1" and "Mrs. Daybird 2" on Gordon's Reserve?[11] Who was Chief Pasquah's "2nd wife"?[12]

Nonetheless, Canadian historians and Aboriginal feminist scholars have begun to analyze the historical relationship between Aboriginal women, the state, public policy, and the broader Canadian context.[13] These scholars identify the patriarchal and gendered nature of state policy and action, and analyze implicit and express forms of racism in laws, policies, and social imagery that affected First Nations women. Not least among these is the construction of contradictory images of Aboriginal women – as "dissolute, dangerous and sinister,"[14] as "beautiful Indian maiden[s],"[15] as commodities who were bought, sold, and enslaved in their marriages to Aboriginal men,[16] where they were "timid, submissive and work worn."[17]

For the Canadian Plains region, it is impossible to consider the nature of the contribution of Canadian state policy in relation to the social position of Aboriginal women historically without considering the towering contribution of Sarah Carter.[18] Carter locates Western Canada squarely within policies, practices, and discourses associated with colonialism, characterizing the North-West Territories as a "colonial dependency of Ottawa."[19] She argues that the "fundamental features of colonialism were clearly present in the extension of the power of the Canadian state and in the maintenance of sharp social, economic, and spatial distinctions between the dominant and subordinate population,"[20] pointing to the "segregationist policies toward the Aboriginal population" and the manner in which these policies constructed Aboriginal women as "dissolute, dangerous and sinister."[21] There emerged a preoccupation with and perception of Aboriginal women as immoral. Carter is careful to point out that while actively promoted by Canadian officials, these sentiments and representations were not shared by everyone; interestingly, she points to the often good relationships, including marriage, that members of the North-West Mounted Police entered into with First Nations women on the Prairies.[22]

Of the many methodological and interpretative challenges in historical work concerning Aboriginal people, perhaps, as Carter has observed, none is more important than the dearth of "first hand voices of the women of this era."[23] Legal and social historians rely heavily on records and documents that were produced by government men, the police and other criminal justice officials, missionaries, and others, in government files and records, official and annual reports, memoirs, press accounts, and so on.[24]

Historians of oppressed, marginalized, and colonized women are of necessity a resourceful and creative lot, because their research involves people whom conventional legal and social history has misinterpreted or ignored. A range of methods and sources must be deployed. Constance Backhouse has made her own important contribution to Canadian legal history, and notably the contribution of the law and the legal profession with respect to racism, sexism, and substantive inequality more generally, through a number of meticulously researched case studies.[25] Backhouse has drawn on legal sources, press accounts, archival records, and – where informants and others are still living – interviews. Joan Sangster is one of the few historians to focus on women in the "criminalization of the colonized" literature, and on the trend toward increasing confinement and over-incarceration of Aboriginal women and girls, notably in Ontario. To do this, she has turned to penal and Indian department government records. Sarah Carter's recent engagement with the legal history of family, marriage, and divorce regulation[26] involves a combination of most of the above. Backhouse's case studies document Aboriginal women's victimization, agency, and resistance; Carter and Sangster make the important point that in these official state records, as well as in religious and missionary records, the voices and perspectives found are those of the "observers," not the Aboriginal women themselves. Carter's pursuit of and respect for their voices is thus a model for others.

Once again, questions remain concerning the relationship and contribution of the criminal law and criminal court and the probative value of criminal court records as a distinct form of official, legal record. Do court records, as argued in the Introduction and Chapter 3, also offer space for voices of the oppressed, such as those of Aboriginal women accused of criminal offences, to be heard? This may be especially difficult for the court records of the nineteenth-century North-West Territories when – for most of the period of this study – accused persons could not testify in their own defence but could only make a Statement of the Accused at the end of a preliminary hearing before justices of the peace.

Lesley Erickson's research, based on a sample of court files from selected judicial districts in Manitoba, Saskatchewan, and Alberta between 1889 and 1940, addresses, among other things, the representation of Aboriginal men and women, victims and accused, in the criminal courts and in the press.[27] She seeks to demonstrate how different ideologies informed legal and public accounts of Aboriginal crime, and how these accounts in turn shaped popular understandings and attitudes. She notes that Prairie judges (Rouleau, Macleod, and Richardson) emphasized the "need for inter-racial equity" in cases where Aboriginal women had been victims of violence, such as murder and sexual violence.[28] She points to Justice Rouleau's charge to the jury in the "Rosalie" case (in which a white man had been charged with the brutal murder of an Aboriginal woman named Rosalie) to "forget the woman's race and consider only the evidence at hand," reminding the jury that "it made no difference whether Rosalie was white or black, and Indian or a negro. In the eyes of the law, every British subject is equal."[29] Erickson quotes an almost verbatim statement by Judge Hugh Richardson in an 1890 rape trial in Regina, when he charged the jury in the trial of George Evense, a German immigrant accused of raping a young Métis woman, as follows: "So long as a woman – be she white or black, Negro,

Indian or Caucasian – conducted herself properly she was as much entitled to protection as the highest lady in the land."[30] (Evense, who was actually charged with assault with intent to rape and indecent assault, attempted to plead guilty to the attempted rape charge, blaming his conduct on being intoxicated at the time.[31]) Despite the language, however, in Erickson's view, statements such as these attributed to Rouleau and Richardson only reinforced public perceptions of racial difference. She concludes that misrepresentation, racist stereotypes, and persecution better capture the experience of Aboriginal women in the West in the period and the records she has studied.

Erickson and Carter also demonstrate the important role and contribution of Indian Department officials in this period. Carter is mindful that the Canadian state and its officials were not of a piece, and that evidence of internal discord can be found. Additionally, in looking at newspaper accounts, North-West Mounted Police (NWMP) records, judicial transcripts, and documents, what was happening on the ground could be quite different from what was promulgated by Parliament or described by government officials in their annual reports. It is important to identify the sites, levels, and forms of Canadian state policy: from the politicians and lawmakers in Ottawa to their local senior bureaucrats – such as Lieutenant-Governor (1881-88) and Indian Commissioner (1879-88) Edgar Dewdney – to the on-the-ground officials in the Territories. In many ways, Indian Department officials in the field were the most powerful people in the lives of Aboriginal women, and their mandated excesses and "iron hands" were the source of much strife and hardship.

The six case studies that follow offer another perspective on the significance of criminalization and sexualization for six Aboriginal women accused of criminal offences and tried by Hugh Richardson during his time on the Territorial bench.

Who Was She? What Was Her Name?

On 4 October 1884, three First Nations prisoners, two men and one woman, were committed by Justice of the Peace Thomas Tweed to stand trial before the stipendiary magistrate in Maple Creek.[32] The court record, on four sheets of NWMP stationery, contains none of the standard legal documents: there are no Informations, no warrants, no date of offence, no indication of the informant or prosecutor, and no clear indication of the name of the accused woman (see Figure 5.1). This court record is one

FIGURE 5.1 Unidentifed Indian woman. | Saskatchewan Archives Board, R-A7857.

of the few that I have read from this period to use the word "Squaw" to describe or name a First Nations woman.

The three prisoners were accused of "housebreaking" into and larceny from the home of Benjamin McCord in Medicine Hat; apparently a string of bells, some curtain stuff, and a buffalo coat had been taken from the house. McCord himself was not indicated as being present at the hearing. The only evidence of the alleged offences appear to have come from the two male prisoners.

Bear Hand, described as an Assiniboine Half-breed, pleaded guilty to larceny but not guilty to the breaking and entering charge. The other two prisoners pleaded not guilty. The men, Bear Hand and Nakiss, each pointed to the other as the person most responsible for breaking into the McCord house. Each also gave evidence that implicated the woman. She appears not to have been called upon to say anything.

The case against Bear Hand is set out in the third person by Peter Girard; given the practice of some interpreters, it is possible that Girard was an interpreter who offered Bear Hand's first-person account as a narrative in the third person. The suggestion from this evidence was that Bear Hand had learned of the house from Nakiss, the Cree prisoner, and that he had gone to the house a week later, and only after Nakiss had told him that he had broken into it: "A Cree Indian said he broke open the door – 'Nakis' – a week after he the prisoner went to the house and found it open [*sic*] He entered the house and took a Buffalo Coat which he gave to Squaw the coat was cut in two. [*sic*] and divided it. The coat was on the bed in House. The Squaw's name I don't know. Little Knoll I think." If I am right about Girard's role, the first-person voice here is his, and it is he (and not Bear Hand) who does not know the name of the woman. On the basis of this evidence, and surely his admission of the theft, Bear Hand was remanded until Wednesday, 8 October, at ten o'clock.

It appears that Bear Hand was then sworn and gave evidence against Nakiss, "Cree Indian," and against "Bone Child," "Cree Squaw," on their charges of housebreaking and larceny in relation to the same house. Nakiss pleaded not guilty to both charges and is recorded to have said: "Prisoner states that he went into the said house with his wife but says he took nothing out of the house." In his evidence before Tweed, Bear Hand stated that "the prisoner told him that he had broken into the above-mentioned house and stolen a string of bells. I saw the Bells and some red curtain stuff also which he said he stole from the said house." It is highly unlikely that Bear Hand employed the legalese reflected by the phrase "the above-mentioned house." Tweed's notes continue: "Prisoner recalled acknowledged stealing the curtain stuff from house" and "Prisoner committed for trial" at Maple Creek for housebreaking and larceny.

Then followed, it seems, the hearing against Bone Child, "Cree Squaw," where she too is recorded as having entered a plea of not guilty. Nakiss,

FIGURE 5.2 Housing fit for a bachelor. The "bachelor shacks" of the new settlers on the Plains were modest structures. | Saskatchewan Archives Board, R-A517.

apparently her husband, told Tweed that "the Squaw was with him when he stole the curtain stuff." In his evidence, Bear Hand stated that "the prisoner 'Squaw' told him that she was with Nakiss when goods were stolen and helped him to do so." She was committed for trial.

There is no record of the proceedings before the stipendiary magistrate other than an endorsement bearing the date of 10 October 1884 that Bear Hand was tried, convicted, and sentenced to six months at the Regina jail for larceny. The same document indicates that Bear Hand faced two charges of larceny and that he admitted to "stealing field glass at Medicine Hat from a Mr. Eamon Edwards" and a "suit of clothes, a buffalo coat from Benjamin McCord."

The NWMP returns for 1884 contain entries recording that Bear Hand was sentenced by Stipendiary Magistrate Richardson to six months' hard labour for larceny; a second entry indicates that "Narkis" and his wife, "The Good Speaker," had their case dismissed due to "insufficient evidence."[33]

Who and where was Benjamin McCord? And without his involvement, how was ownership established either of the shack or the goods that were purportedly stolen? (See Figure 5.2.) The 1901 census indicates that a Ben McCord was a forty-two-year-old single farmer, originally from Ontario, of Scottish Presbyterian stock. So, was he in 1884 a seventeen-year-old bachelor with his own house?[34] Perhaps these cases involve another story of yet another settler's house left unoccupied and untended, apparently for a stretch of time.[35] Although the shack clearly did not belong to the three accused, a conviction should have been predicated on evidence that it was in fact McCord's.

Different inferences can be drawn about how this came to the attention of the NWMP. Perhaps the Cree couple had some new fabric or new bells in their possession; clearly, Bear Hand had acquired a buffalo coat, or a piece of it. But, of course, questions remain – not least about the First Nations woman, or women, who were said to be involved but whose voices we do not hear.

Who was Little Knoll? Was she Bear Hand's wife? Who was The Good Speaker? Was she Bone Child? What was her name? And what were their stories? Were they told in the words ascribed to their men, who were quick to implicate the women, or interpreted or recorded by other men who were too indifferent to them to know, use, or properly record their names? We have, in the words of the NWMP returns, insufficient evidence.

"Are You Positive That I Took Your Money?" Caroline Gouin and Her Employer Accuser

On 3 September 1881, Peter Erasmus, the prominent Cree interpreter who had been hired by Cree chiefs at Treaty 6 to interpret and oversee proceedings for them, was sworn in as the interpreter by the three justices of the peace who were presiding at the hearing in John Alexander McDougall's complaint that about three weeks earlier, Caroline Gouin, a woman described as his servant, had stolen money from him.[36] A warrant to apprehend Gouin had been issued on 3 September, and it must have been executed immediately as she was already named as a prisoner when the hearing into his charge took place that same day.

McDougall said that Gouin, about 10 August, had been scrubbing his house, including the bedroom, and shortly after she left, he noticed that a half-sovereign gold piece and a twenty-five-cent silver coin were missing from his pocketbook on the stand in the bedroom. He immediately suspected Gouin and, acting on this suspicion, went to the Hudson's Bay Company (HBC) post to inform the clerks of his loss and to alert them to watch for the coin, especially the half-sovereign gold piece. He said he named no one as a suspect, but simply asked that they watch in case someone came to the post to spend it. When William Brereton, one of the HBC clerks, sent for him, McDougall felt his suspicions were justly confirmed and, expressing confidence and his theory of the case, he told the justices: "I saw the half Sovereign given to Mr. Brereton and as it is the only one I have seen in the country I felt satisfied it was the one stolen from my place." Caroline Gouin, the prisoner, appears to have been an active and informed participant in the hearing, judging from the fact that she cross-examined three of the four witnesses, including her (presumably former) employer. While McDougall's answer was probably not what she would have preferred, her question did represent a challenge to his charge, raising as it did the difference between direct evidence and the circumstantial nature of the case against her. In this, we see the premise of her defence, and the groundwork laid for her own statement at the end of the hearing:

Q: Are you positive that I took your money?
A: I am.

Joseph McKay, the HBC clerk who had received the gold coin, identified it as the one he had received from the prisoner, and again the theory of the case against Caroline was implicit: he said that he had seen only a few half-sovereign gold coins before, and only one in his time in Edmonton. He recalled that she had made her purchase using it and some other monies, but he could not remember what the latter were. During cross-examination by Caroline, he admitted that he did not remember what amount she had spent that day at the post.

William Brereton deposed that he had called for McDougall when McKay informed him that the half-sovereign gold piece had been presented at the counter. He then showed the coin to Caroline and asked her whether she had presented it, to which she said yes. When McDougall did not appear right away, Brereton, impressively, knew that he "could not keep the Prisoner waiting longer" and so her purchases were completed, and she left. When McDougall arrived, he was shown the coin and he "said he thought it was his." And, as it was a place of commerce, "[t]he coin was put in with the cash sales for the day."

At the hearing, Brereton, like McKay, deposed that he had "seldom seen a half sovereign gold coin in the country ... During the summer I have not seen an other [*sic*] half sovereign gold coin but the one now shown to me by the court."

Leslie Wood, the last deponent before the three justices of the peace, told the justices of the peace that he received cash sales from the shop on the last day of every month, and that on the day before the hearing he had received the half-sovereign gold piece. He identified the coin he was shown: "[I]t is the only one received during the last month. I have not during the year received an other [*sic*] half sovereign gold coin."

At the end of the hearing, Caroline was given the opportunity to give a statement in response to the charge. She spoke at some length, revealing that she also engaged in commerce as well as services:

> When the steamboat arrived first a gentleman from the boat came to my tent and ask [*sic*] me if I had any shoes for sale. I then had two pairs of shoes which I was keeping for my husband who was off on a trip with Donald Macleod. I sold him the two pairs of shoes and washed two pairs of pants and two shirts. When he came for his things after I had washed them he told it was the only money he had and gave me the gold piece in payment asking me if I was satisfied. I told him that I asked one dollar a pair for the shoes and twenty-five cents a piece for the washing He told me that that was the only small coin he had and asked me to accept of it [*sic*]. I then laid the money away and told my uncle of it, and did not make use of it till the day I presented at the Hudson's Bay store. I did not take Mr McDougall's money and can prove that I got it elsewhere. I donot [*sic*] know the name of the person who game [*sic*] me the money.

On the basis of this evidence, Caroline was committed to stand trial on 12 December 1881 at the sitting of the Saskatchewan District Court in Edmonton. A measure of her standing, and possibly the weakness of the case against her, may be gleaned from the fact that she was not remanded in custody to await her trial. She was released on bail: $200 posted by Joseph Gouin and $100 posted by Michel Vivier. Thereafter the court file is silent. Caroline Gouin's trial probably never took place, although the NWMP returns do record that later that fall she was convicted and fined $50 by two justices of the peace, HBC factor Richard Hardisty and NWMP inspector Sévère Gagnon, of the offence of giving intoxicants to Indians.[37]

An Aboriginal Jury of Matrons Investigates: Scholastique's Hidden Pregnancy and Missing Baby

The norms invoked or applied in the territorial court were not simply those imposed by the new dominant social order. Older norms and community values also appear to have found expression and support in the criminal court.

In the spring of 1882, in the remote northwestern community of Lac la Biche in the North-West Territories (which became part of the province of Alberta in 1905), a young "Treaty Half-breed" woman was confronted by a group of women from her community about the pregnancy she had hidden and the fate of her baby. When the baby's body was found, men in the community examined the body. No priest, no medical man, no police officer participated in the investigation, which from the outset appears to have been led by women.

On 1 June 1882, Peter Pruden swore an Information before NWMP inspector and justice of the peace Sévère Gagnon in which he alleged that on 13 May 1882, eighteen-year-old Scholastique Cardinal, described as a "Treaty Half breed," "did feloniously, willfully and of her malice aforethought kill and murder a child of which she had been delivered endeavouring to conceal the birth of said child by secretly burying during the night on the bank of the said Lake La Biche the dead body of said child."[38] The entire hearing appears to have been taken in Gagnon's handwriting, and to have been conducted rather informally, even by territorial standards. At the hearing before Gagnon, the evidence of all six deponents was given through a sworn interpreter, although neither the language nor the interpreter is named. Throughout the transcript, the community is called "Lake La Biche," which suggests that the francophone Gagnon was recording in English even part of the French name of the community. Only two depositions are followed by a signature (those of Peter Pruden and André Fortier), which suggests that they were men with some education and possibly of standing in the community.[39] There is neither a signature nor an "X" beneath the other depositions.

The investigation into Scholastique Cardinal appears to have been led by Mary Pruden, who also seems to have been the lead deponent:

> I saw prisoner only three times during the winter & was always under the impression that she was with child & after I heard that the girl had lost the swelling she had all winter I went over with other women to visit the girl to

> see how she was I asked her you had had a swelling & now the swelling is off it is no use to hide it tell me when I said that the prisoner said nothing but her sister said the [*sic*] had thrown some bloody water. I told the prisoner to tell the story right & she said she could only say what her sister had said I told her again tell us the story right for if you had a child we shall know it by your breasts but she said nothing we got her to show her breast & saw that she had milk & told her that she had had a child but she still said nothing we found she had milk by forcing it from her breast. We told her to go look for the child. & she & the other women went out but I stayed in the house after they found the body of the child they came & called me out.[40]

Scholastique's sister Lisette also gave evidence, telling the justice of the peace that she had not known that her sister had been pregnant until the morning the women had come, and she did not know where her sister had delivered the baby:

> I only knew after some women came over to hunt for a child that my sister had been confined at that time my sister handed over to me the dead body of a child I asked her if it was a boy or a girl. she said it was a girl I saw where the child was buried. It was a side hill & a little mud thrown over the body I do not know where my sister was confined I lived in the same house with prisoner but never noticed that she was with child she was always sickly the whole of last winter.[41]

Lisette apparently attempted to give the baby's body to Mary Pruden, but Mary would not take it from her; she directed her to give it to another woman.

Margaret Fosseneuve[42] also described what transpired that day, and her role in it:

> Some women came for me & I went with them to prisoner's house when we got there I was behind the prisoners [*sic*] sister had the body of a child in her arms she gave the body to me and I gave it to another woman she said we must not take the child but I said we must or the dogs might eat it this took place along the Lake I took a handkerchief from the prisoners head & wrapped the body in it and laid it on the table.[43]

Mary Pruden was the only woman to describe the condition of the baby's body:

> After the woman took the body I saw a little mark on the neck that was all I saw we took the body in the house & laid it on the table rolled up in a handkerchief & that was all I saw I do not know the exact date but it was some time last month.

At the hearing before Gagnon, an unarticulated but no less obvious gendered division of labour emerged from the depositions of the men and women who gave their evidence. Although Mary Pruden said they had visited Scholastique to see how she was, Lisette's characterization of the "hunt for the child" is likely more apt. The women clearly had acted much like a jury of matrons in English criminal law:[44] they had examined Scholastique's body and ascertained, by forcing milk from her breast, that she had recently given birth. They demanded to know what had happened to the baby, and made her show them where the baby was. Once the baby's body was found, they used Scholastique's head scarf to wrap the body and laid the body on a table in her house.

It appears to have been left to the men to determine the cause of death. At least four men examined the body, and three of them described what they saw. It also appears that the examination of the body was carried out over the course of at least a couple of days. Louis Frederick was not the first male deponent, but he may have been among the first men to examine the body:

> The day before, I went over to the prisoners [*sic*] house with several others, I went alone & saw on the top of a box the body of a child wrapped up in a handkerchief I unfolded it & examined the body it was covered with mud all over except a red mark round the neck I had my wife to wash the body & in washing one of the arms the skin came off where there was a red [clot?]. The next day when I went over with others I examined the body again & found the mark around the neck was larger. After we had examined the body I asked prisoner whether it was her child and she said yes.

Another man, André Fortier, pinpointed the day he went to the house with the others as the day before Ascension; he, too, saw the body of the dead child on the table wrapped up. He said that Frederick and another man named Hamelin unfolded the wrap and exposed the body: "I saw that on the left arm the skin was off in two places there was a red mark all round the neck of the body." Peter Pruden described what he saw when he went over to the house on 15 May: "a dead child lying on a table there was a mark around the dead child's neck ... I know nothing more the mark I saw on the body was a red one all round the neck."

By the end of the foregoing evidence, Sévère Gagnon appears to have decided that this was not a case of willful murder, notwithstanding the language used in Pruden's Information. At the end of the depositions and before inviting Scholastique to say anything in response to the charge, his recitation of the summary of the proceedings stipulated that she was delivered of a child on 13 May 1881, and that being so delivered, she "did then unlawfully endeavour to conceal the birth of the said child by secrettly [*sic*] burying during the night on the bank of ... Lake La Biche the dead body of said child." Scholastique described the ordeal of labour and delivery alone, outside, in the night:

> I did not destroy the child on purpose. When I felt the pains of labor the child could not come out at once. When it did come out I lost my strength and fell on the child, but do not know whether it was born alive or not. I fainted and when I came to I found the navel [*sic*] coiled around the child's neck. I cut the cord & untwisted it from the child's neck & tried with my own mouth to induce respiration but found it was dead. I got up and carried the body to the side of the Lake and buried it After I buried it & went home & went in it was about daylight I did not sleep and started that morning for the mission I told no one I had been delivered of a child.[45]

Scholastique was committed for trial. Again, there is no record of the proceedings of the trial, only the following endorsement: "Tried & convicted 13 June 82 Sentence deferred."

There is no mention of who the father might have been, and it also seems that this was not regarded as a relevant issue, which under the circumstances may well have been the case. Perhaps if the baby had lived, such questions would have been pursued. The entire process appears to have been driven by the women of Scholastique Cardinal's community. In any event, the method of investigation and of determining whether Scholastique had recently given birth to a baby was not one that would likely have been employed by the men of the NWMP under Sévère Gagnon's command, had they ever become involved in the matter in the first place. The women of the community brought their knowledge of pregnancy, childbirth, and lactation to the matter, together with a formidable interrogator in the person of Mary Pruden. One might also consider the possibility that one of Lac la Biche's jury of matrons had cause to worry that a husband or son might have been implicated in Scholastique's pregnancy. It is clear that the men who examined the body took care, and the result of their examination appears to have lent support to Scholastique's description of the difficult childbirth and the umbilical cord that was wrapped around her baby's neck. The experience of her appearance before the judge may well have paled in significance compared with the experience of a hidden and apparently difficult pregnancy, labour, and childbirth alone, at night, and outdoors, followed by the arrival of the local jury of matrons led by Mary Pruden. Her punishment had been meted out and her sentence served before she faced the magistrate on 13 June.

Margaret Favel: An Honest Woman and Her Unlikely Ally

E.P. Thompson once observed that "most men have a strong sense of justice, at least with regard to their own interests."[46] On 13 May 1892, Joseph Hollis's sense of justice was offended. On 14 May, he acted on that sense of justice, albeit nervously, and neither to advance nor vindicate his own interests – quite the contrary. On the 13th, Hollis, a justice of the peace in the Touchwood Hills district of the North-West Territories had presided at a hearing into a complaint in which Margaret Favel was accused of stealing many items from the schoolhouse on Poor Man's reserve.[47]

Margaret Favel, named in the Information as the wife of Peter Favel of Fort Qu'Appelle, was also the mother of at least one very young child; she appeared before Hollis as a prisoner, having been apprehended on a warrant that he himself had issued based on an Information sworn by Lucius F. Hardyman. In that Information, Hardyman accused Margaret of stealing a long and detailed list of property – household items and clothing that belonged to him:

> One large silver Table spoon and one large silver Table fork both with a crest viz [*sic*] a greyhound on them. One silver desert [*sic*] spoon with a crest viz [*sic*] an eagle's head with a dolphin in its beak. Also one other silver article with the crest of an eagle with a dolphin in its beak. Five electro plated egg spoons. One large grey government blanket. One patchwork cloth quilt. One down quilt. Two pairs of chamois leather underpants. One chamois leather under vest. One white football jersey with "Red Hand of Ulster" on the breast. Also various items of clothing & four pairs of creton [*sic*] window curtains. Also one brown and black silk neck tie.

Hardyman's Information was silent with respect to the total value of these items, but the warrant for her apprehension as well as Hollis's transcription of the hearing indicate that the amount was fixed at "a total value of more than twenty five dollars." The detail and specificity of Hardyman's itemization was matched by a lack of specificity and vagueness as to when the offence had occurred: she was accused of stealing these things from the schoolhouse on Poor Man's reserve between 10 June 1891 and 2 April 1892.

Hardyman, described in the documents as the "late school master," had been the schoolteacher on Poor Man's reserve. It appears that he left the reserve in mid-June 1891. It also appears he first learned that any of his things were missing during a visit with a Mr. Gooderham to the home of Peter Harper and his wife in Fort Qu'Appelle:

> [W]hilst visiting there I recognized a tie which I knew I had left in my box at the School. I finished my visit. I said to Mr. Gooderham that that was my tie. Mr. Gooderham went back and called Mr. Harper out. I asked Harper where he got the tie, He told me his wife got it from Margaret Favel. I then saw Mrs. Harper who also gave me some creton [*sic*], part of the curtains I had left and she said she had received the creton from Harriet Favel about Easter 1892.

Margaret asked Hardyman one question in cross-examination, pointing to the weakness in the case against her, particularly the basis of his knowledge of her alleged theft: "Did anybody tell you this?" Hardyman's answer showed that Margaret understood the weakness of his evidence better than he did: "No, this is my own evidence." Margaret's point surely had been that although he may have tendered his own evidence, none of it was based on any personal knowledge he had of her involvement. For this, he would need Mrs. Harper. Or, as it happened, her companion "in the crime," Harriet Favel.

Harriet, the other deponent for the prosecution, was described in the documents as a "treaty half-breed." It is not certain that Harriet was a voluntary witness; she may have been told that she had to give evidence against Margaret. In his letter to Hugh Richardson, Hollis later noted that Harriet was not bound over by recognizance "as she is a treaty half-breed but the Indian agent Keith was notified that she would be wanted [to testify at Margaret's trial] and said she could be produced."

Harriet's evidence was taken with the assistance of an interpreter, although none is named. Hardyman's companion, Mr. Gooderham, is also referred to in Harriet Favel's deposition; she gave evidence that it was he who had sent Margaret and her "at hay time last year" to weed the garden at the school. Harriet claimed that the door to the school was always open, but that she and Margaret had gone in through a window so that no one would see them. Harriet also said that she had been frightened, but that Margaret had not been frightened because, she told Harriet, "she was not stealing." Harriet indicated that she had seen Margaret take something from the school but she did not know what, except for the silver spoon found by the police officer at Margaret's house when he arrested her. She added, "I saw a lot of other stuff but cannot say what it was ... There was about half a gunny sack full of things besides the spoon." Harriet also said that Margaret had given her the cretonne curtain fabric, which she then gave to Mrs. Harper to make a dress. Harriet clearly put the blame on Margaret, which evidently troubled Margaret, as seen in her cross-examination of Harriet. Although Margaret made a "rookie's mistake" by asking open-ended questions in cross-examination, her questions conveyed her distress at Harriet's version of events, and she left her best question for last:

Q Are you sure I gave you this creton [*sic*]?
A Yes I am sure.
Q Are you sure I took much things from there?
A Yes I am sure.
Q Are you sure you see [*sic*] me take the neck tie?
A No but I saw you with it after.

The last deponent for the prosecution was NWMP constable Jones, who had arrested Margaret and searched her house. He said he had found a silver spoon answering the description in the warrant; he said she also gave him two other spoons, which she told him she had received from Harriet Favel. The police officer, Jones, also said that Margaret had told him that Harriet had a bag of stuff, and that Margaret had seen these three spoons, which Harriet had given her when she asked for them. Constable Jones said that of the articles described in the warrant, these were the only ones that he found at Margaret's house.

When given the opportunity, and apparently despite Hollis's efforts to dissuade her from saying anything that could be used against her at her trial, Margaret made a long statement. She acknowledged fully that she had entered the house, with Harriet, on three different occasions. Her forthrightness and detailed description are clearly what impressed and worried the justice of the peace; she told a long story in which she admitted everything:

The reason we went in at the window what [*sic*] that we could not open the door. We tried the door and could not open it. We were both there all the time. We lifted the window. We had a talk at the window first. We were both carrying our babies. And when we went into the school, Harriet went up stairs. I followed without her asking me. We went there three times. The first time were [*sic*] we took nothing but looked at the things. We came down stairs again. Then we into the kitchen [*sic*] and looked at everything. Then we left by the window. Harriet first, that was the time we were asked to weed the garden. And we went and weeded it. After we had done we went home. About two days after we went over again. We planned for us both to go. We went again tried to open the door but could not do so. So we went through the window again. I think I went in first. After we were in the school we both went upstairs again and I saw some papers scattered on the floor. I was looking at the papers and noticed Harriet opening a box. She told me to look through the window I suppose because she was frightened some one would catch us in there. I told her it would not matter if any body caught us in here. Then she took everything that was in the box out. I saw the things there and I saw her taking some things so I took some too. I took a little boy's coat and a little vest and a little cap and a dish cloth. I would never have taken any thing unless I had seen Harriet taking something so I thought I would have something too. I saw her take a pillow case and I saw her take a little cap, red. She took a good deal of stuff but I can't say what it was but some of it was men's underclothing. Then we went downstairs again. And went into the kitchen. There was a little box under the table. I saw her take five little spoons out of that box. She took some more spoons. Then we went out again. Then we went home. Soon after we went there the third time and went in through the window again. Then we went upstairs again. Harriet then said she was frightened. We looked at the things again. She opened all the boxes first. We saw some quilts. I did not take anything that time. We went downstairs then and into the kitchen again. Harriet looked all over there. Then we went out and I did not see her take anything this time. We left through the window and went home. We were nearly caught in there that time. We were in a hurry to get out of the window and I saw Harriet put some thing a hole [*sic*] outside that she took. Then we walked off. We turned back and Harriet went for the things she put in the hole. She took those things and put them under her arm as we were carrying our babies. I can't say what she took that time but it was a parsel [*sic*] It [?] before we went home that is to Fort Qu'Appelle. I wanted two spoons she had and asked her for them. She gave them to me. I kept them out of sight all the time. Before I came home from Harriet's house I saw that quilt there.

> It was spread over Harriet's bed. I can't say she took it from there but I think it was the same quilt we saw there.

After Margaret had made her detailed, self-incriminating statement and the justice of the peace had closed the case, the Indian Agent, who had been watching the case "as a Treaty Half-breed had been implicated," spoke to the justice of the peace, saying that Hardyman had left these things on an Indian reserve, "easily ... under nobody's charge & left all over the [school] house there a most strong temptation." Although the court file is faded and fragile and the text here is difficult to make out, it appears that Mr. Keith, the Indian Agent, intimated to Hollis that the victim, Mr. Hardyman, had left behind his things all over the house, in plain view, untended – "in Indian fashion thrown away"; as such, it was tantamount to an invitation or, in Keith's words, a "temptation" for people to take them.

At the end of the hearing, Hollis ordered Margaret to stand trial and remanded her in custody. On 14 May, he forwarded the Information, depositions, and warrant to the attention of Justice Hugh Richardson in Regina. But he sent more than these documents, even as he acknowledged misgivings about whether it was in order for him to do so. In his cover letter to Richardson, he acted, nervously, on his own sense of justice – one that had been offended by the proceedings against Margaret. It was his "first case of this kind," he wrote in a separate note, inquiring about the allowance of fees for interpreters, as both the accused, Margaret Favel, and the prosecution witness Harriet Favel had said they could not properly understand English.

In his longer letter, with which the committal documents were enclosed, to Richardson, the judge who would preside at Margaret Favel's trial, Hollis offered a lengthy assessment of the merits of the case, including his assessment of the credibility of the deponents, his opinion as to the carelessness (at best) of the informant regarding his property (intimating that Hardyman himself was significantly to blame for his loss), and an account of his own unsuccessful efforts to discourage the prisoner from saying anything lest it incriminate her, as well as of his deep distress since she was far from the most culpable party in the case. Hollis did not go so far as to say that the prosecution of Margaret Favel was a travesty of justice, but to a reader one hundred years later, the inference is inescapable.

Hollis was mindful of his place and tried not to pronounce – "I could not judge on the case" – but he could not restrain himself and continued: "[I]t seemed tolerably clear to me that the worst offender was the woman not accused and that is my reason for writing this to you in order that this woman may have the earliest possible opportunity of your considering her case." Finally, Hollis enclosed a note from a medical doctor, dated 14 May, indicating that Mrs. Harper, the other witness who had been summoned to appear, was suffering from congestion of the lungs and was not fit to leave her house at present.

On 19 May 1892, Margaret Favel was indicted by the Crown prosecutor, William Cayley Hamilton of Regina, charged with having stolen a more modest list of items: "four silver spoons and forks, one neck tie, two yards creton, one pillow case and one cap, the property of Lucius F. Hardyman." In the end, she pleaded guilty to stealing one spoon and her sentence was suspended.

Margaret may have learned an important lesson about the way white men regarded their property. It was theirs to do with as they saw fit, and to reclaim at will, even after weeks and months of neglect and disinterest. It may well have seemed that Mr. Hardyman had abandoned his things and had no further use for them, and that they were wasted in the messy, unused schoolhouse. It certainly seems that he had left them untended for almost a year, in a place to where he may or may not have intended to return. Perhaps the items were important to him, but one can well imagine that it would be difficult for a woman who doubtless had little in the way of material comforts or "new" clothes for her baby to understand why a white man – for whose people property seemed to be "sacred" – would treat in this way belongings that he wanted to keep.

And if that was Margaret's view, it may well have been shared by Hollis and even Keith; certainly in the end she pleaded guilty to stealing one small item, a silver spoon. Margaret had not been represented by counsel but she had had an advocate. One wonders whether Margaret, Harriet, and their babies ever walked together again.

Marie Martin Daniel's Windblown Frock

One can well imagine the distress experienced by Robert Williams, secretary of the Central Assiniboia Agricultural Association, when a severe summer storm blew through Fort Qu'Appelle on 2 August 1900. On this very day, the Agricultural Association was holding its annual summer Agricultural Show and Competition. Many local people had entered items, which were on display in a number of tents. Helena L. Symons, for instance, had on exhibit a photograph frame, among other articles. And then the storm struck. Tents were blown down and exhibits scattered by the wind, an always present force of nature on the Plains, powerful and unrelenting in a storm, and often accompanied by its fearsome companions, destruction and pandemonium. Many exhibitors lost to the wind the things they had entered in the show, such as hats, frocks, and blouses.

Williams said he and the association directors did their best to retrieve the windstrewn exhibits; he himself made a public announcement from the judges' stand, presumably in English, "that articles lost or found should be made known to us. I also had a notice inserted in the *Vidette.*" Several exhibitors subsequently made applications for missing items, some of which had been found and returned.

Later that month, Constable Henry Hamilton Crigan of the NWMP received a complaint from Williams, as a result of which he visited two homes at File Hills (Reserve). He found some articles that had been exhibits, specifically a frock and blouse, at Joseph Daniel's home. He also found three ladies' hats at the home of "an Indian named Bellegarde" at File Hills. He was told by Bellegarde's daughter that she had purchased one of the hats from Marie Martin Daniel, and that Marie Martin had given her two others. In his deposition at the hearing into the charge before Justice of the Peace Guernsey, Crigan said that Marie Martin Daniel had stated that "she picked the articles up on the show ground and took them home."[48]

In Williams's Information and complaint of 24 August, Marie Martin Daniel was charged with stealing from the Exhibition Ground three ladies' hats, one photo frame, one pink frock, and one flannelette blouse, the property of exhibitors. Marie Martin Daniel is not identified in the court documents as an Aboriginal woman, but Joseph Martin was sworn to interpret the 25 August hearing at Fort Qu'Appelle into the charge against her, presumably into Cree. She is reported to have waived the reading of the depositions against her, and when asked by the justice of the peace whether she had anything to say in answer to the charge, she said simply, and probably honestly (when silence might have served her better), "I was told by ladies to take the hats as they were no use that is all I have to say."

She was committed for trial by Guernsey, and on 28 August she was indicted by T.C. Johnstone on the charge of theft. She entered a plea of not guilty and was released on bail with two sureties, Joseph Daniel and Alexander Laroque, in the amount of $100. Her trial was set for the November sittings of the North-West Territories Supreme Court at Fort Qu'Appelle, and it took place on 9 November 1900. No record of the evidence taken appears in the court file, but she was convicted by Judge

Richardson, notwithstanding the weaknesses in the Crown's case concerning both the *actus reus* and *mens rea* of the offence, and possibly the evidentiary basis itself.

But for the disruption of the exhibition by an act of nature, and the inability of the white folk to catch the wind, Marie Martin Daniel would never have found herself arrested and prosecuted. One can suppose that for items carried farther afield by the prairie storm, others who found things left by the wind were spared the indignity of criminal prosecution. As for Marie Martin Daniel, any reasonable doubt the court should have entertained as to her formal criminal liability was reflected in her sentence to patriarchal control and supervision. Her sentence was deferred, "convict's husband entering into a recognizance of $50.00 to produce her for sentence when and if required to do so."

Betsy Horsefall's Lost Horse

Many First Nations and Aboriginal men faced criminal charges alleging horse theft. One woman stood alone among them. Betsy Horsefall of George Gordon's band in the Touchwood Hills was one of only seven First Nations and Aboriginal women to appear as an accused person and prisoner before Hugh Richardson during his time on the territorial bench.[49] Unlike most of the others, she did not plead guilty or find herself convicted.

Betsy Horsefall was a First Nations woman of the Touchwood people, whose Chief Ka-ne-on-us-ka-tew (also known as George Gordon) signed Treaty 4 in 1874 on behalf of his followers, a band of Cree and Saulteaux people. Following Treaty 4, George Gordon accepted a reserve in the Little Touchwood Hills. Ten years after the signing of Treaty 4, German immigrants arrived in the neighbouring Last Mountain Hills in the southern North-West Territories. A decade later, on 1 September 1894, Wilhelm Schwandt, a farmer from the Strassburg district[50] in the Last Mountain Hills, accused Betsy Horsefall and her brother, Benjamin Gordon, of stealing a bay mare pony that belonged to him.[51] Betsy Horsefall and her brother were arrested by an NWMP corporal on 2 September 1894 and brought before Justice of the Peace Joseph Hollis for a hearing into the charge; they were committed for trial and remanded in custody.

One potential problem for the trial court should have been that Wilhelm Schwandt (or William, as he was named in the depositions before the justice of the peace) and Betsy Horsefall each claimed ownership of this pony. And, a century before postmodern thinking seized intellectual imaginations in academe, it appears that these apparently irreconcilable claims were both true. Betsy owned the pony. In the Statement of the Accused that she was entitled to make at the end of the hearing before the justice of the peace, she said (possibly through an interpreter, although none is indicated in Hollis's notes):

> I bought the mare from C. Favel [likely Charles Favel, also of the Touchwood Hills] when she was two years old for a cow. After having her for two winters I lost her and she stayed away for one winter. I saw her in the spring after the winter was over. My Father and three others of us died just then so I did not look for the pony.

The pony had not simply stayed away, however. One of the legal innovations brought by the new governance structure of Betsy's peoples' land was a Territorial Ordinance concerning the impounding and sale of stray animals.[52] Thus it was that in the summer of 1894 Schwandt could claim that he owned Betsy's pony.

Schwandt deposed that he had bought the pony in August 1893 from William Doege, the poundkeeper of Strassburg. The court file contains no particulars of how or when the pony came into the possession of the poundkeeper.[53] Different processes were to be followed if the owner of the trespasser (animal) was not known, depending on the kind and age of animal. If the poundkeeper did not know who owned the pony, he was required to post a notice "in three of the most public places in the pound district" and also, if practicable, in the nearest territorial newspaper, giving a full description of the animal.[54] This notice was to be posted for twenty days (in the case of a horse older than two years) or six days (if the horse was younger than two years). If no owner was found, the poundkeeper was authorized to advertise for ten days the sale of the animal by public auction.[55]

Thus, if the poundkeeper deemed this pony's age to be over two years, the notice and advertising period would have been thirty days. In this case, after the necessary advertising, Schwandt deposed that he had paid the poundkeeper $10 for the horse. In his deposition, he estimated that the value of this would be now, a year later, $20. The pony had strayed from his sons about ten months later, when they were herding her and presumably other animals.[56]

Somehow (and again the file is silent), the pony came into the possession of Benjamin Gordon. In August 1894, Alec Gordon, brother of Betsy Horsefall and Benjamin Gordon, had a conversation with the poundkeeper,

Doege, in Strassburg. The depositions of Doege and Alec Gordon were reasonably consistent. The poundkeeper deposed that Alec told him that the bay mare pony was at his brother's place. Doege also suggested before the justice of the peace that Alec had said that he would encourage his siblings to give up the pony. The other evidence as to the second "finding" of the pony came from Schwandt and his son, each of whom deposed that two months after the pony strayed from them, they saw her hitched to a cart driven by an old woman at Benjamin Gordon's place, now bearing Benjamin Gordon's brand, "BG." The Gordon family refused to give her up, despite the admonitions of the poundkeeper and the Indian farm instructor. Before the justice of the peace, this pony was identified by the Schwandts as the pony that the elder Schwandt had bought from the poundkeeper in late summer 1893.

Betsy and Benjamin spent six days in jail awaiting trial. They appeared in court on 8 September without legal counsel, aided by a court interpreter (apparently for Betsy), and entered pleas of not guilty before Judge Richardson. The Crown prosecutor, David Lynch Scott, indicated that he was not ready for trial.[57] He agreed to the prisoners' being released, and so they were, on their recognizance that they would appear again to answer the charge when called upon. Perhaps the Crown prosecutor considered the formidable challenges he faced in establishing that the procedural requisites of the *Stray Animals Ordinance* had been followed in order to have sufficient evidence to prove that Schwandt's acquisition of the pony superseded the prior ownership of Betsy Horsefall. Perhaps he thought it might not be possible to convict Betsy of anything, given the evidence deposed before the justice of the peace – that she lacked the requisite mental element for the offence of theft. Perhaps he thought the pony was in fact still hers and that the physical element of the offence could not be established. Or perhaps he just needed more time to prepare his case. Thereafter the court record is silent, the criminal matter left in abeyance.

Historical research based on sparse lower-court documents requires frequent if cautious inference, interpretation, and some imagination.[58] In this case, one can only imagine Betsy Horsefall's reaction when she was charged with stealing a horse she believed to be hers. And there were the unanswerable questions: What happened to Betsy's pony? What efforts, if any, had the Strassburg poundkeeper made – other than to post a notice in English in the district, and possibly in the territorial newspaper, the Regina *Leader* – to find the owner of this Indian pony? What comfort or lesson was Betsy expected to derive from the publication of the notice, in a language she undoubtedly did not read and likely did not speak, in a newspaper to which she also likely did not have access? What assistance, if any, did the Indian Department officials offer her to find or retrieve her horse, or to protect her when the dispute arose? Why was she charged at all, when the evidence, such as it was, appeared to point to Benjamin? Because she said the horse was hers? What form of gratitude was she expected to feel or express when she was released from jail and allowed to return home, possibly without her pony? And, finally, what light, if any, does her small, legally unresolved criminal case shed on the relationship between nineteenth-century criminal law and Aboriginal women on the Canadian Plains?

In Betsy Horsefall's case, one can see the importance of "low law" and of the critical engagement with criminalization and the construction of criminal law as a central instrument of subordination. The form of law most directly implicated in Betsy Horsefall's criminal prosecution was not criminal law but rather a regulatory ordinance – indeed, she was never convicted of a criminal offence. The legal transformation of the land she and her people called home brought with it the power to legally transform ownership of one's property through a legal fiction that a stray horse belonged to no one. It permitted a new authority, the poundkeeper – for the unknowing and involuntary – to seize a horse, impound it, notify the white settlers of the fact of its impoundment, and then sell it and thereby confer ownership on someone other than the original owner. The ordinance of the North-West Territories Council that created the office of poundkeeper and authorized, and thus rendered legal, this activity – this low law, this low level of legislation – more than any other had the greatest impact in this instance on a hitherto unknown but decidedly unbowed First Nations woman named Betsy Horsefall.

Conclusion

Between 1876 and 1903, only six Aboriginal women and one girl (Julia Coté, who ran away from the industrial school) appeared as accused persons and prisoners before Hugh Richardson, the longest-serving and most experienced magistrate and judge in the North-West Territories. These seven represent about 1 percent of all accused persons (589) and 5 percent of all Aboriginal accused persons (136) who appeared in Richardson's courts during this period. They are not sexualized women; their "crimes," such as they were, reflected the social, material, and economic realities of their hard everyday lives. Most were charged with forms of theft, mostly involving small items or small amounts of money. Betsy Horsefall was charged with horse theft, a serious offence. Scholastique Cardinal was charged with murder and concealment of birth in the death of her newborn infant. The court records of these criminal prosecutions indicate that four were convicted and received deferred or suspended sentences; there is no disposition indicated in two cases, and in Betsy Horsefall's case the prosecution did not proceed in the end.

Although the voices of Scholastique and Bone Child are not heard, and even Betsy's voice is muted, we can see that Caroline Gouin and Margaret Favel were not so intimidated by the legal process or by their status as prisoners that they did not participate. Rather, they challenged their accusers, and in their challenges can be seen very clear theories of their own defences. And even without benefit of counsel, they achieved some measure of success. There is no record that Caroline was ever convicted of the theft of Mr. McDougall's coins, and Margaret Favel – accused of stealing a veritable litany of a schoolteacher's personal property – in the end was convicted of stealing one solitary silver spoon.

In their atypical presence as accused persons, these women paradoxically serve as a reminder that the vast majority of Aboriginal people on the Plains did not find themselves accused in the criminal court. The six women's stories also advance this book's larger story, however: Betsy Horsefall's lost horse and the transformation of property relations and the importance of low law; Scholastique Cardinal's jury of matrons, and the ongoing role of the community in the new legal order; Margaret Favel on white man's property, and Marie Martin Daniel on the importance of the Plain; Caroline Gouin's industry and employment, and her agency and advocacy in court; and, not least, the casually enforced anonymity of the woman alleged to have stolen curtains and bells from a bachelor's shack. Their stories are not a side story, and their numbers serve to remind us that the criminal law was not necessarily the first or most important means of subjugating the First Nations of the Plains.

These women's stories thus demonstrate the larger context and new relations that had arrived: the sanctity of white men's property, new laws that changed how property ownership could be asserted, and new, coercive forms of educating and transforming First Nations children into Indian children. Not every woman was convicted of a criminal offence, but it was not necessary to convict or criminalize each of these women to ensure that this message was delivered.

Conclusion

Criminal law as it was dispensed in ordinary lower courts, such as those of the Fort Qu'Appelle justices of the peace and Hugh Richardson's trial courts, has been overlooked by legal historians interested in the relationship and experience of First Nations people with Canadian law. As this book has shown, and as others have noted, the numbers of Aboriginal accused persons actually prosecuted were not enormous, but they were significant. Unlike many prosecuted for potlatch offences under the *Indian Act,* many Plains First Nations people who experienced actual criminal prosecution appeared in court without counsel or fanfare, other than the occasional report in one of the North-West Territories newspapers. This book has demonstrated that a focus on "low-profile" cases in a lower criminal trial court enables one to develop a fuller understanding of the dimensions and complexity of that relationship and those experiences.

Always mindful of the urgency of today's context, I have looked back to a period when the relationship between the Canadian state and the First Nations was being forged on the ground in the Canadian Plains. The violence and insult of a jail sentence casually imposed by a lay justice of the peace in Fort Qu'Appelle in 1901 on Piapot, then the most senior political and spiritual leader of the Plains Cree, foreshadowed what would follow in the new century – a century that neither promised nor delivered material and cultural well-being, nor hope for them, to his people. This book ends as the twentieth century opened and the two Prairie provinces of Alberta and Saskatchewan were created. The poverty and inordinate hardship that continues to define the lives of the First Nations in Canada is a matter of public record and shame for Canada. If one considers the lives and fate of the apprehended children of the "Sixties Scoop"[1] and the missing Aboriginal women and girls lost to violence and condemned through racist indifference, the legacy and ongoing acts and omissions of the Canadian state ought to impel Canadians to demand redress for their myriad injustices and losses.

In response to the assessment of historians who characterize the historical experience of Aboriginal peoples as one of being criminalized, I have argued that it is essential both to examine the legal forms that are seen to give rise to this characterization and to historicize the processes. While the label of criminalization has been deployed in the historiography to characterize the *Indian Act* offences, the process of actual criminalization has been neglected. One striking if neglected example of such "criminalization" is to be found in the *Indian Act* offence of incitement of Indians to violence, with which Mequanis (The Quill or The Feather) was charged in 1889, but for which he was neither convicted nor tried. When Mequanis was brought to court, he was charged with an offence under the *Indian Act;* three years later, this form of incitement of Indians actually became a criminal offence when it was added for the first time to Canada's first *Criminal Code.*[2]

This neglect of actual criminal law is of great consequence when one considers the legal transformation that occurred over a scant thirty years. Prior to 1870, *inter se* offences involving Aboriginal peoples on the Plains were not dealt with by Anglo-Canadian legal processes. By 1899, a Blood man was convicted of polygamy for his marriage to two women according to the custom of his people.[3] In the period between, many forms of customary and/or routine activity were prosecuted as criminal offences. Through the application of Canadian criminal law, Aboriginal people found themselves in criminal court for conduct ranging from running away from the industrial school, neglecting to read the notices posted by the poundkeeper, failing to return a pony to its owner, killing livestock for food, making off with horses, crossing international boundaries with stolen horses, and taking small pieces of silverware from an apparently abandoned house, to cite but a few from the previous chapters.

This book reinserts criminal law and the specificity of the criminal law as a legal form into the historiography of criminalization and criminal law's relationship with the First Nations. The records examined here shed more light on the role and contribution of the criminal law to the subordination of Aboriginal people in Western Canada during the period, and show that it is but one of many legal forms and state practices deployed in the late nineteenth century to transform the lives and living conditions of the First Nations of the Plains.

I have argued here that the *Indian Act* should not be understood as criminal law. This is not to deny that the provisions regulating or prohibiting some forms of dances created offences with punishment, including custodial sentences, upon conviction. But if one collapses the *Indian Act* into criminal law, one also renders less visible two important developments: first, the increasingly coercive nature of the *Indian Act,* and second, the correspondingly greater power and authority of Indian Agents.[4] Of equal importance, the extension of actual criminal law over aspects of social and economic life is obscured.[5]

Criminalization has become a too readily asserted label affixed to the wrong areas of law, ignores the actual sites of criminalization, and simultaneously neglects the specificity of the transformations of arguably the most fundamental area of legislation affecting Aboriginal peoples, the *Indian Act,* as well as its relationship to criminal law. The offences and prosecutions under the *Indian Act* did not criminalize the First Nations; rather, they "Indianized" the First Nations. They were prosecuted as "Indians" – not as criminals – for violating the *Indian Act,* for not conforming to the new forms of relations and behaviour required of Indians by the legislation.

The use of the criminal law to punish and discipline the people of the Plains First Nations, to constrain their traditional practices and way of life, is seen throughout this book. In addition, the cases in the court records suggest something beyond the role and rule of law: the depth of the material deprivation of the people themselves is revealed, even if it does not speak for itself in the court records. Many cases, however, from the lost daughters of Peaychew in 1878 and of Mr. and Mrs. Bokas in 1901, demonstrate that the criminal law was also invoked by Aboriginal people for help and protection and for vindication of their positions.

Whether one characterizes the alleged activity of Aboriginal accused persons found in the court records as resistance to government policies and practices or as criminalization of aspects of everyday life, or both, one thing is clear from the court records: Aboriginal accused persons found themselves in a criminal court that emerged almost from nowhere in 1876.

These low-law criminal cases from the nineteenth-century Plains demonstrate the complexity of the relations and processes: from Poundmaker's horse race to Peaychew's lost child; from Buffalo Calf's brother-in-law who turned him in, to Is-pinik-hah-kee-toot, who was weary of his brother-in-law's coming to camp and making off with his deceased father's horses; from O-cha-nah-kis, who complained successfully about the Mountie who stole money from her after paying for sexual connection, to Lila Bokas's parents, who felt they had a claim on the services and support of a white man and his law to help them reclaim their daughter from Ce Tan; and from John Eye, who charged a white man with assault after he was struck for refusing to go to the water, to all the leaders – Beardy, Lean Man, Mosquito, Strike Him on the Back, Grizzly Bear's Head, Piapot – who turned to the law or who found themselves ensnared when they attempted to defend their people. Each case comprises and represents complex relationships.

Many findings in this book challenge conventional wisdom and explanations; they should force a re-examination of many assumptions. This work has rendered visible the experiences and relations of many Aboriginal people to the criminal law in the period that have not been told before, but much work remains to be done.

What have I found from the territorial court records? I come away and leave you with two fragmentary images. The first is an image of flexibility, resourcefulness, and expectations of good faith on the part of the First Nations people who turned to the law or who found themselves there unwillingly. For some, Richardson's court was one possible avenue of redress for injuries and wrongs. Their good faith was not always rewarded, but many appear to have obtained the results they were seeking. They were experiencing relations of profound inequality, and I have attempted to illustrate the relational nature of this inequality. The contradictory expressions of these relations merit – indeed, require – identification, analysis, and understanding.

Perhaps more than any other case, Poundmaker's disputed horse race also illustrates the complex and multi-layered nature of social relations in Battleford in 1878: Poundmaker and his brother Yellow Earth Blanket (Yellow Mud Blanket) were involved in horse races with John Ballendine and Goodwin Marchand. The course of the second race with Ballendine was agreed upon; a wager was struck and sealed with a handshake. The court file indicates that a number of men, including Indians, police officers, and cooks, had placed bets on the race. When Poundmaker's horse lost the race, seemingly through the other man's dishonesty, several members of the Battleford community appear to have stepped in to lend him support, including the stipendiary magistrate. The court file does not suggest great support for Ballendine's position while providing some evidence of community support for Poundmaker. The Cree, Métis, North-West Mounted

Police, and a few prominent individuals of Battleford – all men, to be sure – were clearly animated by the race and its aftermath, not least perhaps because the gentlemen's agreement had not been kept and a fair race had not been run.

How are we to interpret the presence of Aboriginal informants and complainants in the court files? I reject the suggestion that, in navigating and negotiating their way or invoking the criminal process, Aboriginal peoples pursued private interests or brokered their own oppression. I have shown that the court records contain a desire for justice and expressions of hope, as well as deprivation, disappointment, misery, and bitterness. And, of course, there are cases in which Aboriginal witnesses attempted, against the odds of a courtroom setting and court interpreters, to make their values, customs, and way of life understood to the white men sitting in judgment of their fellow Cree, Assiniboines, and Saulteaux. An ability to identify, problematize, and analyze human experience, agency, and resistance is of critical importance in socio-legal scholarship, but it is not an easy and uncontested undertaking. To the extent that such agency is juxtaposed with institutional oppression, repression, and suppression, it must be recast. The stories from the territorial criminal court allow – indeed, require – this recasting.

The lower-court records suggest that Aboriginal people turned to criminal law, used it and influenced it when they could, ran from it when they had to, and paid a price when they were caught. Sometimes they experienced a measure of vindication. They were simultaneously victims, actors, informants, interpreters, accused, police guides, and complainants, but in my view, the totality of their involvement in the criminal law (including its lowest courts) needs to be considered. Oppressive relations are still relations. They participated in the criminal law, violated it, turned to it, and resisted it – but it cannot simply be said that the peoples of the Plains oiled the wheels of their own oppression.

The second image, shaped by the first and inspired by E.P. Thompson,[6] suggests the mediating role of (criminal) law in social relations – a legal form that occasionally inhibited the powerful in the interest and at the behest of the less powerful. This is not the dominant image of the relationship between First Nations people and the criminal law, but it may be that the criminal law, in contrast to the *Indian Act,* was one area of law in which First Nations people experienced legal subjectivity and a measure of formal equality in vastly unequal circumstances.

First Nations people did not reacquire self-determination through the rule of law dispensed in the nineteenth-century North-West Territories criminal court. The court records suggest, however, that the role of the criminal law was more complex and contradictory than the images most often associated with it, then and now. In the midst of a transformative, devastating period in the lives of the Plains First Nations, the criminal court has emerged as one of the few sites in the new order that swept over their land in which their voices can be found, and sometimes even heard.

Afterword

A Methodological Note on Sources and Data

Interpreting the Interpreted: Lower-Court Records

Historians who have studied lower-court records and the relationship between indigenous people and criminal law in other colonial contexts have identified interesting, counterintuitive, and paradoxical experiences, and they make some bold claims. For instance, Kathleen Bragdon, writing of seventeenth- and eighteenth-century crime among Indians in Massachusetts, argues that these court records "provide a more intimate and less biased view of Indian life ... than is afforded by other sources. Through them, the Indian emerges with his faults unmagnified by polemic and his actions often vindicated."[1] Writing of another, more recent colonial context, that of colonial Zimbabwe in the 1940s and 1950s, Koni Benson and Joyce Chudya argue that "the [court] records provide us with a rare opportunity to hear African women speaking about their lived experiences."[2] Alan Booth found that young women in twentieth-century colonial Swaziland turned to colonial law courts in preference to traditional tribal courts in their efforts to avoid forced marriage; Booth also found that while young women experienced a measure of success in the colonial courts, older married women were less successful in that forum in their complaints of abusive husbands.[3] Thus, although court records may be quintessential "official" state records, they have been found to contain more voices than simply those of official observers, recorders, and reporters.

The Richardson Court Records

The data for this study are derived largely from two sets of criminal court records:[4] Hugh Richardson's records as stipendiary magistrate, 1876-86 (comprising most of "The Richardson Papers" held by the Saskatchewan Archives Board in Regina),[5] as well as his court records from the Supreme Court of the North-West Territories, from 1887 until his retirement in 1903.[6] These data are supplemented by a number of other archival records, including justice of the peace records (papers and returns),[7] Treaty Annuity Paylists for Treaty 4 and Treaty 6 in the period, census records, prison registers, and other sources discussed below.

Between 1876 and 1883, the court records principally involve criminal prosecutions that arose in and around the settlements and forts in the District of Saskatchewan; after Richardson's move to Regina in 1883, the files derive principally from Regina, Qu'Appelle, Moose Jaw, and surrounding areas. In the early period, when the population of the North-West Territories was overwhelmingly Aboriginal, Aboriginals nonetheless appear as accused persons in significantly smaller numbers. Most accused persons were held in custody in the jail in the police barracks and thus appeared in court as prisoners. Most criminal prosecutions (as opposed to liquor violation prosecutions) were commenced by informants who were private individuals, not North-West Mounted Police officers swearing on information and belief. Most informants knew by name the individual they alleged had committed the offence. It appears that most informants and accused persons had a social or legal relationship prior to and/or giving rise to the matter before the court.

Most property-related offences involved forms of larceny of "subsistence goods" (flour, sugar, bacon, tea, matches, trousers, socks, vests, as well as livestock and horses), but some involved theft of ribbon, watches, buttons, and other readily carried and concealed objects. The major victims of property offences were the major holders of property, the Crown and the Hudson's Bay Company.

While each court record contains, for the most part, most of the requisite legal forms and documents,[8] the language is more informal than formal from these hearings. The depositions appear as first-person accounts, as uninterrupted narratives, but of course they were the product of examination (perhaps by an NWMP officer or a private prosecutor) and some cross-examination. In many of the records, the depositions were taken through Cree and Sioux interpreters, some of whom appear to have been sworn, while others were not. In virtually all the depositions taken from Aboriginal witnesses, an "X" appears in place of a signature.

The records after 1886 from the North-West Territories Supreme Court are not much different in form or content. The Court appears to have acquired more institutional support, and Judge Richardson's handwritten notes, for instance, appear less frequently. The Court acquired a proper court clerk (Dixie Watson),[9] and a Crown prosecutor (David Lynch Scott, later T.C. Johnstone and John Secord) appears more frequently, as do defence counsel (most often T.C. Johnstone in the earlier period, Norman MacKenzie later on). In these records, one finds more typed documents, including transcripts, and more counsel. One finds a bit more process in these records, as one now finds formal indictments signed by the Crown prosecutor in the files.

The "Court Records and Court Reports" of the NWMP and Territorial Press

The court records are admittedly less than exhaustive in their contents and particulars. When one turns to the press reports, supplementary and occasionally fuller and different accounts may be found in the *Saskatchewan Herald* (Battleford) (1878-83) and in the Regina *Leader* (1883-1903). For the most part, with few exceptions, both newspapers contain sparse, cryptic but no less judgmental accounts of the criminal court proceedings. The few exceptions may be found in the "big" or notorious trials (such as the 1885 Rebellion/Resistance trials, The Swift Runner's murder trial and execution in 1879, and Constable Henry Elliott's 1878 trial in Battleford following his elopement with the magistrate's daughter).

The *Herald,* in particular, appeared quicker to proceed to judgment prior to trial, and to offer "insider" information or interpretation of the facts that do not appear in the court records. The *Herald* displayed particular animus toward "troublesome" First Nations leaders such as Big Bear and Beardy, as seen in Chapter 2.

In the Regina *Leader,* reports of the criminal court tended to be snippets, surrounded by items of local interest: comings and goings, picnics, dances, hunting trips, and the like, on the paper's "Town and Country" page. The barest of particulars, either by way of occasional hint of scandal or editorial disapproval, is offered, as in the case of the stepfather who was thought to be the father of his stepdaughter's dead newborn infant; even in this case, the *Leader* did not report on the trial of either the young woman (for concealment of birth) or of the stepfather (for unlawfully disposing of the body of the dead child).[10]

Local and political histories of the region also offer some further evidence of and insight into the social dimensions and transformation in the region, notably the changing demographic composition of the population and the emerging tensions with respect to governance.[11] The biographies, reminiscences, and stories of First Nations people and their leaders, together with ethnographic studies and social histories, provide perspectives and insights that are drawn from their experiences of law and the Canadian state.[12]

The Annual Returns of the North-West Mounted Police

Writing in 1986, Louis Knafla lamented the "haphazard affair" of Western Canadian legal history, dominated by the NWMP and the Riel Rebellions as well as the lack of a critical context and focus for much of what had been written.[13] Some redress of this preoccupation has emerged in the two decades since Knafla's observation, with legal and socio-legal historians addressing, *inter alia,* the particular form of legal colonialism experienced by the Aboriginal peoples, the legacy of colonialism and racism, and the development of the legal profession in Western Canada.[14]

The NWMP continues to loom large in Western Canadian legal history, however. Indeed, it is difficult, if not impossible, to examine the operation of the criminal law and courts in Western Canada without considering the significant role played by the NWMP, especially its officers who were justices of the peace, and its commissioner, James Farquharson Macleod, who was stipendiary magistrate and later judge of the Supreme Court of the North-West Territories. Historians have continued to turn to the records and reports of the NWMP.

For instance, in their recent study of the relationship of Native peoples with, and their integration into, criminal justice in the North-West Territories, R.C. Macleod and Heather Rollason draw heavily on NWMP records and conclude that of 1,355 cases/accused persons in the records, 242 were Native persons (18 percent), and that the conviction rate for Native defendants was 55 percent (as opposed to 62 percent for non-Native accused).[15]

Macleod and Rollason also conclude that Canadian authorities proceeded with caution in the imposition of criminal law on the Native population of the Prairies; importantly, they argue that with the exception of livestock-related offences, Native people were under-represented in criminal prosecutions and were generally treated more leniently when convicted.[16] While they do not suggest that Native peoples "perceived the courts as other than a repressive institution,"[17] they do observe in closing: "There is quite a lot evidence that the Natives adopted an instrumental approach to the law, experimenting with it and using it where it seemed useful."[18]

Macleod and Rollason's research on the NWMP returns, coupled with their more recent work on newspaper coverage in the Territories of criminal trials,[19] provides a broad outline and overview of who appeared in the territorial courts, how the press reported on their cases, and, in particular, how Aboriginal offenders were treated, perceived, and perceived to be treated. The NWMP returns provide a detailed overview of the records of proceedings, of accused, charges, dispositions, and so on. Macleod and Rollason do not tell us, however, other than through the newspaper accounts, what happened in the courtrooms, who the complainants and witnesses were, who required interpreters, who appeared as an informant in one year and as an accused in the next. The significance of the NWMP records and their findings cannot be overstated, but there are important aspects of the form and practice of criminal justice in the North-West Territories that are not to be found in the police returns. This study is informed by and builds upon their work, but looks at other sets of records that were created and kept for another purpose. Also, the depositions and evidence in those records illustrate somewhat different stories, requiring somewhat different analytical and methodological tools.

Conclusion

Court records offer rich but at the same time limited data, depending upon the questions that are asked of them and the hypotheses to be tested. They are quintessential "official" documents. Even in handwritten form, the warrants they contain – warrants for search, warrants for arrest, warrants of committal for trial, warrants of committal following conviction – all gave the bearers thereof the legal authority to search premises, arrest suspects and hold them in custody pending their trial or after their conviction, and of course to execute, in the case of a capital offence.

One must also be mindful of the partial nature of the knowledge that can be gleaned from a court record. An accused person found in the court

FIGURE A.1 Young First Nations soldiers from the File Hills, photographed in Regina in 1915. With them are Mequanis (Feather), seated in the second row, second from left, and Shave Tail, seated directly in front of him, on the floor in the front row. The white man in the middle is W.M. Graham, former Indian Agent for the File Hills Agency, and later Indian Commissioner for the Prairie Provinces. | Saskatchewan Archives Board, R-B582.

records may or may not be etched and defined for life by that experience in the criminal court. Lean Man and Peaychew were long listed as "rebels" in the Treaty Annuity Paylists in the years after 1885, but, judging from the photographs taken in the early years of the twentieth century, Sandfly, Shave Tail, and Mequanis went on with their lives after their appearances in court. Indeed, Mequanis appears to have been an eminent elder of the File Hills First Nations people, and he and Shave Tail both appear in a studio photograph with a prominent government official in 1915 that documented young First Nations soldiers going off to war (see Figure A.1).

Notes

Introduction: One Warrior's Legal History

1 Library and Archives Canada [LAC], RG 10, reel C-7145, vol. 9412, Treaty Annuity Paylists for Treaties 4, 6, and 7 (1877), Treaty 6, Red Pheasant's Band, 294.

2 *Saskatchewan Herald* (12 October 1885) 2 at cols. 3 and 4. See also "Report of the Commissioner of the North-West Mounted Police, 1884," reprinted in Royal Canadian Mounted Police, *Settlers and Rebels: Being the Official Reports to Parliament of the Activities of the Royal* [*sic*] *North-West Mounted Police Force from 1882-1885 by the Commissioners of the Royal* [*sic*] *North-West Mounted Police,* facsimile reprint (Toronto: Coles Publishing, 1973; original ed. Ottawa: Maclean, Roger, 1882-85), Appendix O; Sandra Elizabeth Bingaman, *The North-West Rebellion Trials, 1885* (MA Thesis, University of Saskatchewan [Regina], 1971) [unpublished] at 209 [Bingaman, *Rebellion Trials*]; Blair Stonechild and W.A. Waiser, *Loyal till Death: Indians and the North-West Rebellion* (Saskatoon: Fifth House, 1997) at 263. As with many First Nations persons whose names are found in the court records, other spellings of his name appear in other court and official records and publications. His name is spelled three different ways in the seven-page file 103 concerning his brother-in-law, Robert Saunders, found in Saskatchewan Archives Board, Department of the Attorney General, Regina Judicial Centre: Court Records First Series, 1876-86, files 1-282 [hereinafter SAB AG CR-Regina 1st series, 1876-86]. He appears as *Pee-Yah-Chew* in the Treaty Annuity Paylist (1877) for Red Pheasant's Band (LAC, RG 10, reel C-7145, vol. 9412, Treaty Annuity Paylists for Treaties 4, 6, and 7); *Peachew, Peeyachow* (in the *Saskatchewan Herald*); *Pee-yah-sew, Pe-a-chu,* and *Pee-ah-chew* in SAB AG CR-Regina, 1st series, 1876-86, files 103 and 152; *Pyechiw* (Prisoner 128) in his 7 November 1885 entry in the Manitoba Penitentiary Admitance [*sic*] Register (LAC, RG 73, W87-88/365, Microfilm reel T-11095, vol. 24 [MIKAN no. 134308]); and as *Peaychew* in Stonechild and Waiser at 133, 139. I have elected to use the spelling used by Stonechild and Waiser. I also understand that the family name of his descendants is *Peyachew.*

In recent years, there has been a movement to rename the 1885 North-West Rebellion as the "North-West Resistance"; the library of the University of Saskatchewan maintains a website database devoted to the Northwest Resistance ("Northwest Resistance 1885," http://library2.usask.ca/). Neal McLeod, "Rethinking Treaty 6 in the Spirit of Mistahi Maskwa (Big Bear)" (1999) 19 Canadian Journal of Native Studies 69 at 85 [McLeod, "Rethinking Treaty 6"], writes that the Cree term for the North-West Rebellion is *ê-mâyi-kamikahk* ("where it went wrong"). The Cree phrase captures quite well the nature of the events of 1885, and although I am drawn to it, I have elected, as a non-Cree speaker, to use most often the phrase "the events of 1885," which captures for me all the fighting that was related as well as unrelated to Riel, as well as the legal aftermath. Histories of the events of 1885 include George F.G. Stanley, *The Birth of Western Canada: A History of the Riel Rebellions* (Toronto: University of Toronto Press, 1970); Bob Beal and Rod Macleod, *Prairie Fire: The 1885 North-West Rebellion* (Edmonton: Hurtig Publishers, 1984); Stonechild and Waiser, *ibid.* I am mindful that these authors all employ the discourse of "rebellion."

Many Aboriginal leaders prosecuted in the aftermath of the events of 1885, other than Louis Riel, were charged with the offence of treason-felony. This offence, created by the *Treason Felony Act, 1848,* 11 & 12 Vict., c. 12, provided that conduct that was otherwise treason could be treated as a felony. While the 1848 *Act* did not prevent recourse to the 1351 *Statute of Treasons,* a prosecution under the former avoided the procedural requirements and associated difficulties related to a trial for treason and also the mandatory death sentence upon conviction. The maximum penalty for treason-felony offences was life imprisonment. See Law Reform Commission of Canada, *Crimes against the State Working Paper 49* (Ottawa: Law Reform Commission of Canada, 1986) at 5-7; see also The Law Commission, Working Paper No. 72, Second Programme, Item XVIII, *Codification of the Criminal Law: Treason, Sedition and Allied Offences* (London: Her Majesty's Stationery Office, 1977) at 2-6.

3 Manitoba Penitentiary Admitance [*sic*] Register, *ibid.*

4 Robert Saunders, Joseph Gouin, Louis LeToup (1880), SAB AG CR-Regina, 1st series, 1876-86, file 103. I have used the initials "M-c-s" because I cannot decipher her name from the handwriting.

5 The case of the *Lost Child* bears some similarity, though not in result, to a British Columbia case discussed by Hamar Foster, that of Haatq, the Kit-au-max man who killed a man who had been with his son when the young man drowned. According to the custom of the Kit-au-max people, the man Haatq killed ought to have gone to the drowned man's people "to make known ... what has taken place. If this is not done, it is taken as evidence that there has been foul play." Without suggesting that the same customary practice prevailed among the people of Red Pheasant's band, it does seem that Peaychew, the girl's father, was not pleased that he had learned not from Saunders himself (into whose custody he had given the child) but from another man that she had left the hunting party and had not returned. See Hamar Foster, "'The Queen's Law Is Better than Yours': International Homicide in Early British Columbia" in Susan Lewthwaite, Tina Loo, and Jim Phillips, eds., *Essays in the History of Canadian Law,* vol. 5, *Crime and Criminal Justice in Canadian History* (Toronto: University of Toronto Press, 1994) 41; see also Tina Loo, "Savage Mercy: Native Culture and the Modification of Capital Punishment in Nineteenth-Century British Columbia" in Carolyn Strange, ed., *Qualities of Mercy: Justice, Punishment and Discretion* (Vancouver: UBC Press, 1996) 104 [Loo, "Savage Mercy"].

6 Saunders *et al., supra* note 4.

7 The *Offences Against the Person Act, 1869,* 32-33 Vict., c. 20, s. 57, provided: "Whosoever unlawfully, either by force or fraud, leads or takes away or decoys or entices or detains any

child under the age of fourteen years, with intent to deprive any parent, guardian or other person having the lawful charge of such child, of the possession of such child ... is guilty of felony, and shall be liable to be imprisoned in the penitentiary for any term not exceeding seven years and not less than two years."

8 Saunders *et al., supra* note 4. Richardson had some personal experience with this sort of creativity. In 1878, he had charged a young NWMP constable, Henry Elliott, who had married Richardson's daughter against her parents' wishes, with an offence under s. 54 of the *Offences Against the Person Act, ibid.,* which prohibited the abduction of an heiress against the will of her father. See W.F. Bowker's discussion of this case: "Stipendiary Magistrates and Supreme Court of the North-West Territories, 1868-1907" (1988) 26 Alta. L. Rev. 245 at 263-65. Elliott was also charged with theft of NWMP horses (used in an attempt to retrieve his wife from her parents' home and then to flee); he was acquitted by a jury following a trial over which Richardson and his fellow stipendiary magistrate, James F. Macleod, presided together: Henry R. Elliott (1878), SAB AG CR-Regina, 1st series, 1876-86, file 26.

9 Saunders *et al., ibid.*

10 Gouin might have been known to the NWMP; it is possible he was the same Joseph Gouin who had been convicted in the previous year of theft of a horse belonging to the head chief of the Sarcee, Stamiscotocar (Bull Head): see Joseph Gouin (1879), SAB AG CR-Regina, 1st series, 1876-86, file 69; see also the discussion of that case in R.C. Macleod and Heather Rollason, "'Restrain the Lawless Savages': Native Defendants in the Criminal Courts of the North-West Territories, 1878-1885" (1997) 10 Journal of Historical Sociology 157 at 176-77. He could have been the same man who was charged earlier in 1880 with theft of three fence rails: Joseph Gouin (1886), SAB AG CR-Regina, 1st series, 1876-86, file 93.

11 "A Very Mysterious Case: Disappearance of an Indian Child," *Saskatchewan Herald* (21 June 1880) 1 at col. 4.

12 "Return of the Lost Indian Girl: She Ran Away in Fright, a Fortnight on a Diet of Grass" *Saskatchewan Herald* (5 July 1880) 1 at col. 3.

13 LAC, RG 10, reel C-7145, vol. 9415, Treaty Annuity Paylists for Treaties 4, 6, and 7 (1882), Treaty 6, Red Pheasant's Band, 294.

14 Pee-ah-chew (1882), SAB AG CR-Regina, 1st series, 1876-86, file 152.

15 *Ibid.*

16 *Ibid.*

17 *Saskatchewan Herald* (14 October 1882) 1 at col. 3.

18 Pee-ah-chew, *supra* note 14.

19 *Saskatchewan Herald* (11 November 1882) 1 at col. 4, and 2 at col. 1.

20 See, *e.g.,* Sarah Carter, *The Importance of Being Monogamous: Marriage and Nation Building in Western Canada to 1915* (Edmonton and Athabasca: University of Alberta Press and Athabasca University Press, 2008) [Carter, *Importance*].

21 For the text of the letter, see Sandra E. Bingaman, "The Trials of Poundmaker and Big Bear, 1885" (1975) 28 Saskatchewan History 81 at 83 [Bingaman, "Poundmaker and Big Bear"]. See also Stonechild and Waiser, *supra* note 2 at 139. The last name on the list of signatories was "Pee-yay-chew."

22 Stonechild and Waiser, *ibid.* at 100.

23 This was recounted by Alex Sapp in an interview on Little Pine Reserve in 1982, quoted by Stonechild and Waiser, *ibid.* at 133fn31. Hugh Dempsey's informant, Jimmy Chief, attributes the same call to arms to Wandering Spirit: "'If you don't want to join me, then go home

and put on your wives' dresses!' So they started to agree, saying 'Okay,' 'Okay,' 'Okay.' They started to dance again until it was almost daylight. Then Wandering Spirit stopped the dance again. 'Look here,' he laughed at the ones who were leaving, 'I just made some of our brothers like women'": Hugh A. Dempsey, *Big Bear: The End of Freedom* (Vancouver: Douglas and McIntyre, 1984) at 153-54. See also Rudy Wiebe, *Big Bear* (Toronto: Penguin, 2008) at 158-59 for the same story. One or the other must have said this, or perhaps Cree warriors had such an aversion to wearing women's clothes that both could have said it.

24 Treaty 6, reproduced in Alexander Morris, *The Treaties of Canada with the Indians of Manitoba and the North-West Territories,* facsimile reprint (Toronto: Prospero Books, 2000) at 358.

25 Manitoba Penitentiary Admitance [*sic*] Register, *supra* note 2.

26 Between February and July 1886, thirty-one of the "rebels" convicted in 1885 were pardoned under a general amnesty authorized by Prime Minister John A. Macdonald: Dempsey, *supra* note 23 at 195. Dempsey, *supra* note 23, reports at 195-96 that Big Bear's release was approved by Cabinet on 27 January 1887; too ill to travel, he was actually released in the following week. See also J.R. Miller, *Big Bear [Mistahimusqua]: A Biography* (Toronto: ECW Press, 1996) at 126 [Miller, *Big Bear*]; Wiebe, *supra* note 23. Poundmaker was released in March 1886 after serving seven months of his three-year sentence: Norma Sluman, *Poundmaker* (Toronto: Ryerson Press, 1967) at 280.

27 The 1901 Census of Canada indicates that "Peeaychew" was seventy years of age at the time of the Census: 1901 Census of Canada, North-West Territories, District of Saskatchewan, Battleford Agency Sub-District, Schedule 1, Microfilm T-6555: http://data2.collectionscanada.gc.ca/1901/z/z004/z000184159.pdf.

28 See, *e.g.*, the 1889 Treaty Annuity Paylist: LAC, RG 10, reel 7147, vol. 9422, Treaty Annuity Paylists for Treaties 4, 6, and 7 (1889), Treaty 6, Red Pheasant's Band, 299.

29 Dempsey, *supra* note 23 at 100, says that this happened in 1881. Sluman's account, *supra* note 26 at 73, suggests that Poundmaker left Red Pheasant's band in 1877. Poundmaker, however, appears to be listed, at number 2, as headman to Red Pheasant in the 1877 Treaty Annuity Paylist: LAC, RG 10, reel 7145, vol. 9412, Treaty Annuity Paylists for Treaties 4, 6, and 7 (1877), 294.

30 As I will discuss more fully in Chapter 3, there is no word in Cree for "guilty"; however, many accused Aboriginal persons then as now entered pleas of guilty in court. In a 1990 research paper prepared for the Manitoba Aboriginal Justice Inquiry, Freda Ahenakew and her colleagues reported that the Cree in the Battleford region had devised a word for "guilty" that translates, "Are you going to nod your head?" Freda Ahenakew, Cecil King, and Catherine I. Littlejohn, "Indigenous Languages in the Delivery of Justice in Manitoba: A Paper Presented to the Public Inquiry into the Administration of Justice and Aboriginal People" in *Manitoba Aboriginal Justice Inquiry Research Papers* (Winnipeg, 1990) [unpublished].

31 Blair Stonechild, "The Indian View of the 1885 Uprising" in F. Laurie Barron and James B. Waldram, eds., *1885 and After: Native Society in Transition* (Regina: Canadian Plains Research Center, 1986) 155 [Stonechild, "The Indian View"]; Stonechild and Waiser, *supra* note 2; Blair Stonechild, "Interview" in Myrna Kostash, ed., *The Frog Lake Reader* (Edmonton: NeWest, 2009) at 16 [Stonechild, "Interview"]; Maureen Lux, *Medicine that Walks: Disease, Medicine and Canadian Plains Native People, 1880-1940* (Toronto: University of Toronto Press, 2001) at 53.

32 Stonechild and Waiser, *ibid.* at 190; Sidney L. Harring, *White Man's Law: Native People in Nineteenth-Century Jurisprudence* (Toronto: University of Toronto Press, 1998), 176ff [Harring, *White Man's Law*].

33 Stonechild and Waiser, *ibid.;* Walter Hildebrandt, *Views from Fort Battleford: Constructed Views of an Anglo-Canadian West* (Regina: Canadian Plains Research Center, 1994) 102-3.

34 Hildebrandt, *ibid.*

35 Sidney L. Harring, "'There Seemed to Be No Recognized Law': Canadian Law and the Prairie First Nations" in Louis A. Knafla and Jonathan Swainger, eds., *Laws and Societies in the Canadian Prairie West 1670-1940* (Vancouver: UBC Press, 2005) 92 at 98 [Harring, "No Recognized Law"].

36 Sandra Bingaman quotes the Regina *Leader's* coverage of Poundmaker's trial, including its bizarrely besotted description of him as "noble – nay kingly looking." See Bingaman, "Poundmaker and Big Bear," *supra* note 21 at 81. The *Saskatchewan Herald* was less enthralled with Poundmaker. In the midst of the events of 1885, it described him as a "petted and feted Indian": *Saskatchewan Herald* (23 April 1885) 2 at col. 2. Stonechild, "The Indian View," *supra* note 31 at 166, also quotes this passage at greater length. The following September, after he had been sentenced to three years, the *Herald* offered this assessment of the sentence: "Nominally Poundmaker was sentenced to three year term in the Penitentiary; in reality he is provided with what it is the Indian's highest ambition to attain – plenty to eat and nothing to do": *Saskatchewan Herald* (14 September 1885) 2 at col. 4.

37 See, *e.g.*, Harring, "No Recognized Law," *supra* note 35 at 97-102.

38 Indeed, Harring, *ibid.*, does not suggest that the 1885 trials tell the whole story of the Plains First Nations' experience of Canadian law. In his recent essay, he draws heavily, arguably exclusively, on the evidence marshalled by others, to include the treaties, the *Indian Act,* including the restrictions on religious dances, and the pass system. My issue with Harring is not with the areas he identifies. In his discussion under the heading of "The Legal Assault on Tribal Culture," he observes, "It is difficult to determine the impact of these laws on the daily religious and ceremonial life of Plains Indians," and later notes that "there is no assessment of the effectiveness of these laws in repressing Prairie Indian culture." On my reading of the literature, I am inclined to agree, despite the prominent place s. 114 of the *Indian Act* occupies in the legal historiography.

39 See, *e.g.*, Desmond Morton, *The Queen v. Louis Riel* (Toronto: University of Toronto Press, 1974); J.M. Bumstead, *Louis Riel v. Canada: The Making of a Rebel* (Winnipeg: Great Plains Publishing, 2001); Stanley, *supra* note 2; Stonechild and Waiser, *supra* note 2 at 214.

40 See Bingaman, "Poundmaker and Big Bear," *supra* note 21; Stonechild and Waiser, *ibid.* at 202-5 and 206-9.

41 Beal and Macleod, *supra* note 2; Stonechild, "The Indian View," *supra* note 31 at 66; Stonechild and Waiser, *ibid.* at 199-202.

42 See Stonechild and Waiser, *ibid.* at 209-10.

43 *Ibid.*, Appendix 5 at 261-63 for a list of Indian prisoners tried and convicted following the events of 1885.

44 For thorough and careful analyses of the Frog Lake incident and the subsequent prosecution and execution of the Cree and Assiniboine warriors, see, *e.g.*, Hildebrandt, *supra* note 33; Stonechild and Waiser, *ibid.* at 211-12 and 223-25.

45 Tina Loo, "Don Cranmer's Potlatch: Law as Coercion, Symbol, and Rhetoric in British Columbia" (1992) 73 Canadian Historical Review 125 [Loo, "Don Cranmer's Potlatch"].

46 Katherine Pettipas, *Severing the Ties that Bind: Government Repression of Indigenous Religious Ceremonies on the Prairies* (Winnipeg: University of Manitoba Press 1994); Constance Backhouse, *Colour-Coded: A Legal History of Racism in Canada, 1900-1950* (Toronto: University of Toronto Press, 1999) ch. 3.

47 Douglas Hay, "Time, Inequality and Law's Violence" in Austin Sarat and Thomas R. Kearns, eds., *Law's Violence* (Ann Arbor: University of Michigan Press, 1995) 141 at 166-71 [Hay, "Law's Violence"]; see also, *e.g.,* Douglas Hay, "Legislation, Magistrates and Judges: High Law and Low Law in England and the Empire" in David Lemmings, ed., *The British and Their Laws in the Eighteenth Century* (Woodbridge, Suffolk, UK: Boydell Press, 2005) 59 [Hay, "Legislation, Magistrates"]; Douglas Hay and Paul Craven, "Introduction" in Douglas Hay and Paul Craven, eds., *Masters, Servants, and Magistrates in Britain and the Empire, 1562-1955* (Chapel Hill: University of North Carolina Press, 2004) 1 at 3; Douglas Hay, "England, 1562-1875: The Law and Its Uses" in Douglas Hay and Paul Craven, eds., *Masters, Servants, and Magistrates in Britain and the Empire, 1562-1955* (Chapel Hill: University of North Carolina Press, 2004) 59 [Hay, "England"]; Amanda Glasbeek, *Feminized Justice: The Toronto Women's Court, 1913-34* (Vancouver: UBC Press, 2009) [Glasbeek, *Feminized Justice*].

The records of lower criminal courts are often not preserved, with the result that researchers have to rely on other sources, such as the press, police, or jail records, for a court's activity: see, *e.g.,* Linda Gordon, *Heroes of Their Own Lives: The Politics of Family Violence* (New York: Viking, 1988); Glasbeek, *Feminized Justice, ibid.;* Amanda Glasbeek, "Maternalism Meets the Criminal Law: The Case of the Toronto Women's Court" (1998) 10 C.J.W.L. 480 [Glasbeek, "Maternalism"]; Annalee Golz, "Uncovering and Reconstructing Family Violence: Ontario Criminal Case Files" in Franca Iacovetta and Wendy Mitchinson, eds., *On the Case: Explorations in Social History* (Toronto: University of Toronto Press, 1998) 289 at 289, 291. See also Brad Asher, "'Their Own Domestic Difficulties': Intra-Indian Crime and White Law in Western Washington Territory, 1873-1889" (1996) 27 Western Historical Quarterly 189; Michael Willrich, *City of Courts: Socializing Justice in Progressive Era Chicago* (Cambridge and New York: Cambridge University Press, 2003); Dorothy E. Chunn, *From Punishment to Doing Good: Family Courts and Socialized Justice in Ontario, 1880-1940* (Toronto: University of Toronto Press, 1992); Norman Etherington, "The Gendering of Indirect Rule: Criminal Law and Colonial Fiji, 1875-1900" (1996) 31 Journal of Pacific Studies 42.

48 See, *e.g.,* Boaventura de Sousa Santos, "The Postmodern Transition: Law and Politics" in Austin Sarat and Thomas R. Kearns, eds., *The Fate of Law* (Ann Arbor: University of Michigan Press, 1991) 79 at 110-14.

49 Hay, "Law's Violence," *supra* note 47 at 168.

50 *Ibid.* at 167-68.

51 *Ibid.* at 167.

52 *Ibid.* at 168: "[T]his is the received account of law endemic in class- or status-driven societies, where the most privileged public discourse is insistent that there should be one reading of law's texts, including its rituals ... What is not so privileged is silenced ... The celebration of high justice as if low justice did not exist."

53 In today's context, most criminal prosecutions do not go to trial. In 2006-07 in Canada, for instance, 65 percent of adult criminal cases received a guilty disposition; in the majority of these cases (89 percent), the accused had pleaded guilty: "Adult Criminal Court Statistics, 2006/2007" 28 Juristat, online: Statistics Canada <http://www.statcan.gc.ca/>.

54 Louis A. Knafla, "From Oral to Written Memory: The Common Law Tradition in Western Canada" in Louis A. Knafla, ed., *Law and Justice in a New Land: Essays in Western Canadian Legal History* (Toronto: Carswell, 1986) 31 at 69.
55 I am assisted by W.A. Waiser, who has said in another context that "a distinct sense of place shapes and informs" recent Western Canadian historical scholarship: "Introduction: Place, Process and the New Prairie Realities" (2005) 84 Canadian Historical Review 509 at 515.
56 Baptiste Flammand (1877), SAB AG CR-Regina, 1st series, 1876-86, file 11.
57 Ka-ki-si-kut-chin, The Swift Runner (1879), SAB AG CR-Regina, 1st series, 1876-86, file 65. This case will be discussed in Chapter 2.
58 Charles Cardinal (1877), SAB AG CR-Regina, 1st series, 1876-86, file 6. This case will be discussed in Chapter 2.
59 Kee-Che-Qua-Pie-Ka-wa (1877), SAB AG CR-Regina, 1st series, 1876-86, file 7. This case will be discussed in Chapter 2.
60 Robert Saunders, *et al., supra* note 4.
61 Scholastique Cardinal (1882), SAB AG CR-Regina, 1st series, 1876-86, file 145. This case will be discussed in Chapter 5.
62 Ka-Nah-Pic-Nah-Hew, The Snake Indian (1882), SAB AG CR-Regina, 1st series, 1876-86, file 171. This case will be discussed in Chapter 3.
63 John Saunders and Thomas Horsefall (1877), SAB AG CR-Regina, 1st series, 1876-86, file 10.
64 William Turner (1877), SAB AG CR-Regina, 1st series, 1876-86, file 5.
65 John Ballendine (1878), SAB AG CR-Regina, 1st series, 1876-86, file 29. This case will be discussed in Chapter 4.
66 George Finlay (1882), SAB AG CR-Regina, 1st series, 1876-86, file 156. Finlay was charged with pulling down the house of one John (Jack) Cameron, whom Finlay had accused of "improper intimacy" with his wife. No final disposition is indicated in the file.
67 Francis Oliver (1882), Matthew McCauley *et al.* (1882), Donald R. Fraser (1882), and Joseph Lake (1882), SAB AG CR-Regina, 1st series, 1876-86, files 148, 168, 169, and 170, respectively; see also Bowker, *supra* note 8, who discusses these cases.
68 Margaret Favel (1892) and Antoine Langé (1893), Saskatchewan Archives Board, Supreme Court of North-West Territories (Criminal), Collection R1286 [hereinafter, SAB SCNWT (Crim.), Coll. R1286], files 40 and 63, respectively. This case will be discussed in Chapter 5.
69 This boy, Albert Offord, was convicted in 1895 of break and enter with intent to steal, after he had been found in an empty house. The file is silent with respect to the "intent to steal" element of the offence, and it would appear that Offord's explanation for his presence in the house did not suffice: he told the court, "I wanted a house of my own." Judge Richardson wrote: "Prisoner states he is under 15, an orphan, brought out from St Johns home Ipswich England by one Pady in April'94": Albert Offord (1895), SAB SCNWT (Crim.), Coll. R1286, file 100.
70 George Tyler and Edward Hanley (1883), SAB AG CR-Regina, 1st series, 1876-86, files 186 and 187.
71 Waiser, *supra* note 55.
72 Prior to 1887, *An Act to Amend the "North-West Territories Act, 1875," 1877*, 40 Vict., c. 7, s. 64.3 permitted appeals from the North-West Territories to the Manitoba Court of Queen's Bench only in cases involving convictions where a sentence of death had been imposed.

73 Stephen Robertson, "What's Law Got to Do with It? Legal Records and Sexual Histories" (2005) 12 Journal of the History of Sexuality 161 at 171.

74 *Ibid.*

75 See, *e.g.,* Sarah Carter, *Aboriginal People and the Colonizers of Western Canada to 1900* (Toronto: University of Toronto Press, 1999) [Carter, *Aboriginal People*]; Carter, *Importance, supra* note 20.

76 See, *e.g.,* Lauren Benton, *Law and Colonial Cultures: Legal Regimes in World History, 1400-1900* (Cambridge: Cambridge University Press, 2002) at 15-19. See also Laura F. Gómez, "Race, Colonialism, and Criminal Law: Mexicans and the American Criminal Justice System in Territorial New Mexico" (2000) 34 Law & Soc'y Rev. 1129; Asher, *supra* note 47; Tina Loo, "Tonto's Due: Law, Culture, and Colonialization in British Columbia" in Hamar Foster and John McLaren, eds., *Essays in the History of Canadian Law,* vol. 6, *The Legal History of British Columbia and the Yukon* (Toronto: University of Toronto Press, 1995) 128; reprinted in Catherine Cavanaugh and Jeremy Mouat, eds., *Making Western Canada: Essays on European Colonization and Settlement* (Toronto: Garamond Press, 1996) 62 at 63-64 [Loo, "Tonto's Due"].

77 Macleod and Rollason, *supra* note 10 at 178: "Natives actively negotiated their place within the legal system: a fact that natives seem to have understood more clearly than whites, who took the native position within the system very much for granted. In the period before 1885 natives negotiated from a position of considerable strength. Political, demographic and economic changes after 1885 seriously diminished native bargaining power. How this development affected native crime rates remains to be documented."

78 Loo, "Tonto's Due," *supra* note 76 at 63-64.

79 *Ibid.* at 63 [emphasis added].

80 *Ibid.* at 82. See also Hildrebrandt, *supra* note 33 at 46-47, in relation to Cree chiefs Beardy and Lucky Man.

81 "Report of the Commissioner of the North-West Mounted Police, 1884," reprinted in Royal Canadian Mounted Police, *Settlers and Rebels: Being the Official Reports to Parliament of the Activities of the Royal* [*sic*] *North-West Mounted Police Force from 1882-1885 by the Commissioners of the Royal* [*sic*] *North-West Mounted Police,* facsimile reprint (Toronto: Coles Publishing, 1973; original ed. Ottawa: Maclean, Roger, 1882-85) at 15. In Appendix A of the Returns for 1884, Crow Collar is reported to have been convicted by Superintendent McIllree JP of "malicious injury to property" and sentenced to ten days' imprisonment at hard labour; Bull Head is listed as having been charged with causing a disturbance, which charge was "dismissed, with caution after three days' imprisonment" (at 49).

82 Macleod and Rollason, *supra* note 10 at 176-77.

83 See, *e.g.,* Sally Engle Merry, "Law and Colonialism" (1991) 25 Law & Soc'y Rev. 889; Sally Engle Merry, "The Criminalization of Everyday Life" in Austin Sarat *et al.,* eds., *Everyday Practices and Trouble Cases* (Evanston, IL: Northwestern University Press and the American Bar Foundation, 1998) at 14; Loo, "Tonto's Due," *supra* note 76; Loo, "Don Cranmer's Potlatch," *supra* note 45; Macleod and Rollason, *ibid.;* Asher, *supra* note 47; Gómez, *supra* note 76; Benton, *supra* note 76; Alan R. Booth, "'European Courts Protect Women and Witches': Colonial Law Courts as Redistributors of Power in Swaziland 1920-1950" (1992) 18 Journal of South African Studies 253.

84 See, *e.g.,* Martin Chanock, *Law, Custom and Social Order: The Colonial Experience in Malawi and Zambia* (Cambridge: Cambridge University Press, 1985); Benton, *supra* note 76 at 17. Benton observes at 14: "Conquered peoples showed themselves to be quite adept and sophisticated at interpreting the significance of claims to jurisdiction and strategically taking

positions to undermine those claims ... [*e.g.*,] American Indians at times showed considerable sophistication in their appeals to religious as well as state legal authorities."

85 I acknowledge an explicit debt to E.P. Thompson, *Whigs and Hunters: The Origin of the Black Act* (Middlesex, UK: Penguin Books, 1977) at 266-68.

86 *E.g.*, William Turner (1877), SAB AG CR-Regina, 1st series, 1876-86, file 5; John Smith (1878), SAB AG CR-Regina, 1st series, 1876-86, file 24; James Ford (1889), SAB SCNWT (Crim.), Coll. R1286, file 11; The Little Person, Son of Running Crow (1879), SAB AG CR-Regina, 1st series, 1876-86, file 224.

87 See, *e.g.*, Pierre Bourassa (1894), SAB SCNWT (Crim.), Coll. R1286, file 39; Ka-nah-pic-a-nah-hew or The Snake Indian (1882) SAB AG CR-Regina, 1st series, 1876-86, file 171.

88 Antoine Langé (1893) SAB SCNWT (Crim.), Coll. R1286, file 63. Since Peter Hourie was sworn as a Cree interpreter in this case, I infer that Langé was an Aboriginal person. In this case, Langé intimated that this matter was his wife's affair.

89 Margaret Favel (1892) SAB SCNWT (Crim.), Coll. R1286, file 40 (charged with theft of four silver spoons and forks and other small items from the empty schoolhouse on Poor Man's reserve in the Touchwood Hills; pleaded guilty to stealing one spoon; suspended sentence).

90 Julia Coté (1894) SAB SCNWT (Crim.), Coll. R1286, file 85. Alex Bone (1894) SAB SCNWT (Crim.), Coll. R1286, file 84.

91 Betsy Horsefall and Benjamin Gordon (1894) SAB SCNWT (Crim.), Coll. R1286, file 83.

92 See, *e.g.*, Shelley A.M. Gavigan, "Legal Forms, Family Forms, Gendered Norms: What Is a Spouse?" (1999) 24 C.J.L.S. 129.

93 For scholarship that uses the language of criminalization in relation to the potlatch (in British Columbia) and the giveaway and thirst dances of the Plains, see Loo, "Don Cranmer's Potlatch," *supra* note 45; Backhouse, *supra* note 46 (c. 3 re the prosecution of Wanduta). For careful historical analysis of these *Indian Act* amendments and their implications, see also Katherine Pettipas, *supra* note 46 (who does not use the term "criminalization").

94 In 1884, the *Indian Act* had been amended prohibit the "Potlatch" and the dance known as the "Tamanawas": *An Act Further to Amend the Indian Act, 1884*, 47 Vict., c. 27, s. 3.

95 *An Act Further to Amend the Indian Act, 1895*, 58-59 Vict., c. 35, s. 6 extended the restrictions and created a new s. 114 [emphasis added]: "Every Indian or other person who engages in, or assists in celebrating or encourages either directly or indirectly another to celebrate, any Indian festival, dance or other ceremony of which the *giving away* or paying or giving back of money, goods or articles of any sort forms a part, or is a feature, whether such gift of money, goods or articles takes place before, at, or after the celebration of the same, and every Indian who engages or assists in any celebration or dance of which the *wounding or mutilation* of the dead or living human being or animals forms a part or is a feature, is guilty of an indictable offence and is liable to imprisonment for a term not exceeding six months and not less than two months; but nothing in this section shall be construed to prevent the holding of any agricultural show or exhibition or the giving of prizes for exhibits thereat."

96 E. Brian Titley, *A Narrow Vision: Duncan Campbell Scott and the Administration of Indian Affairs in Canada* (Vancouver: UBC Press, 1986) at 164fn9 and 167 [Titley, *Narrow Vision*]; Pettipas, *supra* note 46. Titley refers to Fine Day (who was David G. Mandelbaum's principal informant in *The Plains Cree: An Ethnographic, Historical and Comparative Study* (Regina: Canadian Plains Research Center, 1979) at 4, where his name is spelled as "Fine-Day"). Mandelbaum and Titley each describe Fine-Day as a great leader of the Sweetgrass Cree, a warrior of formidable reputation, who was said to be "brave in all things." True to his reputation, Fine-Day sponsored seven Thirst Dances during his lifetime despite "official disapproval" (Titley, *Narrow Vision, ibid.* at 164fn9). The 1996 *Report of the Royal Commission*

on Aboriginal Peoples, vol. 1, *Looking Forward, Looking Back* (Ottawa: Minister of Supply and Services, 1996).

97 See, *e.g.,* Frank Pearce, *Crimes of the Powerful* (London: Pluto, 1978); Laureen Snider, *Bad Business: Corporate Crime in Canada* (Scarborough, ON: Nelson Canada, 1993); Frank Pearce and Laureen Snider, eds., *Corporate Crime: Contemporary Debates* (Toronto: University of Toronto Press, 1995); Susan C. Boyd, Dorothy E. Chunn, and Robert Menzies, eds., *Abusing Power: The Canadian Experience* (Halifax: Fernwood, 2001); H.J. Glasbeek, *Wealth by Stealth: Corporate Crime, Corporate Law, and the Perversion of Democracy* (Toronto: Between the Lines, 2002).

98 See, e.g., Robert Menzies, Dorothy E. Chunn and Susan C. Boyd, eds. *Toxic Criminology: Environment, Law and the State of Canada* (Halifax: Fernwood, 2002); Laura Westra, *Ecoviolence and the Law: Supranational Normative Foundations of Ecocrime* (Ardsley, NY: Transnational Publishers, 2004).

99 See Dickson J.'s classic articulation in *R. v. City of Sault Ste Marie* (1978), 40 C.C.C. (2d) 353, 3 C.R. (3d) 30 (S.C.C) (online: QL LexisNexis) at 9 (QL): "The distinction between the true criminal offence and the public welfare offence is one of prime importance. When the offence is criminal, the Crown must establish a mental element, namely, that the accused who committed the prohibited act did so intentionally or recklessly, with knowledge of the facts constituting the offence, or with wilful blindness toward them. Mere negligence is excluded from the concept of the mental element required for conviction."

100 The fact that exclusive jurisdiction to legislate in relation to Indians and to criminal law rested with the Dominion government perhaps blurred the boundaries between the two areas. Perhaps further compounding the "blurriness" in the literature was the federal power in relation to the North-West Territories – notably here, the creation of the NWMP, the form of the administration of justice, and territorial governance until 1905.

101 See, *e.g.,* Backhouse, *supra* note 46 at 60-69; Loo, "Don Cranmer's Potlatch," *supra* note 45 at 128. Harring, "No Recognized Law," *supra* note 35 at 118-23, includes liquor, hunting, and fishing regulations in his discussion of criminal law and Indians in Upper Canada. John Borrows also refers to "the criminalization of their social, economic, and spiritual relations through the enactment of laws against potlatch" in *Recovering Canada: The Resurgence of Indigenous Law* (Toronto: University of Toronto Press, 2002) at 60fn168. Concerning a somewhat later period, see also Joan Sangster, "Criminalizing the Colonized: Ontario Native Women Confront the Criminal Justice System, 1920-60" (1999) 80 Canadian Historical Review 32, who, at 34 (drawing on Chanock, *supra* note 84, characterizes law as the "cutting edge of colonialism," with its "final lesson" of incarceration; Robin Brownlie and Mary-Ellen Kelm, "Desperately Seeking Absolution: Native Agency as Colonialist Alibi?" (1994) 75 Canadian Historical Review 543, reproduce, at 546, in passing and without comment, a reference to criminalization of the potlatch in their critical engagement with Tina Loo. Even in their otherwise penetrating critique, criminalization appears as self-evident, requiring no interrogation.

102 On the pass system, see Sarah Carter, *Lost Harvests: Prairie Indian Reserve Farmers and Government Policy* (Montreal and Kingston: McGill-Queen's University Press, 1990) at 149-58 [Carter, *Lost Harvests*].

103 Backhouse, *supra* note 46 at 60-63; Pettipas, *supra* note 46; Loo, "Don Cranmer's Potlatch," *supra* note 45.

104 See, *e.g.,* Backhouse, *ibid.* at 60; Loo, *ibid.* at 128; Borrows, *supra* note 101 at 20fn168; Brownlie and Kelm, *supra* note 101 at 546.

105 Douglas C. Harris, *Fish, Law, and Colonialism: The Legal Capture of Salmon in British Columbia* (Toronto: University of Toronto Press, 2001), 59.

106 Pettipas, *supra* note 46.

107 *Ibid.* at 110-11.

108 John N. Jennings, *The North-West Mounted Police and Canadian Indian Policy, 1873-1896* (PhD Dissertation, University of Toronto, 1979) [unpublished] at 96-97; Pettipas, *ibid.* at 111.

109 In 1884, the *Indian Act* had been amended to prohibit the "Potlatch" and the dance known as the "Tamanawas": *An Act Further to Amend the Indian Act, 1884,* 47 Vict., c. 27, s. 3. The *Act Further to Amend the Indian Act, 1895,* 58-59 Vict., c. 35, s. 6, extended the restrictions and created a new s. 114, quoted in full at note 95, *supra.*

110 Pettipas, *supra* note 46; Jennings, *supra* note 109.

111 As Harring, "No Recognized Law," *supra* note 35 at 14, says of his own contribution.

112 See, *e.g.,* Benton, *supra* note 76; Merry, *supra* note 83; Jeremy Webber, "Relations of Force and Relations of Justice: The Emergence of Normative Community between Colonists and Aboriginal Peoples" (1995) 33 Osgoode Hall L.J. 623. See also Alan Hunt, *Explorations in Law and Society: Toward a Constitutive Theory of Law* (London: Routledge, 1993) at 225; Dorothy E. Chunn and Shelley A.M. Gavigan, "Welfare Law, Welfare Fraud, and the Moral Regulation of the Never Deserving Poor" (2004) 13 Social and Legal Studies 219 at 230-31.

113 Mary Ellen Turpel, "Patriarchy and Paternalism: The Legacy of the Canadian State for First Nations Women" (1993) 6 C.J.W.L. 174 at 178 has characterized "Indianization" as a central project of the *Indian Act* and the Canadian state.

Chapter 1: Legally Framing the Plains and the First Nations

1 See, *e.g.,* Alberta, *Justice on Trial: Report of the Task Force on the Criminal Justice System and Its Impact on the Indian and Métis People of Alberta* (The Cawsey Report) (March 1991); Canada, Royal Commission on the Donald Marshall, Jr. Prosecution, *Commissioners' Report: Findings and Recommendations* (Halifax: The Commission, 1989); Manitoba, *Report of the Aboriginal Justice Inquiry of Manitoba,* vol. 1, *The Justice System and Aboriginal People* (A.C. Hamilton and C.M. Sinclair, Commissioners) (Winnipeg: Province of Manitoba, 1991) [Manitoba, *Justice Inquiry Report*]; Saskatchewan, *Report of the Saskatchewan Indian Justice Review Committee* (Judge Patricia Linn, Chairperson) (Saskatoon: 1992).

2 Manitoba, *Justice Inquiry Report, ibid.* at 1-7.

3 *Ibid.* at 27.

4 David G. Mandelbaum, *The Plains Cree: An Ethnographic, Historical and Comparative Study* (Regina: Canadian Plains Research Center, 1979) at 122.

5 Mary Ellen Turpel, "Patriarchy and Paternalism: The Legacy of the Canadian State for First Nations Women" (1993) 6 C.J.W.L. 174.

6 See, *e.g.,* Kent McNeil, *Common Law Aboriginal Title* (Oxford: Clarendon Press, 1989) [McNeil, *Common Law Aboriginal Title*]; John Borrows, *Recovering Canada: The Resurgence of Indigenous Law* (Toronto: University of Toronto Press, 2002) [Borrows, *Recovering Canada*].

7 See, *e.g.,* Darlene Johnston, "Litigating Identity: The Challenge of Aboriginality" (Paper presented at the Faculty of Law, University of Toronto, January 2003; L.L.M. Thesis,

University of Toronto, 2003); Sharon Venne, "Understanding Treaty 6: An Indigenous Perspective," in Michael Asch, ed., *Aboriginal and Treaty Rights in Canada: Essays on Law, Equality, and Respect for Difference* (Vancouver: UBC Press, 1997) 173; Harold Cardinal and Walter Hildebrandt, *Treaty Elders of Saskatchewan: Our Dream Is that Our Peoples Will One Day Be Clearly Recognized as Nations* (Calgary: University of Calgary Press, 2000); Treaty 7 Elders and Tribal Council, with Walter Hildebrandt, Dorothy First Rider, and Sarah Carter, *The True Spirit and Original Intent of Treaty 7* (Montreal and Kingston: McGill-Queen's University Press, 1996).

8 See, *e.g.*, John Borrows, "Wampum at Niagara: The Royal Proclamation, Canadian Legal History, and Self-Government" in Michael Asch, ed., *Aboriginal and Treaty Rights in Canada: Essays on Law, Equality, and Respect for Difference* (Vancouver: UBC Press, 1997) 155.

9 See, *e.g.*, Sarah Carter, *Lost Harvests: Prairie Indian Reserve Farmers and Government Policy* (Montreal and Kingston: McGill-Queen's University Press, 1990) [Carter, *Lost Harvests*]; J.R. Miller, *Shingwauk's Vision: A History of Native Residential Schools* (Toronto: University of Toronto Press, 1996) [Miller, *Shingwauk's Vision*]; John S. Milloy, *A National Crime: The Canadian Government and the Residential School System, 1879-1976* (Winnipeg: University of Manitoba Press, 1999); Hugh Shewell, *"Enough to Keep Them Alive": Indian Welfare in Canada: 1873-1965* (Toronto: University of Toronto Press, 2004); Katherine Pettipas, *Severing the Ties that Bind: Government Repression of Indigenous Religious Ceremonies on the Prairies* (Winnipeg: University of Manitoba Press, 1994) [Pettipas, *Severing the Ties*]; Turpel, *supra* note 5; Sarah Carter, "'Complicated and Clouded': The Federal Administration of Marriage and Divorce among the First Nations of Western Canada, 1887-1906" in Sarah Carter, Lesley Erickson, Patricia Roome, and Char Smith, eds., *Unsettled Pasts: Reconceiving the West through Women's History* (Calgary: University of Calgary Press, 2005) 151 [Carter, "Complicated and Clouded"]; Sarah Carter, *The Importance of Being Monogamous: Marriage and Nation Building in Western Canada to 1915* (Edmonton and Athabasca: University of Alberta Press and Athabasca University Press, 2008) [Carter, *Importance of Being Monogamous*]; Maureen Lux, *Medicine that Walks: Disease, Medicine, and Canadian Plains Native People, 1880-1940* (Toronto: University of Toronto Press, 2001).

10 In many ways, government policy and regulation expressed through and under the auspices of the *Indian Act* was the most significant contribution of the Canadian state to the lives of the First Nations. I demonstrate this more fully in Chapter 4.

11 Sarah Carter, *Capturing Women: The Manipulation of Cultural Imagery in Canada's Prairie West* (Montreal and Kingston: McGill-Queen's University Press, 1997) at 20 [Carter, *Capturing Women*]; Sarah Carter, *Aboriginal People and the Colonizers of Western Canada to 1900* (Toronto: University of Toronto Press, 1999) at 106 [Carter, *Aboriginal People*]. See also Lewis Herbert Thomas, *The Struggle for Responsible Government in the North-West Territories*, 2nd ed. (Toronto: University of Toronto Press, 1978).

12 Lieutenant-Governor Alexander Morris to The Gambler, prominent Saulteaux leader and spokesperson for the Cree and Saulteaux at the Treaty 4 negotiations, in Alexander Morris, *The Treaties of Canada with the Indians of Manitoba and the North-West Territories*, facsimile reprint (Saskatoon: Fifth House, 1991) (original ed., Toronto: Belfords, Clarke, 1880) at 103.

13 Together with the right to the "sole trade and commerce of all the seas, straits, bays, rivers, lakes, creeks and sounds, within Hudson's Straits; the lands countries, and territories upon their coasts which were not then actually possessed by the subjects of any Christian Prince or State; all sorts of fish, whales, sturgeons; and all mines, discovered and undiscovered,

of gold, silver, gems and precious stones." Edmund Henry Oliver, ed., *The Canadian North-West: Its Early Development and Legislative Records,* 2 vols. (Ottawa: Government Printing Bureau, 1914) vol. 1 at 22. For Oliver, the *Royal Charter of 1670* was the first and the most important official document relating to Western Canada. Other scholars remind us that the Crown ignored the rights and claims to the land of the indigenous peoples of the region as well as any claims the French might have made, and that the terms of the Charter reveal the framers' profound ignorance of conditions at Hudson Bay: Hamar Foster, "Long Distance Justice: The Criminal Jurisdiction of Canadian Courts West of the Canadas, 1763-1859" (1990) 34 Am. J. Legal Hist. 1 at 2-3 [Foster, "Long Distance Justice"]; Carter, *Aboriginal People, supra* note 11 at 106.

14 Foster, "Long Distance Justice," *ibid.*

15 See, *e.g., ibid.;* D. Colwyn Williams, "The Dawn of Law on the Prairies" (1962) 27 Sask. Bar Rev. 126; (1963) 28 Sask. Bar Rev. 17; (1963) 28 Sask. Bar Rev. 63 [Williams, "Dawn of Law"]; H. Robert Baker, "Creating Order in the Wilderness: Transplanting the English Law to Rupert's Land, 1831-51" (1999) 17 L.H.R. Rev. 209; Russell Smandych and Rick Linden, "Co-Existing Forms of Aboriginal and Private Justice: An Historical Study of the Canadian West," in Kayleen M. Hazelhurst, ed., *Legal Pluralism and the Colonial Legacy* (Aldershot, UK: Avebury, 1995) 1; Tina Loo, *Making Law, Order, and Authority in British Columbia, 1821-1871* (Toronto: University of Toronto Press, 1994) at 18-33 [Loo, *Making Law*]; Oliver, *supra* note 13, vol. 1 at 20-22.

16 Oliver, *ibid.,* vol. 2 at 997fn1. After the Company relinquished formal control of the land, HBC men continued to be appointed as justices of the peace; seven of the first thirteen appointments of justices of the peace made by Lieutenant-Governor David Laird were HBC men (Oliver, *ibid.,* vol. 1 at 56). See also Thomas Reynolds, *Justices of the Peace in the NWT, 1870-1905* (MA Thesis, University of Regina, 1978) [unpublished].

17 Foster, "Long Distance Justice," *supra* note 13 at 3, characterizes the terms of the conferral as "language that was as susceptible to contrary interpretations as the territorial grant"; the judicial power conferred upon the governor and council at each of the Company's establishments was "to judge all persons belonging to the said Governor and Company or that shall live under them in all causes whether Civill or Criminall according to the Lawes of this Kingdome and to execute justice accordingly." Louis Knafla appears to offer a narrower interpretation of the authority conferred by the *Royal Charter.* See Louis A. Knafla, "From Oral to Written Memory: The Common Law Tradition in Western Canada" in Louis A. Knafla, ed., *Law and Justice in a New Land: Essays in Western Canadian Legal History* (Toronto: Carswell, 1986) 31 at 35.

18 Foster, *ibid.* Foster argues at 4-6, 14-32, and 34-37 that two early nineteenth-century pieces of imperial legislation served to compound the problem, as the earlier one provided that courts in Lower and Upper Canada had jurisdiction to try British subjects charged with crimes in the Indian Territories and the later one purported to extend that to Rupert's Land as well. *An Act for Extending the Jurisdiction of the Courts of Justice in the Provinces of Lower and Upper Canada, 1803* (U.K.), 43 Geo. III, c. 138, and *An Act for Regulating the Fur Trade, 1821* (U.K.), 1 and 2 Geo. IV, c. 66, s. 5.

19 Knafla, *supra* note 17 at 35; Foster, *ibid.* at 37-38. According to Thomas, *supra* note 11 at 24, the HBC's "governance" was "primarily concerned with business matters – the company had no intention of transforming Indian society, and ancient customs and tribal organization were not disturbed." See also W. Peter Ward, *The Administration of Justice in the North-West Territories, 1870-1887* (MA Thesis, University of Alberta, 1966) [unpublished]

at 9; Sidney L. Harring, *White Man's Law: Native People in Nineteenth-Century Jurisprudence* (Toronto: University of Toronto Press, 1998) at 242; Dale Gibson and Lee Gibson, *Substantial Justice: Law and Lawyers in Manitoba 1670-1970* (Winnipeg: Peguis Publishers, 1972) at 2.

20 Baker, *supra* note 15 at 213. Baker refers to "three known formal trials over a period of 120 years" (at 215). See also W.F. Bowker, "Stipendiary Magistrates and Supreme Court of the North-West Territories, 1876-1907" (1988) 26 Alta. Law Rev. 245 at 245; Foster, "Long Distance Justice," *supra* note 13 at 48; and Kenneth Bryan Leyton-Brown, *The Origin and Evolution of a System for the Administration of Justice in the North-West Territories, 1870-1905* (PhD Dissertation, Queen's University, 1988) [unpublished] at 5; during the period of its administration, the Company established only the most rudimentary of courts on the prairies; when the need arose, disputes were transferred to a jurisdiction that had a developed system of courts.

21 Irene Spry makes explicit the implications for self-determination of the transition from HBC to Canadian government rule: "The arrival of the NWMP to enforce law and maintain order had one effect that is seldom recognized: the Indians were no longer to be permitted to keep intruders out their country by force": "The Tragedy of the Loss of the Commons in Western Canada" in Ian A.L. Getty and Antoine S. Lussier, eds., *As Long as the Sun Shines and the Water Flows: A Reader in Canadian Native Studies* (Vancouver: UBC Press, 1983) 203 at 212.

22 The late Senator John Tootoosis, speaking at the Treaty 6 Centennial Commemoration in 1976: Norma Sluman and Jean Goodwill, *John Tootoosis: A Biography of a Cree Leader* (Ottawa: Golden Dog Press, 1982) at 1. Senator Tootoosis was the grandson of Yellow Mud Blanket, who was the brother of Chief Poundmaker.

23 These oft-cited words of Chief Sweet Grass, in a message to His Excellency Governor Archibald at Fort Garry (1871) bear repeating here. Alexander Morris, *supra* note 12 at 170. See also Helen Buckley, *From Wooden Ploughs to Welfare: Why Indian Policy Failed in the Prairie Provinces* (Montreal and Kingston: McGill-Queen's University Press, 1992) at 33; Arthur J. Ray, Jim Miller, and Frank J. Tough, *Bounty and Benevolence: A History of Saskatchewan Treaties* (Montreal and Kingston: McGill-Queen's University Press, 2000) at 135; Canada, Royal Commission on Aboriginal Peoples, *Report of the Royal Commission on Aboriginal Peoples,* vol. 1, *Looking Forward, Looking Back* (Ottawa: Indian and Northern Affairs, 1996) pt. 1, ch. 6, "Stage Three, Displacement and Assimilation," online: http://www.collectionscanada.gc.ca/; Deanna Christensen, *Ahtahkakoop: The Epic Account of a Plains Cree Head Chief, His People, and Their Struggle for Survival 1816-1896* (Shell Lake, SK: Ahtahkakoop Publishing, 2000) at 150. Sweet Grass, principal chief of the Fort Pitt area, was one the leading advocates for entering into a treaty and was a signatory to Treaty 6: see J.W. Grant MacEwan, "Sweet Grass: First Western Conservationist," in his *Portraits from the Plains* (Toronto: McGraw-Hill of Canada, 1971) 159 at 162; Hugh A. Dempsey, *Big Bear: The End of Freedom* (Vancouver: Douglas and McIntyre, 1984) at 44, 71-74; J.R. Miller, *Big Bear [Mistahimusqua]: A Biography* (Toronto: ECW Press, 1996) at 47 [Miller, *Big Bear*].

24 Foster, "Long Distance Justice," *supra* note 13 at 3.

25 Carter, *Aboriginal People, supra* note 11.

26 Thomas, *supra* note 11 at 21.

27 See, *e.g.,* the map reproduced in Pettipas, *supra* note 9, following xiv. See also John S. Milloy, *The Plains Cree: Trade, Diplomacy and War, 1790 to 1870* (Winnipeg: University of Manitoba Press, 1990) Map 1.

28 Pettipas, *ibid.* See also Blair Stonechild, "Aboriginal Peoples of Saskatchewan" (2007), online: The Saskatchewan Encylopedia: A Living Legacy <http://esask.uregina.ca/entry/aboriginal_peoplesof_saskatchewan.html>.

29 Carter, *Aboriginal People, supra* note 11 at 109. See also Marcel Giraud, "Métis Settlement in the North-West Territories" (1954) 7 Saskatchewan History 1. While many of the Manitoba Métis were nomadic and active buffalo hunters, they were also distinct from the more indigenous Half-breeds who lived with, travelled with, and identified with Indians. The arrival of the Red River Métis in 1870 and following, and their hunting practices, were experienced as disruptive by many Cree: see Christensen, *supra* note 23 at 135-36, and at 146-47: "[M]any of the chiefs knew that more and more newcomers were arriving in their country each year, and that these people would want to divide the land into pieces for farms and towns. Additionally, it was becoming increasingly evident that many of the newcomers showed little respect for the Indian people. The Métis from the Red River Settlement were not only beginning to act as if they owned the land, but they were trying to take over the buffalo hunt and enforce their laws on the Indian people."

30 Blair Stonechild has argued that in the 1870s, for instance, one would find bands consisting of Cree, Saulteaux, Stoney, and Half-breeds living and travelling together. Blair Stonechild, "The Iron Alliance and Dominion of the Northern Plains 1690-1885: Implications for the Concept of Iskunikan" (2003) [unpublished]. See also Neal McLeod, "Plains Cree Identity: Borderlands, Ambiguous Genealogies and Narrative Irony" (2000) 20 Canadian Journal of Native Studies 437 [McLeod, "Plains Cree Identity"].

31 McLeod, *ibid.* at 446.

32 Poundmaker was the orphaned son of an Assiniboine father and a Cree, or Métis, mother, nephew of Cree chief Mistawasis, and was adopted as an adult by Blackfoot Chief Crowfoot. Piapot was Cree, had been raised by his grandmother in a Sioux camp after they had been captured during a raid, and led a group of Cree-Assiniboine followers. Sweet Grass, one of the principal chiefs of the Crees and spokesperson at the Fort Pitt signing of Treaty 6, is said to have been a full-blooded Crow. Big Bear was the son of Black Powder, a prominent Ojibway leader who had moved from further east (now Ontario). The name and nation of Big Bear's mother is apparently not known, but she may have been Cree, as her son, and his father before him, led a mixed band of Cree and Saulteaux: see Dempsey, *supra* note 23 at 29; McLeod, *ibid;* Norma Sluman, *Poundmaker* (Toronto: Ryerson Press, 1967); Miller, *supra* note 23.

33 Historian Olive Dickason puts the population figures for the Aboriginal population in 1870 at around 35,000, with Métis around 10,000 to 12,000 and whites fewer than 2,000: Olive Patricia Dickason, *Canada's First Nations: A History of Founding Peoples from Earliest Times* (Toronto: McClelland and Stewart, 1992) at 97. See also Spry, *supra* note 21.

Figures provided in the *Report of the Special Committee of the House of Commons, 1857,* of "Establishments of the Hudson's Bay Company in 1856, and Number of Indians frequenting them" indicated that 22,050 Indians attended at the Hudson's Bay posts that figure prominently in Hugh Richardson's court records: Canada, "Report of the Special Committee of the House of Commons, 1857" (Appendix No. 2, 365, 366, and 367) in Statistics Canada, *Censuses of Canada 1865-1871, The Aboriginal Peoples* at 12-13, online: Statistics Canada <http://www.statcan.ca/>. The figures suggest a more significant presence in the northern districts, with figures for the more northern posts – Edmonton (7,500), Carlton (6,000), Fort Pitt (7,000), and Lac la Biche (500) – far exceeding those for the more southern posts – Fort Ellice (250), Qu'Appelle Lakes (250), Touchwood Hills (300), and Egg Lake (200). The Census of 1871 reported that the population of the "Plains Tribes

(Blackfeet, etc.) totalled 25,000." For the year 1871, the total Aboriginal population for Labrador, Rupert's Land, and The Territories was estimated to be 55,500, while "other races" were estimated to number 5,000. *Ibid.* at 16 and 17.

34 *Census of the Three Provisional Districts of the North-West Territories, 1884-1885* (Ottawa: Maclean, Rogers, 1886), Table III at 30. The breakdown of the Indian population between the three districts was: Saskatchewan, 6,260 Indians; Assiniboia, 4,492; Alberta, 9,418. This Census reported that there were 8,397 people of English origin, 8,387 French Half-breeds, 5,285 Irish, 6,788 "Scotch," and 1,520 people of French origin in the North-West Territories (these were the major population groups). Thus by, 1884-85, the population of newcomers (at 21,990) represented by these major population groups in the North-West Territories (excluding the French Métis) eclipsed the population of the First Nations (at 20,170).

35 *Census of Canada 1890-1891* (Ottawa: Queen's Printer, 1893) vol. 1, Table II at 112.

36 *Ibid.,* vol. 2, Table XII at 185.

37 *Ibid.,* vol. 1, Table V at 362. The challenges of ascertaining the Aboriginal population in the 1891 Census because of the elimination of a specific category for "Indian" is discussed by Michelle A. Hamilton and Kris Inwood, "The Identification of the Aboriginal Population in the 1891 Census of Canada" (Paper presented at the Indigenous Identity in Demographic Sources Conference, Umea University, Umea, Sweden, 2006), online: Umea University <http://www.ddb.umu.se/>.

38 Canada, *Fourth Census of Canada 1901* (Ottawa: S.E. Dawson, King's Printer, 1902), Table XI at 392-93.

39 *Ibid.* at 403 (Saskatchewan), 401 (Western Assiniboia), 397 (Eastern Assiniboia), 393 (Alberta). Hugh Richardson presided primarily in the Districts of Saskatchewan and, after 1883, Western Assiniboia. The demographic differences between the two districts were dramatic.

40 See Lux, *supra* note 9 at 51 and 58, and W.A. Waiser, *Saskatchewan: A New History* (Calgary: Fifth House, 2005) at 164, for accounts of the plight of this band after it was moved to the Eagle Hills near Battleford. Lean Man's first encounter with criminal law is discussed in Chapter 4.

41 See Spry, *supra* note 21.

42 Poundmaker at Treaty 6, quoted by Peter Erasmus, *Buffalo Days and Nights, as Told to Henry Thompson* (Calgary: Glenbow-Alberta Institute, 1976) at 244. See also Christensen, *supra* note 23 at 247; Miller, *supra* note 23 at 72.

43 Morris, *supra* note 12 at 183. Morris is referring to the anxieties expressed by the Cree at the outset of the negotiations to Treaty 6 when he first met with them.

44 See, *e.g.,* Sharon Venne, "Understanding Treaty 6: An Indigenous Perspective," in Michael Asch, ed., *Aboriginal and Treaty Rights in Canada: Essays on Law, Equality, and Respect for Difference* (Vancouver: UBC Press, 1997) 172; Harold LeRat, with Linda Ungar, "An 'X' Changes Everything" in Harold LeRat, with Linda Ungar, eds., *Treaty Promises, Indian Reality: Life on a Reserve* (Saskatoon: Purich Publishing, 2005) at 14; Harold Cardinal and Walter Hildebrandt, eds., *Treaty Elders of Saskatchewan: Our Dream Is that Our Peoples Will One Day Be Clearly Recognized as Nations* (Calgary: University of Calgary Press, 2000); Treaty 7 Elders and Tribal Council, with Walter Hildebrandt, Dorothy First Rider, and Sarah Carter, *The True Spirit and Original Intent of Treaty 7* (Kingston and Montreal: McGill-Queen's University Press, 1996); Sidney L. Harring, "'There Seemed to Be No Recognized Law': Canadian Law and the Prairie First Nations" in Louis A. Knafla and

Jonathan Swainger, eds., *Laws and Societies in the Canadian Prairie West 1670-1940* (Vancouver: UBC Press, 2005) 92 at 102-8 [Harring, "No Recognized Law"]; Neal McLeod, "Rethinking Treaty 6 in the Spirit of Mistahi Maskwa (Big Bear)" (1999) 19 Canadian Journal of Native Studies 69 [McLeod, "Rethinking Treaty 6"]; Canada, Royal Commission on Aboriginal Peoples, *supra* note 23. David T. McNab, "Treaties and an Official Use of History" (1993) 12 Canadian Journal of Native Studies 139 at 141.

45 Quoted in Sluman and Goodwill, *supra* note 22 at 8; Dempsey, *supra* note 23 at 63; McLeod, "Rethinking Treaty 6," *ibid.* at 76. See also Rudy Wiebe, *Big Bear* (Toronto: Penguin, 2008).

46 Mistawasis, quoted by Erasmus, *supra* note 42 at 246-47; Christensen, *supra* note 23 at 252; Miller, *supra* note 23 at 72. Peter Erasmus recalled Mistawasis's intervention. Erasmus had been retained by the Cree chiefs to act as their interpreter in the treaty negotiations (Erasmus, *ibid.* at 235-38; Christensen, *ibid.* at 220; 227-31). It has been suggested by some that the chiefs with Christian leanings were the leading advocates of entering into treaty with the government. Neal McLeod, *ibid.,* intimates that Sweet Grass's Christian leanings – he had converted to Roman Catholicism – were a significant factor in his desire to enter into a treaty with the government. It is perhaps worth noting that Ahtahkakoop and Mistawasis, also leading chiefs at Treaty 6, were also converts to Christianity. See Christensen, *ibid.* at 182 (re Ahtahkakoop's conversion to the Anglican faith) and 641 (re Mistawasis's conversion to the Presbyterian faith). See also Dempsey, *supra* note 23 at 59, 62.

47 Mistawasis, quoted by Erasmus, *ibid.* at 248; Christensen, *ibid.* at 254.

48 The following text from Treaty 4, reproduced in Morris, *supra* note 12 at 233 [emphasis added], is virtually identical in all the numbered treaties: "And the undersigned Chiefs and Headmen, on their own behalf, and on behalf of all other Indians inhabiting the tract within ceded ... *They promise and engage that they will, in all respects, obey and abide by the law ... and that they will not molest the person or property of any inhabitant of such ceded tract, or the property of Her Majesty the Queen ... and that they will assist the officers of Her Majesty in bringing to justice and punishment any Indian offending against the stipulations of this treaty, or infringing the laws in force in the country so ceded.*"

49 *Ibid.* [emphasis added]: "And further, Her Majesty agrees that Her said Indians shall have right to pursue their avocations of hunting, trapping and fishing throughout the tract surrendered, *subject to such regulations as may from time to time be made by the Government of the country, acting under the authority of Her Majesty,* and saving and excepting such tracts as may be required or taken up from time to time for settlement, mining or other purposes, under grant or other right given by Her Majesty's said Government."

50 *North-West Territories Act, 1875,* 38 Vict., c. 49, s. 74.

51 Treaty 4, reproduced in Morris, *supra* note 12 at 333 [emphasis added]: "Her Majesty agrees that within the boundary of the Indian reserves, until otherwise determined by the Government of the Dominion of Canada, *no intoxicating liquor shall be allowed to be introduced or sold, and all laws now in force, or hereafter to be enacted, to preserve Her Indian subjects, inhabiting the reserves, or living elsewhere within the North-West Territories, from the evil effects of intoxicating liquor, shall be strictly enforced.*"

52 *Indian Act, 1876,* 39 Vict., c. 18, ss. 79-85.

53 While it cannot be said that the legal historical literature of criminal law in the North-West Territories is voluminous, a small body of scholarship has examined different aspects of nineteenth-century Prairie justice: see, *e.g.,* Ward, *supra* note 19; Reynolds, *supra* note 16; R.C. Macleod, *The North-West Mounted Police and Law Enforcement 1873-1905* (Toronto: University of Toronto Press, 1976) [Macleod, *North-West Mounted Police*]; W.H. McConnell,

Prairie Justice (Calgary: Burroughs, 1980); Leyton-Brown, *supra* note 20. See also Bowker, *supra* note 20; Williams, "Dawn of Law," *supra* note 15; D. Colwyn Williams, "Law and Institutions in the North West Territories (1869-1905)" (1963) 28 Sask. Bar Rev. 109; (1964) 29 Sask. Bar Rev. 51; (1964) 29 Sask. Bar Rev. 83; (1965) 30 Sask. Bar Rev. 51; (1966) 31 Sask. Bar Rev. 1; (1966) 31 Sask. Bar Rev. 137; (1968) 33 Sask. Bar Rev. 145 [Williams, "Law and Institutions"]; C.C. McCaul, "Precursors of the Bench and Bar in the Western Provinces" (1925) Can. Bar Rev. 25. Most recently, see Louis A. Knafla and Jonathan Swainger, eds., *Laws and Societies in the Canadian Prairie West, 1670-1940* (Vancouver: UBC Press, 2005).

54 On 23 June 1870, Rupert's Land and the North-West Territory were admitted by order-in-council to the Dominion of Canada. The groundwork had been laid in 1869 in the *Act for the Temporary Government of Rupert's Land and the North-West Territory when United with Canada, 1869*, 32-33 Vict., c. 3, which authorized the appointment of a Lieutenant-Governor who would be responsible for the administration of justice and make laws and ordinances necessary for the peace, order, and good government of the inhabitants of the Territories, subject to the requirement that all laws and ordinances were to be placed before both Houses. Section 5 of this short statute provided: "All the Laws in force in Rupert's Land and the North-Western Territory, at the time of their admission into the Union shall so far as they are consistent with the British North America Act, 1867, – with the terms and conditions of such admission approved of by the Queen under the 146th section thereof, – and with this Act, – remain in force until altered by the Parliament of Canada, or by the Lieutenant Governor under the authority of this Act." See also Williams, "Law and Institutions," *ibid.* at 109.

55 It is important to note, as Thomas, *supra* note 11 does at 6, that s. 146 of the *British North America Act, 1867* (U.K.), 30-31 Vict., c. 3, recognized the existence of "two different territorial units in the North-West": Rupert's Land (the domain of the HBC) and the North-Western Territory, the boundaries of the two areas not having been "authoritatively settled" and the subject of competing claims by the HBC and the Canadians. The Canadians maintained their claim to the North-Western Territory, the boundaries of which they asserted was "contiguous with Upper Canada and included most of the prairie region from the Red River to the Rockies." Thomas also notes, at 7, that s. 146 provided that the process for admission of Rupert's Land and the North-Western Territory was "to be initiated by unilateral action of the Canadian Parliament and effected by summary action of the Imperial government."

56 Ward, *supra* note 19, at 6.

57 *Ibid.* at 14. Ward cites CSP 1871, no. 20, 26. According to Ward, Lieutenant-Governor Adams Archibald appointed six justices of the peace, but at the time of his writing, Ward was unable to confirm whether these justices ever performed judicial duties between 1870 and 1873.

58 *An Act to Amend the "Act to Make Further Provision for the Government of the North West Territories," 1873*, 36 Vict., c. 34.

59 *Ibid.*, s. 3.

60 *The Department of the Interior Act, 1873*, 36 Vict., c. 4.

61 *Ibid.*, s. 2.

62 *Ibid.*, s. 3.

63 *An Act to Amend the "Act to Make Further Provision for the Government of the North West Territories," 1873*, 36 Vict., c. 34, s. 6, Schedule A.

64 *Ibid.*

65 See, *e.g.*, Macleod, *North-West Mounted Police, supra* note 53; R.C. Macleod, "Canadianizing the West: The North-West Mounted Police as Agents of the National Policy" in Lewis H. Thomas, ed., *Essays on Western History: In Honour of Lewis Gwynne Thomas* (Edmonton: University of Alberta Press, 1976) 101 [Macleod, "Canadianizing the West"]; Ward, *supra* note 19 at 26; Leyton-Brown, *supra* note 20 at 216-19; John Jennings, *The North-West Mounted Police and Canadian Indian Policy, 1873-1896* (PhD Dissertation, University of Toronto, 1979) [unpublished] [Jennings, *North-West Mounted Police*].

66 *An Act Respecting the Administration of Justice, and for the Establishment of a Police Force in the North-West Territories, 1873*, 36 Vict., c. 35. Section 15 of the *Act* specified that "persons" appointed to the Force were to be "of sound constitution, able to ride, active, able-bodied, of good character, and between the ages of eighteen and forty-years" and able to read and write either English or French.

67 *Ibid.*, s. 19.

68 See, *e.g.*, *An Act to Amend and Consolidate the Laws Respecting the North-West Territories, 1875*, 38 Vict., c. 49, s. 68; *An Act to Amend and Consolidate the Several Acts Relating to the North-West Territories, 1880*, 43 Vict., c. 25, ss. 78 and 79.

69 Macleod, *North-West Mounted Police, supra* note 53; McCaul, *supra* note 53; Reynolds, *supra* note 16 at 10-22 reviews the jurisdiction of the justice of the peace in the North-West Territories: justices of the peace could hear many matters under federal law and the penal clauses of many territorial and municipal ordinances; they could adjudicate on master and servant matters as well as on a person's sanity, order the inspections of animals thought to be sick (and two justices could order that a diseased animal be destroyed), order the interdiction (prohibition of sale of alcohol) of anyone apparently abusing alcohol to the detriment of his health and his family, perform marriages (between 1878 and 1882), serve as auctioneer for stray animals, take oaths, and so on.

70 Reynolds, *ibid.* at 58. See the *Indian Act, 1881*, 44 Vict., c. 17, s. 12: the Indian Commissioner, Assistant Indian Commissioner, and every Indian Superintendent, Indian Inspector, and Indian Agent were to be justices of the peace *ex officio* for the purposes of the *Indian Act.*

71 Reynolds, *ibid.* at 113-15. R.C. Macleod and Heather Rollason, "'Restrain the Lawless Savages': Native Defendants in the Criminal Courts of the North-West Territories, 1878-1885" (1997) 10 Journal of Historical Sociology 157 at 159, say that by 1877 six superintendents and twelve inspectors were all appointed justices of the peace.

72 Macleod, *North-West Mounted Police, supra* note 53 at 35.

73 Macleod, *ibid.;* Macleod, "Canadianizing the West," *supra* note 65; Macleod, "Law and Order on the Western Canadian Frontier" in John McLaren, Hamar Foster, and Chet Orloff, eds., *Law for the Elephant, Law for the Beaver: Essays in the Legal History of the North American West* (Regina, SK, and Pasadena, CA: Canadian Plains Research Center and Ninth Judicial District Historical Society, 1992) 90 at 100-1 [Macleod, "Law and Order"]. See also his more recent work with Heather Rollason: Macleod and Rollason, *supra* note 71.

74 Jennings, *North-West Mounted Police, supra* note 65; John Jennings, "The Plains Indians and the Law" in Hugh A. Dempsey, ed., *Men in Scarlet* (Calgary: Historical Society of Alberta and McClelland and Stewart West, 1974) 51 [Jennings, "Plains Indians"]; John Jennings, "The North-West Mounted Police and Indian Policy after the 1885 Rebellion" in F. Laurie Barron and James B. Waldram, eds., *1885 and After: Native Society in Transition* (Regina: Canadian Plains Research Center 1986) 225 [Jennings, "NWMP and Indian Policy"].

75 According to Macleod, *North-West Mounted Police, supra* note 53 at 27: "The police played a major part in the first stage, were almost entirely responsible for the second, and did

what they could toward achieving the third. Their general approach to all three problems was simple but usually very effective. It consisted in giving the Indians first priority at all times. If the protection of the rights of the Indian demanded a policy that annoyed or interfered with the activities of the white settlers, that was unfortunate but it did not prevent the policy from being carried out. The police did not make promises they could not keep and they did all that they could to avoid passage of laws they could not enforce."

76 Macleod, "Law and Order," *supra* note 73 at 101: "The challenges they faced in the 1870s and 1880s were of an entirely different order from those of the HBC era. Immigration was slow at first but reached tens of thousands by the end of the century. The buffalo and the whole Plains Indian economy based on the hunt disappeared with startling suddenness in the early 1880s. Through this great transformation the Mounted Police were outstandingly successful in maintaining order until the Rebellion of 1885."

77 Jennings, "NWMP and Indian Policy," *supra* note 74 at 225. Macleod similarly fixes 1885 as "a natural dividing line because the Canadian Pacific Railway was completed at that time" (Macleod, *North-West Mounted Police, supra* note 53 at 21), coinciding with both the disappearance of the buffalo and the 1885 Rebellion, which itself "was to a considerable extent a product of the coming of the railway and of the economic and social changes that it brought in its wake."

78 Jennings, *ibid.* at 226.

79 Principally, but not exclusively, due to the "authorized" and autobiographical nature of this history, much of which was produced by RCMP historians. See, *e.g.*, Arthur L. Haydon, *The Riders of the Plains: A Record of the Royal North-West Mounted Police of Canada, 1873-1910* (Toronto: Copp Clark, 1920); William Beahan and Stan Horall, *Red Coats on the Prairies: The North-West Mounted Police, 1886-1900* (Regina: Centax Books, 1998) esp. ch. 6; John Peter Turner, *The North-West Mounted Police 1873-1893,* 2 vols. (Ottawa: King's Printer, 1950); Nora Hickson Kelly, *My Mountie and Me: A True Story* (Regina: Centax, 1999); William Kelly, with Nora Hickson Kelly, *Policing the Fringe: A Young Mountie's Story* (Regina: Centax, 1999). For a contrasting view, see Lorne and Caroline Brown, *An Unauthorized History of the RCMP* (Toronto: James Lewis and Samuel, 1973).

80 Walter Hildebrandt, *Views from Fort Battleford: Constructed Visions of an Anglo-Canadian West* (Regina: Canadian Plains Research Center, 1994) at 33.

81 *Ibid.* at 37.

82 *Ibid.* at 36.

83 Jennings, "NWMP and Indian Policy," *supra* note 74 at 228.

84 John L. Tobias, "Canada's Subjugation of the Plains Cree, 1879-1885" in J.R. Miller, ed., *Sweet Promises: A Reader on Indian-White Relations in Canada* (Toronto: University of Toronto Press, 1991) 212 at 221-22. See also Lux, *supra* note 9 at 43, and Hildebrandt's discussion, *supra* note 80 at 46-47, of the arrest of Lucky Man as a result of a provocatively intransigent stance adopted by Indian Farm Instructor Craig in response to Lucky Man's request for provisions for a sick child. The incident to which Hildebrandt refers likely involved Lucky Man's son, Kawaeechataywaymat (Man Who Speaks Our Language) rather than Lucky Man himself: see Dempsey, *supra* note 23 at 6-13. I refer to this incident in Chapter 4, fn1. See Bob Beal and R.C. Macleod, *Prairie Fire: The 1885 North-West Rebellion* (Edmonton: Hurtig Publishers, 1984) at 92-99.

85 Carter, *Aboriginal People, supra* note 11 at 127. Carter re-emphasizes this point at 130: "Yet it remains the case that in Western Canada there simply was not the record of continuous

violence and conquest that characterized not only the western United States but many of Britain's imperial enterprises. This had as much to do with the strategies and actions of the Aboriginal residents as with the policies of government and the actions of a handful of police." See also Hildebrandt's critical engagement with Macleod's characterization of the "benevolent despotism" of the NWMP, *supra* note 80 at 35-37.

86 Carter, *Lost Harvests, supra* note 9 at ix.

87 *Ibid.* See also Frank Laurie Barron, "The Indian Pass System in the Canadian West, 1882-1935" (1988) 13 Prairie Forum 25.

88 Pettipas, *supra* note 9 at 112. Pettipas relies here on Jennings's doctoral dissertation, *The North-West Mounted Police and Canadian Indian Policy, 1873-1896, supra* note 65. John Tobias also notes another instance in which Commissioner Irvine's fair treatment of the Cree, by giving them food, upset Indian Commissioner Edgar Dewdney and officials in Ottawa. See Tobias, *supra* note 84 at 220.

89 Carter, *Lost Harvests, supra* note 9 at 153-54.

90 *Ibid.* at 154.

91 Tobias, *supra* note 84 at 221-22. Historians writing of other jurisdictions demonstrate that Dewdney's views were not unique, and that colonial authorities in other contexts expressed frustration at judicial refusals to enforce discriminatory legislation. See, *e.g.,* John McLaren, "The Early British Columbia Judges, the Rule of Law and the 'Chinese Question': The California and Oregon Connection" in John McLaren, Hamar Foster, and Chet Orloff, eds., *Law for the Elephant, Law for the Beaver: Essays in the Legal History of the North American West* (Regina, SK, and Pasadena, CA: Canadian Plains Research Center and Ninth Judicial District Historical Society, 1992) 237; Sanjay Nigam, "Disciplining and Policing the 'Criminals by Birth,' Part 1: The Making of a Colonial Stereotype – The Criminal Tribes and Castes of North India" (1990) 27 Indian Economic and Social History Review 131; Sanjay Nigam, "Disciplining and Policing the 'Criminals by Birth,' Part 2: The Development of a Disciplinary System, 1871-1900" (1990) 27 Indian Economic and Social History Review 257.

92 Roderick G. Martin, "Macleod at Law: A Judicial Biography of James Farquharson Macleod, 1874-94" in Jonathan Swainger and Constance Backhouse, eds., *People and Place: Historical Influences on Legal Culture* (Vancouver: UBC Press, 2003) 37.

93 Cf. Vic Satzewich, "'Where's the Beef?': Cattle Killing, Rations Policy and First Nations 'Criminality' in Southern Alberta, 1892-1895" (1996) 9 Journal of Historical Sociology 188.

94 *An Act Respecting the Administration of Justice, and for the Establishment of a Police Force in the North-West Territories, 1873*, 36 Vict., c. 35, s. 2.

95 Bowker, *supra* note 20 at 253-54.

96 McCaul, *supra* note 53 at 35. Macleod presided in the Bow River District and was based in Fort Macleod, Ryan (Qu'Appelle District) was based in Shoal Lake, and Richardson (Saskatchewan District) resided in Battleford. In 1883, Charles Borromée Rouleau was appointed to fill the position left vacant when Matthew Ryan quit, or was removed from office, in 1881 following allegations or complaints of bad or improper behaviour. When Rouleau was appointed, he sat in Battleford, by which time Richardson had moved to Regina. Jeremiah Travis was appointed in 1885, and sat in Calgary until the office of stipendiary magistrate was eliminated by statute in 1887: Bowker, *ibid.* at 245 and 271.

97 See *An Act Respecting the Administration of Justice, and for the Establishment of a Police Force in the North-West Territories 1873*, 36 Vict., c. 35, s. 3; *An Act to Amend and Consolidate the Laws Respecting the North-West Territories, 1875*, 38 Vict., c. 49, s. 64; *An Act to Amend*

the "North-West Territories Act, 1875," 1877, 40 Vict., c. 7, ss. 62-64 and 71 (re civil claims); *An Act to Amend and Consolidate the Several Acts Relating to the North-West Territories, 1880,* 43 Vict., c. 25, ss. 76 and 82.

98 *An Act Further to Amend the Law Respecting the North-West Territories, 1886,* 49 Vict., c. 25, ss. 30-32.

99 Initially, the stipendiary magistrate's summary jurisdiction covered minor offences, including: larceny and property-related offences where the value of the property did not exceed $100; attempted larceny; assault with a weapon, assault causing bodily harm, wounding; assault upon a female person of any age, other than rape and attempted rape, and assault upon a male child under 14; assault or obstruction of a range of judicial and law enforcement officers: *An Act Respecting the Administration of Justice, and for the Establishment of a Police Force in the North-West Territories, 1873,* 36 Vict., c. 35, s. 3.

100 *Ibid.*, s. 4.

101 *Ibid.*, s. 5.

102 *North-West Territories Act, 1875,* 38 Vict., c. 49, s. 61ff. consolidated matters governing legal relations and procedure in the Territories. A form of omnibus legislation, this act dealt with everything from wills, estates, and married women's property to the prohibition of manufacture, import, distribution and sale, and possession of intoxicants.

103 Section 64 provided that the Chief Justice of Manitoba or any judge of the Manitoba Court of Queen's Bench and one stipendiary magistrate as Associate had power to try summarily offences for which the maximum punishment was less than five years' imprisonment. With the consent of the accused, they could also try summarily, or with a jury of six if the accused demanded trial by jury, all offences where the maximum punishment was greater than five years' imprisonment but not the death penalty. Where the offences provided for the death penalty upon conviction, a Manitoba judge and a stipendiary magistrate could preside with a jury of eight. A person sentenced to death was able to appeal to the Manitoba Court of Queen's Bench (s. 65).

104 *An Act to Amend the "North-West Territories Act, 1875," 1877,* 40 Vict., c. 7, ss. 63-64.

105 *Ibid.*, s. 64.2.

106 *Ibid.*, s. 64.3.

107 *Ibid.*, s. 78.

108 *An Act to Amend and Consolidate the Several Acts Relating to the North-West Territories, 1880,* 43 Vict., c. 25, ss. 74 and 76. The *Act* provided additional responsibilities to the stipendiary magistrates, who were now, by virtue of s. 82, to act as Coroners (as was the Assistant Commissioner of the NWMP. By operation of ss. 85-89, the stipendiary magistrate could try most forms of civil cases, and all appeals could go to the Manitoba Court of Queen's Bench.

109 *Ibid.*, s. 76.5.

110 Bowker, *supra* note 20 at 262.

111 *North-West Territories Act, 1886,* 43 Vict., c. 50.

112 *Ibid.*, s. 41.

113 *Ibid.*, s. 49.

114 McCaul, *supra* note 53 at 39; Bowker, *supra* note 20 at 277-78.

115 Leyton-Brown, *supra* note 20. Richardson had been passed over for the position of Chief Justice when it was created (McGuire was appointed Chief Justice in 1902). Both Richardson and McGuire retired in 1903. Richardson moved back to Ottawa and died there in 1913: "Deceased Judge Presided at the Trial of Louis Riel" Regina *Leader* (16 July 1913) 1 at col. 3.

See also Thomas Flanagan, "Hugh Richardson" (1910-13) 14 Dictionary of Canadian Biography 872.

116 The court records and press reports in the Regina *Leader* indicate that a number of matters had to be adjourned in July 1902 due to the ill health of Justice Richardson.

117 Bowker, *supra* note 20, suggests at 263 that he came west by late 1876, and then returned to Ottawa late the following spring to bring out his family. The return trip was difficult and long, and they were able to move into their new home in Battleford at the end of September 1877. The earliest dated prosecution before him that I have found in the court records took place in Fort Saskatchewan on 10 October 1877: Regnier Brillon (1877), Department of the Attorney General, Regina Judicial Centre: Court Records First Series, 1878-86, Files 1-282 [SAB AG (GR 11.1) CR-Regina, 1st series, 1876-86], file 4.

118 Flanagan, *supra* note 115; see also Bowker, *supra* note 20; Jonathan Swainger, *The Canadian Department of Justice and the Completion of Confederation 1867-78* (Vancouver: UBC Press, 2000) at 39-40. Swainger suggests that Richardson's long career on the bench illustrates both the calibre of his legal abilities and the kind of legal talent the Department of Justice was able to recruit.

119 See Bob Beal and Barry Wright, "Summary and Incompetent Justice: Legal Responses to the 1885 Crisis" in Barry Wright and Susan Binnie, eds., *Canadian State Trials,* vol. 3, *Political Trials and Security Measures, 1840-1914* (Toronto: University of Toronto Press, 2009) 353; W.A. Waiser, "The White Man Governs: The 1885 Indian Trials" in Barry Wright and Susan Binnie, eds., *Canadian State Trials,* vol. 3, *Political Trials and Security Measures, 1840-1914* (Toronto: University of Toronto Press, 2009) 451.

120 Desmond Morton, *The Queen v. Louis Riel* (Toronto: University of Toronto Press, 1974) at xiv.

121 J.M. Bumstead, *Louis Riel v. Canada: The Making of a Rebel* (Winnipeg: Great Plains Publications, 2001) at 274. Bumstead does not burden his readers with the irritant of footnotes, so one does not know the sources upon which he draws for this assessment. See also Bumstead's more recent contribution: "Another Look at the Riel Trial for Treason" in Barry Wright and Susan Binnie, eds., *Canadian State Trials,* vol. 3, *Political Trials and Security Measures, 1840-1914* (Toronto: University of Toronto Press, 2009) 411 (footnotes now included).

122 *Globe and Mail* (17 July 2006) S8.

123 SAB AG CR-Regina, 1st series, 1876-86, files 176-279. Interspersed within this series of files are ten files from Battleford, Fort Saskatchewan, or Prince Albert; the rest are from the south (*e.g.,* Regina, Moose Jaw, Qu'Appelle, Wood Mountain). In addition to the liquor violations, two Canadian Pacific Railway men were charged with being intoxicated while on duty. Forty-four files involve theft and fraud offences; there are a handful of false pretences and horse-smuggling offences, a few master-and-servant matters involving unpaid wages, among others, including assaults and so on. If a most common matter is to be cited, it would have to be property-related offences, such as theft, fraud, and false pretences.

124 Sandra E. Bingaman, *The North-West Rebellion Trials, 1885* (MA Thesis, University of Saskatchewan [Regina], 1971) [unpublished] at 16-17.

125 Ward, *supra* note 19 at 79.

126 In Bowker's view, "the record shows that Richardson acted with dignity, spoke little and did not demonstrate hostility to Riel, though one can guess that he felt it": Bowker, *supra* note 20 at 273.

127 Unlike his fellow magistrate, Rouleau, who expressed his views as follows in a letter to Lieutenant-Governor Dewdney prior to the trials: "It is high time that those indians [*sic*] should be taught a lesson. I think that General Middleton was altogether too kind to them. My impression is that a *milk and water policy* is a very wrong one. If the indians can commit all the crimes of the Statute with impunity, we may expect a renewal of the same scene in a short period." Quoted by Bingaman, *supra* note 124 at 115 (emphasis added). Bingaman notes that Rouleau suffered losses to both his property (his house in Battleford was burned to the ground during the hostilities) and his reputation during the events of 1885, giving rise to the hostility expressed in his letter. See also Bowker, *ibid.* at 272-73; and Bob Beal and Rod Macleod, *Prairie Fire: The 1885 North-West Rebellion* (Edmonton: Hurtig Publishers, 1984) at 331, who quote from a letter written by the Oblate priest, Father André, to his superior. Father André, who had observed the trials in Regina and Battleford, described Richardson as fair and impartial and condemned Rouleau as a "vindictive man and a servile instrument in the hands of the government."

128 For example, with respect to his jurisdiction to try Daniel Williams for offences that were alleged to have occurred in Fort St. John. Daniel Williams (1879), SAB AG CR-Regina, 1st series, 1876-86, file 179; and *Daniel Williams v. James McDougall and James McKinley* (1879) (false arrest and imprisonment), SAB AG CR-Regina, 1st series, 1876-86, file 107.

129 Goodwin Marchand (1878), SAB AG CR-Regina, 1st series, 1876-86, file 18.

130 Daniel Williams (1879), SAB AG CR-Regina, 1st series, 1876-86, files 79 and 107.

131 This case was covered to a certain extent in the *Saskatchewan Herald.* Only in the *Herald*'s coverage, but not in the court file, do we learn that Daniel Williams was a mixed-race man, "a mulatto" with a racist nickname – "Nigger Dan": see *Saskatchewan Herald* (25 August 1879) 1 at col. 4, and 2 at col. 1.

132 See, *e.g.,* the Case of the Lost or Missing Child, Peaychew's daughter, discussed in the Introduction.

133 George Glover (1891), Saskatchewan Archives Board, Supreme Court of North-West Territories (Criminal), Collection R1286 [hereinafter, SAB SCNWT (Crim.), Coll. R1286], file 31.

134 *Criminal Code, 1892,* 55-56 Vict., c. 29, s. 269 provided that anyone who "carnally knows any girl under the age of fourteen years, not being his wife, whether he believes her to be of or above that age or not," was liable upon conviction to imprisonment for life and to be whipped.

135 Pierre Bourassa (1892), SAB SCNWT (Crim.), Coll. R1286, file 39, trial transcript at 10. Lesley Erickson, *Westward Bound: Sex, Violence, the Law, and the Making of a Settler Society* (Vancouver: UBC Press, 2011), also discusses this case at 51-52.

136 Henry R. Elliott (1878), SAB AG CR-Regina, 1st series, 1876-86, file 26. It appears that Macleod also had some involvement in this case; he appears to have presided with Richardson with a jury at the trial. See also Bowker, *supra* note 20 at 263-65.

137 Kenneth McLeod (1880), SAB AG CR-Regina, 1st series, 1876-86, file 87. Richardson convicted McLeod and sentenced him to two months of hard labour.

Chapter 2: "Of Course No One Saw Them"

1 Felix Plante (1877), Department of the Attorney General, Regina Judicial Centre: Court Records First Series, 1878-86, Files 1-282 [SAB AG (GR 11.1) CR-Regina, 1st series, 1876-86], file 1.

2 Department of Interior, Dominion Land Branch – Applications for Scrip 1886-1901, 1906 made by North-West Half Breeds, Saskchewan Archives Board, R 91-17, Collection R-5.11, file C14943.

3 It is possible that the "December 15, 1877" date is a mistake of transcription on Richardson's part, and that the case was disposed of within one month of the date of the offence. If the date of his guilty plea is incorrect (and should be 15 December 1876 rather than 1877), he may have been held in custody for only two weeks (and thus a relatively short period of time following a serious assault in which to conclude that he was not "dangerous"). When I first read this file in July 2003, I did not query the 1877 date; having read other files since then, I have come to realize that Richardson occasionally misdated his record, especially in the early days of January and occasionally in October. It is likelier that the recorded date is correct in this instance, however. The earliest dated record in this series of court records is that of the inquest into the death of the prisoner Charles Cardinal held at Fort Saskatchewan in July 1877. It is not apparent from this file that Richardson played any role in that proceeding. The earliest dated record in the series in which Richardson appears to have presided is that of Reigner Brillon (1877), SAB AG CR-Regina, 1st series, 1876-86, file 4, whose trial occurred in Battleford on 10 October 1877.

See John Beattie's cautionary admonition in *Crime and the Courts in England, 1660-1800* (Princeton, NJ: Princeton University Press, 1986) at 20-21. Noting that "although much of the information on a criminal indictment is probably reliable (*e.g.,* name of accused and name of victim), other information "cannot be taken at face value," including the date of the alleged offence. In the Richardson files, there is good reason to proceed with Beattie's advice in mind, especially as the Cree and other Aboriginal peoples often described the time of an incident by reference to the season. For example, in her deposition in Kee-chee-qua-pi-e-ka-wa's case, (1877) SAB AG CR-Regina, 1st series, 1876-86, file 7, the deposition of a young girl named Monique explained when the murder of several members of her family by Kee-chee-qua-pi-e-ka-wa, alias Johnny, alias Son of the Big Man, alias Tis-ta-mous-noui, and his brother, Bear, took place: "When the leaves were getting withered and two winters have passed since, my father's family were camped at a small lake between [Lake?] Assiniboine and Lesser Slave Lake."

4 *Saskatchewan Herald* (31 October 1878) 1 at col. 2.

5 The Manitoba Penitentiary admission register is silent as to his age or any particulars, and no release or discharge date is given: Library and Archives Canada [LAC], RG 73, W87-88/365, Microfilm reel T-1108911, vol. 23 (MIKAN no. 134308), "Manitoba Penitentiary Admitance [*sic*] Register," 16 May 1871 – 22 June 1885 at 4; "Report of the Commissioner of the North-West Mounted Police, 1879" reprinted in Royal Canadian Mounted Police, *Opening Up the West: Being the Official Reports to Parliament of the Activities of the Royal* [sic] *North-West Mounted Police from 1874-1881 by The Commissioners of the Royal* [*sic*] *North-West Mounted Police,* facsimile reprint (Toronto: Coles Publishing, 1973; original ed. Ottawa: Maclean, Roger, 1874-81) Appendix C at 42 ["Report of the Commissioner of the NWMP"].

6 David G. Mandelbaum, *The Plains Cree: An Ethnographic, Historical and Comparative Study* (Regina: Canadian Plains Research Center, 1979).

7 Given the genealogy, fluidity, and composition of many bands: Neal McLeod, "Plains Cree Identity: Borderlands, Ambiguous Genealogies and Narrative Irony" (2000) 20 Canadian Journal of Native Studies 455. As noted previously above, some sources suggest that Big Bear may not have been Cree at all, as his father, Black Powder, was an Ojibway originally from Ontario and his mother may also have been Ojibway, although he was clearly raised

as a Cree: see Hugh A. Dempsey, *Big Bear: The End of Freedom* (Vancouver: Douglas and McIntyre, 1984) at 11-15. Dempsey, at 28, tells us as well that Little Pine's mother was a Blackfoot, and Sweet Grass was a full-blooded Crow. Similarly, Poundmaker was of mixed heritage, with an Assiniboine father and a Cree or Half-breed mother.

8 Mandelbaum, *supra* note 6 at 107.

9 Edward Ahenakew, *Voices of the Plains Cree,* edited and with an introduction by Ruth M. Buck (Toronto: McClelland and Stewart, 1973) at 34. This story is titled "Indian Laws."

10 *Ibid.* at 35.

11 Mandelbaum, *supra* note 6 at 107.

12 *Ibid.*

13 *Ibid.* at 108.

14 *Ibid.* at 107-8. Dempsey, *supra* note 7 at 97, also provides a detailed account of the same story. He also makes it clear that Big Bear never forgave the man. See also Rudy Wiebe, *Big Bear* (Toronto: Penguin, 2008).

15 Deanna Christensen, *Ahtahkakoop: The Epic Account of a Plains Cree Head Chief, His People, and Their Struggle for Survival, 1816-1896* (Shell Lake, SK: Ahtahkakoop Publishing, 2000) at 63; Mandelbaum, *supra* note 6 at 111-21.

16 Mandelbaum, *ibid.* at 115. He also notes, however, that an offender who resisted or showed anger during the punishment would receive nothing.

17 *Ibid.* at 123.

18 *Ibid.* at 122.

19 See Manitoba, *Report of the Aboriginal Justice Inquiry of Manitoba,* vol. 1, *The Justice System and Aboriginal People* (A.C. Hamilton and C.M. Sinclair, Commissioners) (Winnipeg: Province of Manitoba, 1991) at 27.

20 Young men known for their bravery or daring, who were not [yet] members of the Warrior Society.

21 Mandelbaum, *supra* note 6 at 122.

22 *Ibid.*

23 *R. v. Bear's Shin Bone* (1899), 3 C.C.C. 329, 4 Terr. L.R. 173 (N.W.T.S.C.). Rouleau J. relied on the case of *R. v. Nan-e-quis-a-ka* (1889), 1 Terr. L.R. 211, in which the Northwest Territories Supreme Court had held that the marriage customs of the Blood were valid and to be legally recognized in the Territories, such that a woman married according to the custom of her people was not competent and not compellable as a witness against her husband.

24 *Ce Tan* (or *Chaton*) (1902), Saskatchewan Archives Board, Supreme Court of North-West Territories (Criminal), Collection R1286 [hereinafter, SAB SCNWT (Crim.), Coll. R1286], file 264.

25 SAB AG CR-Regina, 1st series, 1876-86, files 1-282.

26 One of their cases is discussed in this chapter; the remaining six cases are discussed in detail in Chapter 5.

27 See, *e.g.*, Sylvia van Kirk, *Many Tender Ties: Women in the Fur Trade Society, 1670-1870* (Winnipeg: Watson and Dwyer Publications, 1980); Jennifer S.H. Brown, *Strangers in Blood: Fur Trade Families in Indian Country* (Vancouver: UBC Press, 1980); Theodore Binnema, Gerhard J. Ens, and R.C. Macleod, eds., *From Rupert's Land to Canada* (Edmonton: University of Alberta Press, 2001) (a number of the essays in this collection revisit the construction of Métis identity); Sarah Carter, *The Importance of Being Monogamous: Marriage and Nation Building in Western Canada to 1915* (Edmonton and Athabasca:

University of Alberta Press and Athabasca University Press, 2008) at 32-33, 134-36, 197 [Carter, *Importance*].

28 See, *e.g.*, Alexander Morris, *The Treaties of Canada with the Indians of Manitoba and the North-West Territories,* facsimile reprint (Toronto: Prospero Books, 2000; original ed. Toronto: Belfords Clarke, 1880) at 98 and 186-87, for his record of the interventions on their behalf by The Gambler at Treaty 4 and Mistawasis at Treaty 6. It is my understanding that The Gambler and Mistawasis were speaking on behalf of "Indian Half-breeds," many of whom were relatives and whom they regarded as members of their community, and not the "immigrant" Métis from the Red River Colony (who posed a challenge to the territory and hunt of the First Nations). The Gambler chided the Treaty Commissioner early in the Treaty 4 discussions: "Now when you have come here, you see sitting out there a mixture of Half-breeds, Crees, Saulteaux and Stonies, all are one, and you were slow in taking the hand of a Half-breed." This, for The Gambler, was one of "the many things that are in my way."

29 See, *e.g.,* the Montour cousins and The Youngest Son of the Netmaker, SAB AG CR-Regina, 1st series, 1876-86, file 28; and Baptiste Flammond (Half-Breed), Moses Bunn (Sioux), Simoose (Saulteaux), and Jim Sioux (1877), SAB AG CR-Regina, 1st series, 1876-86, file 11.

30 See, *e.g.,* I-ah-pee-coo-cah (1881), SAB AG CR-Regina, 1st series, 1876-86, file 115; Jean Marie (1881), SAB AG CR-Regina, 1st series, 1876-86, file 118; Hoh-pie-sah-pah, otherwise Blacknest (1882), SAB AG CR-Regina, 1st series, 1876-86, file 185. These cases will be discussed in greater detail in Chapter 3 (I-ah-pee-coo-cah) and Chapter 4 (Jean Marie, Blacknest).

31 SAB AG (GR 11.1) CR-Regina, 1st series, 1876-86: Charles Cardinal (1877), file 6; Ka-ki-si-kut-chin, The Swift Runner (1979), file 65; Joseph Cardinal (1880), file 104; Scholastique Cardinal (1882), file 145. Two of these accused men died in custody prior to trial: Charles Cardinal and Kee-che-qua-pi-e-ka-wa (1877), SAB AG CR-Regina, 1st series, 1876-86, file 7. Two homicide cases involving First Nations accused persons were tried later: Eugana (1885) and Tom Lemac (Wingegee) in 1902; these are discussed more fully in the last section of Chapter 4.

32 Deposition of Alexis Sussey in Kee-che-qua-pi-e-ka-wa (1877), SAB AG CR-Regina, 1st series, 1876-86, file 7.

33 Deposition of George W. Herchmer, MD, *ibid.*

34 Charles Cardinal (1877), SAB AG CR-Regina, 1st series, 1876-86, file 6. Although committed to trial, Cardinal died in custody shortly thereafter, unable, it seems, to cope with the experience of imprisonment and all that it entailed.

35 Deposition of Margaret Gladieu, *ibid.;* Sarah Carter, *Capturing Women: The Manipulation of Cultural Imagery in Canada's Prairie West* (Montreal-Kingston: McGill-Queen's University Press, 1997) at 164-65 [Carter, *Capturing Women*], discusses the "appearance of purchase" in Aboriginal marriages. She quotes Plains ethnologist Robert Lowie: "There was generally rather an appearance of purchase than the reality. The girl's kin often gave back as much property as they received. The significant thing was an exchange of gifts between the two families." In the context of the criminal court file, it is difficult to say whether the second marriage between Cardinal and the second daughter would have been accompanied by the formality of the first, and it is also difficult to say with confidence that Margaret characterized the second marriage in the terms that were attributed to her. See also Carter, *Importance, supra* note 27.

36 This appears to be another instance in which the expertise of the Aboriginal deponent, derived as it was from his experience, was accepted.

37 Ka-ki-si-kut-chin, The Swift Runner (1879), SAB AG CR-Regina, 1st series, 1876-86, file 65.

38 See, *e.g.*, R.G. Evans, "Swift Runner – The Cannibal" in *Outlaws and Lawmen of Western Canada*, vol. 1 (Surrey, BC: Frontier Publishing, 1983) 44; T.W. Paterson, *Outlaws of Western Canada* (Langley, BC: Mr. Paperback, 1982); Colin Argyle Thomson, *Swift Runner* (Calgary: Detselig Enterprises, 1984).

39 "Sad Case of Cannibalism, a Whole Family Slain and Eaten" *Saskatchewan Herald* (30 June 1879) 1, col. 4; "Trial of the Swift Runner for Murder, Found Guilty and Sentenced to Death" *Saskatchewan Herald* (25 August 1879) 1 at col. 4; "Exit the Swift Runner" *Saskatchewan Herald* (12 January 1880) 1 at col. 4, and 2 at cols. 1-3. See also Thomson, *ibid.*, Appendix B at 99-102.

40 Thomson, *ibid.* at 27.

41 *Ibid.* at 28-29.

42 *Ibid.* at 29. Thomson offers this explanation: "The meanings of those signposts remained unrecognized. His strange impulses, delusions, nausea, anorexia and acute depression were all symptoms of the Windigo psychosis. The six-foot, three-inch man was a walking threat."

43 SAB AG CR-Regina, 1st series, 1876-86, file 65.

44 "Voluntary Confession of Ka-ki-si-kut-chin" marked "A," *ibid.* An account of his confession is also reproduced in the *Saskatchewan Herald*'s report of his trial: (25 August 1879) 1 at col. 4.

45 Evidence of Kis-sic-kow-way at the trial of Ka-ki-si-kut-chin, *ibid.*

46 *Saskatchewan Herald* (25 August 1879) 1 at col.4, *supra* note 39.

47 *Saskatchewan Herald* (9 February 1880) 1 at col. 4, and 3 at cols. 1-3.

48 *Ibid.*, 3 at col. 2.

49 *Ibid.*

50 *Ibid.*

51 *Ibid.* at col. 3.

52 *Ibid.*, 1 at col. 4.

53 *Ibid.*, 3 at col. 2.

54 *Saskatchewan Herald* (25 August 1879) 1 at col. 1.

55 *Ibid.* (15 March 1880) 2 at col. 4.

56 Letter from Father E. Groward to W.W. Traill (22 February 1880) in Joseph Cardinal (1880), SAB AG CR-Regina, 1st series, 1876-86, file 104.

57 Letter from Edward Traill J.P. to Superintendent Jarvis, NWMP, Fort Saskatchewan (23 February 1880), *ibid.*

58 Deposition of Angelique Cardinal, *ibid.*

59 Deposition of J-BC, *ibid.*

60 *Ibid.*

61 Deposition of Antoine Cardinal, *ibid.*

62 *Saskatchewan Herald* (10 October 1880) 1 at col. 2: "On Monday, 27th September, Inspector Antrobus and a small party left with two prisoners – Cardinal the murderer, and LaPlante, a lunatic – both sentenced to the Provincial Penitentiary in Manitoba." See also LAC, Manitoba Penitentiary Admitance [*sic*] Register, *supra* note 5 at 4.

63 "Another Murder ... " *Saskatchewan Herald* (15 March 1880) 2 at col. 4.

64 *Saskatchewan Herald* (26 April 1880) 1, col 4.

65 *Ibid.*

66 *Ibid.*

67 SAB AG CR-Regina, 1st series, 1876-86: James Reid (1877), file 12, charged with break, enter, and theft of HBC store, guilty plea (12 months); Jean Baptiste Montour, Joseph Desjarlais, Charles Desjarlais, and Na-ne-ka-qua-nep, The Youngest Son of the Netmaker (also known as Shakes His Wings) (1878), file 28, charged with unlawfully killing an ox, the property of HBC, guilty plea, 3 months' hard labour (Richardson specified that the "hard labor" was to consist of "cutting wood and other ordinary labour for the space of eight hours of every working day during the said time"); Charles Gouin (1879), file 76, break, enter, and theft from HBC (no disposition); Charles Cardinal and Joseph Desjarlais (1879), file 78, break, enter, and theft from HBC, (convicted) 3 years; Daniel Williams (1879), file 79, arson, maiming HBC horses, threatening HBC officers (no disposition); Peecoose (Sandfly), theft from HBC, 2½ years; James Robertson (1881), file 113, break, enter, and theft from HBC warehouse, guilty plea, 1 month; Thomas, a Stony Indian, file 188, theft of fur and bacon from HBC, guilty plea, 1 month.

68 In the initial letter in file 28, *ibid.*, the four are described as "sons of Abram Montour, Baptiste Montour, Abram Montour Junior and the Netmaker."

69 As Hugh Dempsey has observed, *supra* note 7 at 39: "In spite of vast distances and problems of communication, news could travel like a prairie fire across the plains."

70 *Supra* note 67.

71 See Napesis (or Joseph) (1881), SAB AG CR-Regina, 1st series, 1876-86, files 131, 152, and 154.

72 Thomas (1883), SAB AG CR-Regina, 1st series, 1876-86, file 188.

73 Not every Aboriginal person accused of theft from an employer was convicted. It appears that Caroline Gouin, charged with stealing two coins from her employer's pocketbook, never went to trial. Peter Erasmus is named as an interpreter in the file, and thus I infer that she was either a First Nations or Métis woman (and my further inference would be the latter). Caroline Gouin (1881), SAB AG CR-Regina, 1st series, 1876-86, file 124.

74 In the days of HBC rule, the factor might have dispensed a form of private Company justice or possibly even let the matter go, as the goods were retrieved.

75 Peecoose (Sandfly) (1880), SAB AG CR-Regina, 1st series, 1876-86, file 88.

76 *Ibid.*

77 *Saskatchewan Herald* (7 June 1880) 2 at col. 2.

78 Dempsey, *supra* note 7 at 117; Carter, *Capturing Women, supra* note 35 at 57-58; Walter Hildebrandt, *Views from Fort Battleford: Constructed Visions of an Anglo-Canadian West* (Regina: Canadian Plains Research Center, 1994) at 62; Wiebe, *supra* note 14; Myrna Kostash, ed., *The Frog Lake Reader* (Edmonton: NeWest Press, 2009) at 29.

79 Dempsey, *supra* note 7.

80 *Ibid.*

81 Kostash, *supra* note 78.

82 See also Carter, *Capturing Women, supra* note 35. Theresa Delaney and Theresa Gowanlock, *Two Months in the Camp of Big Bear* (Regina: Canadian Plains Research Center, 1999).

83 The account provided by Dempsey is also referred to by Hildebrandt, *supra* note 78 at 62. Blair Stonechild and W.A. Waiser, *Loyal till Death: Indians and the North-West Rebellion* (Saskatoon: Fifth House, 1997) refer at 108 to Delaney's affair with "Sand Fly's wife" but make no mention of the theft charge.

84 *Saskatchewan Herald* (5 July 1880) 2 at col. 4.

85 See, *e.g.*, Dempsey, *supra* note 7 at 161; Stonechild and Waiser, *supra* note 83 at 108; Kostash, *supra* note 78. The *Saskatchewan Herald* offered a different assessment of Delaney's

relationship with the Indians. Reporting on the men who had been killed at Frog Lake, the *Herald* said of Delaney that "[h]e was looked upon as having been successful in civilizing and humanizing the band of miserable wretches amongst whom he labored so diligently. That they killed their best friends [referring also to Thomas Quinn *et al.*] first shows them to be utterly depraved and not to be trusted in anything": *Saskatchewan Herald* (23 April 1885) 2 at col. 1. See also Theresa Delaney's description of her late husband, and how "respected and really beloved" he was by those "under his care," *supra* note 82 at 64. Delaney's death was later overshadowed by the national celebration of his widow's "rescue" from Big Bear's camp: see Carter, *Capturing Women, supra* note 35. Carter, with her characteristic evenhandedness, reminds her readers that Delaney had been disciplined by his superiors on at least one occasion for giving out rations without work.

86 "Report of the Commissioner of the NWMP, 1885," Appendix O at 115. See also Dempsey, *supra* note 7 at 161, who says that Peecoose (Sandfly) was in the village of Frog Lake at the time of the killings on 2 April 1885.

87 LAC, Manitoba Penitentiary Admitance [*sic*] Register, *supra* note 5, Microfilm reel T-11095, vol. 24.

88 The court files use the names of Aboriginal child prisoners and witnesses. In today's proceedings, publication of their names would not be permitted without a court order. While I have reservations about reproducing their names, on balance I have elected to use the names as they appear in the court files, as they are already a matter of public record. Where I have not been able to decipher the names, I have used initials.

89 John Thomas and Thomas A. Beckett (1881), SAB AG CR-Regina, 1st series, 1876-86, file 116.

90 *Ibid.*

91 John Thomas's evidence, *ibid.*

92 In a sprinkling of files, the ages of very young accused are indicated. In Regina in 1894, two brothers, Philip Rothenbusch and Gustav Rothenbusch (the younger of whom was said to be thirteen), were tried on charges in respect of an alleged rape of a young neighbour girl at their farm and were acquitted by Richardson: SAB SCNWT (Crim.), Coll. R1286, files 88 and 89. Fifteen-year-old Albert Offord was convicted in 1895 of break and enter with intent to steal, after he had been found in an empty house. Judge Richardson sentenced him to two months in jail, noting on the back of the indictment that the boy had said he was under fifteen, an orphan, who had been brought to Canada from England in the previous year (SAB SCNWT (Crim.), Coll. R1286, file 100). See also Edward (Ted) Sweetway (under sixteen) (1901), SAB SCNWT (Crim.), Coll. R1286, file 252, convicted of theft of horses and later sentenced to a year in jail and a further two-year recognizance to keep the peace and be of good behaviour (if no surety came forward, he was to serve another year consecutive to the first year) for another theft conviction as well as the previous conviction (SAB SCNWT (Crim.), Coll. R1286, file 271).

93 "Report of the Commissioner of the North-West Mounted Police, 1882" reprinted in Royal Canadian Mounted Police, *Settlers and Rebels: Being the Official Reports to Parliament of the Activities of the Royal* [*sic*] *North-West Mounted Police Force from 1882-1885 by the Commissioners of the Royal* [*sic*] *North-West Mounted Police,* facsimile reprint (Toronto: Coles Publishing, 1973; original ed. Ottawa: Maclean, Roger, 1882-85) Appendix A at 51.

94 "Report of the Commissioner of the North-West Mounted Police, 1883" reprinted in Royal Canadian Mounted Police, *ibid.,* Appendix D at 38 (cases tried at Fort Macleod) and at 40 (cases tried at Fort Calgary), respectively.

95 John S. Milloy, *A National Crime: The Canadian Government and the Residential School System, 1879-1986* (Winnipeg: University of Manitoba Press, 1999) at 154.

96 Alex Bone (1894), SAB SCNWT (Crim.), Coll. R1286, file 84.

97 Julia Coté (1894), SAB SCNWT (Crim.), Coll. R1286, file 85.

98 *An Act Further to Amend the Indian Act, 1894,* 57-58 Vict., c. 32, s. 11.

99 LAC, RG 10, reel C-7148, vol. 9427, Treaty Annuity Paylists for Treaties 4, 6, and 7 (1894), Treaty 4, Pasquah's Band, 112. Alex Bone is listed at No. 128 as a single male person, and the paylist for the following year indicates that he continued to be a member of that band. The 1895 paylist makes no reference to his treaty payment going to anyone but himself, so perhaps he had finished with the school by the following year: LAC, RG 10, reel C-7148, vol. 9428, Treaty Annuity Paylists for Treaties 4, 6, and 7 (1895), Treaty 4, Pasquah's Band, 211.

100 This form of ingenuity was, of course, not unique to Indian Department officials. See, *e.g.*, D. Murray, "Hands across the Border: The Abortive Extradition of Solomon Moseby" (2000) 30 Canadian Review of American Studies 187, for an account of the criminal prosecution of a runaway slave for theft of the horse on which he escaped.

101 Statement of the Accused, Ka-ka-wusk (1880), SAB AG CR-Regina, 1st series, 1876-86, file 120. Eighteen-year-old Ka-ka-wusk, Prisoner 71, was sentenced to five years in the Manitoba Penitentiary, where he died on 2 June 1882, before the expiration of his sentence: LAC, Manitoba Penitentiary Admitance [*sic*] Register, *supra* note 5 at 4.

102 R.C. Macleod and Heather Rollason, "'Restrain the Lawless Savages': Native Defendants in the Criminal Courts of the North-West Territories, 1878-1885" (1997) 10 Journal of Historical Sociology 157 at 170; Brian Hubner, "Horse Stealing and the Borderline: The NWMP and the Control of Indian Movement, 1874-1900" (1995) 20 Prairie Forum 281 at 285. For the importance of the "raid," see also Mandelbaum, *supra* note 6 at 239-45.

103 Mandelbaum, *ibid.* at 239.

104 Hubner, *supra* note 102 at 285.

105 *Ibid.* at 288.

106 "Annual Report of the Commissioner of the North-West Mounted Police, 1883," *supra* note 94, Appendix A at 38.

107 *Ibid.* at 37, 45.

108 He was possibly a signatory to Treaty 4. See Morris, *supra* note 28 at 334, where one "Cha-ca-chas" is listed as a signatory to Treaty 4. If so, if he was a chief or headman or a man of stature, this might shed some light on the relatively minor sentence he and his co-accused received.

109 Chac-a-Chas *et al.* (1882), SAB AG CR-Regina, 1st series, 1876-86, file 143.

110 "Report of the Commissioner of the North-West Mounted Police, 1883," *supra* note 94 at 8-9.

111 Deposition of Jean Louis Légaré, in The Man That Walks There *et al.* (1882), SAB AG CR-Regina, 1st series, 1876-86, file 143. Légaré (whose name was spelled "Legarie" in the court file) was a prominent member of the growing francophone community and a trader in the area since 1871; he had provided financial support to Sitting Bull and his people during their time in Canada: Waiser, *supra* note 40 at 40.

112 *Supra* note 94.

113 Statement of the Accused, The Man that Walks There *et al.* re Légaré charges, taken 12 May 1882, *supra* note 111.

114 Statement of the Accused, The Man that Walks There *et al.* re Champagne and Sansregret charges, taken 12 May 1882, *ibid.*

115 SAB AG CR-Regina, 1st series, 1876-86: Ar-ki-tap (or Ah-kee-tap) (1884), file 221; The Cree (1884), file 224; Ah-sti-ni-ah (1884), file 225; The Rock, Little Fish, and Is-te-wah (1884), file 226; Day Thunder (1884), file 227; Little Fish [again] (1884), file 228. The accused man in file 221 (Ar-ki-tap) appears to be the same man, Ah-kee-tap, who was the principal witness against Buffalo Calf (*infra* note 117).

116 "Report of the Commissioner of the North-West Mounted Police, 1884" reprinted in Royal Canadian Mounted Police, *supra* note 93, Appendix A at 46.

117 Buffalo Calf, an Assiniboine Indian (1884), SAB AG CR-Regina, 1st series, 1876-86, file 219. John Jennings also refers to Buffalo Calf in his dissertation, *The North-West Mounted Police and Canadian Indian Policy, 1873-1896* (PhD Dissertation, University of Toronto, 1979) [unpublished] at 188.

118 This letter contained in the court file was written on stationery bearing the letterhead of the Commissioner of the NWMP.

119 "Report of the Commissioner of the North-West Mounted Police, 1884," *supra* note 116 at 46.

120 *Ibid.*

121 *Ibid.* The Richardson court records include the Peltier and Brier Informations, but nothing else is contained in the file: SAB AG CR-Regina, 1st series, 1876-86, file 212.

122 LAC, Manitoba Penitentiary Admitance [*sic*] Register, *supra* note 5.

123 The Rock, Little Fish, and Is-te-wah, 3 Cree Indians (1884), SAB AG CR-Regina, 1st series, 1876-86, file 226.

124 Ah-sti-ni-ah, Cree Indian (1884), SAB AG CR-Regina, 1st series, 1876-86, file 225.

125 Day Thunder, a Cree Indian (1884), SAB AG CR-Regina, 1st series, 1876-86, file 227.

126 Little Fish, Cree Indian (1884), SAB AG CR-Regina, 1st series, 1876-86, file 228.

127 Statement of the Accused, Ar-ki-tap, Assiniboine Indian (1884), SAB AG CR-Regina, 1st series, 1876-86, file 221.

128 Statement of the Accused, The Rock (1884), SAB AG CR-Regina, 1st series, 1876-86, file 226.

129 Statement of the Accused, Ah-sti-ni-ah (1884), SAB AG CR-Regina, 1st series, 1876-86, file 225. Nowhere in the records does the identity of the Big Bull appear, although he may have been "Boss Bull."

130 Statement of the Accused, The Cree, Cree Indian (1884), SAB AG CR-Regina, 1st series, 1876-86, file 224.

131 The Little Person, Son of Running Crow (1879), SAB AG CR-Regina, 1st series, 1876-86, file 73.

132 Letter from James Walker, Supt, NWMP, to Richardson (10 September 1979), *ibid.*

133 "A Small Bull," "A Soul," "The Thunders Home Son," and "A Deceiving Man" (1881), SAB AG CR-Regina, 1st series, 1876-86, file 133. This file contains only the Information. In the trial of The Ghost (1881), SAB AG CR-Regina, 1st series, 1876-86, file 135, the police witness, Sergeant Parker, testified in cross-examination: "There were 2 large and 1 small [?] forming the camp on the north side. There were 3 men besides the prisoner at this camp. There were horses belonging to the mail carrier nearby but not belonging with those described." It is possible that this was a reference to Peter Ballendine, who was the mail carrier for Battleford. In 1883, Ballendine, "mail contractor," charged and prosecuted Joseph Alexander with abandoning the mail; the accused offered an explanation, he was cautioned, and the prosecution was allowed to be dropped: SAB AG CR-Regina, 1st series, 1876-86, file 180.

134 *Saskatchewan Herald* (31 October 1881) 1 at col. 4.

135 A Bull that Walks Painted Red (1881), SAB AG CR-Regina, 1st series, 1876-86, file 136.

136 The relevant provisions of the *Indian Act, 1876,* 39 Vict., c. 18, ss. 74-78, permitted a judge to accept the unsworn evidence of a non-Christian Indian ("who is destitute of the knowledge of God and of any fixed and clear belief in religion or in a future state of rewards and punishments") upon the solemn declaration or affirmation by the Indian to tell the truth. Prior to the receipt of the evidence, the court was required to caution every Indian that he would be liable to punishment if he did not tell the truth. In the files that I have read, I have not found one in which Richardson declined to receive the evidence of a non-Christian Indian.

137 The Ghost (1881), SAB AG CR-Regina, 1st series, 1876-86, file 135.

138 Evidence of Chief Mosquito, Esktope (1881), SAB AG CR-Regina, 1st series, 1876-86, file 134.

139 "Report of the Commissioner of the North-West Mounted Police, 1880," reprinted in Royal Canadian Mounted Police, *supra* note 5, Appendix D at 39.

140 The next two issues of the *Saskatchewan Herald* appeared on 12 November and 26 November 1881. No report of this court proceeding is contained in either issue.

141 E. Brian Titley, *The Frontier World of Edgar Dewdney* (Vancouver: UBC Press, 1999)at 65; E. Brian Titley, *A Narrow Vision: Duncan Campbell Scott and the Administration of Indian Affairs in Canada* (Vancouver: UBC Press, 1986) at 65fn16, and at 167-71. Sarah Carter, *Lost Harvests: Prairie Indian Reserve Farmers and Government Policy* (Montreal and Kingston: McGill-Queen's University Press, 1990) at 153-54, for NWMP resistance to the policies regarding "passes" and dances. See also Sidney L. Harring, "'There Seemed to Be No Recognized Law': Canadian Law and the Prairie First Nations" in Louis A. Knafla and Jonathan Swainger, eds., *Laws and Societies in the Canadian Prairie West 1670-1940* (Vancouver: UBC Press, 2005) 92 at 119.

Chapter 3: "Prisoner Never Gave Me Anything for What He Done"

1 John Ballendine (1878), Saskatchewan Archives Board, Department of the Attorney General, Regina Judicial Centre: Court Records First Series, 1876-86, Files 1-282 [hereinafter SAB AG CR-Regina, 1st Series, 1876-86], file 29.

2 I conclude that "The Pondmaker" and "Poundmaker" are one and the same man for several reasons, despite the fact that the Informant was described as a "Christian Indian" (and I understand that Poundmaker is said to have converted to Christianity later, while in prison). The Informant in this file was clearly a Cree man of standing, given the prominent men he was able to mobilize on his behalf (Peter Erasmus, Hugh Richardson, Mr. Brelland) in his attempt to retrieve his horse. The court file refers to The Pondmaker's brother as "Yellow Earth Blanket"; Poundmaker's brother was known as Yellow Mud Blanket. Alexander Morris names him as "Oo-pee-too-kerah-han-ap-ee-wee-yin" (The Pondmaker): *The Treaties of Canada with the Indians of Manitoba and the North-West Territories,* facsimile reprint (Toronto: Prospero Books, 2000; original ed. Toronto: Belfords Clarke, 1880) at 210; at 219, he appears as "Oo-pee-too-korah-hair-ap-ee-wee-yin" (The Pond-maker). The many spellings of Poundmaker's name in translation illustrate how difficult it is to assert with confidence the identity of the persons named in the court files. Poundmaker himself arguably illustrates, as well, the fluidity of relations among the First Peoples of the Prairies, and why it is a trap for the unwary to insist upon rigid distinctions between "Indian" and

"Métis," Cree and Saulteaux. Even the description of him as a "Cree" may not be one that he would have used: he was the son of Sikakwayan, an Assiniboine shaman, and a mixed-blood Cree mother, nephew of the prominent Chief Mistawasis (his mother's brother), and adopted son of the chief of the Blackfoot, Crowfoot. See Christian Thompson, "Poundmaker" in Christian Thompson, ed., *Saskatchewan First Nations: Lives Past and Present* (Regina: Canadian Plains Research Center, 2004) at 108-9. His brother, Yellow Mud Blanket (or, as he was named in the court file, Yellow Earth Blanket), like Poundmaker was also prosecuted after the 1885 North-West Rebellion. Unlike Poundmaker, who was sentenced to three years in the Manitoba Penitentiary, Yellow Mud Blanket was released by the court on the recommendation of Crown counsel; see Sandra E. Bingaman, *The North-West Rebellion Trials, 1885* (MA Thesis, University of Saskatchewan [Regina], 1971) [unpublished] Appendix A at 206; see also Sandra E. Bingaman, "The Trials of Poundmaker and Big Bear, 1885" (1975) 28 Saskatchewan History 81; Blair Stonechild and W.A. Waiser, *Loyal till Death: Indians and the North-West Rebellion* (Saskatoon: Fifth House, 1997); Bob Beal and R.C. Macleod, *Prairie Fire: The 1885 North-West Rebellion* (Edmonton: Hurtig Publishers, 1984).

3 Peter Erasmus had acted as interpreter for the First Nations during the Treaty 6 negotiations: see, *e.g.*, Morris, *ibid.* at 196.

4 Lewis H. Thomas, *The Struggle for Responsible Government in the North-West Territories*, 2nd ed. (Toronto: University of Toronto Press, 1978).

5 The exception, of course, may be found in the files in which the alleged offence is one of unlawful carnal knowledge with a female person under the age of twelve years, as in the case of Ka-nah-pic-a-nah-haw, or "The Snake Indian," in November 1882 – SAB AG CR-Regina, 1st series, 1876-86, file 171 – or fourteen years – as in the case of Pierre Bourassa (1892), SAB AG CR-Regina, 1st series, 1876-86, file 39.

6 See, *e.g.*, Frederick Kidd's questions of witnesses before the justices of the peace: Frederick Kidd (1877), SAB AG CR-Regina, 1st series, 1876-86, file 8; and Pierre Bourassa's efforts, *ibid.*, through the interpreter Peter Hourie during his trial.

7 William Turner (1877), SAB AG CR-Regina, 1st series, 1876-86, file 5. In 1878, William Turner was again before Richardson on two other matters. In May 1878, he was placed on a peace bond of $100 for one year following a complaint by Michael McGinnis of Battleford, also a labourer. Later that fall, Peter Ballendine charged him with unlawfully cutting timber on Dominion lands, to which he pleaded guilty and received a fine of $1.50 and $2.50 in costs. See William Turner (1878), SAB AG CR-Regina, 1st series, 1876-86, files 22 and 47, respectively.

8 William Turner (1877), *ibid.*, file 5.

9 *Ibid.*

10 *Ibid.*

11 See, *e.g.*, Patricia A. Monture-Okanee and Mary Ellen Turpel, "Aboriginal Peoples and Canadian Criminal Law: Rethinking Justice" (1992) 26 U.B.C. L. Rev. 239. The evidence in Tom Lemac's case (1902), including the interpreter's "evidence," is discussed more fully in Chapter 3.

12 See, *e.g.*, Paula Jane Byrne, *Criminal Law and Colonial Subject: New South Wales, 1810-1930* (Cambridge: Cambridge University Press, 1993) at 9. See also Edward Muir and Guido Ruggiero, "Afterword: Crime and the Writing of History" in Edward Muir and Guido Ruggiero, eds., *History from Crime* (Baltimore: The Johns Hopkins University Press, 1994) 226 at 230:

> It could well be argued that every judicial document in a case is a tissue of lies: defendants reconstructing their past to make it as innocent sounding as possible; accusers recasting events to make the accused seem as guilty as possible; investigators working to fit individuals and events into preconceived notions of crime; witnesses shaping their testimony because of animosities, friendships, the desire to please the powerful, or the need to thwart them.
>
> In the face of such an apparently endless range of possibilities, it might seem that reconstructing any sort of history from such documentation would be extremely problematic.

13 Carolyn Strange, "Stories of Their Lives: The Historian and the Capital Case File" in Franca Iacovetta and Wendy Mitchinson, eds., *On the Case: Explorations in Social History* (Toronto: University of Toronto Press, 1998) 25.

14 Muir and Ruggiero, *supra* note 12. Similarly, Muir and Ruggiero (like Byrne) are not paralyzed in the face of the possibility of falsehood and fiction in the court documents: "Crime documents over and over again construct narratives that have a large fictional component and which are directed toward pleasing a certain audience. Both accusations and investigations try to force the details of an event into the mold of what was required or perceived to be required to designate a specific action as a crime. Testimonies might have the opposite goal of exculpation ... The task is always in some sense rhetorical, that is, to convince a jury, judge, or broader public that something criminal did or did not occur" (at 235).

15 John Beattie, *Crime and the Courts in England, 1660-1800* (Princeton, NJ: Princeton University Press, 1986) at 21.

16 See the medical officer's evidence in Paskada (otherwise Whitehead) (1880), SAB AG CR-Regina, 1st series, 1876-86, file 91.

17 Tom Lemac (1902), Saskatchewan Archives Board, Supreme Court of North-West Territories (Criminal), Collection R1286 [hereinafter, SAB SCNWT (Crim.), Coll. R1286], file 266. I discuss this case later in this chapter and in Chapter 4.

18 *E.g.*, Samuel Flack (1897), SAB SCNWT (Crim.), Coll. R1286, file 154; Charles Langdon (1900), SAB SCNWT (Crim.), Coll. R1286, file 226.

19 See, *e.g.*, Rev. Henry Steinhauer's evidence in Charles Cardinal (1877), SAB AG CR-Regina, 1st series, 1876-86, file 6. I discuss this case in Chapter 2.

20 See the witnesses in Tom Lemac's trial (1902), SAB SCNWT (Crim.), Coll. R1286, file 266. I discuss this case in Chapters 3 and 4.

21 Jim Phillips, "Women, Crime and Criminal Justice in Early Halifax, 1750-1800" in Susan Lewthwaite, Tina Loo, and Jim Phillips, eds., *Essays in the History of Canadian Law,* vol. 5, *Crime and Criminal Justice in Canadian History* (Toronto: University of Toronto Press, 1994) 174 at 174: "I wish also to use the records of crime as a prism through which to analyse both male and female attitudes to women and the related issues of women's experience in this society." See also Robert Menzies and Dorothy E. Chunn, "The Gender Politics of Criminal Insanity: 'Order-in-Council' Women" (1998) 31 Social History 241 at 250-51 [Menzies and Chunn, "Order-in-Council Women"]:

> Despite their statistical rarity and virtual invisibility in the writing of feminist history, these Order-in-Council women offer a unique understanding about women's lives in late nineteenth- and early twentieth century British Columbia. Specifically, these women's biographies of disorder and disrepute, the regulatory discourses and

practices that enveloped them, and their own, along with official, accounts of their transactions with forensic authorities can tell us much about two issues. First, by studying the forensic careers of these "double deviants," we can learn about the assumptions and practices governing "normal" womanhood over time. Secondly, we can gain critical insight into the relationship between gender, crime, and madness in the province's segregative institutions of medico-legal control during a period of social transformation.

22 Apistatim (1878), SAB AG CR-Regina, 1st series, 1876-86, file 42.

23 See, *e.g.,* cases discussed below; SAB AG (GR 11.1) CR-Regina, 1st series, 1876-86: I-ah-pee-koo-caw (1881), file 115; Jean Marie (1881), file 118; Hoh-pie-sah-pah, otherwise Blacknest (1882), file 155.

24 Paskada (otherwise Whitehead) (1880), SAB AG CR-Regina, 1st series, 1876-86, file 91.

25 As I have indicated in previous chapters, R.C. Macleod and Heather Rollason, "'Restrain the Lawless Savages': Native Defendants in the Criminal Courts of the North-West Territories, 1878-1885" (1997) 10 Journal of Historical Sociology 157 at 176-77, discuss how Blackfoot chief Stamiscotocar (Bull Head) made use of the criminal law in his prosecution of Joseph Gouin. Stamiscotocar consciously invoked the "Queen's law" when he charged Gouin with theft of a horse, which arose out of an incident that reflected either a misunderstanding or a breakdown in their relationship and the meaning of gifts that had been exchanged between them. Gouin was convicted by Richardson and sentenced to three months of hard labour. This case is in the first series of Richardson's records, Joseph Gouin (1879), SAB AG CR-Regina, 1st series, 1876-86, file 72.

26 Francis Deschaw (1878), SAB AG CR-Regina, 1st series, 1876-86, file 57.

27 Library and Archives Canada [LAC], RG 10, reel C-7145, vol. 9412, Treaty Annuity Paylists for Treaties 4, 6, and 7 (1878), Treaty 6, Strike Him on the Back's Band, 443.

28 Ka-nah-pic-a-nah-hew, or "The Snake Indian" (1882), SAB AG CR-Regina, 1st series, 1876-86, file 172. It is not clear from the file who Kaa-out-a-pew was; given that the mother's name is somewhat different, this may be the name of Kutenay's father.

29 The NWMP record of his name is "Ka-na-pic-a-nahon." The entry in the "Report of the Commissioner of the NWMP" indicates that a witness named [Ka-nah-neh-can-mokin] was released on the same day that Ka-na-pic-a-nahon (Snake Indian) was convicted: "Report of the Commissioner of the North-West Mounted Police, 1882," reprinted in Royal Canadian Mounted Police, *Settlers and Rebels: Being the Official Reports to Parliament of the Activities of the Royal* [*sic*] *North-West Mounted Police Force from 1882-1885 by the Commissioners of the Royal* [*sic*] *North-West Mounted Police,* facsimile reprint (Toronto: Coles Publishing, 1973; original ed. Ottawa: Maclean, Roger, 1882-85) Appendix D at 41. This witness may have been the child's mother, who was described by an English name in the court file.

30 *Ibid.*

31 See LAC, RG 73, W87-88/365, Microfilm reel T-1108911, vol. 23 (MIKAN no. 134308), Manitoba Penitentiary Admitaance [*sic*] Register, 16 May 1871 – 22 June 1885 at 5.

32 William Williams (1882), SAB AG CR-Regina, 1st series, 1876-86, file 172.

33 Wa-Chin (1891), SAB SCNWT (Crim.), Coll. R1286, file 28.

34 *Ibid.*

35 *Ibid.*

36 James B. Mahoney (1878), SAB AG CR-Regina, 1st series, 1876-86, file 54.

37 John Smith (1878), SAB AG CR-Regina, 1st series, 1876-86, file 24.

38 He also acted as the prosecutor in a subsequent case in 1882, in which Madeleine charged that William Mitchell and William Peterson had attempted to rape her: SAB AG CR-Regina, 1st series, 1876-86, file 144. The prisoners were committed for trial but released on bail. The matter seems not to have ever gone to trial.

39 Lawrence Clarke outlined Wallace's story and requested that a police officer be sent if Richardson considered "it right to have the man arrested." Apparently this was not Richardson's view, as Hayter Reed served the summons on his client.

40 It has been suggested by the historian of the Law Society of Saskatchewan that Hayter Reed was, in 1881, one of the first two practising lawyers in Prince Albert: Iain A. Mentiplay, *A Century of Integrity: The Law Society of Saskatchewan 1907 to 2007* (Regina: Law Society of Saskatchewan, 2007) at 17. Reed later became Indian Agent for Battleford, Assistant Indian Commissioner, and later Commissioner of Indian Affairs. He was also appointed to the North-West Territories Council. His nickname among the Cree, Saulteaux, and Assiniboine people of the Battleford area was "Iron Heart." See Walter Hildebrandt, *Views from Fort Battleford: Constructed Visions of an Anglo- Canadian West* (Regina: Canadian Plains Research Center, 1994), photographic entry after 86. I discuss his role as a legal professional in Chapter 4.

41 John Smith, *supra* note 37.

42 *Ibid.*

43 *Ibid.*

44 See, *e.g.*, Carolyn Strange, "Patriarchy Modified: The Criminal Prosecution of Rape in York County, Ontario, 1880-1930" in Susan Lewthwaite, Tina Loo, Jim Phillips, eds., *Essays in the History of Canadian Law*, vol. 5, *Crime and Criminal Justice in Canadian History* (Toronto: University of Toronto Press, 1994) 207 at 210fn13.

45 Including $2 for the interpreter's fee.

46 Hoh-pie-sah-pah, otherwise Blacknest (1882), SAB AG CR-Regina, 1st series, 1876-86, file 155.

47 *Saskatchewan Herald* (22 July 1882) 1 at col. 4.

48 Jean Marie (1881), SAB AG CR-Regina, 1st series, 1876-86, file 118.

49 *Saskatchewan Herald* (10 October 1880) 1 at cols. 1 and 2.

50 I-ah-pee-coo-caw (1881), SAB AG CR-Regina, 1st series, 1876-86, file 115.

51 *Ibid.*

52 See, *e.g.*, Interview of Rudy Wiebe, in Myrna Kostash, ed., *The Frog Lake Reader* (Edmonton: NeWest Press, 2009) at 68-69.

53 Sarah Carter, "First Nations Women of Prairie Canada in the Early Reserve Years, the 1870s to 1920: A Preliminary Inquiry" in Christine Miller and Patricia Chuchryk, with Marie Smallface Marule, Brenda Manyfingers, and Cheryl Deering, eds., *Women of the First Nations: Power, Wisdom, and Strength* (Winnipeg: University of Manitoba Press, 1996) 51 at 70 [Carter, "First Nations Women"]: "DIA files reveal that there were some agents and farm instructors who abused their positions of authority. In 1882 Chief Crowfoot of the Blackfoot complained that farm instructor John Horrish was exchanging extra rations for sexual services. The woman's family was issued a ration ticket for seven when there were only four in the family. Norrish was dismissed from his position. Similar complaints against the farm instructors on his reserve were raised by Chief Thunderchild in 1893."

54 James Ford (1889), SAB SCNWT (Crim.), Coll. R1286, file 11.

55 "James Ford," LAC, RG 18-G, vol. 10041, R196-158-9-E, 1873-1999, Sub-series North West [*sic*] Mounted Police (NWMP) – Personnel Records, 1873-1904, online: LAC <http://www.collectionscanada.gc.ca/>. Ford's regimental number was 1348. The "Report of the Commissioner of the North-West Mounted Police, 1886," reprinted in Royal Canadian Mounted Police, *Law and Order: Being the Official Reports to Parliament of the Royal* [*sic*] *North-West Mounted Police from 1886-1887 by the Commissioners of the Royal* [*sic*] *North-West Mounted Police,* facsimile reprint (Toronto: Coles Publishing, 1973; original ed. Ottawa: Maclean, Roger, 1886-87) Appendix AA, confirms that "Jas. Ford" was convicted by Stipendiary Magistrate McLeod on 20 January 1886 for "shooting at peace officers in the execution of their duty" and sentenced to three months' hard labour at the Regina jail.

56 Letter from James Conrick, Proprietor, Dufferin Stables, Montreal (4 May 1885), "James Ford," LAC, *ibid.* at 4.

57 *Ibid.* at 30-31.

58 Sarah Carter, *Capturing Women: The Manipulation of Cultural Imagery in Canada's Prairie West* (Montreal and Kingston: McGill-Queen's University Press, 1997) at 5 [Carter, *Capturing Women*].

59 Jean Barman, "Taming Aboriginal Sexuality: Gender, Power, and Race in British Columbia, 1850-1900" in Mary-Ellen Kelm and Lorna Townsend, eds., *In the Days of Our Grandmothers: A Reader in Aboriginal Women's History in Canada* (Toronto: University of Toronto Press, 2006) 270; Joan Sangster, "Native Women, Sexuality and the Law" in Mary-Ellen Kelm and Lorna Townsend, eds., *ibid.* 301. Of an earlier period in New France, see Karen Anderson, *Chain Her by One Foot: The Subjugation of Native Women in Seventeenth-Century New France* (New York: Routledge, 1991).

60 Barman, *ibid.* at 274.

61 James Ford, *supra* note 54.

62 Memorandum from Superintendent Sévère Gagnon to the Commissioner of the NWMP, 5 November 1889, in "James Ford," LAC, *supra* note 55.

63 See, *e.g.,* Baptiste Robillard (1898), SAB SCNWT (Crim.), Coll. R1286, file 184; Thomas Desjarlais the Younger (1900), SAB SCNWT (Crim.), Coll. R1286, file 228.

64 Baptiste Robillard, *ibid.*

65 This appears to be the Cree word "kîmôcisâkiskwewin" or "kîmôcisâkiskwewina," which means the act of loving on the sly, secret love: Earle Waugh, ed., *Nancy LeClaire and George Cardinal, Alberta Elders' Cree Dictionary* (Edmonton: University of Alberta Press, 1998) at 54.

66 Baptiste apparently named names for his counsel, which Hamilton put to Maria Thorne in cross-examination, to which she replied: "I never had connection with other boys. I never had connection with Isadore Blondin, nor with Thomas Desjarlais, nor with Patrick Swan."

67 The entry Criminal Docket Book for the Supreme Court of the North-West Territories indicates only the date that the documents were received at the Court.

68 Darlene M. Johnston, *Litigating Identity: The Challenge of Aboriginality* (L.L.M. Thesis, University of Toronto, 2003). Patricia Monture-Okanee expresses it this way: "In the First Nations system, you do not admit guilt, but you admit honesty: "I have done wrong." Patricia Monture-Okanee, "Reclaiming Justice: Aboriginal Women and Justice Initiatives in the 1990s" in Canada, Royal Commission on Aboriginal Peoples, *Aboriginal Peoples and the Justice System: Report of the National Round Table on Aboriginal Justice Issues* (Ottawa: Minister of Supply and Services Canada, 1993) 105 at 121. See also Tracey Lindberg, "Rooms

with 'Traditional Views': Justice L'Heureux-Dubé and the Extension of Interpretative Principles Related to Equality in the Context of Indigenous Rights" in Elizabeth Sheehy, ed., *Adding Feminism to Law: The Contributions of Justice Claire L'Heureux-Dubé* (Toronto: Irwin Law, 2004) 367 at 367.

69 Monture-Okanee, *ibid.* For instance, in today's context, the Supreme Court of the North-West Territories has developed a list of legal terms with their translation into, and "back translation" from, five indigenous languages (Chipewayan, Dogrib, Loucheux, North Slavey, and South Slavey). The back translation for "not guilty" from the indigenous languages is "Did you not do it?" (Chipewayan); "Did you do not do it?"(Dogrib); "Person says he did not do wrong" (Loucheux); "I did not act in that manner" (North Slavey); and "I did not do it" (South Slavey). Although there is, to be sure, an emphasis on the physical (as opposed to mental) elements of the offence in these translations, it is also clear that there are differences as well as similarities in the back translations. These and other cultural and linguistic challenges were discussed by Justice John Vertes, "Northern Justice: "Jury Trials in Aboriginal Communities" (Paper presented at the Faculty of Law, University of British Columbia, 25 January 2007). The list of translations and back translations that was distributed by Justice Vertes at his lecture is on file with the author.

70 Freda Ahenakew, Cecil King, and Catherine I. Littlejohn, "Indigenous Languages in the Delivery of Justice in Manitoba: A Paper Presented to the Public Inquiry into the Administration of Justice and Aboriginal Peoples" in *Manitoba Aboriginal Justice Inquiry Research Papers* (Winnipeg, 1991) [unpublished] at 32.

71 Blair Stonechild and W.A. Waiser, *Loyal till Death: Indians and the North-West Rebellion* (Saskatoon: Fifth House, 1997); Bob Beal and R.C. Macleod, *Prairie Fire: The 1885 North-West Rebellion* (Edmonton: Hurtig Publishers, 1984). See also W.A. Waiser, "The White Man Governs: The 1885 Indian Trials" in Barry Wright and Susan Binnie, eds., *Canadian State Trials,* vol. 3, *Political Trials and Security Measures, 1840-1914* (Toronto: University of Toronto Press, 2009) 451 at 463.

72 Peter Erasmus, *Buffalo Days and Nights, as Told to Henry Thompson* (Calgary: Glenbow-Alberta Institute, 1976) at 241. See also Deanna Christensen, *Ahtahkakoop: The Epic Account of a Plains Cree Head Chief, His People, and Their Struggle for Survival 1816-1896* (Shell Lake, SK: Ahtahkakoop Publishing, 2000) at 237.

73 See, *e.g.,* Hugh A. Dempsey, *Big Bear: The End of Freedom* (Vancouver: Douglas and McIntyre, 1984) at 74; J.R. Miller, *Big Bear [Mistahimusqua]: A Biography* (Toronto: ECW Press, 1996) at 80-83.

74 See Tina Loo, "Tonto's Due: Law, Culture, and Colonization in British Columbia" in Hamar Foster and John McLaren, eds., *Essays in the History of Canadian Law,* vol. 6, *The Legal History of British Columbia and the Yukon* (Toronto: University of Toronto Press, 1995) 128; reprinted in Catherine Cavanaugh and Jerome Mouat, eds., *Making Western Canada: Essays on European Colonization and Settlement* (Toronto: Garamond Press, 1996) 62 at 77; Nancy E. Wright, "The Problem of Aboriginal Evidence in Early Colonial New South Wales" in Diane Kirkby and Catharine Coleborne, eds., *Law, History, Colonialism: The Reach of Empire* (Manchester, UK: Manchester University Press, 2001) 140.

75 Notable exceptions include Hamar Foster, "The Queen's Law Is Better than Yours": International Homicide in Early British Columbia" in Susan Lewthwaite, Tina Loo, and Jim Phillips, eds., *Essays in the History of Canadian Law,* vol. 5, *Crime and Criminal Justice in Canadian History* (Toronto: University of Toronto Press, 1994) 41 at 66ff; Diana Eades, "'I Don't Think the Lawyers Were Communicating with Me': Misunderstanding Cultural

Differences in Communicative Style" (2003) 52 Emory L.J. 1109; Ahenakew *et al., supra* note 70.

76 Erasmus, *supra* note 72 at 241.

77 In the six court files in the early period in which Ballendine appears as informant, he is described variously as "merchant" – Ernest E. Wood (1877), SAB AG CR-Regina, 1st series, 1876-86, file 3 (an enforcement of a debt matter); as the government timber agent – Peter Boyer (1878), file 27 (charged with theft of timber; convicted and fined $1 and costs), William Turner (1878), file 47 (unlawfully cut timber on Dominion lands; fine of $1.50 and $2.50 in costs), Louis Sayer (1879), file 66 (theft of timber, *i.e.,* cutting timber without a licence; convicted and fined $1 and $8 in costs, including costs of the interpreter); as the property owner when he charged Robert Saunders in 1880 (file 82) with breaking and entering and theft at his home in Battleford (no disposition); and as mail contractor – Joseph Alexander (1883), file 180 (charged with abandoning the mail; prosecution allowed to be dropped and accused discharged after he offered an explanation and received a caution; Ballendine is listed as representing the Crown in this case).

78 See Beal and Macleod, *supra* note 71 at 314.

79 Ballendine, a former HBC employee who arrived in 1874, was one of the first settlers and merchants in Telegraphs Flats, which later became the Battleford townsite. He served as an interpreter for Alexander Morris during the Treaty 6 negotiations in 1876, as "secret agent" for Lieutenant-Governor Dewdney, and as a witness for the Crown in Poundmaker's trial in 1885. See Arlean McPherson, *The Battlefords: A History* (Saskatoon: Modern Press, 1967) at 35-36; Beal and Macleod, *ibid.* at 119-20; E. Brian Titley, *The Frontier World of Edgar Dewdney* (Vancouver: UBC Press, 1999) at 62; Alexander Morris, *The Treaties of Canada with the Indians of Manitoba and the North-West Territories,* facsimile reprint (Toronto: Prospero Books, 2000; original ed. Toronto: Belfords Clark, 1880) at 196.

80 The *Indian Act, 1876,* 39 Vict., c. 18, ss. 74-78 governed this process. Section 74 permitted the receipt of evidence on the affirmation to tell the truth: "[I]t shall be lawful for any court, judge, stipendiary magistrate, coroner, or justice of the peace to receive the evidence of an Indian or non-treaty Indian, who is destitute of the knowledge of God and of any fixed and clear belief in religion or in a future state of rewards and punishments, without administering the usual form of oath to any such Indian, or non-treaty Indian, as aforesaid, upon his solemn declaration to tell the truth."

81 Ka-nah-pic-a-nah-haw, or The Snake Indian (1882), SAB AG CR-Regina, 1st series, 1876-86, file 172.

82 Tom Lemac (1902), SAB SCNWT (Crim.), Coll. R1286, file 266.

83 This continues to be an issue of relevance. See, *e.g.,* Patricia Monture-Okanee, *supra* note 68 at 121.

84 Lemac was likely the man to whom Squaspekoke (whose case I discuss in this chapter, below) complained that Wa-chin had taken her pony, and who took her to the justice of the peace.

85 LAC, RG 73, W87-88/365, Microfilm reel T-11095, vol. 24 (MIKAN no. 134308), Manitoba Penitentiary Admitance [*sic*] Register, Prisoner No. 15 (or 884), Tom Lemac (Wingegee).

86 See also Tina Loo, "Savage Mercy: Native Culture and the Modification of Capital Punishment in Nineteenth-Century British Columbia" in Carolyn Strange, ed., *Qualities of Mercy: Justice, Punishment and Discretion* (Vancouver: UBC Press, 1996) 104.

87 Jeremy Webber, "Relations of Force and Relations of Justice: The Emergence of Normative Community between Colonists and Aboriginal Peoples" (1995) 33 Osgoode Hall L.J. 623.

Chapter 4: "Make a Better Indian of Him"

1 See, *e.g.*, R.C. Macleod, *The North-West Mounted Police and Law Enforcement 1873-1905* (Toronto: University of Toronto Press, 1976) [Macleod, *NWMP*]; R.C. Macleod, "Canadianizing the West: The North-West Mounted Police as Agents of the National Policy" in Lewis H. Thomas, ed., *Essays on Western History: In Honour of Lewis Gwynne Thomas* (Edmonton: University of Alberta Press, 1976) 101 [Macleod, "Canadianizing the West"]; W. Peter Ward, *The Administration of Justice in the North-West Territories, 1870-1887* (MA Thesis, University of Alberta, 1966) [unpublished] at 26; Kenneth B. Leyton-Brown, *The Origin and Evolution of a System for the Administration of Justice in the North-West Territories, 1870-1905* (PhD Dissertation, Queen's University, 1988) [unpublished] at 216-19; John Jennings, *The North-West Mounted Police and Canadian Indian Policy, 1873-1896* (PhD Dissertation, University of Toronto, 1979)[unpublished] [Jennings, *North-West Mounted Police*].

2 See, for instance, the accounts under the heading "Indians" and "Assistance to Indian Department" in the "Report of the Commissioner of the North-West Mounted Police, 1884," reprinted in Royal Canadian Mounted Police, *Settlers and Rebels: Being the Official Reports to Parliament of the Activities of the Royal* [*sic*] *North-West Mounted Police Force from 1882-1885 by the Commissioners of the Royal* [*sic*] *North-West Mounted Police,* facsimile reprint (Toronto: Coles Publishing, 1973; original ed. Ottawa: Maclean, Roger, 1882-85) at 6-13 ["Report of the Commissioner of the NWMP"]. This report contains the police version of the famous incident involving the altercation at a Thirst Dance organized by Big Bear between Indian farm instructor John Craig and the son of Lucky Man due to Craig's refusal to provide him with more rations. Lucky Man delivered up his son, Kawaeechatawaymat (Man Who Speaks Our Language), who was arrested, charged with assault, and sentenced to seven days. Hugh A. Dempsey, *Big Bear: The End of Freedom* (Vancouver: Douglas and McIntyre, 1984) at 132, quotes the *Saskatchewan Herald*'s account of the incident; the paper reported that the presiding magistrate (likely C.B. Rouleau) is reported to have accepted that Craig precipitated the incident: "From the evidence before me, he said I believe that Craig was in a great measure to blame in this matter. But if Craig pushed or struck an Indian, it was the Indian's duty to complain to his agent or to a magistrate and then he would be punished." Dempsey says that Man Who Speaks Our Language, who died at the Battle of Frenchman's Butte in 1885, was responsible for the deaths of two men at Frog Lake (at 156-57 and 176). See also Blair Stonechild, "The Indian View of the 1885 Uprising" in F. Laurie Barron and James B. Waldram, eds., *1885 and After: Native Society in Transition* (Regina: Canadian Plains Research Center, 1986) 155 at 167.

3 See also E. Brian Titley, *A Narrow Vision: Duncan Campbell Scott and the Administration of Indian Affairs in Canada* (Vancouver: UBC Press, 1986) at 167 [Titley, *A Narrow Vision*], for an example of the NWMP's differing with Indian Agents on the question of Indian dancing, the former taking a more tolerant position. The *Report of the Royal Commission on Aboriginal Peoples,* vol. 1, *Looking Forward, Looking Back* (Ottawa: Minister of Supply and Services, 1996) at 298 [RCAP, *Report*], echoes Titley on this point, noting that while some Indian Agents were petty despots, others were persons of integrity who resisted and opposed the *Indian Act* prohibitions of the potlatch and other aspects of the government's Indian policies.

4 I have discussed these cases in Chapter 2: Alex Bone (1894), Saskatchewan Archives Board, Supreme Court of North-West Territories (Criminal), Collection R1286 [hereinafter, SAB

SCNWT (Crim.), Coll. R1286], file 84; Julia Coté (1894), SAB SCNWT (Crim.), Coll. R1286, file 85.

5 Simon Crow Moccasin (1898), SAB SCNWT (Crim.), Coll. R1286, file 180. Crow Moccasin entered a guilty plea before Richardson and was sentenced to one year's hard labour for theft of Chaquay's pony.

6 Deposition of William Graham, *ibid.*

7 Fortunately for the prosecution, Chaquay, the man who lost the pony, had provided a sworn deposition that he had lent the horse to Crow Moccasin but that it had not been returned; he denied Crow Moccasin's suggestion put to him under cross-examination at the hearing before the justice of the peace that he had given him permission to sell the horse.

8 Alexander Morris, *The Treaties of Canada with the Indians of Manitoba and the North-West Territories,* facsimile reprint (Toronto: Prospero Books, 2000; original ed. Toronto: Belfords Clarke, 1880) at 183.

9 *Indian Act, 1876,* 39 Vict., c. 18.

10 RCAP, *Report, supra* note 3 at 257.

11 *Ibid.* at 278.

12 *Ibid.* at 276-81.

13 See, *e.g., ibid.* See also Sarah Carter, *Lost Harvests: Prairie Indian Reserve Farmers and Government Policy* (Montreal and Kingston: McGill-Queen's University Press, 1990) [Carter, *Lost Harvests*]; Sarah Carter, *Aboriginal People and the Colonizers of Western Canada to 1900* (Toronto: University of Toronto Press, 1999) at 101 [Carter, *Aboriginal People*] (Carter, at 117, repeats the description of the *Indian Act* as a "formidable dossier of repression"); J.R. Miller, *Skyscrapers Hide the Heavens: A History of Indian-White Relations in Canada,* 3rd ed. (Toronto: University of Toronto Press, 2000) at 225-82 [Miller, *Skyscrapers*]; J.R. Miller, *Shingwauk's Vision: A History of Native Residential Schools* (Toronto: University of Toronto Press, 1996) [Miller, *Shingwauk's Vision*]; Kathryn Pettipas, *Severing the Ties that Bind: Government Repression of Indigenous Religious Ceremonies on the Prairies* (Winnipeg: University of Manitoba Press, 1994); E. Brian Titley, *The Frontier World of Edgar Dewdney* (Vancouver: UBC Press, 1999) [Titley, *Edgar Dewdney*]; Titley, *A Narrow Vision, supra* note 3; Hugh Shewell, *"Enough to Keep Them Alive": Indian Welfare in Canada, 1873-1965* (Toronto: University of Toronto Press, 2004); John L. Tobias, "Canada's Subjugation of the Plains Cree, 1879-1885" in J.R. Miller, ed., *Sweet Promises: A Reader on Indian-White Relations in Canada* (Toronto: University of Toronto Press, 1991) 212 at 221-22 [Tobias, "Canada's Subjugation"]; John L. Tobias, "Protection, Civilization, Assimilation: An Outline History of Canada's Indian Policy" in Ian A.L. Getty and Antoine S. Lussier, eds., *As Long as the Sun Shines and Water Flows: A Reader in Canadian Native Studies* (Vancouver: UBC Press, 1983) 39 at 44-45; Helen Buckley, *From Wooden Ploughs to Welfare: Why Indian Policy Failed in the Prairie Provinces* (Montreal and Kingston: McGill-Queen's University Press, 1992); RCAP, *Report, supra* note 3 at 256-409 (chapters on the *Indian Act* and the residential schools); Manitoba, *Report of the Aboriginal Justice Inquiry of Manitoba,* vol. 1, *The Justice System and Aboriginal People* (A.C. Hamilton and C.M. Sinclair, Commissioners) (Winnipeg: Province of Manitoba, 1991) at 201-5, 301-5 [Manitoba, *Justice Inquiry Report*]; F. Laurie Barron, "A Summary of Federal Indian Policy in the Canadian West, 1867-1984" (1985) 1 Native Studies Review 28; Sidney L. Harring, "'There Seemed to Be No Recognized Law': Canadian Law and the Prairie First Nations" in Louis A. Knafla and Jonathan Swainger, eds., *Laws and Societies in the Canadian Prairie West 1670-1940* (Vancouver: UBC Press, 2005) 92 [Harring, "No Recognized Law"]; Constance Backhouse, *Colour-Coded:*

A Legal History of Racism in Canada, 1900-1950 (Toronto: University of Toronto Press, 1999); Maureen Lux, *Medicine that Walks: Disease, Medicine, and Canadian Plains Native People, 1880-1940* (Toronto: University of Toronto Press, 2001).

14 *Indian Act, 1876,* 39 Vict., c. 18; *Indian Act, 1881,* 44 Vict., c. 17, s. 12. See Thomas Reynolds, *Justices of the Peace in the NWT, 1870-1905* (MA Thesis, University of Regina, 1978) [unpublished] at 58.

15 *An Act Further to Amend the Indian Act, 1895,* 58-59 Vict., c. 35, s. 7.

16 Laurie Barron argues that Quinn, who was killed at Frog Lake, was "intensely disliked for personal reasons." He reminds his readers that Quinn was related by marriage to Lone Man (Big Bear's son-in-law) and that Payne also had family ties to the Assiniboine. See F. Laurie Barron, "Indian Agents and the North-West Rebellion" in F. Laurie Barron and James B. Waldram, eds., *1885 and After: Native Society in Transition* (Regina: Canadian Plains Research Center, 1986) 139 at 149. John Delaney, who was also disliked, nonetheless was disciplined by Quinn when Quinn discovered that he was distributing rations without requiring work (*ibid.*). See also Walter Hildebrandt, *Views from Fort Battleford: Constructed Visions of an Anglo-Canadian West* (Regina: Canadian Plains Research Center, 1994); see Dempsey, *supra* note 2, and Stonechild, *supra* note 2 at 159, for their accounts of the personal grievances against Payne and Delaney, respectively.

17 Douglas Leighton, "A Victorian Civil Servant at Work: Lawrence Vankoughnet and the Canadian Indian Department, 1874-1893" in Ian A.L. Getty and Antoine S. Lussier, eds., *As Long as the Sun Shines and Water Flows: A Reader in Canadian Native Studies* (Vancouver: UBC Press, 1983) 104 at 106.

18 *Ibid.* at 107; Shewell, *supra* note 13 at 69; Titley, *Edgar Dewdney, supra* note 13 at 51-55.

19 Tobias, "Canada's Subjugation," *supra* note 13 at 221; Titley, *ibid.* at 52-54.

20 Titley, *ibid.* at 65.

21 *Ibid.*

22 *Ibid.* at 7; Leighton, *supra* note 17 at 107. For another reference to saucy Indians, see Laura Peer, *The Ojibwa of Western Canada, 1780-1870* (Winnipeg: University of Manitoba Press, 1994) at 144. Peer observes that mixed-group camps of Cree and Ojibwa (Saulteaux) were regarded by traders as "saucy and independent." Big Bear's father was the Ojibwa chief Black Powder, who led a mixed band of Cree and Ojibwa that combined the cultural traditions of both the Plains Cree and the "woodland" Ojibwa.

23 This is the spelling of his name appears in Treaty 4. John Tobias spells his name Kamyistowesit, or Beardy, Chief of the Willow Band of the Plains Cree: Dictionary of Canadian Biography, online: <http://www.biographi.ca/>. See also J.W. Grant McEwen, *Portraits from the Plains* (Toronto: McGraw-Hill, 1971) at 150-58.

24 See, *e.g., Saskatchewan Herald* (6 February 1880) 1 at col. 3; "A Bit of Indian Ugliness," *Saskatchewan Herald* (16 August 1880) 1 at col. 4.

25 Beardy (1879), Saskatchewan Archives Board, Department of the Attorney General, Regina Judicial Centre: Court Records First Series, 1876-86, files 1-282 [hereinafter SAB AG CR-Regina, 1st series, 1876-86], file 72. The second proceeding against Beardy occurred on 28 July 1880 before two justices of the peace at Duck Lake, following the killing of cattle on the reserve. The record contains no Information, only the depositions of two men who stated that they had killed the cattle on the instructions of Beardy and two other chiefs. This document is contained (misfiled, it seems) in a file concerning Robert Saunders (1880), SAB AG CR-Regina, 1st series, 1876-86, file 82 (an Information sworn on 29 July 1880 at Battleford by Peter Ballendine against Robert Saunders for entering Ballendine's house without permission and "disappearing from the neighbourhood" with Ballendine's

double-barrelled muzzle-loading short gun and bark canoe). There is no disposition of this matter. I have placed my copy of the 28 July 1880 record concerning Beardy, One Arrow, and Cut Nose in my file containing a copy of the 1879 record (file 72) concerning Beardy's earlier matter.

26 Francis Deschaw (1878), SAB AG CR-Regina, 1st series, 1876-86, file 57. I discussed this case in Chapter 3.

27 Beardy (1879), *supra* note 25.

28 Deposition of Omenakaw before Justices of the Peace Herchmer and Hughes, on 28 July 1880, contained in my file Beardy (1879), SAB AG CR-Regina, 1st series, 1876-86, file 72. See also Carter, *Lost Harvests, supra* note 13 at 121-22, who says that this view was shared by the Indians, who maintained that the contents of the reserve storehouses belonged to them.

29 "Report of the Commissioner of the North-West Mounted Police, 1880" reprinted in Royal Canadian Mounted Police, *Opening Up the West: Being the Official Reports to Parliament of the Activities of the Royal* [*sic*] *North-West Mounted Police from 1874-1881 by The Commissioners of the Royal* [*sic*] *North-West Mounted Police,* facsimile reprint (Toronto: Coles Publishing, 1973; original ed. Ottawa: Maclean, Roger, 1874-81) at 41. It appears that only Omenakaw was convicted.

30 In the following year, the *Saskatchewan Herald* (16 August 1880) at 1 at col. 4, celebrated Beardy's arrest on yet another charge with the following scathing characterization:

> Of the Indian Chiefs on the Saskatchewan few have a wider and at the same time less enviable reputation than The Beardy, of Duck Lake. His name is associated with all the troubles that have arisen in that neighbourhood, and is looked upon as synonymous with everything that is base and dishonest. Fidelity to promises is a principle entirely unknown to him ... He has had several narrow escapes from arrest, but has hitherto stopped short of committing any overt act; but mistaking the leniency of the authorities for fear, he this time overstepped the mark and this time laid himself open to punishment.

Despite the *Herald*'s confidence and fervent hope, Beardy was not imprisoned.

31 McEwen, *supra* note 23 at 157-58.

32 Norbert Delorme (1881), SAB AG (GR 11.1) CR-Regina, 1st series, 1876-86, file 112.

33 See Reed's list, reproduced in Blair Stonechild and W.A. Waiser, *Loyal till Death: Indians and the North-West Rebellion* (Saskatoon: Fifth House, 1997) Appendix 4 at 257.

34 Blair Stonechild, "The Indian View of the 1885 Uprising" in F. Laurie Barron and James B. Waldram, eds., *1885 and After: Native Society in Transition* (Regina: Canadian Plains Research Center, 1986) 155.

35 Stamiscotocar (Bull Head) also turned to the criminal law to enforce his rights in his successful prosecution of a Métis man for theft of his horse: Joseph Gouin (1879), SAB AG CR-Regina, 1st series, 1876-86, file 69. R.C. Macleod and Heather Rollason, "'Restrain the Lawless Savages': Native Defendants in the Criminal Courts of the North-West Territories, 1878-1885" (1997) 10 Journal of Historical Sociology 157 at 176-77, also refer to this case, citing it as "evidence that the Natives adopted an instrumental approach to the law; experimenting with it and using it when it seemed useful" (at 176).

36 "Report of the Commissioner of the NWMP, 1884," *supra* note 2 at 15. In Appendix A of the Returns for 1884, Crow Collar is reported to have been convicted by Superintendent McIllree J.P. of "malicious injury to property" and sentenced to ten days' imprisonment

at hard labour; Bull Head is listed as having been charged with causing a disturbance, which charge was "dismissed, with caution after three days' imprisonment" (at 49).

37 See, *e.g.*, Stonechild and Waiser, *supra* note 33 at 51fn15; Bob Beal and R.C. Macleod, *Prairie Fire: The 1885 North-West Rebellion* (Edmonton: Hurtig Publishers, 1984) at 76.

38 Titley, *Edgar Dewdney, supra* note 13 at 46; Stonechild and Waiser, *ibid.* at 50-51.

39 See Lux, *supra* note 13 at 37-41.

40 Stonechild and Waiser, *supra* note 33.

41 Lux, *supra* note 13.

42 Lean Man, an Assiniboine Indian (1883), SAB AG CR-Regina, 1st series, 1876-86, file 193.

43 *Ibid.*

44 Lean Man is referring here to the medal he received as a signatory to the treaty.

45 Statement of the Accused, *ibid.*

46 *Saskatchewan Herald* (9 June 1883) 1 at col. 4.

47 See the Rebellion conviction tables in Sandra E. Bingaman, *The North-West Rebellion Trials, 1885* (MA Thesis, University of Regina, 1971) [unpublished] at 204-10; Stonechild and Waiser, *supra* note 33, Appendix 5 at 261-63; "Report of the Commissioner of the North-West Mounted Police, 1885," reprinted in Royal Canadian Mounted Police, *Settlers and Rebels: Being the Official Reports to Parliament of the Activities of the Royal* [*sic*] *North-West Mounted Police Force from 1882-1885 by the Commissioners of the Royal* [*sic*] *North-West Mounted Police,* facsimile reprint (Toronto: Coles Publishing, 1973; original ed. Ottawa: Maclean, Roger, 1882-85) Appendix O.

48 For accounts, see Stonechild and Waiser, *ibid.* at 98-99; Dempsey, *supra* note 2 at 161; Beal and Macleod, *supra* note 37 at 183.

49 Hildebrandt, *supra* note 16 at 84-85.

50 The *Saskatchewan Herald*'s report of Itka's statement in court is a bit different yet again. The *Herald* reported that Itka said at the time of his plea that he had asked Payne for some shot and flour, and that Payne would not give him any: "then my heart got bad and Payne got vexed; I told him not to get vexed; he said he would not give me flour for ten days; I went away and got my gun and came back." Itka reported that they struggled, and he shot Payne. *Saskatchewan Herald* (12 October 1885) 2 at cols. 3 and 4.

51 Stonechild and Waiser, *supra* note 33 at 98.

52 Norma Sluman and Jean Goodwill, *John Tootoosis: A Biography of a Cree Leader* (Ottawa: Golden Dog Press, 1982) at 37.

53 *Saskatchewan Herald, supra* note 50. The admonition attributed by the *Herald* to Rouleau is similar to that attributed by Hugh Dempsey (relying on the *Herald*) to an unnamed magistrate (probably Rouleau) who sentenced The Man Who Talks Our Language following the incident with John Delaney at the Thirst Dance in June 1884: Dempsey, *supra* note 2.

54 *Saskatchewan Herald* (14 February 1881) 2 at col. 2.

55 Bazil Lafond (1878), SAB AG CR-Regina, 1st series, 1876-86, file 16.

56 *Indian Act, 1876,* 39 Vict., c. 18, s. 79, made it an offence for anyone to sell, exchange with, barter, or supply any kind of intoxicant to any Indian or non-Treaty Indian in Canada. A stipendiary magistrate or two justices of the peace could convict on the evidence of one credible witness other than the informer or prosecutor. Upon conviction, one could be liable to a sentence of not less than one month and not more than six months, and to a fine of not less than $50 and not more than $300, plus the costs of the prosecution.

57 Arlean McPherson, *The Battlefords: A History* (Saskatoon: Modern Press, 1967) at 48.

58 *Indian Act, 1876,* 39 Vict., c. 18, s. 79: "[O]ne moiety of the fine to go to the informer or prosecutor, and the other moiety to Her Majesty, to form part of a fund for the benefit of that body of Indians ... with respect to one or more members of which the offence was committed."

59 See James Falster (1881), SAB AG CR-Regina, 1st series, 1876-86, file 109 (this matter was tried before Hayter Reed J.P.). The informant against Falster was farm instructor Daniel Clink, who claimed that Falster, a labourer, had come to Moosomin's reserve near Battleford and offered him a drink of liquor, which Clink refused; Falster told Clink he was off to the chief's tent, and stayed there all night. Clink claimed that nearly all the Indians on the reserve "are this morning drunk or more or less on the influence of liquor and from the information supplied by such of the Indians who are fit to speak of it," he believed that Falster was the cause of it. One wonders, of course, why Clink would have allowed Falster to stay on the reserve in the first place.

John M. Rae [Indian Agent] (1881), SAB AG CR-Regina, 1st series, 1876-86, file 110, charged with supplying liquor to Indians (informant Reverend John Hines); Reverend John Hines (1881), SAB AG CR-Regina, 1st series, 1876-86, file 111, charged with selling intoxicating liquor (informant John M. Rae). Rae and Hines were convicted. Hines was the Anglican missionary invited by Cree Chief Ahtahkakoop to build a school and church on his reserve. He is favourably represented in Deanna Christensen, *Ahtahkakoop: The Epic Account of a Plains Cree Head Chief, His People, and Their Struggle for Survival 1816-1896* (Shell Lake, SK: Ahtahkakoop Publishing, 2000); see, for instance, his remarkably sympathetic approach to the baptism of the first and oldest of Sasakamoose's two wives: as she had only one husband, he decided he could baptize her (at 183-84). Sasakamoose was the older brother of Ahtahkakoop.

60 Wachan (1882), SAB AG CR-Regina, 1st series, 1876-86, file 165; Noel Duquette (1881), SAB AG CR-Regina, 1st series, 1876-86, file 139 (breach of contract of employment, Hayter Reed, Indian Agent, informant). Reed had been trained as a lawyer and was a member of the Manitoba Bar. Although Sarah Carter, *Lost Harvests, supra* note 13 at 142, suggests that Reed had never been active as a lawyer, the Richardson court files, including these prosecutions, provide evidence that he prosecuted and defended cases before Richardson in Battleford. Before his 1881 appointment as Indian Agent in Battleford, Reed had acted as defence counsel in at least three cases: SAB AG (GR 11.1) CR-Regina, 1st series, 1876-86: John Smith (1878), file 24 (accused of assault with intent to rape); J.B. Mahoney (1878), file 21; and Henry R. Elliott (1878), file 26. Elliott was Richardson's aspirant son-in-law, who was charged with a series of offences related to his attempt to marry and leave with Luders Richardson: SAB AG CR-Regina, 1st series, 1876-86, file 26. It appears that Mahoney never went to trial on the charge of (indecently) assaulting Mary Hamblyn; Smith was convicted and fined modestly, but Reed's defence of Elliott was successful. Reed also appeared for the prosecutrix in the prosecution of Chystotome Poitras, SAB AG CR-Regina, 1st series, 1876-86, file 70. In April 1881, he also appeared with John Thomas and Thomas A. Beckett (the widow Conata's son), who were charged with shooting and wounding John Burnett: SAB AG CR-Regina, 1st series, 1876-86, file 116. (I discuss this case in Chapter 3.) It is likely that he appeared with the boys in his capacity as Indian Agent, not as a privately retained counsel.

61 Ah-tim-musis-se-quine (1881), SAB AG CR-Regina, 1st series, 1876-86, file 117.

62 Peecoose (Sandfly) (1879), SAB AG CR-Regina, 1st series, 1876-86, file 88. This case was discussed in Chapter 2. Peecoose was sentenced to two and one-half years in the penitentiary for theft of goods from the HBC post at Fort Pitt. He escaped from prison shortly after

he was sentenced, and was reported by the *Saskatchewan Herald* on 16 August 1880 (1 at col. 3) to have been back in his community the day before Treaty payments, "but did not stay to interview the police." He was still at large in 1885, until sentenced to more time in the penitentiary for treason-felony subsequent to the events of 1885.

63 The Dancing Bull and Moostus (1882), SAB AG CR-Regina, 1st series, 1876-86, file 153.

64 I-ah-pee-coo-caw (1881), SAB AG CR-Regina, 1st series, 1876-86, file 115.

65 Dempsey, *supra* note 2 at 117. Dempsey reports that Dancing Bull received a sentence of four months, but the court record indicates a sentence of two months for him.

66 Their trial was covered in the Regina *Leader* (6 March 1884) 3 at cols. 3 and 4. Isabel Andrews has written about this case and its background and context in her article "Indian Protest against Starvation: The Yellow Calf Incident of 1884" (1975) 28 Saskatchewan History 41.

67 Tom Gopher (1884), SAB AG CR-Regina, 1st series, 1876-86, file 213.

68 Regina *Leader* (6 March 1884) 3 at cols. 2 and 3.

69 Jean Felix Callilouis (1882), SAB AG CR-Regina, 1st series, 1876-86, file 175.

70 Tom Gopher (1884), SAB AG CR-Regina, 1st series, 1876-86, file 213.

71 Of all the descriptions of the events of 1885 ("Riel Rebellion," "1885 Uprising," "North-West Rebellion," "North-West Resistance"), I find that this phrase – *ê-mâyi-kamikahk* – best expresses the nature of the events, their implications, and their aftermath. I am indebted to Neal McLeod, "Rethinking Treaty 6 in the Spirit of Mistahi Maskwa (Big Bear)" (1999) 19 Canadian Journal of Native Studies 69 at 84.

72 Carter, *Lost Harvests, supra* note 13 at 130-58, esp. 141ff. At 141, Carter describes Reed as the "major architect of Indian policy in the North-West in the decades following the rebellion." She cites an 1885 memorandum prepared by Reed for Vankoughnet, in which he advocated "extremely repressive measures" for the future management of Indians, measures that were initially supposed to be temporary and punitive, targeted to the "rebel bands," but which became "permanent and universal" (at 145). The two cornerstones of Reed's agenda were the attack on traditional forms of band leadership and authority and the introduction of the "pass system" to restrict Aboriginal movement and interaction (at 146-56) and to isolate them from the broader society. Reed's memorandum is reproduced in Stonechild and Waiser, *supra* note 33, Appendix 3 at 250-53.

73 Mequanis (The Little Quill) (1889), SAB SCNWT (Crim.), Coll. R1286, file 10.

74 Library and Archives Canada [LAC], RG 10, reel C-7148, vol. 9424, Treaty Annuity Paylists for Treaties 4, 6, and 7 (1891), Peepeekeesis's Band, 160-61. In later years, he was named simply as "Mequanis The Quill": *ibid.*, vol. 9427, Treaty Annuity Paylists for Treaties 4, 6, and 7 (1894), Peepeekeesis's Band, 163-70.

75 Shave Tail (1896), SAB SCNWT (Crim.), Coll. R1286, file 128.

76 Jean Baptiste (1896), SAB SCNWT (Crim.), Coll. R1286, file 130.

77 *Ibid.*

78 *Ibid.*

79 Eopiassis, Son of the Old Blind Man (1896), SAB SCNWT (Crim.), Coll. R1286, file 122.

80 In sentencing Pierre Bourassa (1892) for unlawful carnal knowledge: SAB SCNWT (Crim.), Coll. R1286, file 39.

81 In offering this interpretation, I am mindful that on at least two occasions, he did sentence men charged with similar offences to jail: young Jean Felix Callilouis, who said he killed the farm instructor's ox because his family was starving; his mistake was that he had thought the ox belonged to the government (and thus to the reserve), and he received six months – SAB AG CR-Regina, 1st series, 1876-86, file 175; as discussed above, Gopher Tom (also known as Tom Gopher) was also sentenced to one month's hard labour in 1884 for breaking

into and stealing flour and bacon from the reserve's ration storehouse (having been delivered up by his chief) – SAB AG CR-Regina, 1st series, 1876-86, file 213.

82 Shave Tail (1903), SAB SCNWT (Crim.), Coll. R1286, file 316.

83 Etchease (1903), SAB SCNWT (Crim.), Coll. R1286, file 314. His conviction attracted a small piece in the *Leader:* "Imprisoned for Breach of Indian Act" Regina *Leader* (4 June 1903) 5.

84 In addition to the Riel treason trial in 1885, Stipendiary Magistrate Richardson presided with a justice of the peace at the trials of Ka-ka-si-kut-chin (The Swift Runner) (1879), SAB AG CR-Regina, 1st series, 1876-86, file 65 (convicted and executed at Fort Saskatchewan for the murder of his wife and children, and other members of his family in the bush in the region of Lac la Biche. The case excited interest in the press because of the allegations that he was a cannibal and wendigo); Joseph Cardinal (1880), SAB AG CR-Regina, 1st series, 1876-86, file 104, for the murder of his teenage son, Moise (convicted at Lac la Biche of manslaughter, and sentenced to an unknown term in the Manitoba Penitentiary) (see Chapter 3); Scholastique Cardinal (1882), SAB AG CR-Regina, 1st series, 1876-86, file 145 (initially charged with murder and concealment of birth of her newborn infant; convicted of concealment of birth; sentence deferred) (see Chapter 6); George Stevenson and John Stevenson (1883) tried and convicted for murder and sentenced to death, Annual Report of the Commissioner of the NWMP, 1883, Appendix A, in Royal Canadian Mounted Police, *Settlers and Rebels: Being the Official Reports to Parliament of the Activities of the Royal [sic] North-West Mounted Police Force from 1882-1885 by the Commissioners of the Royal [sic] North-West Mounted Police,* facsimile reprint (Toronto: Coles Publishing, 1973; original ed. Ottawa: Maclean, Roger, 1882-85); John Connor, *R. v. Connor,* [1884] 1 Terr. L.R. 4 (Man. Q.B.); and Eugana (The Fast Runner) (1885), Library and Archives Canada, RG 13, vol. 1421, Capital Case file 193; also found in Saskatchewan Archives Board, Department of the Attorney General, Regina Judicial Centre: Court Records, Collection R996, file 284L [hereinafter SAB, Coll. R996] (convicted of murdering Eagle Child). As a judge of the North-West Territories Supreme Court, he presided at the murder trial of John McDonald (1893), SAB SCNWT (Crim.), Coll. R1286, file 64 (charged with murder of Vincent Weidman, convicted of manslaughter, and sentenced to five years in the penitentiary); Tom Lemac (Winegee) (1902), SAB SCNWT (Crim.), Coll. R1286, file 266 (LAC, RG 13, vol. 1442, Capital Case file 337a) (convicted of murdering Josiah Matoney (Oskinaway). Not every one of these cases, including Eugana's case, which I will discuss here, is found in the two SAB collections that form the basis of my research. I cannot explain why, in particular, Eugana's trial in October 1885 is found in another collection (that of the Attorney General files, Coll. R996), but it is clear that Richardson, with justice of the peace (and coroner) Dr. Dodd, presided at the Regina trial and wrote the report to the Executive Council after Eugana's conviction and death sentence.

85 The commutation decision for each of the two men, Eugana and Tom Lemac, can be found in the "capital case" files housed at Library and Archives Canada in Ottawa. These records are a rich source of material that has been invaluable to criminal justice historians, including those whose research focuses on the experience of Aboriginal prisoners sentenced to death. See, *e.g.,* Carolyn Strange, ed., *Qualities of Mercy, Justice, Punishment and Discretion* (Vancouver: UBC Press, 1996); Carolyn Strange, "Stories of Their Lives: The Historian and the Capital Case File" in Franca Iacovetta and Wendy Mitchinson, eds., *On the Case: Explorations in Social History* (Toronto: University of Toronto Press, 1998) 25; Karen Dubinsky and Franca Iacovetta, "Murder, Womanly Virtue, and Motherhood: The Case

of Angelina Napolitano, 1911-1922" in Tina Loo and Lorna R. McLean, eds., *Historical Perspectives on Law and Society in Canada* (Toronto: Copp Clark Longman, 1994) 161; Hamar Foster, "'The Queen's Law Is Better than Yours': International Homicide in Early British Columbia" in Susan Lewthwaite, Tina Loo, and Jim Phillips, eds., *Essays in the History of Canadian Law,* vol. 5, *Crime and Criminal Justice in Canadian History* (Toronto: University of Toronto Press, 1994) 41; Tina Loo, "Savage Mercy: Native Culture and the Modification of Capital Punishment in Nineteenth-Century British Columbia" in Carolyn Strange, ed., *Qualities of Mercy: Justice, Punishment and Discretion* (Vancouver: UBC Press, 1996) 104 [Loo, "Savage Mercy"]; Alan Grove, "'Where Is the Justice, Mr. Mills?': A Case Study of *R. v. Nantuck*" in Hamar Foster and John McLaren, eds., *Essays in the History of Canadian Law: The Legal History of British Columbia and the Yukon* (Toronto: University of Toronto Press, 1995) 87; Jonathan Swainger, "A Distant Edge of Authority: Capital Punishment and the Prerogative of Mercy in British Columbia, 1872-1880" in Hamar Foster and John McLaren, eds., *Essays in the History of Canadian Law: The Legal History of British Columbia and the Yukon* (Toronto: University of Toronto Press, 1995) 204.

86 Eugana, *supra* note 84.

87 The assertion that the facts of the case were well known raises the question of how this was so. As this was the only reference to Eugana I could find in the Regina *Leader* (1 October 1885, 4 at col. 2, under the headline "The Gallows"), one may infer again that news travelled like a prairie fire, but not necessarily through the press. See Dempsey, *supra* note 2 at 39.

88 The Indian Agent said of him that "an active and good working Indian is gone. He was about completing the best house on the reserve and working at it when he was shot. From then to his death his mind was on his house giving instructions how it should be finished off." Quoted by Edgar Dewdney, Commissioner of Indian Affairs, North-West Territories, in his letter of 19 August 1885 to the Superintendent General of Indian Affairs. Eugana, *supra* note 84.

89 Letter from Edgar Dewdney, Indian Commissioner, to Superintendent General of Indian Affairs (19 August 1885), *ibid.,* quoting from the account of incident provided to him by the Indian Agent.

90 *Ibid.*

91 *Ibid.*

92 Letter from John Secord to Lieutenant-Governor (and Indian Commissioner) Edgar Dewdney (29 September 1885), *ibid.* Secord's second line of defence, not repeated after the trial, involved a long shot, a causation issue based on his argument that the Indian medicine, and not the injury, had caused the man's death.

93 Transcript of the trial, *ibid.* at 3.

94 *Ibid.* at 6.

95 *Ibid.* These words are similar to ones uttered by the deceased, which gave rise to and supported the defence of provocation in a recent Supreme Court of Canada decision in *R v. Thibert,* [1996] 1 S.C.R. 37 (SCC). Mr. Thibert had shot his wife's lover, as the latter had walked toward him with his hands on Mrs. Thibert's shoulders. His evidence in part was that the deceased had taunted him by saying, "You want to shoot me? Go ahead and shoot me," and, "Come on big fellow, shoot me."

96 Transcript of the trial, *supra* note 93 at 11.

97 *Ibid.* at 12.

98 *Ibid.*

99 *Ibid.* at 13.

100 *Ibid.* at 14-15.
101 *Ibid.* at 18.
102 *Ibid.* at 19.
103 *Ibid.* at 20.
104 Petition of John Secord (29 September 1885), *ibid.*
105 Letter from Lieutenant-Governor Edgar Dewdney to the Secretary of State (9 October 1885), *ibid.*
106 Letter from the Office of the Indian Commissioner, North-West Territories, Hayter Reed to the Superintendent General of Indian Affairs (13 August 1888), *ibid.*
107 *Ibid.* at 3.
108 Memorandum from Robert W. Sedgewick, Deputy Minister of Justice (1 September 1888) to the Secretary of State, *ibid.*
109 Memorandum from Robert W. Sedgewick, Deputy Minister of Justice, to the Under Secretary of State (3 September 1888), *ibid.*
110 Tom Lemac (Winegee) (1902), SAB SCNWT (Crim.), Coll. R1286, file 266.
111 Memorandum from Reginald Rimmer, Law Clerk, Department of Indian Affairs, to the Minister of Justice, The Hon. C. Fitzpatrick (7 June 1902), *ibid.*
112 *Ibid.* at 7.
113 *Ibid.* at 8.
114 "Report of Wm. Graham, Indian Agent, Qu'Appelle Agency, N.W.T." in *Dominion of Canada Annual Report of the Department of Indian Affairs for the Year Ended June 30 1902* (Ottawa: King's Printer, 1902) at 162, online: Library and Archives Canada <http://www.collectionscanada.gc.ca/>.
115 Chief Piapot, at his trial in Fort Qu'Appelle on 21 October 1901, where he was charged with and convicted of interfering with a police officer in discharge of duty: *J.W. Fyffe (complt) v. Piapot (Deft),* SAB, Justice of the Peace Papers (unprocessed), H-3503 (1901) [*J.W. Fyffe (complt) v. Piapot (Deft)*].
116 On Piapot's importance and enduring stature as a leader, see John L. Tobias, "PAYIPWAT (Piapot, Hole in the Sioux, Kisikawasan, Flash in the Sky), Plains Cree chief" (1901-10) 13 Dictionary of Canadian Biography, online: <http://www.biographi.ca/>; Christian Thompson, "Piapot" in *Saskatchewan First Nations: Lives Past and Present* (Regina: Canadian Plains Research Center, 2004) 105; Abel Watetch. *Payepot and His People* (Saskatoon: Modern Press, 1959; repr. Regina: Canadian Plains Research Center, 2007); David Lee, "Piapot: Man and Myth" (1992) 17 Prairie Forum 251.
117 Evidence of Charles Fox at his trial at Fort Qu'Appelle on 21 October 1901 before Justices of the Peace G.W. Guernsey and John North: *D.J. Grant v. Charles Fox* charge: engaging in a giveaway dance: SAB, Justice of the Peace Papers (unprocessed), H-3503 (1901).
118 Evidence of NWMP Staff Sergeant J.W. Fyffe at Piapot's trial, *J.W. Fyffe (complt) v. Piapot (Deft), supra* note 115.
119 See Christian Thompson, "Piapot" in Christian Thompson, ed., *Saskatchewan First Nations: Lives Past and Present* (Regina: Canadian Plains Research Center, 2004) 105 at 108; Lux, *supra* note 13 at 88; Pettipas, *supra* note 13 at 118-19.

Chapter 5: Six Women, Six Stories

1 E.P. Thompson, "Folklore, Anthropology, and Social History" (1978) 3 Indian Historical Review 247 at 254.

2 Sarah Carter, "First Nations Women of Prairie Canada in the Early Reserve Years, the 1870s to 1920: A Preliminary Inquiry" in Christine Miller and Patricia Chuchryk, with Marie Smallface Marule, Brenda Manyfingers, and Cheryl Deering, eds., *Women of the First Nations: Power, Wisdom, and Strength* (Winnipeg: University of Manitoba Press, 1996) 51 at 55 [Carter, "First Nations Women"].
3 See, *e.g.*, Dorothy E. Chunn and Dany Lacombe, eds., *Law as a Gendering Practice* (Oxford: Oxford University Press, 2000).
4 A notable exception is found in Joan Sangster's research into Aboriginal girls and women in early to mid-twentieth-century Ontario. See Joan Sangster, "Criminalizing the Colonized: Ontario Native Women Confront the Criminal Justice System, 1920-60" (1999) 80 Canadian Historical Review 32, and "'She Is Hostile to Our Ways': First Nations Girls Sentenced to the Ontario Training School for Girls, 1933-1960" (2002) 20 Law and History Review 59.
5 Val Napoleon, "Aboriginal Discourse: Gender, Identity, and Community" in Benjamin J. Richardson, Shin Imai, and Kent McNeil, eds., *Indigenous Peoples and the Law: Comparative and Critical Perspectives* (Oxford: Hart Publishing, 2009) 233 at 235.
6 *Ibid.* at 241.
7 Jean Barman, "Taming Aboriginal Sexuality: Gender, Power, and Race in British Columbia, 1850-1900" in Mary-Ellen Kelm and Lorna Townsend, eds., *In the Days of Our Grandmothers: A Reader in Aboriginal Women's History in Canada* (Toronto: University of Toronto Press, 2006) 270 at 271.
8 *Ibid.*
9 To borrow from Sheila Rowbotham's early contribution to women's history: Sheila Rowbotham, *Hidden from History: Three Hundred Years of Women's Oppression and the Fight Against It* (Middlesex, UK: Penguin Books, 1975).
10 Hugh A. Dempsey, *Big Bear: The End of Freedom* (Vancouver: Douglas and McIntyre, 1984) at 11.
11 See, *e.g.*, Day Bird's entry at number 2 for himself, his two wives, and nine children, on the 1876 Treaty Paylist for Gordon's Band: Day Bird, Head Man to Chief George Gordon, Library and Archives Canada [LAC], RG 10, reel C-7145, vol. 9412, Treaty Annuity Paylists for Treaties 4, 6, and 7 (1877), Treaty 4, Gordon's Band, 50-51.
12 *Ibid.*, reel C-7148, vol. 9424 (1891), Treary 4, Pasqua's Band, 79-83: "Pasquah's 2nd wife" at number 101 received a treaty payment of $5 for herself (at 82).
13 See *e.g.*, Patricia A. Monture and Patricia D. McGuire, eds., *First Voices: An Aboriginal Women's Reader* (Toronto: Inanna Publications, 2009); Mary-Ellen Kelm and Lorna Townsend, eds., *In the Days of Our grandmothers: A Reader in Aboriginal Women's History in Canada* (Toronto: University of Toronto Press, 2006). Sarah Carter has made a towering contribution to the field: Sarah Carter, *The Importance of Being Monogamous: Marriage and Nation Building in Western Canada to 1915* (Edmonton and Athabasca: University of Alberta Press and Athabasca University Press, 2008) [Carter, *Importance*]; Sarah Carter, *Aboriginal People and the Colonizers of Western Canada to 1900* (Toronto: University of Toronto Press, 1999) [Carter, *Aboriginal People*]; Sarah Carter, "'Complicated and Clouded': The Federal Administration of Marriage and Divorce among the First Nations of Canada, 1887-1906" in Sarah Carter, Lesley Erickson, Patricia Roome, and Char Smith, eds., *Unsettled Pasts: Reconceiving the West through Women's History* (Calgary: University of Calgary Press, 2005) 151 [Carter, "Complicated and Clouded"]; Carter, "First Nations Women, *supra* note 2; Sarah Carter, "Two Months in Big Bear's Camp, 1885: Narratives of 'Indian Captivity' and the Articulation of 'Race' and 'Gender' Hierarchies in Western Canada" in Lorry W.

Felske and Beverly Rapsowich, eds., *Challenging Frontiers: The Canadian West* (Calgary: University of Calgary Press, 2004) 69 [Carter, "Two Months"]; Sarah Carter, "Categories and Terrains of Exclusion: Constructing the 'Indian Woman' in the Early Settlement Era in Western Canada" in Joy Parr and Mark Rosenfeld, eds., *Gender and History in Canada* (Toronto: Copp Clark, 1996) 31 [Carter, "Categories and Terrains"]; Sarah Carter, "The Exploitation and Narration of the Captivity of Theresa Delaney and Theresa Gowanlock, 1885" in Catherine Cavanaugh and Jeremy Mouat, eds., *Making Western Canada: Essays on European Colonialization and Settlement* (Toronto: Garamond Press, 1996) 31 [Carter, "Exploitation"]; Sarah Carter, *Capturing Women: The Manipulation of Cultural Imagery in Canada's Prairie West* (Montreal and Kingston: McGill-Queen's University Press, 1997) [Carter, *Capturing Women*]. See also Lesley Erickson, "Murdered Women and Mythic Villains: The Criminal Case and the Imaginary Criminal in the Canadian West, 1886-1930" in Jonathan Swainger and Constance Backhouse, eds., *People and Place: Historical Influences on Legal Culture* (Vancouver: UBC Press, 2003) 95 [Erickson, "Murdered Women"]; Mary Ellen Turpel, "Patriarchy and Paternalism: The Legacy of the Canadian State for First Nations Women" (1993) 6 C.J.W.L. 174.

14 Carter, *Capturing Women, ibid.* at 159.

15 Kristen Burnet, "Aboriginal and White Women in the Publications of John Maclean, Egerton Ryerson Young, and John McDougall" in Sarah Carter, Lesley Erickson, Patricia Roome, and Char Smith, eds., *Unsettled Pasts: Reconceiving the West through Women's History* (Calgary: University of Calgary Press, 2005) 101.

16 Burnet, *ibid.;* Carter, "Complicated and Clouded," *supra* note 13 at 154.

17 Burnet, *ibid.* at 112.

18 See Sarah Carter citations, *supra* note 13.

19 Carter, *Capturing Women, supra* note 13 at 20.

20 *Ibid.* at 19.

21 *Ibid.* at 159

22 *Ibid.*

23 Carter, "First Nations Women," *supra* note 2 at 55.

24 See Franca Iacovetta and Wendy Mitchinson, eds., *On the Case: Explorations in Social History* (Toronto: University of Toronto Press, 1998).

25 Of particular relevance in this context are her studies that illuminate the experiences and struggles of First Nations women. See, *e.g.,* "'Sordid' but 'Understandable in the Circumstances': Kohnke, Croft and Wilson, 1967" in Constance Backhouse, *Carnal Crimes: Sexual Assault Law in Canada, 1900-1975* (Toronto: Irwin Law, 2008) 227; Eliza Sero's legal fight in "They Are a People Unacquainted with Subordination: First Nations Sovereignty Claims: *Sero v. Gault,* 1921" in *Colour-Coded: A Legal History of Racism in Canada, 1900-1950* (Toronto: University of Toronto Press, 1999) 103; Suzanne Connelly's case, in Constance Backhouse, *Petticoats and Prejudice: Women and Law in Nineteenth-Century Canada* (Toronto: Women's Press, 1991).

26 Carter, "Complicated and Clouded," *supra* note 13; Carter, *Importance, supra* note 13.

27 See, *e.g.,* Erickson, "Murdered Women," *supra* note 13; Lesley Erickson, *Westward Bound: Sex, Violence, the Law, and the Making of a Settler Society* (Vancouver: UBC Press, 2011) at 52 [Erickson, *Westward Bound*].

28 Erickson, "Murdered Women," *ibid.* at 98.

29 *Ibid.*

30 Quoted by Erickson, *ibid.*

31 George Evense (1890), Saskatchewan Archives Board, Supreme Court of North-West Territories (Criminal), Collection R1286 [hereinafter, SAB SCNWT (Crim.), Coll. R1286], file 21.

32 Bear Hand, Nakiss, and Bore Child (1884), Saskatchewan Archives Board, Department of the Attorney General, Regina Judicial Centre: Court Records First Series, 1876-86, files 1-282 [hereinafter SAB AG CR-Regina, 1st Series, 1876-86], file 233.

33 "Report of the Commissioner of the North-West Mounted Police, 1884" reprinted in Royal Canadian Mounted Police, *Settlers and Rebels: Being the Official Reports to Parliament of the Activities of the Royal* [*sic*] *North-West Mounted Police Force from 1882-1885 by the Commissioners of the Royal* [*sic*] *North-West Mounted Police,* facsimile reprint (Toronto: Coles Publishing, 1973; original ed. Ottawa: Maclean, Roger, 1882-85), Appendix A at 45 ["Report of the Commissioner of the North-West Mounted Police"].

34 The 1901 Census of Canada contains an entry for Ben McCord, aged 42 and single, of Medicine Hat; online: <http://data2.collectionscanada.gc.ca/1891/pdf/30953_148228-00312.pdf>.

35 Margaret Favel's case, described later, similarly involved a white man's belongings left unattended for almost a year in an apparently unused schoolhouse on her reserve in the Touchwood Hills.

36 Caroline Gouin (1881), SAB AG CR-Regina, 1st series, 1876-86, file 124.

37 "Report of the Commissioner of the North-West Mounted Police, 1881," reprinted in Royal Canadian Mounted Police, *Opening Up the West: Being the Official Reports to Parliament of the Activities of the Royal* [*sic*] *North-West Mounted Police from 1874-1881 by The Commissioners of the Royal* [*sic*] *North-West Mounted Police,* facsimile reprint (Toronto: Coles Publishing, 1973; original ed. Ottawa: Maclean, Roger, 1874-81) Appendix D.

38 Scholastique Cardinal (1882), SAB AG CR-Regina, 1st series, 1876-86, file 145.

39 The 1891 Census of Canada records for Lac la Biche, subdistrict of Alberta, in the North-West Territories, contains entries for Peter Pruden, trader, aged 47, religion Church of England; Mary Pruden is listed as his wife, aged 52 (religion Roman Catholic); online: <http://data2.collectionscanada.gc.ca/1891/pdf/30953_148227-00513.pdf>.

40 Scholastique Cardinal, *supra* note 38.

41 *Ibid.*

42 Earlier and later in the transcript, her name is spelled "Marguerite": *ibid.*

43 *Ibid.*

44 The role and practices of the jury of matrons is discussed in Thomas R. Forbes, "A Jury of Matrons'" (1988) 32 Medical History 23; Shelley A.M. Gavigan, "Petit Treason in Eighteenth-Century England and Women's Inequality before the Law" (1989) 3 C.J.W.L. 335, and "The Criminal Sanction as It Relates to Human Reproduction: The Genesis of the Statutory Prohibition of Abortion" (1984) 5 J. Legal Hist. 20.

45 *Ibid.*

46 E.P. Thompson, *Whigs and Hunters: The Origin of the Black Act* (Middlesex, UK: Penguin Books, 1977) at 263.

47 Margaret Favel (1892), SAB SCNWT (Crim.), Coll. R1286, file 40.

48 Marie Martin Daniel (1900), SAB SCNWT (Crim.), Coll. R1286, file 229.

49 Betsy Horsefall and Benjamin Gordon (1894), SAB SCNWT (Crim.), Coll. R1286, file 83.

50 Now Strasbourg, Saskatchewan. The spelling of the community's name was changed from the German to the French version in 1919, following the First World War.

51 Betsy Horsefall and Benjamin Gordon (1894), *supra* note 49.

52 *An Ordinance Respecting Trespassing and Stray Animals, No. 6 of 1881.*

53 If the legal process required by the Territorial Ordinance concerning stray animals was followed, an aggrieved property owner whose land had suffered damage from a trespassing animal could seize the trespasser and deliver it to the district poundkeeper: *ibid.*

54 *Ibid.*, s. 9(2).

55 *Ibid.*

56 Deposition of Herman Schwandt, son of William Schwandt, in the court file, *supra* note 49.

57 This may have been one of his last prosecutions, as he was appointed to the North-West Territories Supreme Court later that month. Louis A. Knafla, "David Lynch Scott," (1921-30) 15 Dictionary of Canadian Biography, online: <http://www.biographi.ca/>.

58 I derive inspiration and a measure of confidence here from two disparate sources. Richard Rathbone, writing of a 1949 trial in the Gold Coast of Africa that resulted in the convictions of eight men, all accused of murder, expressed his anxiety this way: "We cannot hear the hesitations, or see the downcast eyes, nor do we receive any real sense of the court room during the period of the trial from 8 November to 1 December 1944. The jury, who were privy to these things, were at least convinced of the prosecution's case and found it proved against all eight defendants. The scholar can only remain uncomfortably neutral and cannot be certain of guilt or innocence beyond reasonable doubt": Richard Rathbone, "A Murder in the Colonial Gold Coast: Law and Politics in the 1940s" (1989) 30 Journal of African History 445 at 459.

See also Carlo Ginzberg, "Checking the Evidence: The Judge and the Historian" (1991) 18 Critical Inquiry 79:

> It must be stressed that historians – whether they deal with distant, recent, or even ongoing phenomena – never take a direct approach to reality. Their work is necessarily inferential. A piece of historical evidence can be either involuntary (a skull, a footprint, a food relic) or voluntary (a chronicle, a notarial act, a fork). But in both cases a specific interpretive framework is needed, which must be related (in the latter case) to the specific code according to which the evidence has been constructed. (at 84)
>
> ...
>
> The use of court records, therefore, does not imply that historians, disguised as judges, should try to reenact the trials of the past – an aim that would be pointless, if it were not intrinsically impossible ... The specific aim of this kind of historical research should be, I think, the reconstruction of the relationship (about which we know so little) between individual lives and the contexts in which they unfold. (at 90)

Conclusion

1 A phrase that was coined to describe the now well documented period in the history of the relationship between the First Nations and the Canadian state when thousands of First Nations children were taken from their families and communities in the care of the provincial child welfare authorities, often to be adopted into white families. See Royal Commission on Aboriginal Peoples, *Report of the Royal Commission on Aboriginal Peoples,*

vol. 1, *Looking Forward, Looking Back* (Ottawa: Minister of Supply and Services, 1996), vol. 3, ch. 2, online: http://www.collectionscanada.gc.ca/.

2 Mequanis (The Quill) (1899), Saskatchewan Archives Board, Supreme Court of North-West Territories (Criminal), Collection R1286, [hereinafter, SAB SCNWT (Crim.), Coll. R1286], file 10. I discussed this case in Chapter 4. In 1892, the new *Criminal Code, 1892,* 55-56 Vict., c. 29, s. 98, introduced this offence into Canadian criminal law.

3 *R v. Bear's Shin Bone* (1899), 3 C.C.C. 329, 4 Terr. L.R. 173 (N.W.T.S.C.).

4 The "criminalization" thesis neglects this important aspect of the "criminalization of the *Indian Act*" – the increasing judicial power of the Indian Agents. The 1876 *Indian Act* was silent on this, but in 1881 the Indian Commissioner and senior Indian Department officials, including Indian Agents, were made justices of the peace, *ex officio,* for the purposes of offences under the *Indian Act, 1876,* 39 Vict., c. 18, s. 12). By 1895, this magisterial role had been expanded to empower Indian Agents to hear offences under Parts XIII and XV of the *Criminal Code* (offences against morality and vagrancy offences), as well as two sections of the *Criminal Code* dealing with the prostitution of Indian women: *An Act to Further Amend the Indian Act, 1895,* 58-59 Vict., c. 35, s. 7. The amendment that empowered the Indian Agent to sit as a justice of the peace extended to the entire North-West Territories; in other words, his authority was not confined to matters involving Indians under his jurisdiction. This significant expansion of the legal powers of the Indian Agents may well have reflected some dissatisfaction with the justice enforced and dispensed in the regular criminal courts.

5 I am indebted in the development of this argument to an early article by Jock Young, a piece that has informed and influenced my thinking and writing from the time I first read it in 1980: "Left Idealism, Reformism and Beyond: From New Criminology to Marxism" in Bob Fine *et al.*, eds., *Capitalism and the Rule of Law: From Deviancy Theory to Marxism* (London: Hutchinson, 1979) 11.

6 E.P. Thompson, *Whigs and Hunters: The Origin of the Black Act* (Middlesex, UK: Penguin Books, 1977).

Afterword: A Methodological Note on Sources and Data

1 Kathleen Joan Bragdon, "Crime and Punishment among the Indians of Massachusetts, 1675-1750" (1981) 28 Ethnohistory 23 at 23.

2 Koni Benson and Joyce M. Chudya, "Ukubhinya: Gender and Sexual Violence in Bulawayo, Colonial Zimbabwe, 1946-1956" (2005) 31 Journal of Southern African Studies 587 at 587. Benson and Chudya found in the cases of sexual violence against African women and girls, 99 percent of which involved assaults by African men, a few in which the women and girls also complained of white men raping them and saw the latter sentenced to jail.

3 Alan R. Booth, "'European Courts Protect Women and Witches': Colonial Law Courts as Redistributors of Power in Swaziland 1920-1950" (1992) 18 Journal of South African Studies 253.

4 A number of records relating to the collection of debt and unpaid wages have not been included.

5 This collection is located at the Saskatchewan Archives Board (SAB) (Regina), in the Records of the Department of the Attorney General, Regina Judicial Centre: Court Records, First Series, 1876-86, files 1-282 [hereinafter SAB AG CR-Regina, 1st Series, 1876-86].

6 This collection is located at the Saskatchewan Archives Board, Supreme Court of North-West Territories (Criminal), Collection R1286 [hereinafter, SAB SCNWT (Crim.), Coll. R1286].

7 These include a set of unprocessed "papers" (which include some records of proceedings before and "returns" of justices of the peace (who were not also NWMP officers) found in Collections H-3501, Location 1202.2.1, and H-3503 at the SAB (Regina).

8 Each court file contains the handwritten record of the proceedings before the justices of the peace who committed the accused for trial; these justices of the peace more often than not were senior officers of the NWMP. Included are the Information, Warrant to Apprehend (where relevant), the occasional Warrant to Search (again where relevant), the Depositions of the Informant and other witnesses, frequently the Statement of the Accused, the Warrant of Committal for trial, the warrant to the jailer (commanding officer) to hold the prisoner until the next sittings; occasionally, again, a Recognizance releasing the accused pending trial, a Recognizance to prosecute, and, finally and infrequently, a cover letter from the committing justice. Orders involving recognizances almost invariably required sureties and money. The record of the actual trial is much less detailed. The informants tended to be present at the hearing before the justices of the peace, but it is not clear that they were present at the trials. Often, the phrase "tried and convicted" is all that appears, or "guilty plea" together with a record of the sentence and calculation of the court costs – and sometimes not even that. Before 1887, there is seldom reference in the court file to prosecuting counsel (who the NWMP returns suggest would have been a senior NWMP officer). Often the bulk of the record is that of the pre-trial hearing held before one or more justices of the peace to determine whether the prisoner should be committed for trial.

9 SAB SCNWT (Crim.), Coll. R1286 includes "Criminal Docket" Books of the Supreme Court of the North-West Territories commencing in 1901. Given the similarity in the handwriting in both the court files and the docket book, I believe these docket books were created and maintained by Dixie Watson.

10 Regina *Leader* (29 April 1897) 8 at col. 3 reported, under the heading "A Serious Charge," a small item: "A sensational investigation is under way in Moose Jaw ... There is suspicion that the step father of the girl – a young woman of about 24 years – is the father of the child. The girl's mother is alive but has lived in Ontario for year past." Nothing further on the case was reported. The legal result may be read perhaps as a juridical apportioning of responsibility and blame in the matter. The young woman, Maggie Coulter, was acquitted by a jury of the charge of neglect to obtain assistance in childbirth and concealment of birth: (1897) SAB SCNWT (Crim.), Coll. R1286, file 149; her stepfather, Samuel Flack, pleaded guilty before Richardson on 26 June 1897 to unlawfully disposing of the body of the child, and was sentenced to one day's imprisonment and a $200 fine, payable forthwith; in default of payment, three months' hard labour in the Regina jail. See SAB SCNWT (Crim.), Coll. R1286, file 154.

11 See, *e.g.*, Lewis H. Thomas, *The Struggle for Responsible Government in the North-West Territories*, 2nd ed. (Toronto: University of Toronto Press, 1978); Arlean McPherson, *The Battlefords: A History* (Saskatoon: Modern Press, 1967); Walter Hildebrandt, *Views from Fort Battleford: Constructed Visions of an Anglo-Canadian West* (Regina: Canadian Plains Research Center, 1994); F. Laurie Barron and James B. Waldram, eds., *1885 and After: Native Society in Transition* (Regina: Canadian Plains Research Center, 1986). For instance, from McPherson, *ibid.*, we learn that Goodwin Marchant, freighter, who appears as an accused in two importing-of-liquor cases – SAB AG CR-Regina, 1st series, 1876-86, file 18 – was

regarded as "a man of repute" (at 59), and that Robert C. Wyld became a prominent Battleford "farmer following his two terms with the Mounted Police" (at 53). Needless to say, W.A. Waiser, *Saskatchewan: A New History* (Saskatoon: Fifth House, 2005) is an invaluable addition to the historiography of Saskatchewan, not least because of the exquisite attention to and seamless integration of the contributions and experience of the First Nations and Métis peoples in the history of the province. Researchers owe an enormous debt to the Canadian Plains Research Center at the University of Regina for its contribution to the knowledge of the region and its history through its many publications, including the comprehensive *Encyclopedia of Saskatchewan: A Living Legacy* (Regina: Canadian Plains Research Center, 2007) (http://www.esask.uregina.ca/).

12 I have drawn heavily on a number of these sources, notably: Deanna Christensen, *Ahtahkakoop: The Epic Account of a Plains Cree Head Chief, His People, and Their Struggle for Survival 1816-1896* (Shell Lake, SK: Ahtahkakoop Publishing, 2000); Hugh A. Dempsey, *Big Bear: The End of Freedom* (Vancouver: Douglas and McIntyre, 1984); Norma Sluman and Jean Goodwill, *John Tootoosis: A Biography of a Cree Leader* (Ottawa: Golden Dog Press, 1982); Peter Erasmus, *Buffalo Days and Nights, as told to Henry Thompson* (Calgary: Glenbow-Alberta Institute, 1976); Dan Kennedy (Ochankugahe), *Recollections of an Assiniboine Chief,* edited and with an introduction by James R. Stevens (Toronto: McClelland and Stewart, 1972); Harold LeRat, with Linda Unger, *Treaty Promises, Indian Reality: Life on a Reserve* (Saskatoon: Purich Publishing, 2005); Edward Ahenakew, *Voices of the Plains Cree,* edited and with an introduction by Ruth M. Buck (Toronto: McClelland and Stewart, 1973); J.W. Grant MacEwan, *Portraits from the Plains* (Toronto: McGraw-Hill of Canada, 1971); J.R. Miller, *Big Bear [Mistahimusqua]: A Biography* (Toronto: ECW Press, 1996); Rudy Wiebe, *Big Bear* (Toronto: Penguin, 2008); David G. Mandelbaum, *The Plains Cree: An Ethnographic, Historical and Comparative Study* (Regina: Canadian Plains Research Center, 1979); David Lee, "Piapot: Man and Myth" (1992) 17 Prairie Forum 251; Christian Thompson, ed., *Saskatchewan First Nations: Lives Past and Present* (Regina: Canadian Plains Research Center, 2004); Abel Watetch, *Payepot and His People* (Saskatoon: Modern Press, 1959; repr. Regina: Canadian Plains Research Center, 2007); Gerry Radison, *Kā-Pēpāmahchakwēw Wandering Spirit: Plains War Chief* (Yorkton, SK: Smoke Ridge Books, 2009). I have also consulted a number of electronic sources, including: "First Nations Bands of Saskatchewan" (http://www.sicc.sk.ca/bands/); "Poundmaker" (http://www.collectionscanada.ca/2/6/h6-234-e.html); and "North-West Resistance" (http://library2.usask.ca/northwest/background/backgrd.htm).

13 Knafla argued that the preoccupation with the NWMP and Riel had "deflected research and writing on more fundamental as well as broader legal subjects." See Louis A. Knafla, "From Oral to Written Memory: The Common Law Tradition in Western Canada" in Louis A. Knafla, ed., *Law and Justice in a New Land: Essays in Western Canadian Legal History* (Toronto: Carswell, 1986) 31 at 35.

14 See, *e.g.,* W.F. Bowker, "Stipendiary Magistrates and Supreme Court of the North-West Territories, 1876-1907" (1988) 26 Alta. L. Rev. 245; Lesley Erickson, "Murdered Women and Mythic Villains: The Criminal Case and the Imaginary Criminal in the Canadian West, 1886-1930" in Jonathan Swainger and Constance Backhouse, eds., *People and Place: Historical Influences on Legal Culture* (Vancouver: UBC Press, 2003) 95; Sidney L. Harring, "'There Seemed to Be No Recognized Law': Canadian Law and the Prairie First Nations" in Louis A. Knafla and Jonathan Swainger, eds., *Laws and Societies in the Canadian Prairie West 1670-1940* (Vancouver: UBC Press, 2005) 92 at 102-8 [Harring, "No Recognized

Law"]; Sidney L. Harring, *White Man's Law: Native People in Nineteenth-Century Jurisprudence* (Toronto: University of Toronto Press, 1998) [Harring, *White Man's Law*]; Roderick G. Martin, "Macleod at Law: A Judicial Biography of James Farquharson Macleod, 1874-94" in Jonathan Swainger and Constance Backhouse, eds., *People and Place: Historical Influences on Legal Culture* (Vancouver: UBC Press, 2003); Louis A. Knafla and Jonathan Swainger, eds. *Laws and Societies in the Canadian Prairie West, 1670-1940* (Vancouver: UBC Press, 2005).

15 See R.C. Macleod and Heather Rollason, "'Restrain the Lawless Savages': Native Defendants in the Criminal Courts of the North-West Territories, 1878-1885" (1997) 10 Journal of Historical Sociology 157. Their sources include NWMP returns of criminal court cases (starting in 1878); newspaper articles on criminal activities in four regional newspapers (eighty-three additional case reports were found in the newspapers that had not been reported in the police returns); annual summaries of activities submitted by Indian Agents to the Canadian government.

Macleod and Rollason rely on the names that appeared in the NWMP returns to distinguish between Native and non-Native accused persons. This is not always accurate; for example, Robert Saunders, John Thomas, Thomas A. Beckett, Moses Bunn, and John Eye, to cite but a few, were all Aboriginal accused persons who appeared in Richardson's court.

16 *Ibid.* at 173.

17 *Ibid.* at 173-74.

18 *Ibid.* at 176.

19 R.C. Macleod and Heather Rollason Driscoll, "Natives, Newspapers and Crime Rates in the North-West Territories, 1878-1885" in Theodore Binnema, Gerhard J. Ens, and R.C. Macleod, eds., *From Rupert's Land to Canada* (Edmonton: University of Alberta Press, 2001) 249.

Bibliography

Legislation

Canada

Act for the Temporary Government of Rupert's Land and the North-West Territory when United with Canada, 1869, 32-33 Vict., c. 3.

An Act Further to Amend the Indian Act, 1884, 47 Vict., c. 27.

An Act Further to Amend the Indian Act, 1894, 57-58 Vict., c. 32.

An Act Further to Amend the Indian Act, 1895, 58-59 Vict., c. 35.

An Act Further to Amend the Law Respecting the North-West Territories, 1886, 49 Vict., c. 25.

An Act Respecting the Administration of Justice, and for the Establishment of a Police Force in the North-West Territories, 1873, 36 Vict., c. 35.

An Act to Amend and Consolidate the Laws Respecting the North-West Territories, 1875, 38 Vict., c. 49.

An Act to Amend and Consolidate the Several Acts Relating to the North-West Territories, 1880, 43 Vict., c. 25.

An Act to Amend the "Act to Make Further Provision for the Government of the North West Territories," 1873, 36 Vict., c. 34.

An Act to Amend the "North-West Territories Act, 1875," 1877, 40 Vict., c. 7.

Criminal Code, 1892, 55-56 Vict. (1892) c. 29.

Indian Act, 1876, 39 Vict., c. 18.

Indian Act, 1881, 44 Vict., c. 17.

North-West Territories Act, 1875, 38 Vict., c. 49.

North-West Territories Act, 1886, 43 Vict., c. 50.

Offences Against the Person Act, 1869, 32-33 Vict., c. 20, ss. 55, 57.

The Department of the Interior Act, 1873, 36 Vict., c. 4.

United Kingdom

An Act for Extending the Jurisdiction of the Courts of Justice in the Provinces of Lower and Upper Canada, 1803 (U.K.), 43 Geo. III, c. 138.

An Act for Regulating the Fur Trade, 1821 (U.K.), 1 and 2 Geo. IV, c. 66.
British North America Act, 1867 (U.K.), 30-31 Vict., c. 3.
Treason Felony Act, 1848, 11 & 12 Vict., c. 12.

Jurisprudence

R. v. Bear's Shin Bone (1899), 3 C.C.C. 329, 4 Terr. L.R. 173 (N.W.T.S.C.).
R. v. City of Sault Ste Marie (1978), 40 C.C.C. (2d) 353, 3 C.R. (3d) 30 (S.C.C) (online: QL LexisNexis).
R. v. Connor, [1884] 1 Terr. L.R. 4 (Man. Q.B.).
R. v. Thibert, [1996] 1 S.C.R. 37.

Primary and Archival Sources

Library and Archives Canada [LAC]

Census of Canada, 1901, North-West Territories, District of Saskatchewan, Battleford Agency Sub-District, Schedule 1, Microfilm reel T-6555; online: <http://www.collectionscanada.gc.ca/databases/census-1901/index-e.html>.
Department of Indian Affairs. Annual Report for the Year Ended June 30 1902 (Ottawa: King's Printer, 1902); online: <http://www.collectionscanada.gc.ca/>.
Department of Indian Affairs, Treaty Annuity Paylists, Treaties 4, 6, and 7, 1874-1903, RG 10, Microfilm reels C-7145-51, vols. 9413-36.
Department of Justice, Capital Punishment Case Files, Archival Reference no. R188-53-2-E (former Archival Reference no. RG 13-13-1, vol. 1421).
Department of the Solicitor General, Manitoba Penitentiary, Inmate Admitance [*sic*] Book, 22 June 1885 – 27 March 1913, RG 73, W87-88/365, Microfilm reels T-1108391 and T-11095, vols. 23 and 24 (MIKAN no. 134308).
North-West Mounted Police (NWMP) – Personnel Records, 1873-1904, RG 18, vol. 10037-10047, and RG 18 1997-98/386/box 33; online: <http://www.collectionscanada.gc.ca/databases/nwmp-pcno/index-e.html>.

Saskatchewan Archives Board [SAB]

Department of the Attorney General, Regina Judicial Centre: Court Records First Series, 1878-86, files 1-282.
Department of the Attorney-General, Regina Judicial Centre: Court Records, Collection R996.
Department of Interior, Dominion Land Branch – Applications for Scrip 1886-1901, 1906 made by North-West Half Breeds, R 91-17, Collection R-5.11.
Justice of the Peace Papers (unprocessed), H-3503 (1901).
Regina *Leader*, 1883-1903, 1913.
Saskatchewan Herald, 1876-85.
Supreme Court of North-West Territories (Criminal), Collection R1286, including Criminal Docket Book.

Government Publications

Alberta. *Justice on Trial: Report of the Task Force on the Criminal Justice System and Its Impact on the Indian and Métis People of Alberta* (The Cawsey Report) (March 1991).

Canada. *Census of Canada 1890-1891* (Ottawa: Queen's Printer, 1893).

–. *Census of the Three Provisional Districts of the North-West Territories, 1884-1885* (Ottawa: Maclean, Rogers, 1886).

–. *Fourth Census of Canada 1901* (Ottawa: S.E. Dawson, King's Printers, 1902).

–. "Report of the Special Committee of the House of Commons, 1857" (Appendix No. 2, pages 365, 366, and 367) in Statistics Canada, *Censuses of Canada 1865-1871, The Aboriginal Peoples* at 12-13, online: Statistics Canada <http://www.statcan.ca/>.

Canada. Law Reform Commission of Canada. *Crimes against the State Working Paper 49* (Ottawa: Law Reform Commission of Canada, 1986).

Canada. Royal Commission on Aboriginal Peoples. *Report of the Royal Commission on Aboriginal Peoples,* vol. 1, *Looking Forward, Looking Back* (Ottawa: Minister of Supply and Services, 1996), online: http://www.collectionscanada.gc.ca/.

Canada. Royal Commission on the Donald Marshall, Jr. Prosecution. *Commissioners' Report: Findings and Recommendations* (Halifax: The Commission, 1989).

Manitoba. *Report of the Aboriginal Justice Inquiry of Manitoba,* vol. 1, *The Justice System and Aboriginal People* (A.C. Hamilton and C.M. Sinclair, Commissioners) (Winnipeg: Province of Manitoba, 1991).

Royal Canadian Mounted Police. *Law and Order: Being the Official Reports to Parliament of the Royal* [*sic*] *North-West Mounted Police from 1886-1887 by the Commissioners of the Royal* [*sic*] *North-West Mounted Police,* facsimile reprint (Toronto: Coles Publishing, 1973; original ed. Ottawa: Maclean, Roger, 1886-87).

–. *Opening Up the West: Being the Official Reports to Parliament of the Activities of the Royal [sic] North-West Mounted Police from 1874-1881 by The Commissioners of the Royal [sic] North-West Mounted Police,* facsimile reprint (Toronto: Coles Publishing, 1973; original ed. Ottawa: Maclean, Roger, 1874-81).

–. *Settlers and Rebels: Being the Official Reports to Parliament of the Activities of the Royal [sic] North-West Mounted Police Force from 1882-1885 by the Commissioners of the Royal [sic] North-West Mounted Police,* facsimile reprint (Toronto: Coles Publishing, 1973; original ed. Ottawa: Maclean, Roger, 1882-85).

Saskatchewan. *Report of the Saskatchewan Indian Justice Review Committee* (Judge Patricia Linn, Chairperson) (Saskatoon: 1992).

United Kingdom. *The Commission, Working Paper No. 72,* Second Programme, Item XVIII, Codification of the Criminal Law: Treason, Sedition and Allied Offences (London: Her Majesty's Stationery Office, 1977).

Secondary Sources

Ahenakew, Edward. *Voices of the Plains Cree,* edited and with an introduction by Ruth M. Buck (Toronto: McClelland and Stewart, 1973).

Ahenakew, Freda, Cecil King, and Catherine I. Littlejohn. "Indigenous Languages in the Delivery of Justice in Manitoba: A Paper Presented to the Public Inquiry into the

Administration of Justice and Aboriginal People" in *Manitoba Aboriginal Justice Inquiry Research Papers* (Winnipeg, 1991) [unpublished].

Anderson, Karen. *Chain Her by One Foot: The Subjugation of Native Women in Seventeenth-Century New France* (London: Routledge, 1991).

Andrews, Isabel. "Indian Protest against Starvation: The Yellow Calf Incident of 1884" (1975) 28 Saskatchewan History 41.

Asher, Brad. "'Their Own Domestic Difficulties': Intra-Indian Crime and White Law in Western Washington Territory, 1873-1889" (1996) 27 Western Historical Quarterly 189.

Backhouse, Constance. *Carnal Crimes: Sexual Assault Law in Canada, 1900-1975* (Toronto: Irwin Law, 2008).

–. *Colour-Coded: A Legal History of Racism in Canada, 1900-1950* (Toronto: University of Toronto Press, 1999).

–. *Petticoats and Prejudice: Women and Law in Nineteenth-Century Canada* (Toronto: Women's Press, 1991).

Baker, H. Robert. "Creating Order in the Wilderness: Transplanting the English Law to Rupert's Land, 1835-1851" (1999) 17 L.H.R. 209

Barman, Jean. "Taming Aboriginal Sexuality: Gender, Power, and Race in British Columbia, 1850-1900" in Mary-Ellen Kelm and Lorna Townsend, eds., *In the Days of Our Grandmothers: A Reader in Aboriginal Women's History in Canada* (Toronto: University of Toronto Press, 2006) 270.

Barron, F. Laurie. "A Summary of Federal Indian Policy in the Canadian West, 1867-1984" (1985) 1 Native Studies Review 28.

–. "Indian Agents and the North-West Rebellion" in F. Laurie Barron and James B. Waldram, eds., *1885 and After: Native Society in Transition* (Regina: Canadian Plains Research Center, 1986) 139.

–. "The Indian Pass System in the Canadian West, 1888-1935" (1988) 13 Prairie Forum 25.

Barron, F. Laurie, and James B. Waldram, eds. *1885 and After: Native Society in Transition* (Regina: Canadian Plains Research Center, 1986).

Beahan, William, and Stan Horall. *Red Coats on the Prairies: The North-West Mounted Police, 1886-1900* (Regina: Centax Books, 1998).

Beal, Bob, and R.C. Macleod. *Prairie Fire: The 1885 North-West Rebellion* (Edmonton: Hurtig Publishers, 1984).

Beal, Bob, and Barry Wright. "Summary and Incompetent Justice: Legal Responses to the 1885 Crisis" in Barry Wright and Susan Binnie, eds., *Canadian State Trials*, vol. 3, *Political Trials and Security Measures, 1840-1914* (Toronto: University of Toronto Press, 2009) 353.

Beattie, John. *Crime and the Courts in England, 1660-1800* (Princeton, NJ: Princeton University Press, 1986).

Benson, Koni, and Joyce M. Chudya. "Ukubhinya: Gender and Sexual Violence in Bulawayo, Colonial Zimbabwe, 1946-1956" (2005) 31 Journal of Southern African Studies 587.

Benton, Lauren A. *Law and Colonial Cultures: Legal Regimes in World History, 1400-1900* (Cambridge: Cambridge University Press, 2002).

Bingaman, Sandra E. *The North-West Rebellion Trials, 1885* (MA Thesis, University of Saskatchewan, [Regina] 1971) [unpublished].

–. "The Trials of Poundmaker and Big Bear, 1885" (1975) 28 Saskatchewan History 81.

Binnema, Theodore, Gerhard J. Ens, and R.C. Macleod, eds. *From Rupert's Land to Canada* (Edmonton: University of Alberta Press, 2001).

Booth, Alan R. "'European Courts Protect Women and Witches': Colonial Law Courts as Redistributors of Power in Swaziland 1920-1950" (1992) 18 Journal of South African Studies 253.

Borrows, John. *Recovering Canada: The Resurgence of Indigenous Law* (Toronto: University of Toronto Press, 2002).

–. "Wampum at Niagara: The Royal Proclamation, Canadian Legal History, and Self-Government" in Michael Asch, ed., *Aboriginal and Treaty Rights in Canada: Essays on Law, Equality, and Respect for Difference* (Vancouver: UBC Press, 1997) 155.

Bowker, W.F. "Stipendiary Magistrates and Supreme Court of the North-West Territories, 1876-1907" (1988) 26 Alta L. Rev. 245.

Boyd, Susan C., Dorothy E. Chunn, and Robert Menzies, eds. *Abusing Power: The Canadian Experience* (Halifax: Fernwood, 2001).

Bragdon, Kathleen Joan. "Crime and Punishment among the Indians of Massachusetts, 1675-1750" (1981) 28 Ethnohistory 23.

Brown, Jennifer S.H. *Strangers in Blood: Fur Trade Families in Indian Country* (Vancouver: UBC Press, 1980).

Brown, Lorne, and Caroline Brown. *An Unauthorized History of the RCMP* (Toronto: James Lewis and Samuel, 1973).

Brownlie, Robin Jarvis. *A Fatherly Eye: Indian Agents, Government Power, and Aboriginal Resistance in Ontario, 1918-1939* (Toronto: Oxford University Press, 2003).

Brownlie, Robin, and Mary-Ellen Kelm. "Desperately Seeking Absolution: Native Agency as Colonialist Alibi?" (1994) 75 Canadian Historical Review 543.

Buckley, Helen. *From Wooden Ploughs to Welfare: Why Indian Policy Failed in the Prairie Provinces* (Montreal and Kingston: McGill-Queen's University Press, 1992).

Bumstead, J.M. "Another Look at the Riel Trial for Treason" in Barry Wright and Susan Binnie, eds., *Canadian State Trials*, vol. 3, *Political Trials and Security Measures, 1840-1914* (Toronto: University of Toronto Press, 2009) 411.

–. *Louis Riel v. Canada: The Making of a Rebel* (Winnipeg: Great Plains Publications, 2001).

Burnet, Kristen. "Aboriginal and White Women in the Publications of John Maclean, Egerton Ryerson Young, and John McDougall" in Sarah Carter, Lesley Erickson, Patricia Roome, and Char Smith, eds., *Unsettled Pasts: Reconceiving the West through Women's History* (Calgary: University of Calgary Press, 2005) 101.

Byrne, Paula Jane. *Criminal Law and Colonial Subject: New South Wales, 1810-1930* (Cambridge: Cambridge University Press, 1993).

Cardinal, Harold, and Walter Hildebrandt. *Treaty Elders of Saskatchewan: Our Dream Is that Our Peoples Will One Day Be Clearly Recognized as Nations* (Calgary: University of Calgary Press, 2000).

Carter, Sarah. *Aboriginal People and the Colonizers of Western Canada to 1900* (Toronto: University of Toronto Press, 1999).

–. *Capturing Women: The Manipulation of Cultural Imagery in Canada's Prairie West* (Montreal and Kingston: McGill-Queen's University Press, 1997).

–. "Categories and Terrains of Exclusion: Constructing the 'Indian Woman' in the Early Settlement Era in Western Canada" in Joy Parr and Mark Rosenfeld, eds., *Gender and History in Canada* (Toronto: Copp Clark, 1996) 31.

–. "'Complicated and Clouded': The Federal Administration of Marriage and Divorce among the First Nations of Western Canada, 1887-1906" in Sarah Carter, Lesley Erickson,

Patricia Roome, and Char Smith, eds., *Unsettled Pasts: Reconceiving the West through Women's History* (Calgary: University of Calgary Press, 2005) 151.
–. "First Nations Women of Prairie Canada in the Early Reserve Years, the 1870s to 1920: A Preliminary Inquiry" in Christine Miller and Patricia Chuchryk, with Marie Smallface Marule, Brenda Manyfingers, and Cheryl Deering, eds., *Women of the First Nations: Power, Wisdom, and Strength* (Winnipeg: University of Manitoba Press, 1996) 51.
–. *Lost Harvests: Prairie Indian Reserve Farmers and Government Policy* (Montreal and Kingston: McGill-Queen's University Press, 1990).
–. "The Exploitation and Narration of the Captivity of Theresa Delaney and Theresa Gowanlock, 1885" in Catherine Cavanaugh and Jeremy Mouat, eds., *Making Western Canada: Essays on European Colonialization and Settlement* (Toronto: Garamond Press, 1996) 31.
–. *The Importance of Being Monogamous: Marriage and Nation Building in Western Canada to 1915* (Edmonton and Athabasca: University of Alberta Press and Athabasca University Press, 2008).
–. "Two Months in Big Bear's Camp, 1885: Narratives of 'Indian Captivity' and the Articulation of 'Race' and 'Gender' Hierarchies in Western Canada" in Lorry W. Felske and Beverly Rapsowich, eds., *Challenging Frontiers: The Canadian West* (Calgary: University of Calgary Press, 2004) 69.
Chanock, Martin. *Law, Custom and Social Order: The Colonial Experience in Malawi and Zambia* (Cambridge: Cambridge University Press, 1985).
Christensen, Deanna. *Ahtahkakoop: The Epic Account of a Plains Cree Head Chief, His People, and Their Struggle for Survival 1816-1896* (Shell Lake, SK: Ahtahkakoop Publishing, 2000).
Chunn, Dorothy E. *From Punishment to Doing Good: Family Courts and Socialized Justice in Ontario, 1880-1940* (Toronto: University of Toronto Press, 1992).
–. "Welfare Law, Welfare Fraud, and the Moral Regulation of the Never Deserving Poor" (2004) 13 Social and Legal Studies 219.
Chunn, Dorothy E., and Dany Lacombe, eds., *Law as a Gendering Practice* (Oxford: Oxford University Press, 2000).
Cole, Douglas, and Ira Chaikin. *An Iron Hand upon the People: The Law against the Potlatch on the Northwest Coast* (Vancouver: Douglas and McIntyre, 1994).
de Sousa Santos, Boaventura. "The Postmodern Transition: Law and Politics" in Austin Sarat and Thomas Kearns, eds., *The Fate of Law* (Ann Arbor: University of Michigan Press, 1991) 79.
Delaney, Theresa, and Theresa Gowanlock. *Two Months in the Camp of Big Bear* (Regina: Canadian Plains Research Center, 1999).
Dempsey, Hugh A. *Big Bear: The End of Freedom* (Vancouver: Douglas and McIntyre, 1984).
–, ed. *Men in Scarlet* (Calgary: Historical Society of Alberta and McClelland and Stewart West, 1974).
Dickason, Olive Patricia. *Canada's First Nations: A History of Founding Peoples from Earliest Times* (Toronto: McClelland and Stewart, 1992).
Dubinsky, Karen, and Franca Iacovetta. "Murder, Womanly Virtue, and Motherhood: The Case of Angelina Napolitino, 1911-1922" in Tina Loo and Lorna R. McLean, eds., *Historical Perspectives on Law and Society in Canada* (Toronto: Copp Clark Longman, 1994) 161.
Eades, Diana. "'I Don't Think the Lawyers Were Communicating with Me': Misunderstanding Cultural Differences in Communicative Style" (2003) 52 Emory L.J. 1109.

Erasmus, Peter. *Buffalo Days and Nights, as Told to Henry Thompson* (Calgary: Glenbow-Alberta Institute, 1976).
Erickson, Lesley. "Murdered Women and Mythic Villains: The Criminal Case and the Imaginary Criminal in the Canadian West, 1886-1930" in Jonathan Swainger and Constance Backhouse, eds., *People and Place: Historical Influences on Legal Culture* (Vancouver: UBC Press, 2003) 95.
–. "'Under the Queen's Law': The Impact of Canadian Criminal Justice on Native Women and Their Communities, 1889-1940 (Paper presented at the annual meeting of the Canadian Law and Society Association, University of Manitoba, 2-5 June 2004).
–. *Westward Bound: Sex, Violence, the Law, and Making of a Settler Society* (Vancouver: UBC Press, 2011).
Etherington, Norman. "The Gendering of Indirect Rule: Criminal Law and Colonial Fiji, 1875-1900" (1996) 31 Journal of Pacific Studies 42.
Evans, R.G. "Swift Runner – The Cannibal" in *Outlaws and Lawmen of Western Canada*, vol. 1 (Surrey, BC: Frontier Books, 1983) 34.
Flanagan, Thomas. "Hugh Richardson" (1910-13) 14 *Dictionary of Canadian Biography* 872.
Forbes, Thomas R. "A Jury of Matrons" (1988) 32 Medical History 23.
Foster, Hamar. "Long Distance Justice: The Criminal Jurisdiction of Canadian Courts West of the Canadas, 1763-1859" (1990) 34 Am. J. Legal Hist. 1.
–. "'The Queen's Law Is Better than Yours': International Homicide in Early British Columbia" in Susan Lewthwaite, Tina Loo, and Jim Phillips, eds., *Essays in the History of Canadian Law*, vol. 5, *Crime and Criminal Justice in Canadian History* (Toronto: University of Toronto Press, 1994) 41.
Gavigan, Shelley A.M. "Legal Forms, Family Forms, and Gendered Norms: What Is a Spouse?" (1999) 14 C.J.L.S. 129.
–. "Petit Treason in Eighteenth-Century England and Women's Inequality before the Law" (1989) 3 C.J.W.L. 335.
–. "The Criminal Sanction as It Relates to Human Reproduction: The Genesis of the Statutory Prohibition of Abortion" (1984) 5 J. Legal Hist. 20.
Gibson, Dale, and Lee Gibson. *Substantial Justice: Law and Lawyers in Manitoba 1670-1970* (Winnipeg: Peguis Publishers, 1972).
Ginzberg, Carlo. "Checking the Evidence: The Judge and the Historian" (1991) 18 Critical Inquiry 79.
Giraud, Marcel. "Métis Settlement in the North-West Territories" (1954) 7 Saskatchewan History 1.
Glasbeek, Amanda. *Feminized Justice: The Toronto Women's Court, 1913-34* (Vancouver: UBC Press, 2009).
–. "Maternalism Meets the Criminal Law: The Case of the Toronto Women's Court" (1998) 10 C.J.W.L. 480.
Glasbeek, H.J. *Wealth by Stealth: Corporate Crime, Corporate Law, and the Perversion of Democracy* (Toronto: Between the Lines, 2002).
Golz, Annalee. "Uncovering and Reconstructing Family Violence: Ontario Criminal Case Files" in Franca Iacovetta and Wendy Mitchinson, eds., *On the Case: Explorations in Social History* (Toronto: University of Toronto Press, 1998) 289.
Gómez, Laura F. "Race, Colonialism, and Criminal Law: Mexicans and the American Criminal Justice System in Territorial New Mexico" (2000) 34 Law & Soc'y Rev. 1129.

Gordon, Linda. *Heroes of Their Own Lives: The Politics of Family Violence* (New York: Viking, 1988).

Grove, Alan. "Where Is the Justice, Mr. Mills? A Case Study of *R. v. Nantuck*" in Hamar Foster and John McLaren, eds., *Essays in the History of Canadian Law,* vol. 6, *The Legal History of British Columbia and the Yukon* (Toronto: University of Toronto Press, 1995) 87.

Hamilton, Michelle A., and Kris Inwood, "The Identification of the Aboriginal Population in the 1891 Census of Canada" (Paper presented at the Indigenous Identity in Demographic Sources Conference, Umea University, Umea, Sweden, 2006), online: Umea University <http://www.ddb.umu.se/>.

Harring, Sidney, L. "'There Seemed to Be No Recognized Law': Canadian Law and the Prairie First Nations" in Louis A. Knafla and Jonathan Swainger, eds., *Laws and Societies in the Canadian Prairie West 1670-1940* (Vancouver: UBC Press, 2005) 92.

–. *White Man's Law: Native People in Nineteenth-Century Jurisprudence* (Toronto: University of Toronto Press, 1998).

Harris, Douglas C. *Fish, Law, and Colonialism: The Legal Capture of Salmon in British Columbia* (Toronto: University of Toronto Press, 2001).

Hay, Douglas. "Legislation, Magistrates, and Judges: High Law and Low Law in England and the Empire" in David Lemmings, ed., *The British and Their Laws in the Eighteenth Century* (Woodbridge, Suffolk, UK: Boydell Press, 2005) 59.

–. "Property, Authority and Criminal Law" in Douglas Hay *et al.*, eds., *Albion's Fatal Tree: Crime and Society in Eighteenth-Century England* (London: Pantheon, 1975) 17.

–. "Time, Inequality and Law's Violence" in Austin Sarat and Thomas R. Kearns, eds., *Law's Violence* (Ann Arbor: University of Michigan Press, 1995) 141.

Hay, Douglas, and Paul Craven. *Masters, Servants, and Magistrates in Britain and the Empire, 1562-1955* (Chapel Hill: University of North Carolina Press, 2004).

Haydon, A.L. *The Riders of the Plains: A Record of the Royal North-West Mounted Police of Canada, 1873-1910* (Toronto: Copp Clark, 1910).

Hildebrandt, Walter. *Views from Fort Battleford: Constructed Visions of an Anglo-Canadian West* (Regina: Canadian Plains Research Center, 1994).

Hubner, Brian. "Horse Stealing and the Borderline: The NWMP and the Control of Indian Movement, 1874-1900" (1995) 20 Prairie Forum 281.

Hunt, Alan. *Explorations in Law and Society: Toward a Constitutive Theory of Law* (London: Routledge, 1993).

Iacovetta, Franca, and Karen Dubinsky. "Introduction" in Franca Iacovetta and Wendy Mitchinson, eds., *On the Case: Explorations in Social History* (Toronto: University of Toronto Press, 1998) 3.

Iacovetta, Franca, and Wendy Mitchinson, eds. *On the Case: Explorations in Social History* (Toronto: University of Toronto Press, 1998).

Jennings, John N. *The North-West Mounted Police and Canadian Indian Policy, 1873-1896* (PhD Dissertation, University of Toronto, 1979) [unpublished].

–. "The North-West Mounted Police and Indian Policy after the 1885 Rebellion" in F. Laurie Barron and James B. Waldram, eds., *1885 and After: Native Society in Transition* (Regina: Canadian Plains Research Center, 1986) 225.

–. "The Plains Indians and the Law" in Hugh A. Demspey, ed., *Men in Scarlet* (Calgary: Historical Society of Alberta and McClelland and Stewart West, 1974) 51.

Johnston, Darlene M. *Litigating Identity: The Challenge of Aboriginality* (L.L.M. Thesis, University of Toronto, 2003).

–. "Litigating Identity: The Challenge of Aboriginality" (Paper presented at the Faculty of Law, University of Toronto, January 2003).

Karsten, Peter. *Between Law and Custom: High and Low Legal Cultures in the Lands of the British Diaspora – the United States, Canada, Australia, and New Zealand, 1600-1900* (Cambridge: Cambridge University Press, 2002).

Kelly, Nora Hickson. *My Mountie and Me: A True Story* (Regina: Centax, 1999).

Kelly, William, with Nora Hickson Kelly. *Policing the Fringe: A Young Mountie's Story.* (Regina: Centax, 1999).

Kelm, Mary-Ellen, and Lorna Townsend, eds. *In the Days of Our Grandmothers: A Reader in Aboriginal Women's History in Canada* (Toronto: University of Toronto Press, 2006).

Kennedy, Dan (Ochankugahe). *Recollections of an Assiniboine Chief,* edited and with an introduction by James R. Stevens (Toronto: McClelland and Stewart, 1972).

Knafla, Louis A. "David Lynch Scott," (1921-30) 15 Dictionary of Canadian Biography, online: <http://www.biographi.ca/>

–. "From Oral to Written Memory: The Common Law Tradition in Western Canada" in Louis Knafla, ed., *Law and Justice in a New Land: Essays in Western Canadian Legal History* (Toronto: Carswell, 1986) 31.

Knafla, Louis A., and Jonathan Swainger, eds. *Laws and Societies in the Canadian Prairie West, 1670-1940* (Vancouver: UBC Press, 2005).

Kostash, Myrna, ed. *The Frog Lake Reader* (Edmonton: NeWest Press, 2009).

Lacey, Nicola. "Historicising Criminalisation: Conceptual and Empirical Issues" (2009) 72 Modern L. Rev. 736

Lee, David. "Piapot: Man and Myth" (1992) 17 Prairie Forum 251.

Leighton, Douglas. "A Victorian Civil Servant at Work: Lawrence Vankoughnet and the Canadian Indian Department, 1874-1893" in Ian A.L. Getty and Antoine S. Lussier, eds., *As Long as the Sun Shines and Water Flows: A Reader in Canadian Native Studies* (Vancouver: UBC Press, 1983) 104.

LeRat, Harold, with Linda Ungar. *Treaty Promises, Indian Reality: Life on a Reserve* (Saskatoon: Purich Publishing, 2005).

Lewthwaite, Susan, Tina Loo, and Jim Phillips, eds. *Essays in the History of Criminal Law,* vol. 5, *Crime and Criminal Justice in Canadian History* (Toronto: University of Toronto Press, 1994).

Leyton-Brown, Kenneth Bryan. *The Origin and Evolution of a System for the Administration of Justice in the North-West Territories, 1870-1905* (PhD Dissertation, Queen's University, 1988) [unpublished].

Lindberg, Tracey. "Rooms with 'Traditional Views': Justice L'Heureux-Dubé and the Expansion of Interpretative Principles Related to Equality in the Context of Indigenous Rights" in Elizabeth Sheehy, ed., *Adding Feminism to Law: The Contributions of Justice Claire L'Heureux-Dubé* (Toronto: Irwin Law, 2004) 367.

Loo, Tina. "Dan Cranmer's Potlatch: Law as Coercion, Symbol, and Rhetoric in British Columbia" (1992) 73 Canadian Historical Review 125.

–. *Making Law, Order, and Authority in British Columbia, 1821-1871* (Toronto: University of Toronto Press, 1994).

–. "Savage Mercy: Native Culture and the Modification of Capital Punishment in Nineteenth-Century British Columbia" in Carolyn Strange, ed., *Qualities of Mercy: Justice, Punishment and Discretion* (Vancouver: UBC Press, 1996) 104.

–. "Tonto's Due: Law, Culture, and Colonialization in British Columbia" in Hamar Foster and John McLaren, eds., *Essays in the History of Canadian Law,* vol. 6, *The Legal History of British Columbia and the Yukon* (Toronto: University of Toronto Press, 1995) 128; reprinted in Catherine Cavanaugh and Jeremy Mouat, eds., *Making Western Canada: Essays on European Colonization and Settlement* (Toronto: Garamond Press, 1996) 62.

Loo, Tina, and Lorna R. McLean, eds. *Historical Perspectives on Law and Society in Canada* (Toronto: Copp Clark Longman, 1994).

Looy, Anthony J. *The Indian Agent and His Role in the Administration of the North-West Superintendency, 1876-1893* (PhD Dissertation, Queen's University, 1976) [unpublished].

Lux, Maureen. *Medicine that Walks: Disease, Medicine, and Canadian Plains Native People, 1880-1940* (Toronto: University of Toronto Press, 2001).

MacEwan, J.W. Grant. *Portraits from the Plains* (Toronto: McGraw-Hill of Canada, 1971).

Macleod, R.C. "Canadianizing the West: The North-West Mounted Police as Agents of the National Policy" in Lewis H. Thomas, ed., *Essays on Western History: In Honour of Lewis Gwynne Thomas* (Edmonton: University of Alberta Press, 1976) 101.

–. "Law and Order on the Western Canadian Frontier" in John McLaren, Hamar Foster, and Chet Orloff, eds., *Law for the Elephant, Law for the Beaver: Essays in the Legal History of the North American West* (Regina, SK, and Pasadena, CA: Canadian Plains Research Center and Ninth Judicial Circuit Historical Society, 1992) 90.

–. *The North-West Mounted Police and Law Enforcement 1873-1905* (Toronto: University of Toronto Press, 1976).

Macleod, R.C., and Heather Rollason. "Natives, Newspapers and Crime Rates in the North-West Territories, 1878-1885" in Theodore Binnema, Gerhard J. Ens, and R.C. MacLeod, eds., *From Rupert's Land to Canada* (Edmonton: University of Alberta Press, 2001) 249.

Macleod, R.C., and Heather Rollason-Driscoll. "'Restrain the Lawless Savages': Native Defendants in the Criminal Courts of the North-West Territories, 1878-1885" (1997) 10 Journal of Historical Sociology 157.

Mandelbaum, David G. *The Plains Cree: An Ethnographic, Historical and Comparative Study* (Regina: Canadian Plains Research Center, 1979).

Martin, Roderick G. "Macleod at Law: A Judicial Biography of James Farquharson Macleod, 1874-94" in Jonathan Swainger and Constance Backhouse, eds., *People and Place: Historical Influences on Legal Culture* (Vancouver: UBC Press, 2003) 37.

McCaul, C.C. "Precursors of the Bench and Bar in the Western Provinces" (1925) Can. Bar Rev. 25.

McConnell, W.H. *Prairie Justice* (Calgary: Burroughs, 1980).

McEwen, J.W. Grant. *Portraits from the Plains* (Toronto: McGraw-Hill, 1971).

McLaren, John. "The Early British Columbia Judges, the Rule of Law and the 'Chinese Question': The California and Oregon Connection" in John McLaren, Hamar Foster, and Chet Orloff, eds., *Law for the Elephant, Law for the Beaver: Essays in the Legal History of the North American West* (Regina, SK, and Pasadena, CA: Canadian Plains Research Center and Ninth Judicial Circuit Historical Society, 1992) 237.

McLeod, Neal. "Plains Cree Identity: Borderlands, Ambiguous Genealogies and Narrative Irony" (2000) 20 Canadian Journal of Native Studies 437.

–. "Rethinking Treaty 6 in the Spirit of Mistahi Maskwa (Big Bear)" (1999) 19 Canadian Journal of Native Studies 69.

McNab, David T. "Treaties and an Official Use of History" (1993) 13 Canadian Journal of Native Studies 139.

McNeil, Kent. *Common Law Aboriginal Title* (Oxford: Clarendon Press, 1989).
McPherson, Arlean. *The Battlefords: A History* (Saskatoon: Modern Press, 1967).
Mentiplay, Iain A. *A Century of Integrity: The Law Society of Saskatchewan 1907 to 2007* (Regina: Law Society of Saskatchewan, 2007).
Menzies, Robert, and Dorothy E. Chunn. "The Gender Politics of Criminal Insanity: 'Order-in-Council' Women" (1998) 31 Social History 241.
Menzies, Robert, Dorothy E. Chunn, and Susan Boyd, eds. *Toxic Criminology: Environment, Law and the State of Canada* (Halifax: Fernwood, 2002).
Merry, Sally Engle. "Law and Colonialism" (1991) 25 Law & Soc'y Rev. 889.
–. "The Criminalization of Everyday Life" in Austin Sarat et al., eds., *Everyday Practices and Trouble Cases* (Evanston, IL: Northwestern University Press and the American Bar Foundation, 1998) 14.
Miller, J.R. *Big Bear [Mistahimusqua]: A Biography* (Toronto: ECW Press, 1996).
–. *Shingwauk's Vision: A History of Native Residential Schools* (Toronto: University of Toronto Press, 1996).
–. *Skyscrapers Hide the Heavens: A History of Indian-White Relations in Canada,* 3rd ed. (Toronto: University of Toronto Press, 2000).
–, ed. *Sweet Promises: A Reader in Indian-White Relations in Canada* (Toronto: University of Toronto Press, 1991).
Milloy, John S. *A National Crime: The Canadian Government and the Residential School System, 1879-1976* (Winnipeg: University of Manitoba Press, 1999).
–. *The Plains Cree: Trade, Diplomacy and War, 1790-1870* (Winnipeg: University of Manitoba Press, 1990).
Monture, Patricia A., and Patricia D. McGuire, eds. *First Voices: An Aboriginal Women's Reader* (Toronto: Inanna Publications, 2009).
Monture-Okanee, Patricia A. "Reclaiming Justice: Aboriginal Women and Justice Initiatives in the 1990s" in Canada, Royal Commission on Aboriginal Peoples, *Aboriginal Peoples and the Justice System: Report of the National Round Table on Aboriginal Justice Issues* (Ottawa: Minister of Supply and Services Canada, 1993) 105.
Monture-Okanee, Patricia A., and Mary Ellen Turpel. "Aboriginal Peoples and Canadian Criminal Law: Rethinking Justice" (1992) 26 U.B.C. L. Rev. 239.
Morris, Alexander. *The Treaties of Canada with the Indians of Manitoba and the North-West Territories,* facsimile reprint (Toronto: Prospero Books, 2000; original ed. Toronto: Belfords Clarke, 1880).
Morton, Desmond. *The Queen v. Louis Riel* (Toronto: University of Toronto Press, 1974).
Muir, Edward, and Guido Ruggiero, eds. *History from Crime* (Baltimore: The Johns Hopkins University Press, 1994).
Murray, David. "Hands across the Border: The Abortive Extradition of Solomon Moseby" (2000) 30 Canadian Review of American Studies 187.
Napoleon, Val. "Aboriginal Discourse: Gender, Identity, and Community" in Benjamin J. Richardson, Shin Imai, and Kent McNeil, eds., *Indigenous Peoples and the Law: Comparative and Critical Perspectives* (Oxford: Hart Publishing, 2009) 233.
Nigam, Sanjay. "Disciplining and Policing the 'Criminals by Birth,' Part 1: The Making of a Colonial Stereotype – The Criminal Tribes and Castes of North India" (1990) 27 Indian Economic and Social History Review 131.
–. "Disciplining and Policing the 'Criminals by Birth,' Part 2: The Development of a Disciplinary System, 1871-1900" (1990) 27 Indian Economic and Social History Review 257.

Oliver, Edmund Henry, ed. *The Canadian North-West: Its Early Development and Legislative Records,* 2 vols. (Ottawa: Government Printing Bureau, 1914).

Paterson, T.W. *Outlaws of Western Canada* (Langley, BC: Mr. Paperback, 1982).

Payment, Diane. "Batoche after 1885: A Society in Transition" in F. Laurie Barron and James B. Waldram, eds., *1885 and After: Native Society in Transition* (Regina: Canadian Plains Research Center, 1986) 173.

Pearce, Frank. *Crimes of the Powerful* (London: Pluto, 1976).

Pearce, Frank, and Laureen Snider, eds. *Corporate Crime: Contemporary Debates* (Toronto: University of Toronto Press, 1995).

Peers, Laura. *The Ojibwa of Western Canada, 1780-1870* (Winnipeg: University of Manitoba Press, 1994).

Pettipas, Katherine. *Severing the Ties that Bind: Government Repression of Indigenous Religious Ceremonies on the Prairies* (Winnipeg: University of Manitoba Press, 1994).

Radison, Garry. *Kā-Pēpāmahchakwēw Wandering Spirit: Plains War Chief* (Yorkton, SK: Smoke Ridge Books, 2009).

Rathbone, Richard. "A Murder in the Colonial Gold Coast: Law and Politics in the 1940s" (1989) 30 Journal of African History 445.

Ray, Arthur J., Jim Miller, and Frank J. Tough. *Bounty and Benevolence: A History of Saskatchewan Treaties* (Montreal and Kingston: McGill-Queen's University Press, 2000).

Reynolds, Thomas. *Justices of the Peace in the NWT, 1870-1905* (MA Thesis, University of Regina, 1978) [unpublished].

Robertson, Stephen. "What's Law Got to Do with It? Legal Records and Sexual Histories" (2005) 12 Journal of the History of Sexuality 161.

Rowbotham, Sheila. *Hidden from History: Three Hundred Years of Women's Oppression and the Fight Against It* (Middlesex, UK: Penguin Books, 1977).

Sangster, Joan. "Criminalizing the Colonized: Ontario Native Women Confront the Criminal Justice System, 1920-60" (1999) 80 Canadian Historical Review 32.

–. "Native Women, Sexuality and the Law" in Mary-Ellen Kelm and Lorna Townsend, eds., *In the Days of Our Grandmothers: A Reader in Aboriginal Women's History in Canada* (Toronto: University of Toronto Press, 2006) 301.

–. "'She Is Hostile to Our Ways': First Nations Girls Sentenced to the Ontario Training School for Girls, 1933-1960" (2002) 20 Law and History Review 59.

Satzewich, Vic. "'Where's the Beef?': Cattle Killing, Rations Policy and First Nations 'Criminality' in Southern Alberta, 1892-1895" (1996) 9 Journal of Historical Sociology 188.

Shewell, Hugh. *"Enough to Keep Them Alive": Indian Welfare in Canada, 1873-1965* (Toronto: University of Toronto Press, 2004).

Sluman, Norma. *Poundmaker* (Toronto: Ryerson Press, 1967).

Sluman, Norma, and Jean Goodwill. *John Tootoosis: A Biography of a Cree Leader* (Ottawa: Golden Dog Press, 1982).

Smandych, Russell, and Rick Linden. "Co-existing Forms of Aboriginal Justice and Private Justice: An Historical Study of the Canadian West" in Kayleen M. Hazelhurst, ed., *Legal Pluralism and the Colonial Legacy* (Aldershot, UK: Avebury, 1995).

Snider, Laureen. *Bad Business: Corporate Crime in Canada* (Scarborough, ON: Nelson Canada, 1993).

Spry, Irene. "The Tragedy of the Loss of the Commons in Western Canada" in Ian A.L. Getty and Antoine S. Lussier, eds., *As Long as the Sun Shines and Water Flows: A Reader in Canadian Native Studies* (Vancouver: UBC Press, 1983) 203.

Stanley, George F.G. *The Birth of Western Canada: A History of the Riel Rebellions* (Toronto: University of Toronto Press, 1960).

Stonechild, Blair. "Aboriginal Peoples of Saskatchewan" (2007), online: The Saskatchewan Encylopedia: A Living Legacy <http://esask.uregina.ca/>.

–. "Interview" in Myrna Kostash, ed., *The Frog Lake Reader* (Edmonton: NeWest, 2009).

–. "The Indian View of the 1885 Uprising" in F. Laurie Barron and James B. Waldram, eds., *1885 and After: Native Society in Transition* (Regina: Canadian Plains Research Center, 1986) 155.

–. "The Iron Alliance and Dominion of the Northern Plains 1690-1885: Implications for the Concept of Iskunikan" (2002) [unpublished].

Stonechild, Blair, and W.A. Waiser. *Loyal till Death: Indians and the North-West Rebellion* (Saskatoon: Fifth House, 1997).

Strange, Carolyn. "Patriarchy Modified: The Criminal Prosecution of Rape in York County, Ontario, 1880-1930" in Susan Lewthwaite, Tina Loo, and Jim Phillips, eds., *Essays in the History of Criminal Law,* vol. 5, *Crime and Criminal Justice in Canadian History* (Toronto: University of Toronto Press, 1994) 207.

–, ed. *Qualities of Mercy, Justice, Punishment and Discretion* (Vancouver: UBC Press, 1996).

–. "Stories of Their Lives: The Historian and the Capital Case File" in Franca Iacovetta and Wendy Mitchinson, eds., *On the Case: Explorations in Social History* (Toronto: University of Toronto Press, 1998) 25.

Swainger, Jonathan. "A Distant Edge of Authority: Capital Punishment and the Prerogative of Mercy in British Columbia, 1872-1880" in Hamar Foster and John McLaren, eds., *Essays in the History of Canadian Law,* vol. 6, *The Legal History of British Columbia and the Yukon* (Toronto: University of Toronto Press, 1995) 204.

–. *The Canadian Department of Justice and the Completion of Confederation 1867-78* (Vancouver: UBC Press, 2000).

Thomas, Lewis Herbert. *The Struggle for Responsible Government in the North-West Territories,* 2nd ed. (Toronto: University of Toronto Press, 1978).

Thompson, Christian, ed., *Saskatchewan First Nations: Lives Past and Present* (Regina: Canadian Plains Research Center, 2004).

Thompson, E.P. "Folklore, Anthropology, and Social History (1978) 3 Indian Historical Review 247.

–. *Whigs and Hunters: The Origin of the Black Act* (Middlesex, UK: Penguin Books, 1977).

Thomson, Colin Argyle. *Swift Runner* (Calgary: Detselig Enterprises, 1984).

Titley, E. Brian. *A Narrow Vision: Duncan Campbell Scott and the Administration of Indian Affairs in Canada* (Vancouver: UBC Press, 1986).

–. *The Frontier World of Edgar Dewdney* (Vancouver: UBC Press, 1999).

Tobias, John L. "Canada's Subjugation of the Plains Cree, 1879-1885" in J.R. Miller, ed., *Sweet Promises: A Reader on Indian-White Relations in Canada* (Toronto: University of Toronto Press, 1991) 212.

–. "Kam-yistowesit, or Beardy, Chief of the Willow Band of the Plains Cree" (1881-90) 11 Dictionary of Canadian Biography, online: <http://www.biographi.ca/>.

–. "PAYIPWAT (Piapot, Hole in the Sioux, Kisikawasan, Flash in the Sky), Plains Cree chief" (1901-10) 13 Dictionary of Canadian Biography, online: <http://www.biographi.ca/>.

–. "Protection, Civilization, Assimilation: An Outline History of Canada's Indian Policy" in Ian A.L. Getty and Antoine S. Lussier, eds., *As Long as the Sun Shines and Water Flows: A Reader in Canadian Native Studies* (Vancouver: UBC Press, 1983) 39.

–. "Protection, Civilization, Assimilation: An Outline History of Canada's Indian Policy" in Tina Loo and Lorna R. McLean, eds., *Historical Perspectives on Law and Society in Canada* (Toronto: Copp Clark Longman, 1994) 290; reprinted from (1976) 6 Western Canadian Journal of Anthropology 13.

–. "The Origins of the Treaty Rights Movement in Saskatchewan" in F. Laurie Barron and James B. Waldram, eds., *1885 and After: Native Society in Transition* (Regina: Canadian Plains Research Center, 1986) 241.

Tomlins, Christopher. "Introduction: The Many Legalities of Colonization: A Manifesto of Destiny for Early American Legal History" in Christopher L. Tomlins and Bruce H. Mann, eds., *The Many Legalities of Early America* (Chapel Hill: University of North Carolina Press, 2001) 1.

Treaty 7 Elders and Tribal Council, with Walter Hildebrandt, Dorothy First Rider, and Sarah Carter. *The True Spirit and Original Intent of Treaty 7* (Montreal and Kingston: McGill-Queen's University Press, 1996).

Turner, John Peter. *The North-West Mounted Police 1873-1893*, 2 vols. (Ottawa: King's Printer, 1950).

Turpel, Mary Ellen. "Patriarchy and Paternalism: The Legacy of the Canadian State for First Nations Women" (1993) 6 C.J.W.L. 174.

van Kirk, Sylvia. *Many Tender Ties: Women in the Fur Trade Society, 1670-1870* (Winnipeg: Watson and Dwyer Publications, 1980).

Venne, Sharon. "Understanding Treaty 6: An Indigenous Perspective" in Michael Asch, ed., *Aboriginal and Treaty Rights in Canada: Essays in Law, Equality, and Respect for Difference* (Vancouver: UBC Press, 1997) 172.

Vertes, The Honourable Justice John. "Northern Justice: Jury Trials in Aboriginal Communities" (Paper presented at the Faculty of Law, University of British Columbia, 25 January 2007).

Waiser, W.A. "Introduction: Place, Process and the New Prairie Realities" (2005) 84 Canadian Historical Review 509.

–. *Saskatchewan: A New History* (Saskatoon: Fifth House, 2005).

–. "The White Man Governs: The 1885 Indian Trials" in Barry Wright and Susan Binnie, eds., *Canadian State Trials*, vol. 3, *Political Trials and Security Measures, 1840-1914* (Toronto: University of Toronto Press, 2009) 451.

Ward, Peter. *The Administration of Justice in the North-West Territories, 1870-1887* (MA Thesis, University of Alberta, 1966) [unpublished].

Watetch, Abel. *Payepot and His People* (Saskatoon: Modern Press, 1959; repr. Regina: Canadian Plains Research Center, 2007).

Waugh, Earle, ed. *Nancy LeClaire and George Cardinal, Alberta Elders' Cree Dictionary* (Edmonton: University of Alberta Press, 1998).

Webber, Jeremy. "Relations of Force and Relations of Justice: The Emergence of Normative Community between Colonists and Aboriginal Peoples" (1995) 33 Osgoode Hall L.J. 623.

Westra, Laura. *Ecoviolence and the Law: Supranational Normative Foundations of Ecocrime* (Ardsley, NY: Transnational Publishers, 2004).

Wiebe, Rudy. *Big Bear* (Toronto: Penguin, 2008).

Williams, D. Colwyn. "Law and Institutions in the North West Territories (1869-1905)" (1963) 28 Sask. Bar Rev. 109; (1964) 29 Sask. Bar Rev. 51; (1964) 29 Sask. Bar Rev. 83;

(1965) 30 Sask. Bar Rev. 51; (1966) 31 Sask. Bar Rev. 1; (1966) 31 Sask. Bar Rev. 137; (1968) 33 Sask. Bar Rev. 145.

–. "The Dawn of Law on the Prairies" (1962) 27 Sask. Bar Rev. 126; (1963) 28 Sask. Bar Rev. 17; (1963) 28 Sask. Bar Rev. 63.

Willrich, Michael. *City of Courts: Socializing Justice in Progressive Era Chicago* (Cambridge and New York: Cambridge University Press, 2003).

Wright, Barry, and Susan Binnie, eds. *Canadian State Trials*, vol. 3, *Political Trials and Security Measures, 1840-1914* (Toronto: University of Toronto Press, 2009).

Wright, Nancy E. "The Problem of Aboriginal Evidence in Early Colonial New South Wales" in Diane Kirkby and Catharine Coleborne, eds., *Law, History, Colonialism: The Reach of Empire* (Manchester, UK: Manchester University Press, 2001) 140.

Young, Jock. "Left Idealism, Reformism and Beyond: From New Criminology to Marxism" in Bob Fine *et al.*, eds., *Capitalism and the Rule of Law: From Deviancy Theory to Marxism* (London: Hutchinson, 1979) 11.

Index

Note: "(f)" after a page number indicates a figure; "(m)" after a page number indicates a map; NWMP stands for North-West Mounted Police; "(t)" after a page number indicates a table

PUBLICATIONS OF THE OSGOODE SOCIETY FOR CANADIAN LEGAL HISTORY

2012 R. Blake Brown, *Arming & Disarming: A History of Gun Control in Canada*

Eric Tucker, Bruce Ziff, and James Muir, eds., *Property on Trial: Canadian Cases in Context*

Shelley A.M. Gavigan, *Hunger, Horses, and Government Men: Criminal Law on the Aboriginal Plains, 1870-1905*

Barrington Walker, ed., *The African-Canadian Legal Odyssey: Historical Essays*

2011 Robert J. Sharpe, *The Lazier Murder: Prince Edward County, 1884*

Philip Girard, *Lawyers and Legal Culture in British North America: Beamish Murdoch of Halifax*

John McLaren, *Dewigged, Bothered and Bewildered: British Colonial Judges on Trial*

Lesley Erickson, *Westward Bound: Sex, Violence, the Law and the Making of a Settler Society*

2010 Judy Fudge and Eric Tucker, eds., *Work on Trial: Canadian Labour Law Struggles*

Christopher Moore, *The British Columbia Court of Appeal: The First Hundred Years*

Frederick Vaughan, *Viscount Haldane: The Wicked Step-Father of the Canadian Constitution*

Barrington Walker, *Race on Trial: Black Defendants in Ontario's Criminal Courts, 1850-1950*

2009 William Kaplan, *Canadian Maverick: The Life and Times of Ivan C. Rand*

R. Blake Brown, *A Trying Question: The Jury in Nineteenth-Century Canada*

Barry Wright and Susan Binnie, eds., *Canadian State Trials. Volume 3: Political Trials and Security Measures, 1840-1914*

Robert J. Sharpe, *The Last Day, the Last Hour: The Currie Libel Trial*

2008 Constance Backhouse, *Carnal Crimes: Sexual Assault Law in Canada, 1900-1975*

Jim Phillips, R. Roy McMurtry, and John Saywell, eds., *Essays in the History of Canadian Law. Volume 10: A Tribute to Peter N. Oliver*

Gregory Taylor, *The Law of the Land: Canada's Receptions of the Torrens System*

Hamar Foster, Benjamin Berger, and A.R. Buck, eds., *The Grand Experiment: Law and Legal Culture in British Settler Societies*

2007 Robert Sharpe and Patricia McMahon, *The Persons Case: The Origins and Legacy of the Fight for Legal Personhood*

Lori Chambers, *Misconceptions: Unmarried Motherhood and the Ontario Children of Unmarried Parents Act, 1921-1969*

Jonathan Swainger, ed., *The Alberta Supreme Court at 100: History and Authority*

Martin Friedland, *My Life in Crime and Other Academic Adventures*

2006 Donald Fyson, *Magistrates, Police and People: Everyday Criminal Justice in Quebec and Lower Canada, 1764-1837*

Dale Brawn, *The Court of Queen's Bench of Manitoba 1870-1950: A Biographical History*

R.C.B. Risk, *A History of Canadian Legal Thought: Collected Essays*, edited and introduced by G. Blaine Baker and Jim Phillips

2005 Philip Girard, *Bora Laskin: Bringing Law to Life*

Christopher English, ed., *Essays in the History of Canadian Law. Volume 9: Two Islands, Newfoundland and Prince Edward Island*

Fred Kaufman, *Searching for Justice: An Autobiography*

2004 John D. Honsberger, *Osgoode Hall: An Illustrated History*

Frederick Vaughan, *Aggressive in Pursuit: The Life of Justice Emmett Hall*

Constance Backhouse and Nancy Backhouse, *The Heiress versus the Establishment: Mrs. Campbell's Campaign for Legal Justice*

Philip Girard, Jim Phillips, and Barry Cahill, eds., *The Supreme Court of Nova Scotia, 1754-2004: From Imperial Bastion to Provincial Oracle*

2003 Robert Sharpe and Kent Roach, *Brian Dickson: A Judge's Journey*

George Finlayson, John J. Robinette: *Peerless Mentor*

Peter Oliver, *The Conventional Man: The Diaries of Ontario Chief Justice Robert A. Harrison, 1856-1878*

Jerry Bannister, *The Rule of the Admirals: Law, Custom and Naval Government in Newfoundland, 1699-1832*

2002 John T. Saywell, *The Law Makers: Judicial Power and the Shaping of Canadian Federalism*

David Murray, *Colonial Justice: Justice, Morality and Crime in the Niagara District, 1791-1849*

F. Murray Greenwood and Barry Wright, eds., *Canadian State Trials. Volume 2: Rebellion and Invasion in the Canadas, 1837-38*

Patrick Brode, *Courted and Abandoned: Seduction in Canadian Law*

2001 Ellen Anderson, *Judging Bertha Wilson: Law as Large as Life*

Judy Fudge and Eric Tucker, *Labour before the Law: Collective Action in Canada, 1900-1948*

Laurel Sefton MacDowell, *Renegade Lawyer: The Life of J.L. Cohen*

2000 Barry Cahill, *"The Thousandth Man": A Biography of James McGregor Stewart*

A.B. McKillop, *The Spinster and the Prophet: Florence Deeks, H.G. Wells, and the Mystery of the Purloined Past*

Beverley Boissery and F. Murray Greenwood, *Uncertain Justice: Canadian Women and Capital Punishment*

Bruce Ziff, *Unforeseen Legacies: Reuben Wells Leonard and the Leonard Foundation Trust*

1999 Constance Backhouse, *Colour-Coded: A Legal History of Racism in Canada, 1900-1950*

G. Blaine Baker and Jim Phillips, eds., *Essays in the History of Canadian Law. Volume 8: In Honour of R.C.B. Risk*

Richard W. Pound, *Chief Justice W.R. Jackett: By the Law of the Land*

David Vanek, *Fulfilment: Memoirs of a Criminal Court Judge*

1998 Sidney Harring, *White Man's Law: Native People in Nineteenth-Century Canadian Jurisprudence*

Peter Oliver, *"Terror to Evil-Doers": Prisons and Punishments in Nineteenth-Century Ontario*

1997 James W. St. G. Walker, *"Race," Rights and the Law in the Supreme Court of Canada: Historical Case Studies*

Lori Chambers, *Married Women and Property Law in Victorian Ontario*

Patrick Brode, *Casual Slaughters and Accidental Judgments: Canadian War Crimes and Prosecutions, 1944-1948*

Ian Bushnell, *The Federal Court of Canada: A History, 1875-1992*

1996 Carol Wilton, ed., *Essays in the History of Canadian Law. Volume 7: Inside the Law – Canadian Law Firms in Historical Perspective*

William Kaplan, *Bad Judgment: The Case of Mr. Justice Leo A. Landreville*

Murray Greenwood and Barry Wright, eds., *Canadian State Trials. Volume 1: Law, Politics and Security Measures, 1608-1837*

1995 David Williams, *Just Lawyers: Seven Portraits*

Hamar Foster and John McLaren, eds., *Essays in the History of Canadian Law. Volume 6: The Legal History of British Columbia and the Yukon*

W.H. Morrow, ed., *Northern Justice: The Memoirs of Mr. Justice William G. Morrow*

Beverley Boissery, *A Deep Sense of Wrong: The Treason, Trials and Transportation to New South Wales of Lower Canadian Rebels after the 1838 Rebellion*

1994 Patrick Boyer, *A Passion for Justice: The Legacy of James Chalmers McRuer*

Charles Pullen, *The Life and Times of Arthur Maloney: The Last of the Tribunes*

Susan Lewthwaite, Tina Loo, and Jim Phillips, eds., *Essays in the History of Criminal Law. Volume 5: Crime and Criminal Justice in Canadian History*

Brian Young, *The Politics of Codification: The Lower Canadian Civil Code of 1866*

1993 Greg Marquis, *Policing Canada's Century: A History of the Canadian Association of Chiefs of Police*

Murray Greenwood, *Legacies of Fear: Law and Politics in Quebec in the Era of the French Revolution*

1992 Brendan O'Brien, *Speedy Justice: The Tragic Last Voyage of His Majesty's Vessel Speedy*

Robert Fraser, ed., *Provincial Justice: Upper Canadian Legal Portraits from the Dictionary of Canadian Biography*

1991 Constance Backhouse, *Petticoats and Prejudice: Women and Law in Nineteenth-Century Canada*

1990 Philip Girard and Jim Phillips, eds., *Essays in the History of Canadian Law. Volume 3: Nova Scotia*
Carol Wilton, ed., *Essays in the History of Canadian Law. Volume 4: Beyond the Law – Lawyers and Business in Canada 1830-1930*

1989 Desmond Brown, *The Genesis of the Canadian Criminal Code of 1892*
Patrick Brode, *The Odyssey of John Anderson*

1988 Robert Sharpe, *The Last Day, the Last Hour: The Currie Libel Trial*
John D. Arnup, *Middleton: The Beloved Judge*

1987 C. Ian Kyer and Jerome Bickenbach, *The Fiercest Debate: Cecil A. Wright, the Benchers and Legal Education in Ontario, 1923-1957*

1986 Paul Romney, *Mr. Attorney: The Attorney General for Ontario in Court, Cabinet and Legislature, 1791-1899*
Martin Friedland, *The Case of Valentine Shortis: A True Story of Crime and Politics in Canada*

1985 James Snell and Frederick Vaughan, *The Supreme Court of Canada: History of the Institution*

1984 Patrick Brode, *Sir John Beverley Robinson: Bone and Sinew of the Compact*
David Williams, *Duff: A Life in the Law*

1983 David H. Flaherty, ed., *Essays in the History of Canadian Law. Volume 2*

1982 Marion MacRae and Anthony Adamson, *Cornerstones of Order: Courthouses and Town Halls of Ontario, 1784-1914*

1981 David H. Flaherty, ed., *Essays in the History of Canadian Law. Volume 1*

LAW AND SOCIETY

2012 David R. Boyd, *The Right to a Healthy Environment: Revitalizing Canada's Constitution*

David Milward, *Aboriginal Justice and the Charter: Realizing a Culturally Sensitive Interpretation of Legal Rights*

Steven Bittle, *Still Dying for a Living: Corporate Criminal Liability after the Westray Mine Disaster*

Jacqueline D. Krikorian, *International Trade Law and Domestic Policy: Canada, the United States, and the WTO*

Michael Boudreau, *City of Order: Crime and Society in Halifax, 1918-35*

David R. Boyd, *The Environmental Rights Revolution: A Global Study of Constitutions, Human Rights, and the Environment*

2011 Lesley Erickson, *Westward Bound: Sex, Violence, the Law, and the Making of a Settler Society*

Elaine Craig, *Troubling Sex: Toward a Legal Theory of Sexual Integrity*

Laura DeVries, *Conflict in Caledonia: Aboriginal Land Rights and the Rule of Law*

Jocelyn Downie and Jennifer J. Llewellyn, eds., *Being Relational: Reflections on Relational Theory and Health Law and Policy*

Grace Li Xiu Woo, *Ghost Dancing with Colonialism: Decolonization and Indigenous Rights at the Supreme Court of Canada*

Fiona J. Kelly, *Transforming Law's Family: The Legal Recognition of Planned Lesbian Motherhood*

Colleen Bell, *The Freedom of Security: Governing Canada in the Age of Counter-Terrorism*

2010 Andrew S. Thompson, *In Defence of Principles: NGOs and Human Rights in Canada*

Aaron Doyle and Dawn Moore, eds., *Critical Criminology in Canada: New Voices, New Directions*

Joanna R. Quinn, *The Politics of Acknowledgement: Truth Commissions in Uganda and Haiti*

Patrick James, *Constitutional Politics in Canada after the Charter: Liberalism, Communitarianism, and Systemism*

Louis A. Knafla and Haijo Westra, eds., *Aboriginal Title and Indigenous Peoples: Canada, Australia, and New Zealand*

Janet Mosher and Joan Brockman, eds., *Constructing Crime: Contemporary Processes of Criminalization*

2009 Stephen Clarkson and Stepan Wood, *A Perilous Imbalance: The Globalization of Canadian Law and Governance*

Amanda Glasbeek, *Feminized Justice: The Toronto Women's Court, 1913-34*

Kimberley Brooks, ed., *Justice Bertha Wilson: One Woman's Difference*

Wayne V. McIntosh and Cynthia L. Cates, *Multi-Party Litigation: The Strategic Context*

Renisa Mawani, *Colonial Proximities: Crossracial Encounters and Juridical Truths in British Columbia, 1871-1921*

James B. Kelly and Christopher P. Manfredi, eds., *Contested Constitutionalism: Reflections on the Canadian Charter of Rights and Freedoms*

2008 Catherine E. Bell and Robert K. Paterson, eds., *Protection of First Nations Cultural Heritage: Laws, Policy, and Reform*

Richard J. Moon, ed., *Law and Religious Pluralism in Canada*

Catherine E. Bell and Val Napoleon, eds., *First Nations Cultural Heritage and Law: Case Studies, Voices, and Perspectives*

Douglas C. Harris, *Landing Native Fisheries: Indian Reserves and Fishing Rights in British Columbia, 1849-1925*

Peggy J. Blair, *Lament for a First Nation: The Williams Treaties in Southern Ontario*

2007 Lori G. Beaman, *Defining Harm: Religious Freedom and the Limits of the Law*

Stephen Tierney, ed., *Multiculturalism and the Canadian Constitution*

Julie Macfarlane, *The New Lawyer: How Settlement Is Transforming the Practice of Law*

Kimberley White, *Negotiating Responsibility: Law, Murder, and States of Mind*

Dawn Moore, *Criminal Artefacts: Governing Drugs and Users*

Hamar Foster, Heather Raven, and Jeremy Webber, eds., *Let Right Be Done: Aboriginal Title, the Calder Case, and the Future of Indigenous Rights*

Dorothy E. Chunn, Susan B. Boyd, and Hester Lessard, eds., *Reaction and Resistance: Feminism, Law, and Social Change*
Margot Young, Susan B. Boyd, Gwen Brodsky, and Shelagh Day, eds., *Poverty: Rights, Social Citizenship, and Legal Activism*
Rosanna L. Langer, *Defining Rights and Wrongs: Bureaucracy, Human Rights, and Public Accountability*
C.L. Ostberg and Matthew E. Wetstein, *Attitudinal Decision Making in the Supreme Court of Canada*
Chris Clarkson, *Domestic Reforms: Political Visions and Family Regulation in British Columbia, 1862-1940*

2006 Jean McKenzie Leiper, *Bar Codes: Women in the Legal Profession*
Gerald Baier, *Courts and Federalism: Judicial Doctrine in the United States, Australia, and Canada*
Avigail Eisenberg, ed., *Diversity and Equality: The Changing Framework of Freedom in Canada*

2005 Randy K. Lippert, *Sanctuary, Sovereignty, Sacrifice: Canadian Sanctuary Incidents, Power, and Law*
James B. Kelly, *Governing with the Charter: Legislative and Judicial Activism and Framers' Intent*
Dianne Pothier and Richard Devlin, eds., *Critical Disability Theory: Essays in Philosophy, Politics, Policy, and Law*
Susan G. Drummond, *Mapping Marriage Law in Spanish Gitano Communities*
Louis A. Knafla and Jonathan Swainger, eds., *Laws and Societies in the Canadian Prairie West, 1670-1940*
Ikechi Mgbeoji, *Global Biopiracy: Patents, Plants, and Indigenous Knowledge*
Florian Sauvageau, David Schneiderman, and David Taras, with Ruth Klinkhammer and Pierre Trudel, *The Last Word: Media Coverage of the Supreme Court of Canada*
Gerald Kernerman, *Multicultural Nationalism: Civilizing Difference, Constituting Community*
Pamela A. Jordan, *Defending Rights in Russia: Lawyers, the State, and Legal Reform in the Post-Soviet Era*
Anna Pratt, *Securing Borders: Detention and Deportation in Canada*
Kirsten Johnson Kramar, *Unwilling Mothers, Unwanted Babies: Infanticide in Canada*
W.A. Bogart, *Good Government? Good Citizens? Courts, Politics, and Markets in a Changing Canada*

Catherine Dauvergne, *Humanitarianism, Identity, and Nation: Migration Laws in Canada and Australia*

Michael Lee Ross, *First Nations Sacred Sites in Canada's Courts*

Andrew Woolford, *Between Justice and Certainty: Treaty Making in British Columbia*

2004 John McLaren, Andrew Buck, and Nancy Wright, eds., *Despotic Dominion: Property Rights in British Settler Societies*

Georges Campeau, *From UI to EI: Waging War on the Welfare State*

Alvin J. Esau, *The Courts and the Colonies: The Litigation of Hutterite Church Disputes*

Christopher N. Kendall, *Gay Male Pornography: An Issue of Sex Discrimination*

Roy B. Flemming, *Tournament of Appeals: Granting Judicial Review in Canada*

Constance Backhouse and Nancy L. Backhouse, *The Heiress vs the Establishment: Mrs. Campbell's Campaign for Legal Justice*

Christopher P. Manfredi, *Feminist Activism in the Supreme Court: Legal Mobilization and the Women's Legal Education and Action Fund*

Annalise Acorn, *Compulsory Compassion: A Critique of Restorative Justice*

2003 Jonathan Swainger and Constance Backhouse, eds., *People and Place: Historical Influences on Legal Culture*

Jim Phillips and Rosemary Gartner, *Murdering Holiness: The Trials of Franz Creffield and George Mitchell*

David R. Boyd, *Unnatural Law: Rethinking Canadian Environmental Law and Policy*

Ikechi Mgbeoji, *Collective Insecurity: The Liberian Crisis, Unilateralism, and Global Order*

2002 Rebecca Johnson, *Taxing Choices: The Intersection of Class, Gender, Parenthood, and the Law*

John McLaren, Robert Menzies, and Dorothy E. Chunn, eds., *Regulating Lives: Historical Essays on the State, Society, the Individual, and the Law*

2001 Joan Brockman, *Gender in the Legal Profession: Fitting or Breaking the Mould*

Printed and bound in Canada by Friesens

Set in Garamond by Artegraphica Design Co. Ltd.

Copy editor: Francis Chow

Proofreader: Lara Kordic